MW00605607

Editorial project:
2022 © **booq** publishing, S.L.
c/ Domènech, 7-9, 2º 1ª
08012 Barcelona, Spain
T: +34 93 268 80 88
www.booqpublishing.com

ISBN: 978-84-9936-683-8

Editorial coordinator:
Claudia Martínez Alonso

Art director:
Mireia Casanovas Soley

Editor:
Francesc Zamora Mola

Layout:
Francesc Zamora Mola
Cristina Simó Perales

Translation:
© **booq** publishing, S.L.

Printing in Spain

Architect: © Kendle Design Collaborative; photographer: © Rick Brazil

The Southwest region, encompassing the states of Arizona, Colorado, Nevada, New Mexico, Texas, and Utah, is a land full of contrasts and complexity. Comprised of rolling hills, high mountain peaks, red rock canyons, mesas, and basins, there is a rugged beauty that holds people as diverse as its landscapes. It has served as inspiration for poets, artists, scientists, and explorers and kept families knit to the land for generations.

Though the Southwest encompasses land from 70 feet —Sonoran Desert—to 14,440 feet—Rocky Mountains—above sea level, most of the region ranks as the driest in the nation, with Nevada receiving less than ten inches of precipitation per year. Utah's claim to "the greatest snow on earth" is attributed to over 500 inches of snowfall on its high peaks. However, it is precisely due to the low water content of the snow that creates the coveted "powder," leaving the state average of fifteen inches of precipitation among the driest.

The Colorado River and the Rio Grande are the main tributaries for the watershed encompassing much of the region, providing for agricultural irrigation and human consumption for millions of people. Due to climate change and misuse, this life-giving resource is rapidly dwindling, creating an urgent demand to address conservation strategies and reduce activities that impact climate change.

Currently, the fastest-growing states in the nation include Arizona, Nevada, Utah, and Texas. Many are drawn to the offered quality of life with access to nature, recreation, and vibrant urban centers. As a result, development is expanding across the landscape, defined as the wildland-urban interface zone. As the built environment encroaches on previously wild places, conflicts arise with habitat loss and human-wildlife interactions. In addition, wildfires pose a threat to communities located at these edges and to air quality throughout the region, especially as the climate becomes dryer.

These conditions offer unique design challenges, opportunities, and responsibilities to create landscapes and buildings that respect and honor the natural environment. This imperative calls us to sustain the planet with all its life forms, including ourselves. Tools such as conservation land trusts, transfer of development rights, and sensitive land use zoning are attempting to meet the growing demand while addressing the limits of natural resources. Designing for resiliency creates a built environment that is durable, utilizes passive and renewable systems, and can adapt to the changing climate. Some cities have set goals for phasing out carbon-sourced energy, investing in renewable infrastructure, and expanding public transportation.

Appropriate technology provides another piece of the puzzle toward our sustainable future. Individual property owners are providing self-sufficient power to their homes and businesses, while large-scale utility systems are tapping into geothermal, solar, and wind to replace carbon-producing energy sources. Exciting developments with building science and material innovations are becoming available to the mainstream construction industry, such as carbon capture use in concrete, recycled building blocks, engineered structural composites, energy and material-efficient prefabricated systems, 3D printing, and many more.

With the knowledge of our connectedness to all life on earth, we can no longer be passive observers of the loss of species or habitats without realizing the harm to ourselves. We can't produce products and dispose of waste that contains harmful chemicals without making ourselves sick. Clean air and water are not nice-to-haves but essential. With this awareness, backed by science, there is an urgency that will soon reveal whether we have acted in time. The thrill of this opportunity is the potential for our actions to turn away from minimizing the negative impact of our existence to creating positive outcomes because of our existence.

Examples in these pages offer glimpses into the possibilities for architecture and landscapes to create a meaningful sense of place. Belonging to a place creates a bond that inspires people to act for its preservation. Rather than seeing the challenges before us as barriers, we must see them as opportunities to draw on our most creative, empathic, and inspired selves. At its best, building a place called home is an expression of our ideals and vision for the future we wish to see.

Angela Dean, AIA, LEED AP;
Principal at AMD Architecture

Der Südwesten, der die Bundesstaaten Arizona, Colorado, Nevada, New Mexico, Texas und Utah umfasst, ist ein Land voller Kontraste und Komplexität. Sie besteht aus sanften Hügeln, hohen Berggipfeln, Canyons aus rotem Gestein, Mesas und Becken und hat eine raue Schönheit, die Menschen anzieht, die so unterschiedlich sind wie ihre Landschaften. Sie hat Dichter, Künstler, Wissenschaftler und Entdecker inspiriert und die Familien über Generationen hinweg mit dem Land verbunden.

Obwohl der Südwesten eine Fläche von 70 Fuß umfasst. Sonoran-Wüste bis 14.440 Fuß -(Rocky Mountains) über dem Meeresspiegel liegt, ist der größte Teil der Region die trockenste des Landes, wobei Nevada weniger als zehn Zoll Niederschlag pro Jahr erhält. Utahs Anspruch, das „schneereichste Land der Welt" zu sein, ist auf die mehr als 500 Zoll Schnee zurückzuführen, der auf den hohen Gipfeln fällt. Doch gerade der geringe Wassergehalt des Schnees sorgt für den begehrten „Pulverschnee", so dass die durchschnittliche Niederschlagsmenge von fünfzehn Zoll zu den trockensten des Landes gehört.

Der Colorado River und der Rio Grande sind die Hauptzuflüsse des Wassereinzugsgebiets, das einen großen Teil der Region umfasst und Millionen von Menschen mit landwirtschaftlichen Bewässerungsanlagen und Nahrungsmitteln versorgt. Aufgrund des Klimawandels und des Missbrauchs nimmt diese lebenswichtige Ressource rapide ab, so dass es dringend erforderlich ist, Schutzstrategien zu entwickeln und Aktivitäten, die den Klimawandel beeinflussen, zu reduzieren.

Die derzeit am schnellsten wachsenden Bundesstaaten sind Arizona, Nevada, Utah und Texas. Viele werden von der Lebensqualität angezogen, die sie mit ihrem Zugang zu Natur, Erholung und pulsierenden Stadtzentren bieten. Infolgedessen breitet sich die Bebauung in der Landschaft aus, die als „wildland-urban interface zone" bezeichnet wird. In dem Maße, wie die bebaute Umwelt in ehemals wilde Gebiete eindringt, kommt es zu Konflikten über den Verlust von Lebensraum und die Interaktion zwischen Mensch und Wildtieren. Darüber hinaus stellen Waldbrände eine Bedrohung für die Gemeinden an diesen Rändern und für die Luftqualität in der gesamten Region dar, insbesondere wenn das Klima trockener wird.

Diese Bedingungen bieten einzigartige Herausforderungen, Chancen und Verantwortlichkeiten für die Gestaltung von Landschaften und Gebäuden, die die natürliche Umwelt respektieren und achten. Dieser Imperativ ruft uns dazu auf, den Planeten mit all seinen Lebensformen, einschließlich uns selbst, zu erhalten. Mit Instrumenten wie Land Conservation Trusts, der Übertragung von Erschließungsrechten und sensiblen Flächennutzungsplänen wird versucht, die wachsende Nachfrage zu befriedigen und gleichzeitig die Grenzen der natürlichen Ressourcen zu berücksichtigen. Resilienzdesign schafft eine bauliche Umgebung, die dauerhaft ist, passive und erneuerbare Systeme nutzt und sich an den Klimawandel anpassen kann. Einige Städte haben sich Ziele für den Ausstieg aus der kohlenstoffhaltigen Energie, Investitionen in erneuerbare Infrastrukturen und den Ausbau des öffentlichen Nahverkehrs gesetzt.

Die richtige Technologie ist ein weiteres Puzzlestück unserer nachhaltigen Zukunft. Einzelne Hausbesitzer versorgen ihre Häuser und Unternehmen mit autarker Energie, während große Versorgungssysteme Erdwärme, Sonnen- und Windenergie nutzen, um kohlenstoffproduzierende Energiequellen zu ersetzen. Die Bauindustrie erlebt spannende Entwicklungen sowohl in der Wissenschaft als auch bei den Materialinnovationen, wie z. B. die Verwendung von Kohlenstoffabscheidung in Beton, recycelten Bausteinen, technischen Verbundwerkstoffen, effizienten vorgefertigten Systemen, 3D-Druck und vielem mehr.

Da wir wissen, dass wir mit allem Leben auf der Erde verbunden sind, können wir den Verlust von Arten und Lebensräumen nicht länger passiv beobachten, ohne uns des Schadens bewusst zu werden, der uns dadurch entsteht. Wir können keine Produkte herstellen und keine Abfälle entsorgen, die schädliche Chemikalien enthalten, ohne selbst krank zu werden. Saubere Luft und sauberes Wasser sind nicht nur schön, sie sind lebenswichtig. Mit diesem Bewusstsein, das durch die Wissenschaft gestützt wird, entsteht eine Dringlichkeit, die bald zeigen wird, ob wir rechtzeitig gehandelt haben. Das Spannende an dieser Möglichkeit ist, dass wir durch unser Handeln nicht nur die negativen Auswirkungen unserer Existenz minimieren, sondern auch positive Ergebnisse erzielen können.

Die Beispiele auf diesen Seiten geben einen Einblick in die Möglichkeiten von Architektur und Landschaft, einen sinnvollen Sinn für den Ort zu schaffen. Die Zugehörigkeit zu einem Ort schafft eine Bindung, die die Menschen dazu inspiriert, sich für seine Erhaltung einzusetzen. Wir sollten die vor uns liegenden Herausforderungen nicht als Hindernisse betrachten, sondern als Gelegenheit, unsere kreativste, einfühlsamste und inspirierendste Seite zum Vorschein zu bringen. Im besten Fall ist der Bau eines Hauses Ausdruck unserer Ideale und der Vision der Zukunft, die wir uns wünschen.

Angela Dean, AIA, LEED AP;
Principal at AMD Architecture

La région du Sud-Ouest, qui englobe les États de l'Arizona, du Colorado, du Nevada, du Nouveau-Mexique, du Texas et de l'Utah, est une terre de contrastes et de complexité. Composée de collines ondulantes, de hauts sommets, de canyons de roche rouge, de mesas et de bassins, elle possède une beauté sauvage qui attire des personnes aussi diverses que ses paysages. Elle a inspiré des poètes, des artistes, des scientifiques et des explorateurs et a permis aux familles de rester attachées à la terre pendant des générations.

Bien que le Sud-Ouest englobe des terres allant de 70 pieds. -Désert de Sonoran à 14.440 pieds (montagnes Rocheuses) au-dessus du niveau de la mer, la majeure partie de la région est la plus sèche du pays, le Nevada recevant moins de dix pouces de précipitations par an. Si l'Utah se targue d'être « le pays le plus enneigé du monde », c'est parce qu'il tombe plus de 500 pouces de neige sur ses hauts sommets. Cependant, c'est précisément la faible teneur en eau de la neige qui crée la « poudre » tant convoitée, laissant la moyenne de quinze pouces de précipitations de l'État parmi les plus sèches.

Le fleuve Colorado et le Rio Grande sont les principaux affluents du bassin versant qui couvre une grande partie de la région, fournissant l'irrigation agricole et la consommation humaine à des millions de personnes. En raison du changement climatique et d'une mauvaise utilisation, cette ressource vitale diminue rapidement, créant une demande urgente de stratégies de conservation et de réduction des activités ayant un impact sur le changement climatique.

Actuellement, les États dont la croissance est la plus rapide sont l'Arizona, le Nevada, l'Utah et le Texas. Beaucoup sont attirés par la qualité de vie qu'ils offrent, avec un accès à la nature, aux loisirs et à des centres urbains dynamiques. En conséquence, le développement s'étend à travers le paysage, défini comme la zone d'interface entre les zones urbaines et sauvages. À mesure que l'environnement bâti empiète sur des lieux autrefois sauvages, la perte d'habitat et les interactions entre l'homme et la faune sauvage suscitent des conflits. En outre, les incendies de forêt constituent une menace pour les communautés situées le long de ces frontières et pour la qualité de l'air dans toute la région, d'autant plus que le climat devient plus sec.

Ces conditions offrent des défis uniques en matière de conception, des opportunités et des responsabilités pour créer des paysages et des bâtiments qui respectent et honorent l'environnement naturel. Cet impératif nous appelle à soutenir la planète avec toutes ses formes de vie, y compris nous-mêmes. Des outils tels que les fiducies de conservation des terres, le transfert des droits de développement et le zonage sensible de l'utilisation des terres tentent de répondre à la demande croissante tout en tenant compte des limites des ressources naturelles. La conception pour la résilience crée un environnement bâti qui est durable, utilise des systèmes passifs et renouvelables, et peut s'adapter au changement climatique. Certaines villes ont fixé des objectifs pour éliminer progressivement les énergies carbonées, investir dans des infrastructures renouvelables et développer les transports publics.

La bonne technologie est une autre pièce du puzzle de notre avenir durable. Les particuliers fournissent une énergie autosuffisante à leur maison et à leur entreprise, tandis que les grands réseaux d'électricité exploitent l'énergie géothermique, solaire et éolienne pour remplacer les sources d'énergie productrices de carbone. Le secteur de la construction connaît des avancées passionnantes en matière d'innovations scientifiques et matérielles, telles que l'utilisation du captage du carbone dans le béton, les blocs de construction recyclés, les composites structurels techniques, les systèmes préfabriqués efficaces, l'impression 3D et bien d'autres encore.

Grâce à la connaissance de notre lien avec toute vie sur Terre, nous ne pouvons plus être des observateurs passifs de la disparition d'espèces ou d'habitats sans prendre conscience du mal qu'ils nous font. Nous ne pouvons pas fabriquer des produits et éliminer des déchets contenant des substances chimiques nocives sans nous rendre malades. Un air et une eau propres ne sont pas seulement agréables, ils sont essentiels. Avec cette prise de conscience, étayée par la science, il y a une urgence qui révélera bientôt si nous avons agi à temps. Ce qui est passionnant dans cette opportunité, c'est la possibilité pour nos actions de passer de la minimisation de l'impact négatif de notre existence à la création de résultats positifs grâce à elle.

Les exemples présentés dans ces pages donnent un aperçu des possibilités qu'offrent l'architecture et les paysages pour créer un sentiment d'appartenance significatif. L'appartenance à un lieu crée un lien qui incite les gens à agir pour sa conservation. Plutôt que de considérer les défis qui se présentent à nous comme des obstacles, nous devrions les voir comme des occasions de faire ressortir notre côté le plus créatif, empathique et inspirant. Au mieux, la construction d'un lieu appelé "maison" est l'expression de nos idéaux et de la vision de l'avenir que nous souhaitons.

Angela Dean, AIA, LEED AP;
Principal at AMD Architecture

La región del Suroeste, que abarca los estados de Arizona, Colorado, Nevada, Nuevo México, Texas y Utah, es una tierra llena de contrastes y complejidad. Compuesta por colinas onduladas, altos picos montañosos, cañones de roca roja, mesas y cuencas, posee una belleza agreste que atrae a personas tan diversas como sus paisajes. Ha servido de inspiración a poetas, artistas, científicos y exploradores y ha mantenido a las familias unidas a la tierra durante generaciones.

Aunque el Suroeste abarca tierras que van desde los 70 pies -desierto de Sonora- hasta los 14.440 pies -Montañas Rocosas- por encima del nivel del mar, la mayor parte de la región es la más seca del país, y Nevada recibe menos de diez pulgadas de precipitación al año. La afirmación de Utah de ser «la mayor tierra nevada del mundo» se atribuye a los más de 500 pulgadas de nieve que caen en sus altas cumbres. Sin embargo, es precisamente el bajo contenido en agua de la nieve lo que crea el codiciado «polvo», dejando la media estatal de quinze pulgadas de precipitación entre las más secas.

El río Colorado y el Río Grande son los principales afluentes de la cuenca hidrográfica que abarca gran parte de la región, y proporcionan el riego agrícola y el consumo humano de millones de personas. Debido al cambio climático y al mal uso, este recurso vital está disminuyendo rápidamente, lo que crea una demanda urgente para abordar las estrategias de conservación y reducir las actividades que repercuten en el cambio climático.

En la actualidad, los estados de mayor crecimiento de la nación son Arizona, Nevada, Utah y Texas. Muchos se sienten atraídos por la calidad de vida que ofrecen con acceso a la naturaleza, el ocio y los vibrantes centros urbanos. Como resultado, el desarrollo se está expandiendo a través del paisaje, definido como la zona de interfaz silvestre-urbana. A medida que el entorno construido invade lugares que antes eran salvajes, surgen conflictos por la pérdida de hábitat y las interacciones entre el hombre y la fauna. Además, los incendios forestales suponen una amenaza para las comunidades situadas en estos bordes y para la calidad del aire en toda la región, especialmente a medida que el clima se vuelve más seco.

Estas condiciones ofrecen retos de diseño, oportunidades y responsabilidades únicas para crear paisajes y edificios que respeten y honren el entorno natural. Este imperativo nos llama a sostener el planeta con todas sus formas de vida, incluidos nosotros mismos. Herramientas como los fideicomisos para la conservación de tierras, la transferencia de derechos de desarrollo y la zonificación sensible del uso de la tierra intentan satisfacer la creciente demanda al tiempo que abordan los límites de los recursos naturales. El diseño para la resiliencia crea un entorno construido que es duradero, utiliza sistemas pasivos y renovables y puede adaptarse al cambio climático. Algunas ciudades han fijado objetivos para eliminar progresivamente la energía procedente del carbono, invertir en infraestructuras renovables y ampliar el transporte público.

La tecnología adecuada es otra pieza del rompecabezas de nuestro futuro sostenible. Los propietarios individuales están proporcionando energía autosuficiente a sus hogares y empresas, mientras que los sistemas de servicios públicos a gran escala están aprovechando la energía geotérmica, solar y eólica para sustituir las fuentes de energía que producen carbono. La industria de la construcción está experimentando avances emocionantes, tanto en la parte científica y en las innovaciones de los materiales, como en el uso de la captura de carbono en el hormigón, los bloques de construcción reciclados, los compuestos estructurales de ingeniería, los sistemas prefabricados eficientes, la impresión en 3D y muchos más.

Con el conocimiento de nuestra conexión con toda la vida en la Tierra, ya no podemos ser observadores pasivos de la pérdida de especies o hábitats sin darnos cuenta del daño que nos causa. No podemos fabricar productos y eliminar residuos que contienen sustancias químicas nocivas sin enfermarnos. El aire y el agua limpios no son algo agradable, sino esencial. Con esta conciencia, respaldada por la ciencia, existe una urgencia que pronto revelará si hemos actuado a tiempo. Lo emocionante de esta oportunidad es el potencial de que nuestras acciones pasen de minimizar el impacto negativo de nuestra existencia a crear resultados positivos gracias a ella.

Los ejemplos de estas páginas ofrecen una visión de las posibilidades de la arquitectura y los paisajes para crear un sentido significativo del lugar. La pertenencia a un sitio crea un vínculo que inspira a las personas a actuar para su conservación. En lugar de ver los retos que tenemos ante nosotros como barreras, debemos verlos como oportunidades para sacar nuestro lado más creativo, empático e inspirador. En el mejor de los casos, la construcción de un lugar llamado hogar es una expresión de nuestros ideales y de la visión del futuro que deseamos.

Angela Dean, AIA, LEED AP;
Principal at AMD Architecture

# 180 DEGREES
## DESIGN + BUILD

012
v

**ECHO CANYON**

Architect:
180 Degrees Design + Build
Builder:
180 Degrees Design + Build
Photographer:
An Pham Photography

016
v

**COLACHIS**

Architect:
Al Beadle (original) and
180 Degrees Design + Build (renovation)
Builder:
180 Degrees Design + Build
Photographer:
Matt Winquist

020
v

**ROCKRIDGE**

Architect:
180 Degrees Design + Build
Builder:
180 Degrees Design + Build
Photographer:
An Pham Photography

180degreesinc.com 180degreesinc

180 Degrees Design + Build is an award-winning, architect-led design-build firm that provides the highest level of quality design and construction for discerning clients who value innovation, sustainability, and craft. Our practice—formed by a team of licensed architects, architecturally trained specialists, and fabricators—is driven by sensitivity to client needs, high-performance demands, an intense climate, and the urge to create beautiful solutions for challenging problems. Our experience as master builders gives us tremendous insight into how architecture works, helping bridge the gaps that often occur between a client's vision, a realistic budget, and the skillful execution of significant and sincere architectural works.
At 180 Degrees Design + Build, our work embodies our brand values of Rigor, Restraint, Craftsmanship, and Patience.

180 Degrees Design + Build ist ein preisgekröntes, von Architekten geführtes Design- und Bauunternehmen, das anspruchsvollen Kunden, die Wert auf Innovation, Nachhaltigkeit und Handwerk legen, ein Höchstmaß an Qualität bei Design und Bau bietet. Unser Team aus lizenzierten Architekten, architektonisch geschulten Fachleuten und Verarbeitern wird von der Sensibilität für die Bedürfnisse unserer Kunden, den hohen Leistungsanforderungen, dem intensiven Klima und dem Drang angetrieben, schöne Lösungen für anspruchsvolle Probleme zu schaffen. Unsere Erfahrung als Baumeister gibt uns einen enormen Einblick in die Funktionsweise der Architektur und hilft uns, die Lücken zu schließen, die oft zwischen der Vision eines Kunden, einem realistischen Budget und der geschickten Ausführung bedeutender und ehrlicher architektonischer Werke entstehen.
Die Arbeit von 180 Degrees Design + Build verkörpert unsere Markenwerte: Strenge, Zurückhaltung, Handwerkskunst und Geduld.

180 Degrees Design + Build est une société de conception-construction primée, dirigée par des architectes, qui offre un niveau de qualité élevé en matière de conception et de construction à des clients exigeants qui apprécient l'innovation, la durabilité et l'artisanat. Notre pratique - formée par une équipe d'architectes agréés, de spécialistes formés à l'architecture et de fabricants - est motivée par la sensibilité aux besoins des clients, les exigences de haute performance, un climat intense et l'envie de créer de belles solutions à des problèmes difficiles. Notre expérience en tant que maîtres d'œuvre nous donne un aperçu extraordinaire du fonctionnement de l'architecture, ce qui nous aide à combler les écarts qui se produisent souvent entre la vision d'un client, un budget réaliste et l'exécution habile d'œuvres architecturales significantes et sincères.
Chez 180 Degrees Design + Build, notre travail incarne les valeurs de notre marque, à savoir la rigueur, la retenue, l'artisanat et la patience.

180 Degrees Design + Build es una galardonada empresa de diseño y construcción dirigida por arquitectos que ofrece el más alto nivel de calidad para clientes exigentes que valoran la innovación, la sostenibilidad y la artesanía. Nuestro estudio, formado por un equipo de arquitectos licenciados, especialistas con formación arquitectónica y fabricantes, está impulsado por la sensibilidad a las necesidades del cliente, las demandas de alto rendimiento, un clima intenso y el impulso de crear soluciones hermosas para los problemas desafiantes. Nuestra experiencia como maestros de obras nos da una enorme visión de cómo funciona la arquitectura, ayudando a cerrar las brechas que a menudo se producen entre la visión de un cliente, un presupuesto realista, y la hábil ejecución de obras arquitectónicas significativas y sinceras.
En 180 Degrees Design + Build, nuestro trabajo encarna los valores de nuestra marca: Rigor, Restricción, Artesanía y Paciencia.

## ECHO CANYON

Phoenix, Arizona, United States // Lot area: 14,929 sq ft; building area: 4,929 sq ft

This renovated 1960s home captures the grandeur of Camelback Mountain and long vistas of the Phoenix valley, while creating various spatial experiences for the owners and their guests. The experience begins in the street, where the architecture and massing proportions are simplified to respect the textural and colorful mountain. Ascending through the first of two steel portals, you are greeted with a large courtyard highlighted by key stopping points to view some of the well-known Camelback Mountain's rock features. The second steel portal, painted in vibrant yellow to mimic the yellow blooms of the desert plants, compresses as you enter the home. As you maneuver around the feature fireplace, the roof line tilts upward, revealing the dynamic vertical face of the mountain.

Cette maison rénovée des années 1960 capture la grandeur de Camelback Mountain et les longues vues de la vallée de Phoenix, tout en créant diverses expériences spatiales pour les propriétaires et leurs invités. L'expérience commence dans la rue, où l'architecture et les proportions de masse sont simplifiées pour respecter la montagne texturée et colorée. En passant par le premier des deux portails en acier, vous êtes accueillis par une grande cour soulignée par des points d'arrêt clés pour voir certaines des caractéristiques rocheuses bien connues de Camelback Mountain. Le deuxième portail en acier, peint en jaune vif pour imiter les fleurs jaunes des plantes du désert, se comprime lorsque vous entrez dans la maison. Lorsque vous vous déplacez autour de la cheminée, la ligne de toit s'incline vers le haut, révélant la face verticale dynamique de la montagne.

Dieses renovierte Haus aus den 1960er Jahren fängt die Erhabenheit des Camelback Mountain und weite Ausblicke auf das Phoenix-Tal ein und schafft gleichzeitig vielfältige räumliche Erlebnisse für die Eigentümer und ihre Gäste. Das Erlebnis beginnt bereits auf der Straße, wo die Architektur und die Proportionen des Hauses vereinfacht wurden, um den strukturierten und farbenfrohen Berg zu respektieren. Wenn man durch das erste von zwei Stahlportalen aufsteigt, wird man von einem großen Innenhof begrüßt, in dem sich wichtige Haltepunkte befinden, von denen aus man einige der bekannten Felsen des Camelback Mountain betrachten kann. Das zweite Stahlportal, das in leuchtendem Gelb gestrichen ist, um die gelben Blüten der Wüstenpflanzen zu imitieren, verdichtet sich, wenn man das Haus betritt. Wenn man sich um den Kamin herum bewegt, neigt sich die Dachlinie nach oben und gibt den Blick auf die dynamische vertikale Bergwand frei.

Esta casa renovada de los años 60 captura la grandeza de la montaña Camelback y las largas vistas del valle de Phoenix, al tiempo que crea diversas experiencias espaciales para los propietarios y sus invitados. La experiencia comienza en la calle, donde la arquitectura y las proporciones de la masa se simplifican para respetar la textura y el colorido de la montaña. Al ascender por el primero de los dos portales de acero, uno se encuentra con un gran patio resaltado por puntos de parada clave para disfrutar de las vistas de algunas de las conocidas características rocosas de Camelback Mountain. El segundo portal de acero, pintado en amarillo vibrante para imitar las flores amarillas de las plantas del desierto, se comprime al entrar en la casa. Al rodear la chimenea, la línea del techo se inclina hacia arriba, revelando la cara vertical de la montaña.

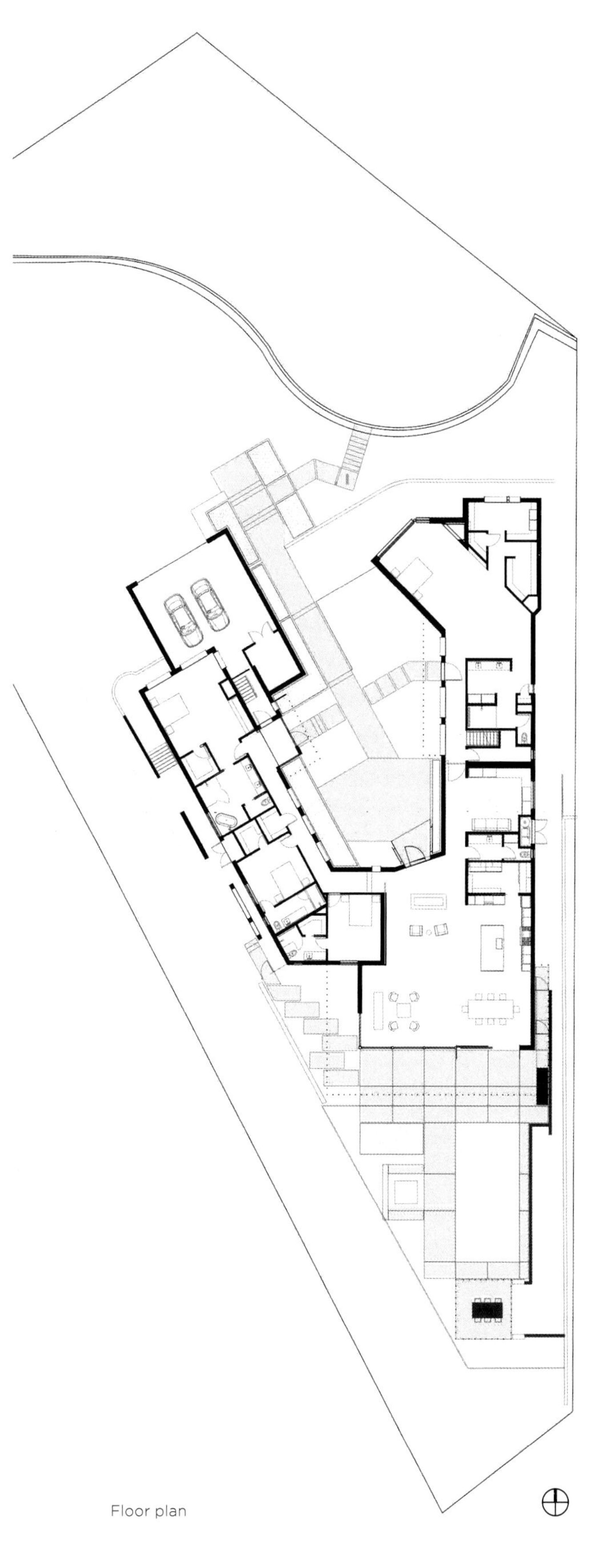

Floor plan

## COLACHIS

Phoenix, Arizona, United States // Lot area: 36,769 sq ft; building area: 3,917 sq ft

The house is sited to capture the stunning foothill panoramas of Camelback Mountain in Phoenix, Arizona. This residence was originally designed by Alfred Newman Beadle, who is often considered one of the most prolific Modernist architects of the Southwest. The home features many of Beadle's signature design elements of self-contained space, combined with expanse and glass. The extensive remodel of this almost fifty-year-old home preserves the original design concept. In addition to a general refresh, the client wanted to add a master suite and expand the restricting kitchen to allow for more functional entertaining. When adding onto historically significant homes, 180 Degrees Design + Build's ethos is not to imitate other architectural masters but to create complementary new and beautiful spaces that will stand the test of time.

La maison est située de manière à capturer les superbes panoramas des contreforts de Camelback Mountain à Phoenix, Arizona. Cette résidence a été conçue à l'origine par Alfred Newman Beadle, qui est souvent considéré comme l'un des architectes modernistes les plus prolifiques du Sud-Ouest. La maison présente de nombreux éléments de conception caractéristiques de Beadle, à savoir des espaces autonomes, combinés à des surfaces étendues et vitrées. Le remodelage complet de cette maison de près de cinquante ans préserve le concept de design original. En plus d'un rafraîchissement général, le client souhaitait ajouter une suite parentale et agrandir la cuisine trop étroite pour permettre des réceptions plus fonctionnelles. Lorsqu'il s'agit d'ajouter des maisons d'importance historique, la philosophie de 180 Degrees Design + Build n'est pas d'imiter d'autres maîtres de l'architecture, mais de créer de nouveaux espaces complémentaires et magnifiques qui résisteront à l'épreuve du temps.

Das Haus ist so platziert, dass es das atemberaubende Vorgebirgspanorama des Camelback Mountain in Phoenix, Arizona, einfängt. Das Haus wurde ursprünglich von Alfred Newman Beadle entworfen, der oft als einer der produktivsten modernistischen Architekten des Südwestens gilt. Das Haus weist viele von Beadles charakteristischen Designelementen auf, die einen in sich geschlossenen Raum mit Weite und Glas kombinieren. Bei der umfassenden Umgestaltung dieses fast fünfzig Jahre alten Hauses wurde das ursprüngliche Designkonzept beibehalten. Neben einer allgemeinen Erneuerung wollte der Bauherr eine Master-Suite einrichten und die beengte Küche erweitern, um mehr Raum für funktionale Unterhaltung zu schaffen. Bei der Erweiterung von historisch bedeutsamen Häusern ist es der Ethos von 180 Degrees Design + Build, nicht andere architektonische Meister zu imitieren, sondern ergänzende neue und schöne Räume zu schaffen, die dem Test der Zeit standhalten werden.

La casa captura los impresionantes panoramas de la montaña Camelback en Phoenix, Arizona. Esta residencia fue diseñada originalmente por Alfred Newman Beadle, que suele ser considerado uno de los arquitectos modernistas más prolíficos del suroeste. La casa presenta muchos de los elementos de diseño característicos de Beadle, como el espacio autónomo, combinado con la amplitud y el cristal. La amplia remodelación de esta casa de casi cincuenta años conserva el concepto de diseño original. Además de una renovación general, el cliente quería añadir una suite principal y ampliar la restringida cocina para permitir un entretenimiento más funcional. Cuando se añaden casas de importancia histórica, el espíritu de 180 Degrees Design + Build no es imitar a otros maestros de la arquitectura, sino crear espacios nuevos y hermosos que resistan el paso del tiempo.

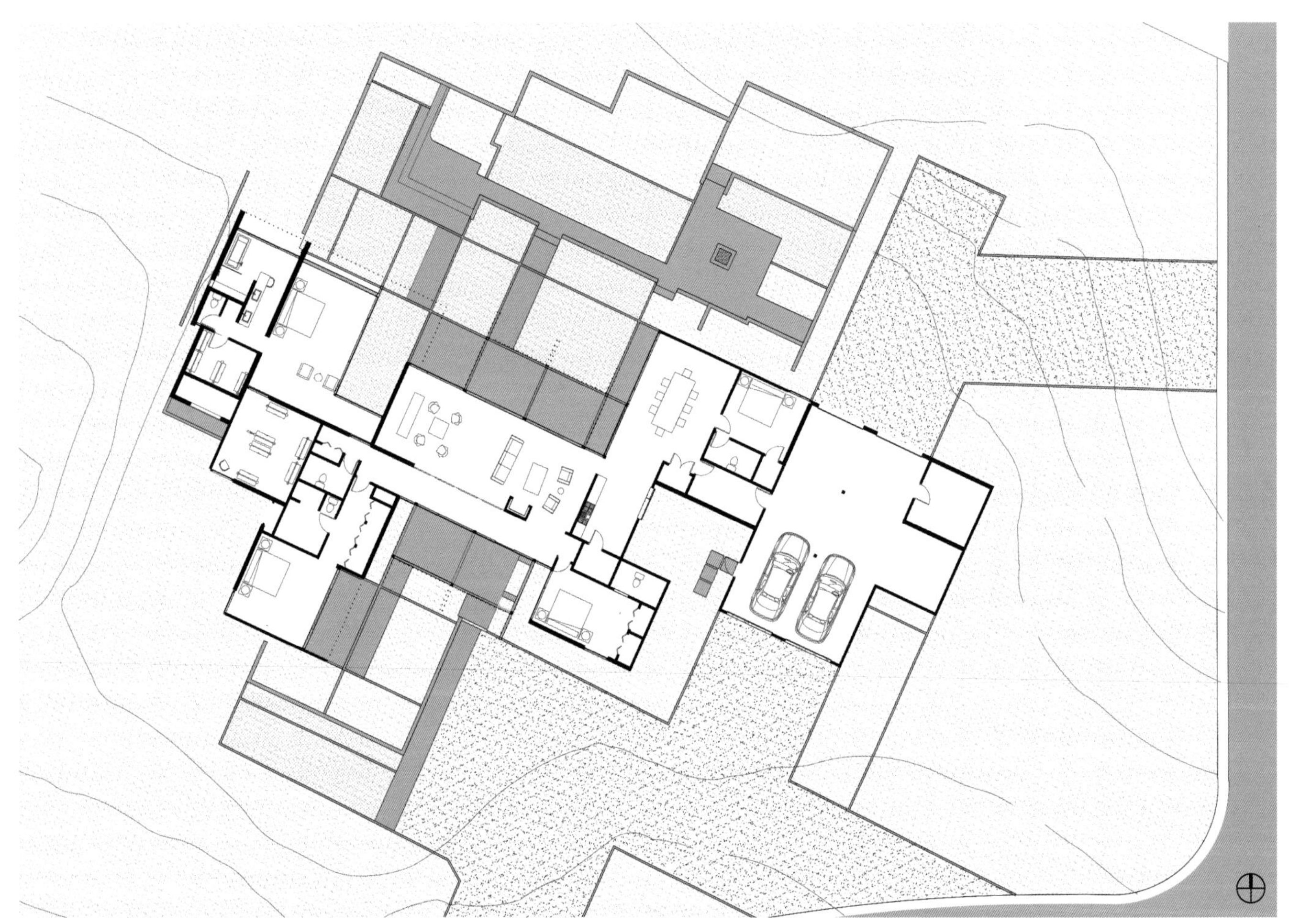

Floor plan

## ROCKRIDGE

Phoenix, Arizona, United States // Lot area: 37,398 sq ft; building area: 4,951 sq ft

This residence rests on a spectacular lot at the base of the iconic Camelback Mountain in Phoenix, Arizona. The owners wanted the property to fully embody al fresco living, taking advantage of the "resort" climate this part of the Southwest offers much of the year. To maximize the indoor/outdoor lifestyle, the design aimed at integrating and capturing the existing natural elements of this magnificent desert setting into the daily living experience through a wall of glass that can be completely hidden from sight. Frank Lloyd Wright stated: "I believe a house is more of a home by being a work of art." In the Rockridge residence's case, "nature is the work of art, and we simply captured it with a functional glass vessel that became the home," says James Trahan, Principal at 180 Degrees Design + Build.

Cette résidence se trouve sur un terrain spectaculaire au pied de l'emblématique Camelback Mountain à Phoenix, en Arizona. Les propriétaires voulaient que la propriété incarne pleinement la vie al fresco, en profitant du climat de « station balnéaire » que cette partie du Sud-Ouest offre une grande partie de l'année. Pour maximiser le style de vie intérieur/extérieur, la conception visait à intégrer et à capturer les éléments naturels existants de ce magnifique cadre désertique dans l'expérience de vie quotidienne grâce à un mur de verre qui peut être complètement caché de la vue. Frank Lloyd Wright a déclaré : « Je crois qu'une maison est davantage un foyer en étant une œuvre d'art ». Dans le cas de la résidence de Rockridge, « la nature est l'œuvre d'art, et nous l'avons simplement capturée avec un récipient en verre fonctionnel qui est devenu la maison », explique James Trahan, directeur de 180 Degrees Design + Build.

Dieses Haus befindet sich auf einem spektakulären Grundstück am Fuße des berühmten Camelback Mountain in Phoenix, Arizona. Die Eigentümer wollten, dass das Haus ein Leben im Freien verkörpert und die Vorteile des „Resort"-Klimas nutzt, das dieser Teil des Südwestens die meiste Zeit des Jahres bietet. Um den Lebensstil im Innen- und Außenbereich zu maximieren, zielte der Entwurf darauf ab, die vorhandenen natürlichen Elemente dieser herrlichen Wüstenlandschaft durch eine Glaswand, die vollständig aus dem Blickfeld verschwinden kann, in das tägliche Wohnerlebnis zu integrieren und einzufangen. Frank Lloyd Wright sagte: „Ich glaube, ein Haus ist mehr als ein Zuhause, wenn es ein Kunstwerk ist." Im Fall der Rockridge-Residenz „ist die Natur das Kunstwerk, und wir haben sie einfach mit einem funktionalen Glasgefäß eingefangen, das zum Zuhause wurde", sagt James Trahan, Leiter von 180 Degrees Design + Build.

Esta residencia se encuentra en un terreno espectacular en la base de la icónica montaña Camelback en Phoenix, Arizona. Los propietarios querían que la propiedad encarnara plenamente la vida al aire libre, aprovechando el clima de «resort» que esta parte del suroeste ofrece la mayor parte del año. Para maximizar el estilo de vida interior/exterior, el diseño tenía como objetivo integrar y capturar los elementos naturales existentes de este magnífico entorno desértico en la experiencia de vida diaria a través de una pared de cristal que se puede ocultar completamente. Frank Lloyd Wright declaró: «Creo que una casa es más un hogar al ser una obra de arte». En el caso de la residencia Rockridge, «la naturaleza es la obra de arte, y nosotros simplemente la capturamos con un recipiente de vidrio funcional que se convirtió en hogar», dice James Trahan, director de 180 Degrees Design + Build.

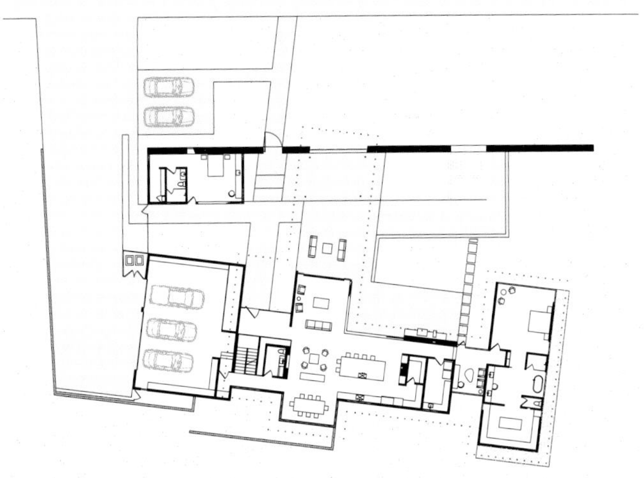

Ground floor plan

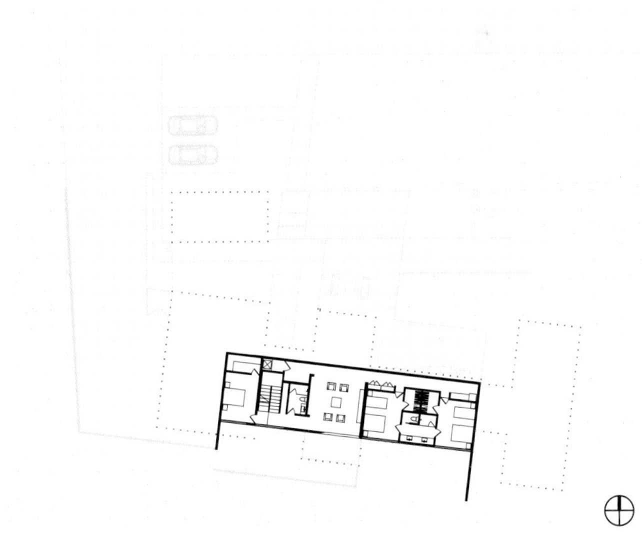

Lower level floor plan

# SOLOWAY DESIGNS INC.
# CELAYA | SOLOWAY INTERIORS

026
v

**CONTEMPORARY HACIENDA**

Architecture and Interior Design Team:
Soloway Designs Inc.,
Celaya|Soloway Interiors
Landscape Architect:
Soloway Designs Inc.
Builder:
One-Oak
Photographer:
© Kurt Munger

030
v

**GALLERY-INSPIRED MODERN**

Architecture and Interior Design Team:
Soloway Designs Inc.,
Celaya|Soloway Interiors
Landscape Architect:
Soloway Designs Inc.
Builder:
CAOS Construction
Photographer:
© Kurt Munger and Jaret Miller

034
v

**RUSTIC CONTEMPORARY**

Architecture and Interior Design Team:
Soloway Designs Inc.,
Celaya|Soloway Interiors
Landscape Architect:
Soloway Designs Inc.
Builder:
CAOS Construction
Photographer:
© Kurt Munger

www.soloway-designs.com

Marc Soloway, AIA

Esthela Celaya, ASID/NKBA

Soloway Designs Inc and Celaya|Soloway Interiors are award-winning Arizona-based Architecture and Interior Design firms that work seamlessly together under the motto: "A unique pairing for the Southwest and beyond." The team provides clients with uniquely satisfying experiences, recognizing that Architecture and Interior Design are inseparable disciplines that must coalesce to identify, create, and instantiate the anticipated mood for each space in the home. Marc Soloway is the practical visionary who conceives uniquely dynamic architecture that blends client wants and needs while creating a fusion of architecture and nature. Founded in 1996, Soloway Designs has completed over 1200 projects, including custom homes, major remodels, and commercial buildings. Esthela Celaya collaborates closely with each client to create the design and environment tailored to each client's individual needs, aesthetics, and lifestyle. Founded in 2014, Celaya|Soloway Interiors has completed over 200 custom home projects.

Soloway Designs Inc und Celaya|Soloway Interiors sind preisgekrönte Architektur- und Innenarchitekturbüros mit Sitz in Arizona, die nahtlos zusammenarbeiten unter dem Motto: „Eine einzigartige Kombination für den Südwesten und darüber hinaus". Das Team bietet seinen Kunden eine einzigartige Erfahrung, denn Architektur und Innenarchitektur sind untrennbare Disziplinen, die zusammenwachsen müssen, um die erwartete Stimmung für jeden Raum im Haus zu identifizieren, zu schaffen und umzusetzen. Marc Soloway ist ein praktischer Visionär, der eine einzigartige dynamische Architektur entwirft, die die Wünsche und Bedürfnisse der Kunden berücksichtigt und gleichzeitig eine Verschmelzung von Architektur und Natur schafft. Das 1996 gegründete Unternehmen Soloway Designs hat über 1200 Projekte realisiert, darunter Eigenheime, umfangreiche Umbauten und gewerbliche Gebäude. Esthela Celaya arbeitet eng mit jedem Kunden zusammen, um ein Design und eine Umgebung zu schaffen, die auf die individuellen Bedürfnisse, die Ästhetik und den Lebensstil jedes einzelnen Kunden zugeschnitten sind. Seit der Gründung im Jahr 2014 hat Celaya|Soloway Interiors über 200 Projekte für Eigenheime abgeschlossen.

Soloway Designs Inc. et Celaya|Soloway Interiors sont des cabinets d'architecture et de design d'intérieur primés, basés en Arizona, qui travaillent ensemble de manière transparente sous la devise : « Une paire unique pour le Sud-Ouest et au-delà ». L'équipe offre à ses clients une expérience unique et satisfaisante, en reconnaissant que l'architecture et le design d'intérieur sont des disciplines indissociables qui doivent s'unir pour identifier, créer et concrétiser l'ambiance prévue pour chaque espace de la maison. Marc Soloway est le visionnaire pratique qui conçoit une architecture unique et dynamique qui allie les désirs et les besoins du client tout en créant une fusion entre l'architecture et la nature. Fondé en 1996, Soloway Designs a réalisé plus de 1200 projets, dont des maisons personnalisées, des rénovations majeures et des bâtiments commerciaux. Esthela Celaya collabore étroitement avec chaque client pour créer le design et l'environnement adaptés aux besoins individuels, à l'esthétique et au style de vie de chaque client. Fondée en 2014, Celaya|Soloway Interiors a réalisé plus de 200 projets de maisons personnalisées.

Soloway Designs Inc y Celaya|Soloway Interiors son empresas galardonadas de arquitectura y diseño de interiores con sede en Arizona que trabajan juntas a la perfección bajo el lema: «Un binomio único para el suroeste y más allá». El equipo proporciona a los clientes experiencias únicas y satisfactorias, reconociendo que la Arquitectura y el Diseño de Interiores son disciplinas inseparables que deben unirse para identificar, crear e influir el estado de ánimo previsto para cada espacio del hogar. Marc Soloway es el visionario práctico que concibe una arquitectura única y dinámica que combina los deseos y las necesidades de los clientes y crea una fusión de arquitectura y naturaleza. Fundada en 1996, Soloway Designs ha completado más de 1.200 proyectos, incluyendo casas a medida, remodelaciones importantes y edificios comerciales. Esthela Celaya colabora estrechamente con cada cliente para crear el diseño y el entorno adaptado a las necesidades individuales de toda ellos, la estética y el estilo de vida. Fundada en 2014, Celaya|Soloway Interiors ha completado más de 200 proyectos de casas personalizadas.

## CONTEMPORARY HACIENDA

Oro Valley, Arizona, United States // Lot area: 1.5 acres; building area: 6,432 sq ft

This rugged desert building site set the stage for a contemporary interpretation of traditional Hacienda architecture. The client wanted a unique home that fitted effortlessly into its surroundings. Rock outcropping presented siting challenges, but the use of stone reflecting local geology allowed the structure to create a true sense of place. Hacienda hallmarks of a clay tile roof, rough wood beams, and an exquisite wood entry door greet visitors and portent what to anticipate inside. Interior design emphasizes rustic romantic beauty with rich colors, natural materials accented with traditional wood and metal detailing. The expansive rear patio and curvilinear pool provide ample space for socializing and taking in the rugged desert mountain views. Day or night, inside or out, amazing views to savor.

Ce site de construction désertique accidenté a préparé le terrain pour une interprétation contemporaine de l'architecture traditionnelle Hacienda. Le client souhaitait une maison unique qui s'intègre parfaitement à son environnement. Les affleurements rocheux ont posé des problèmes d'implantation, mais l'utilisation de pierres reflétant la géologie locale a permis à la structure de créer un véritable sentiment d'appartenance. Le toit en tuiles d'argile, les poutres en bois brut et la porte d'entrée en bois exquis, caractéristiques d'une hacienda, accueillent les visiteurs et laissent présager ce qui les attend à l'intérieur. Le design intérieur met l'accent sur la beauté rustique et romantique avec des couleurs riches, des matériaux naturels accentués par des détails traditionnels en bois et en métal. Le vaste patio arrière et la piscine curviligne offrent un grand espace pour se retrouver et profiter de la vue imprenable sur les montagnes du désert. Jour et nuit, à l'intérieur ou à l'extérieur, des vues incroyables à savourer.

Dieses schroffe Wüstengrundstück bildete die Grundlage für eine zeitgenössische Interpretation der traditionellen Hacienda-Architektur. Der Kunde wollte ein einzigartiges Haus, das sich in die Umgebung einfügt. Die Felsvorsprünge stellten eine Herausforderung für den Standort dar, aber durch die Verwendung von Steinen, die die örtliche Geologie widerspiegeln, konnte das Gebäude ein echtes Gefühl für den Ort vermitteln. Die typischen Merkmale einer Hacienda - ein Dach aus Tonziegeln, raue Holzbalken und eine exquisite Eingangstür aus Holz - begrüßen die Besucher und lassen erahnen, was sie im Inneren erwartet. Das Innendesign betont die rustikale, romantische Schönheit mit satten Farben und natürlichen Materialien, die mit traditionellen Holz- und Metalldetails akzentuiert werden. Der weitläufige Garten und der geschwungene Pool bieten viel Platz, um Kontakte zu knüpfen und die Aussicht auf die Bergwüste zu genießen. Ob bei Tag oder Nacht, drinnen oder draußen, genießen Sie die herrliche Aussicht.

Este emplazamiento en el desierto escarpado estableció el escenario para una interpretación contemporánea de la arquitectura tradicional de la Hacienda. El cliente quería una casa única que encajara en su entorno. El afloramiento de rocas supuso un reto para el emplazamiento, pero el uso de la piedra, que refleja la geología local, permitió que la estructura creara un verdadero sentido del lugar. El tejado de tejas de arcilla, las vigas de madera y la exquisita puerta de entrada también de madera acogen a los visitantes y presagian lo que les espera en el interior. El diseño interior realza la belleza rústica y romántica con ricos colores y materiales naturales acentuados con detalles tradicionales de madera y metal. El amplio patio trasero y la piscina curvilínea proporcionan un amplio espacio para socializar y disfrutar de las vistas del desierto montañoso. De día o de noche, en el interior o al aire libre, la vivienda ofrece vistas increíbles para el deleite.

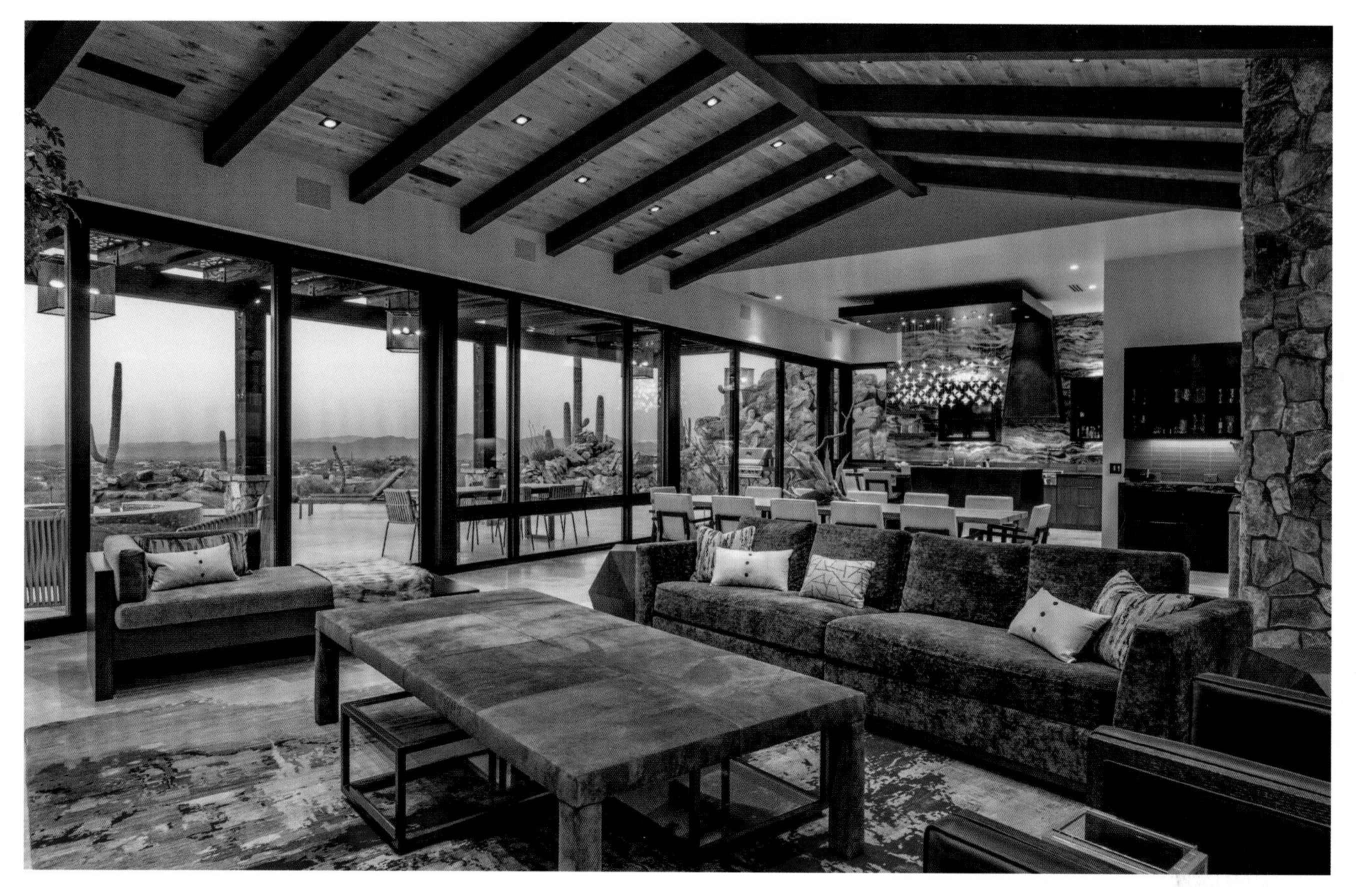

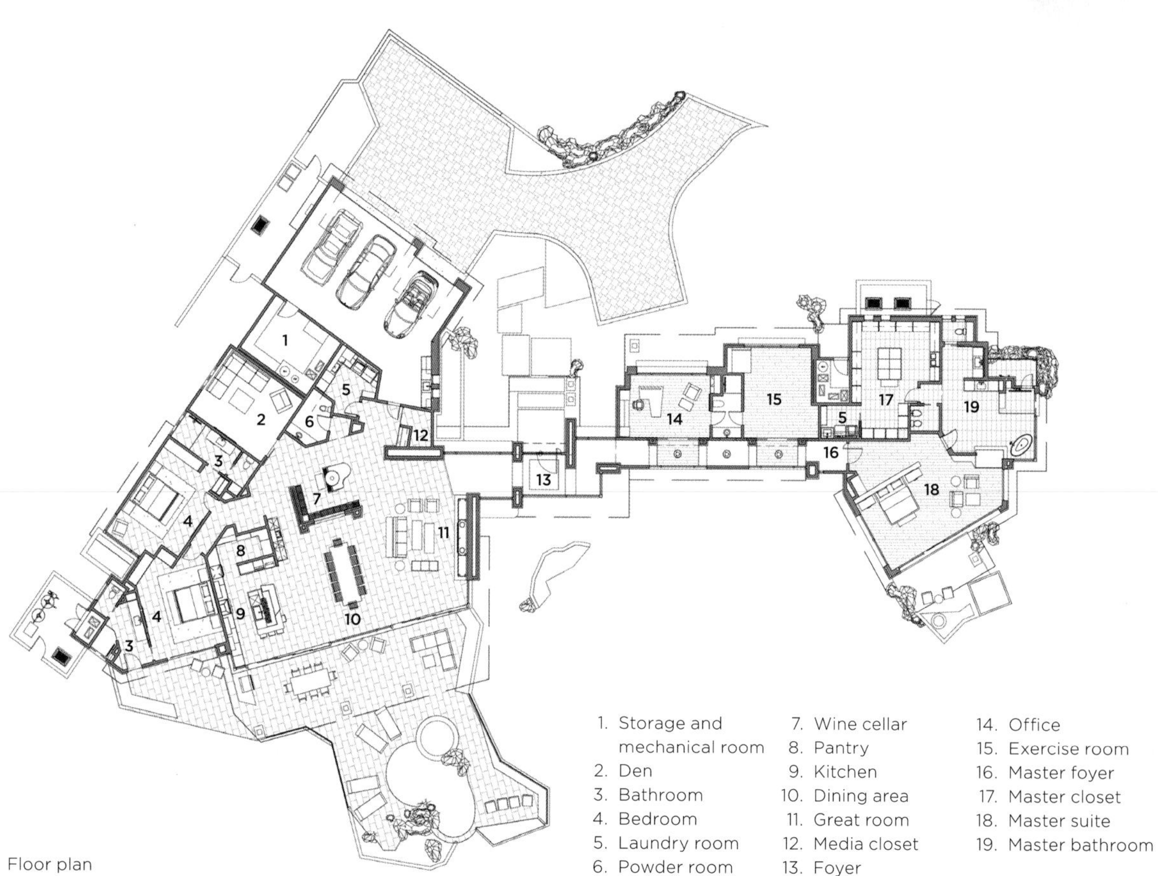
1. Storage and mechanical room
2. Den
3. Bathroom
4. Bedroom
5. Laundry room
6. Powder room
7. Wine cellar
8. Pantry
9. Kitchen
10. Dining area
11. Great room
12. Media closet
13. Foyer
14. Office
15. Exercise room
16. Master foyer
17. Master closet
18. Master suite
19. Master bathroom

Floor plan

## GALLERY-INSPIRED MODERN

Tucson, Arizona, United States // Lot area: 1.5 acres; building area: 5,086 sq ft

The client's vision was to create a pristine gallery-feeling home in the rugged Sonoran Desert. While large boulder outcroppings and mature native cacti presented some siting challenges, the design resulted in a clean, modern home with mesquite blend stone accent walls merging with the surrounding geology. Walls of glass bring the desert inside, presenting an everchanging palate of shapes and colors as sunrise transitions to sunset. Environmental concerns guided two aspects of the home: the construction of concrete masonry walls that significantly reduces energy usage and the use of a hybrid solar system—composed of solar panels augmented with an integrated battery—that facilitates solar energy storage, reducing reliance on the grid.

La vision du client était de créer une maison à l'allure d'une galerie d'art dans le désert sauvage de Sonoran. Bien que de grands affleurements rocheux et des cactus indigènes matures aient posé quelques problèmes d'emplacement, la conception a abouti à une maison moderne et épurée, dont les murs d'accent en pierre de mesquite se fondent dans la géologie environnante. Des murs de verre amènent le désert à l'intérieur, présentant une palette de formes et de couleurs en constante évolution lorsque le soleil se lève et se couche. Les préoccupations environnementales ont guidé deux aspects de la maison : la construction de murs en maçonnerie de béton qui réduit considérablement la consommation d'énergie et l'utilisation d'un système solaire hybride - composé de panneaux solaires et d'une batterie intégrée - qui facilite le stockage de l'énergie solaire, réduisant ainsi la dépendance au réseau.

Die Vision des Bauherrn war es, in der zerklüfteten Sonoran-Wüste ein ursprüngliches Haus mit Galeriecharakter zu schaffen. Große Felsbrocken und ausgewachsene einheimische Kakteen stellten zwar eine Herausforderung für den Standort dar, doch der Entwurf führte zu einem klaren, modernen Haus mit Akzentwänden aus Mesquite-Stein, die mit der umgebenden Geologie verschmelzen. Glaswände bringen die Wüste ins Innere und bieten eine sich ständig verändernde Palette von Formen und Farben, wenn der Sonnenaufgang in den Sonnenuntergang übergeht. Bei zwei Aspekten des Hauses wurden Umweltaspekte berücksichtigt: der Bau von Wänden aus Betonmauerwerk, die den Energieverbrauch erheblich reduzieren, und die Verwendung eines hybriden Solarsystems, das aus Solarpanelen und einer integrierten Batterie besteht, die die Speicherung von Solarenergie ermöglicht und so die Abhängigkeit vom Stromnetz verringert.

La visión del cliente era crear una casa prístina inspirada en una galería en el escarpado desierto de Sonora. Aunque los grandes afloramientos de rocas y los cactus autóctonos maduros plantearon algunos retos de ubicación, el diseño dio lugar a una casa limpia y moderna con paredes de acento de mezcla de mezquite que se funden con la geología circundante. Las paredes de cristal traen el desierto al interior, presentando un paladar siempre cambiante de formas y colores a medida que el amanecer pasa a la puesta de sol. La preocupación por el medio ambiente ha guiado dos aspectos de la casa: la construcción de muros de mampostería de hormigón, que reduce significativamente el uso de energía, y el uso de un sistema solar híbrido -compuesto por paneles solares aumentados con una batería integrada- que facilita el almacenamiento de energía solar, reduciendo la dependencia de la red.

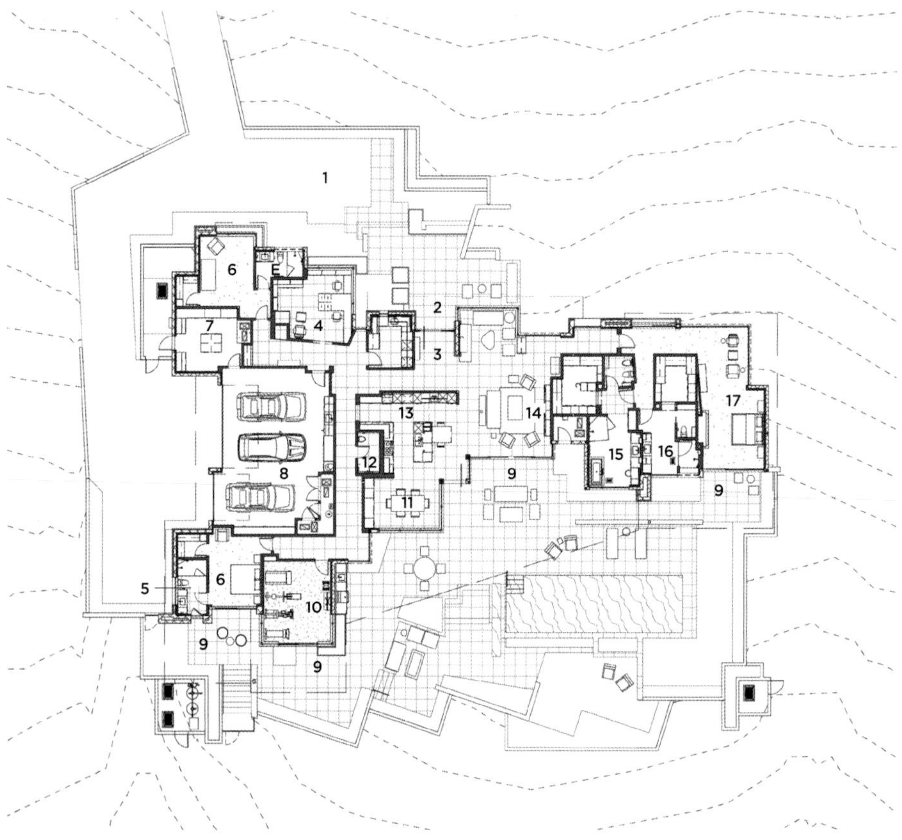


Floor plan

1. Guest parking
2. Covered entry
3. Foyer
4. Office
5. Bathroom
6. Bedroom
7. Storage/shop
8. Three-car garage
9. Covered patio
10. Exercise room
11. Dining area
12. Powder room
13. Kitchen
14. Great room
15. Master bathroom (hers)
16. Master bathroom (his)
17. Master bedroom

## RUSTIC CONTEMPORARY

Oro Valley, Arizona, United States // Lot area: 2 acres; building area: 5,412 sq ft

The client wanted a home that capitalized on the views with minimal disruption to the desert landscape —mainly native saguaro cacti and massive rock outcroppings. The house presents a truly biophilic design —from the entry courtyard through all the rooms in the house— that merges indoors and outdoors and emphasizes natural materials while creating a unique sense of place. A large, curved steel trellis and the custom-designed massive glass and metal entry door echo the curves of the rugged mountainous terrain. The house interior exudes a feeling of grandeur, displaying open, expansive spaces, floor-to-ceiling windows, and heavily wood-beamed ceilings blurring the boundaries between inside and outside.

Der Bauherr wünschte sich ein Haus, das die Aussicht nutzt und die Wüstenlandschaft - hauptsächlich einheimische Saguaro-Kakteen und massive Felsen - möglichst wenig stört. Das Haus präsentiert ein wahrhaft biophiles Design - vom Eingangshof bis hin zu allen Räumen des Hauses -, das Innen- und Außenbereiche miteinander verschmelzen lässt, natürliche Materialien betont und gleichzeitig ein einzigartiges Gefühl für den Ort schafft. Ein großes, geschwungenes Stahlgitter und die maßgefertigte massive Eingangstür aus Glas und Metall spiegeln die Kurven des zerklüfteten Berggeländes wider. Das Innere des Hauses strahlt ein Gefühl von Erhabenheit aus, mit offenen, weitläufigen Räumen, raumhohen Fenstern und hohen Holzbalkendecken, die die Grenzen zwischen Innen und Außen verwischen.

Le client voulait une maison qui capitalisait sur les vues avec une perturbation minimale du paysage désertique - principalement des cactus saguaro indigènes et des affleurements rocheux massifs. La maison présente un design biophilique - de la cour d'entrée à toutes les pièces de la maison - qui fusionne l'intérieur et l'extérieur et met l'accent sur les matériaux naturels tout en créant un effet d'appartenance unique. Un grand treillis en acier incurvé et la porte d'entrée massive en verre et en métal conçue sur mesure font écho aux courbes du terrain montagneux accidenté. L'intérieur de la maison dégage un sentiment de grandeur, affichant des espaces ouverts et expansifs, des baies vitrées et des plafonds à poutres apparentes qui brouillent les frontières entre l'intérieur et l'extérieur.

El cliente quería una casa que aprovechara las vistas con la mínima interrupción del paisaje desértico, principalmente *cactus saguaro* nativos y afloramientos rocosos masivos. La casa presenta un diseño verdaderamente biofílico, desde el patio de entrada a través de todas las habitaciones de la casa, que fusiona el interior y el exterior y enfatiza los materiales naturales mientras crea un sentido único del lugar. Un gran enrejado de acero curvo y la puerta de entrada de metal y vidrio macizo de diseño personalizado hacen eco de las curvas del accidentado terreno montañoso. El interior de la casa emana una sensación de grandeza, mostrando espacios abiertos y amplios, ventanas del suelo al techo y tejados con vigas de madera maciza que difuminan los límites entre interior y exterior.

1. Guest parking
2. Autocourt
3. Garage
4. Bathroom
5. Bedroom
6. Patio
7. Office
8. Storage
9. Game room
10. Powder room
11. Kitchen
12. Covered entry
13. Foyer
14. Dining area
15. Covered patio
16. Laundry room
17. Master bathroom
18. Master suite
19. Great room

Floor plan

# KENDLE DESIGN COLLABORATIVE

040
v

**DANCING LIGHT RESIDENCE**

Architect:
Brent Kendle/Kendle Design Collaborative
Interior Designer:
David Michael Miller
Landscape Designer:
GBTwo Landscape Architects
Builder:
Desert Star Construction
Photographer:
© Alexander Vertikoff

044
v

**DESERT WING**

Architect:
Brent Kendle/Kendle Design Collaborative
Interior Designer:
Jack Wozniak
Landscape Architect:
Floor and Associates
Builder:
Construction Zone
Photographer:
© Rick Brazil

048
v

**RAMMED EARTH MODERN**

Architect:
Kendle Design Collaborative
Interior Furnishings:
Gabe Holland, Design Within Reach
Builder:
Mackos Architecture and Construction
Photographer:
© Winquist Photography

www.kendledesign.com kendledesign

Founded by Brent Kendle, AIA, LEED AP, in 2002, Kendle Design Collaborative is located in Scottsdale, Arizona and is an internationally acclaimed architectural firm specializing in regionally inspired modern design. Our work is not defined by imported historic styles or the latest fashion trends, but instead, each home is a creative response to our clients' unique needs and the spirit of the land they have chosen to call home. We strive to create designs that appear timeless while also being an authentic reflection of their specific place and time. We believe homes should be both pragmatic and poetic, connecting occupants to nature and providing unique experiences that change with the passing of the sun or the seasons. We seek to clearly understand our clients' priorities, values, and aspirations, in the pursuit of understanding what brings them joy. Only then can we carefully design a home that transcends shelter, enhancing their daily living and bringing them joy in their most intimate moments as well as times of gathering and celebration.

Die 2002 von Brent Kendle, AIA, LEED AP, gegründete Kendle Design Collaborative mit Sitz in Scottsdale, Arizona, ist ein international anerkanntes Architekturbüro, das sich auf regional inspiriertes modernes Design spezialisiert hat. Unsere Arbeit wird nicht durch importierte historische Stile oder die neuesten Modetrends bestimmt, sondern jedes Haus ist eine kreative Antwort auf die einzigartigen Bedürfnisse unserer Kunden und den Geist des Landes, das sie als ihr Zuhause gewählt haben. Wir streben danach, Entwürfe zu schaffen, die zeitlos erscheinen und gleichzeitig ein authentisches Spiegelbild des jeweiligen Ortes und der jeweiligen Zeit sind. Wir sind der Meinung, dass Häuser sowohl pragmatisch als auch poetisch sein sollten, um die Bewohner mit der Natur zu verbinden und vielfältige einzigartige Erfahrungen zu bieten, die sich mit dem Lauf der Sonne oder der Jahreszeiten verändern. Wir versuchen, die Prioritäten, Werte und Wünsche unserer Kunden genau zu verstehen, um herauszufinden, was ihnen Freude bereitet. Nur dann können wir ein Haus entwerfen, das mehr ist als nur eine Behausung, das ihr tägliches Leben bereichert und ihnen Freude in ihren intimsten Momenten, aber auch in Zeiten des Zusammenseins und des Feierns bringt.

Fondé par Brent Kendle, AIA, LEED AP, en 2002, Kendle Design Collaborative est situé à Scottsdale, Arizona et est un cabinet d'architecture de renommée internationale spécialisé dans le design moderne d'inspiration régionale. Notre travail n'est pas défini par des styles historiques importés ou les dernières tendances, mais chaque maison est une réponse créative aux besoins uniques de nos clients et à l'esprit de la terre qu'ils ont choisi d'appeler leur foyer. Nous créons des modèles qui sont intemporels tout en étant un reflet de leur lieu et de leur époque spécifiques. Nous pensons que les maisons doivent être à la fois pragmatiques et poétiques, reliant les occupants à la nature et offrant de expériences uniques qui changent au gré du soleil ou des saisons. Nous cherchons à comprendre clairement les priorités, les valeurs et les aspirations de nos clients, dans le but de comprendre ce qui leur apporte de la joie. Ce n'est qu'alors que nous pouvons concevoir avec soin une maison qui transcende l'abri, améliore leur vie quotidienne et leur apporte de la joie dans leurs moments les plus intimes ainsi que dans les moments de rassemblement et de célébration.

Fundada por Brent Kendle, AIA, LEED AP, en 2002, Kendle Design Collaborative se encuentra en Scottsdale, Arizona, y es una empresa de arquitectura aclamada internacionalmente que se especializa en el diseño moderno de inspiración regional. Nuestro trabajo no se define por los estilos históricos importados o las últimas tendencias, sino que cada casa es una respuesta creativa a las necesidades únicas de nuestros clientes y al espíritu de la tierra que han elegido y llaman hogar. Creamos diseños que parezcen intemporales y que, al mismo tiempo, son un reflejo de su lugar y su época. Creemos que las casas deben ser a la vez pragmáticas y poéticas, conectando a los ocupantes con la naturaleza y proporcionando experiencias únicas que cambian con el paso del sol o las estaciones. Tratamos de entender claramente las prioridades, los valores y las aspiraciones de nuestros clientes, en la búsqueda de comprender lo que les produce alegría. Sólo entonces podemos diseñar cuidadosamente un hogar que trascienda el refugio, mejorando su vida diaria y aportándoles alegría en sus momentos más íntimos, así como en los momentos de reunión y celebración.

## DANCING LIGHT RESIDENCE

Paradise Valley, Arizona, United States // Lot area: 3 acres; main house: 5,700 sq ft; casita: 500 sq ft

The poetically named Dancing Light house celebrates nature through striking geometric shapes that mirror the surrounding mountains and other details, paying homage to the desert landscape. The eye-catching element of the entire structure, a floating roof canopy, gives a sculptural accent to the design. At the same time, it creates a perfect balance between the cozy living spaces with a lower ceiling and the sweeping views created by the large windows and elevated roof. Tectonic-like shapes reference both the local geology and monsoon cloud formations. Apart from the topography and features of the land, the house also draws inspiration from natural light. Layered rammed-earth walls link the modern interior to the desert, while concrete, metal, and glass provide a counterbalance to the organic forms.

La maison Dancing Light, au nom poétique, célèbre la nature par des formes géométriques saisissantes qui reflètent les montagnes environnantes et d'autres détails, rendant ainsi hommage au paysage désertique. L'élément qui attire l'attention sur l'ensemble de la structure, un toit flottant, donne un accent sculptural à la conception. En même temps, il crée un équilibre parfait entre les espaces de vie confortables avec un plafond plus bas et les vues panoramiques créées par les grandes fenêtres et le toit surélevé. Les formes de type tectonique font référence à la fois à la géologie locale et aux formations nuageuses de la mousson. Outre la topographie et les caractéristiques du terrain, la maison s'inspire également de la lumière naturelle. Des murs de terre battue en couches relient l'intérieur moderne au désert, tandis que le béton, le métal et le verre font contrepoids aux formes organiques.

Das Haus mit dem poetischen Namen Dancing Light zelebriert die Natur durch markante geometrische Formen, in denen sich die umliegenden Berge und andere Details spiegeln, und ist eine Hommage an die Wüstenlandschaft. Das auffällige Element der gesamten Struktur, ein schwebendes Dachdach, verleiht dem Entwurf einen skulpturalen Akzent. Gleichzeitig schafft es ein perfektes Gleichgewicht zwischen den gemütlichen Wohnräumen mit niedrigeren Decken und den weiten Ausblicken, die durch die großen Fenster und das erhöhte Dach entstehen. Tektonisch anmutende Formen nehmen Bezug auf die örtliche Geologie und die Wolkenformationen des Monsuns. Abgesehen von der Topografie und den Merkmalen des Grundstücks lässt sich das Haus auch vom natürlichen Licht inspirieren. Geschichtete Stampflehmwände verbinden das moderne Innere mit der Wüste, während Beton, Metall und Glas ein Gegengewicht zu den organischen Formen bilden.

La casa Dancing Light, de nombre poético, celebra la naturaleza a través de llamativas formas geométricas que reflejan las montañas circundantes y otros detalles, rindiendo homenaje al paisaje del desierto. El elemento más llamativo de toda la estructura, un tejado flotante, aporta un acento escultural al diseño. Al mismo tiempo, crea un equilibrio perfecto entre los acogedores espacios habitables con un techo más bajo y las amplias vistas creadas por los grandes ventanales y el techo elevado. Las formas tectónicas hacen referencia tanto a la geología local como a las formaciones nubosas del monzón. Además de la topografía y las características del terreno, la casa también se inspira en la luz natural. Los muros de tierra apisonada en capas vinculan el moderno interior con el desierto, mientras que el hormigón, el metal y el vidrio proporcionan un contrapeso a las formas orgánicas.

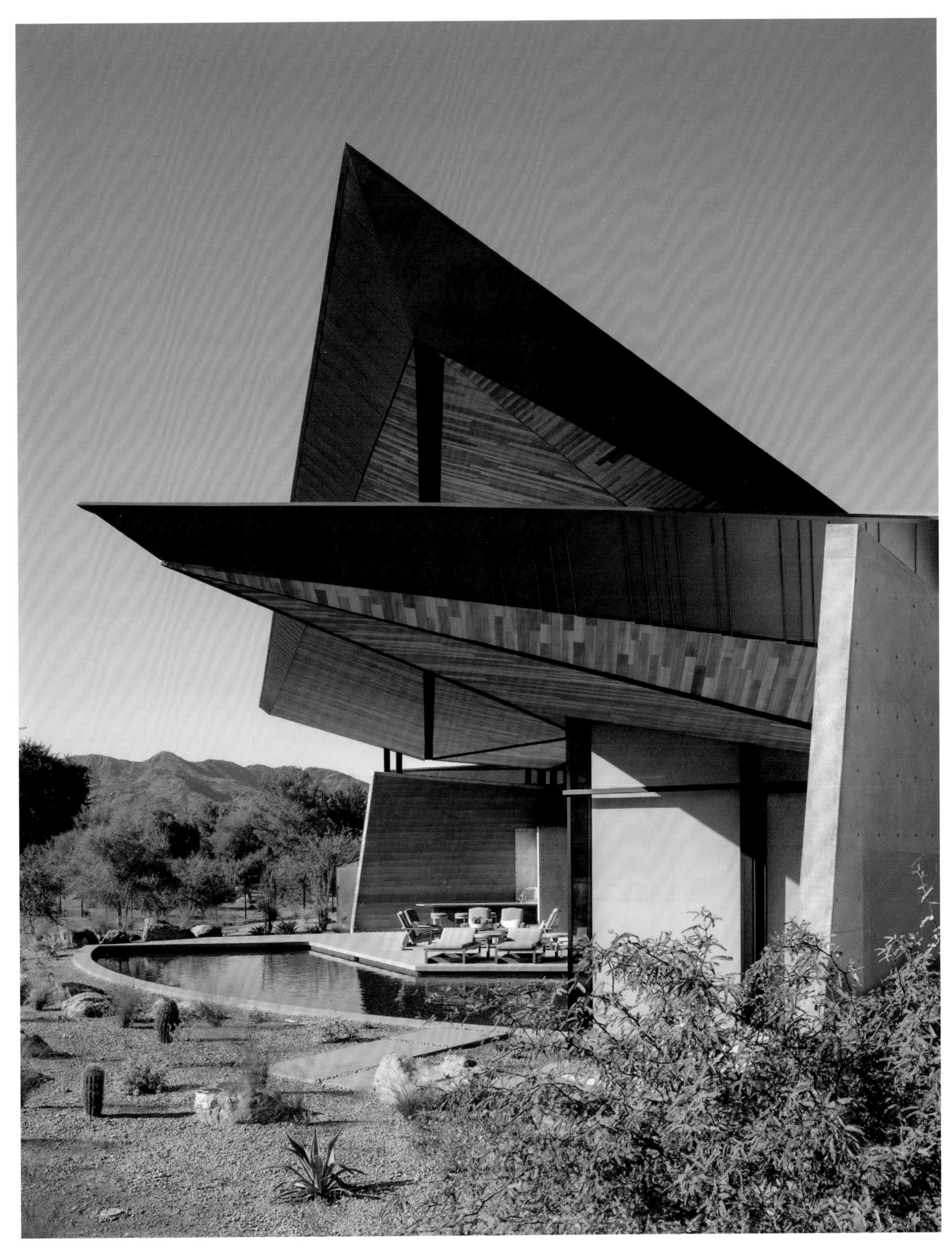

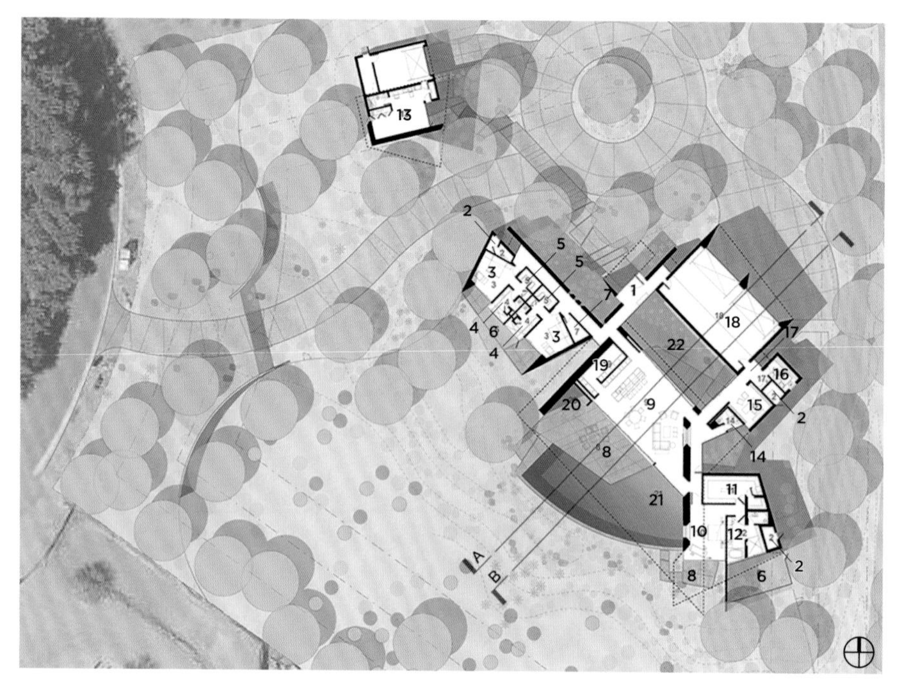

Site plan

1. Foyer
2. Mechanical room
3. Guest bedroom
4. Bathroom
5. Walk-in-closet
6. Garden
7. Storage
8. Terrace
9. Kitchen/ great room
10. Master bedroom
11. Master closet
12. Master bathroom
13. Guest house
14. Powder room
15. Office
16. Laundry room
17. Vestibule
18. Four-car garage
19. Pantry
20. Barbecue area
21. Pool
22. Atrium

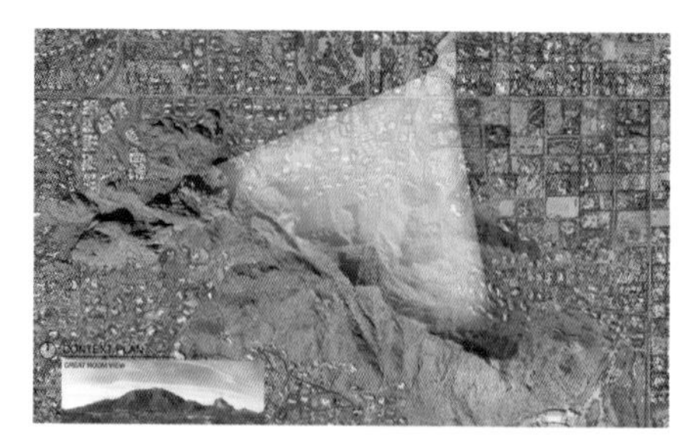

Contextual illustration

Section A

Section B

Inspirational imagery

## DESERT WING

Scottsdale, Arizona, United States // Lot area: 1 acre; building area: 8,300 sq ft

Programmatically, the home is split into two zones, a residence for the owners—a couple requiring a low maintenance lifestyle—and another zone for their extended family and friends who visit the Arizona sunshine. This home speaks to its specific place in the Sonoran Desert displaying forms derived by programmatic and climatic forces. Solid earth and concrete walls block out the harsh desert sun and views of surrounding structures. Folded planar roof forms catch rainwater and disperse it to surrounding vegetation. Large expanses of glass, shaded by deep overhangs, blur the boundaries between indoor and outdoor living, while focusing on near and distant views of nature and the wonder of city lights in the distant valley. The result is a home that is truly in harmony with its site and is expressive of its unique place in the world.

D'un point de vue programmatique, la maison est divisée en deux zones, une résidence pour les propriétaires - un couple qui a besoin d'un style de vie nécessitant peu d'entretien - et une autre zone pour leur famille élargie et les amis qui visitent le soleil de l'Arizona. Cette maison parle de son emplacement spécifique dans le désert de Sonoran en affichant des formes dérivées des forces programmatiques et climatiques. Des murs massifs en terre et en béton bloquent le dur soleil du désert et les vues sur les structures environnantes. Des formes de toit planes et pliées récupèrent l'eau de pluie et la dispersent dans la végétation environnante. De grandes étendues de verre, ombragées par de profonds surplombs, estompent les frontières entre l'intérieur et l'extérieur, tout en offrant des vues proches et lointaines sur la nature et sur les lumières de la ville dans la vallée. Le résultat est une maison qui est véritablement en harmonie avec son site et qui exprime sa place unique dans le monde.

Programmatisch ist das Haus in zwei Bereiche aufgeteilt: ein Wohnbereich für die Eigentümer - ein Paar, das einen pflegeleichten Lebensstil bevorzugt - und ein weiterer Bereich für die Großfamilie und Freunde, die die Sonne Arizonas besuchen. Dieses Haus spricht zu seinem spezifischen Ort in der Sonoran-Wüste und zeigt Formen, die von programmatischen und klimatischen Kräften abgeleitet sind. Massive Erd- und Betonwände schirmen die raue Wüstensonne und die Sicht auf die umliegenden Strukturen ab. Gefaltete, ebene Dachformen fangen das Regenwasser auf und leiten es an die umliegende Vegetation weiter. Große Glasflächen, die durch tiefe Überhänge beschattet werden, lassen die Grenzen zwischen Innen- und Außenbereich verschwimmen, während sie den Blick auf die nahe und ferne Natur und die Lichter der Stadt im fernen Tal lenken. Das Ergebnis ist ein Haus, das wirklich in Harmonie mit seinem Standort steht und seinen einzigartigen Platz in der Welt zum Ausdruck bringt.

Programáticamente, la casa se divide en dos zonas, una residencia para los propietarios -una pareja que requiere un estilo de vida de bajo mantenimiento- y otra zona para su familia y amigos que visitan el sol de Arizona. Esta casa habla de su lugar específico en el desierto de Sonora mostrando formas derivadas de las fuerzas programáticas y climáticas. Los sólidos muros de tierra y hormigón bloquean el duro sol del desierto y las vistas de las estructuras circundantes. Los tejados planos plegados recogen el agua de lluvia y la dispersan hacia la vegetación circundante. Las grandes extensiones de cristal, sombreadas por profundos voladizos, desdibujan los límites entre la vida interior y la exterior, a la vez que se centran en las vistas cercanas y lejanas de la naturaleza y la maravilla de las luces de la ciudad en el valle en la lejanía. El resultado es una casa en armonía con su emplazamiento y que expresa su lugar único en el mundo.

Context plan

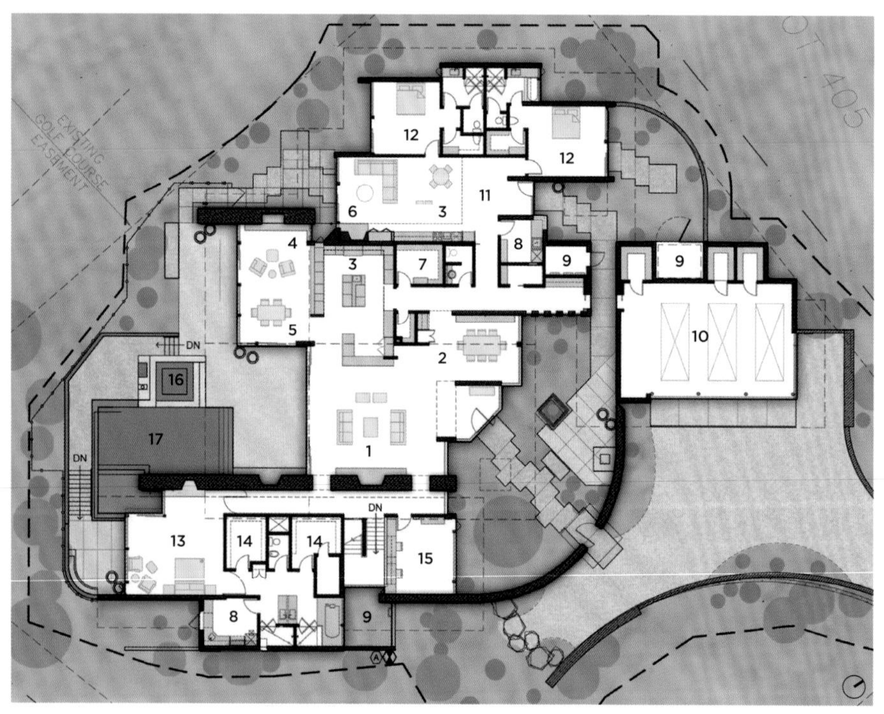


First floor plan

1. Great room
2. Dining area
3. Kitchen
4. Family room
5. Breakfast nook
6. Living area
7. Pantry
8. Laundry room
9. Mechanical room
10. Garage
11. Guest bedroom
12. Bedroom
13. Master bedroom
14. Walk-in closet
15. Office
16. Spa
17. Play pool

## RAMMED EARTH MODERN

Paradise Valley, Arizona, United States // Lot area: 1 acre; building area: 4,700 sq ft

This project consisted of a modest single-story hillside home for a family wishing to downsize and simplify. The feel of this home is evocative of the mid-century modern dwellings which once dominated the surrounding area before the McMansion craze of the last decade. Humble, natural materials such as rammed earth walls, limestone floors, and Douglas fir wood ceilings are woven inside and out in a sophisticated play of interlocking interior and exterior living spaces. The scale of the home is decidedly "cozy" and visually calm with a minimalist approach to materials and detailing, allowing the focus to be on art and nature, meeting the owners' goal of creating a home of simple, sophisticated elegance without being boastful.

Ce projet consistait en une modeste maison de plain-pied à flanc de colline pour une famille qui souhaitait réduire ses effectifs et se simplifier la vie. L'ambiance de cette maison évoque les habitations modernes du milieu du siècle dernier qui dominaient autrefois les environs avant la folie des constructions de type McMansion de la dernière décennie. Des matériaux humbles et naturels tels que des murs en terre battue, des sols en pierre calcaire et des plafonds en bois de sapin de Douglas sont tissés à l'intérieur et à l'extérieur dans un jeu sophistiqué d'espaces de vie intérieurs et extérieurs imbriqués. L'échelle de la maison est résolument « cozy » et visuellement calme avec une approche minimaliste des matériaux et des détails, permettant de se concentrer sur l'art et la nature, répondant ainsi à l'objectif des propriétaires de créer une maison d'une élégance simple et sophistiquée sans être prétentieuse.

Bei diesem Projekt handelte es sich um ein bescheidenes einstöckiges Haus in Hanglage für eine Familie, die sich verkleinern und vereinfachen wollte. Die Atmosphäre dieses Hauses erinnert an die modernen Häuser aus der Mitte des Jahrhunderts, die vor dem McMansion-Wahn des letzten Jahrzehnts in der Umgebung vorherrschten. Bescheidene, natürliche Materialien wie Stampflehmwände, Kalksteinböden und Decken aus Douglasienholz sind innen und außen zu einem raffinierten Spiel ineinandergreifender Innen- und Außenwohnräume verwoben. Der Maßstab des Hauses ist entschieden „gemütlich" und visuell ruhig mit einem minimalistischen Ansatz für Materialien und Details, so dass der Fokus auf Kunst und Natur liegt, was dem Ziel der Eigentümer entspricht, ein Haus von einfacher, anspruchsvoller Eleganz zu schaffen, ohne prahlerisch zu sein.

Este proyecto consistió en una modesta casa de una sola planta en la ladera para una familia que deseaba simplificar. La sensación de esta vivienda evoca las construcciones modernas de mediados de siglo que dominaban los alrededores antes de la moda de las McMansiones de la última década. Los materiales naturales y humildes, como las paredes de adobe, los suelos de piedra caliza y los techos de madera de abeto Douglas, se entrelazan en el interior y el exterior en un sofisticado juego de espacios interiores y exteriores. La escala de la casa es decididamente «acogedora» y visualmente tranquila, con un enfoque minimalista de los materiales y los detalles, lo que permite centrarse en el arte y la naturaleza, cumpliendo el objetivo de los propietarios de crear una casa de elegancia sencilla y sofisticada sin ser ostentosa.

Site plan

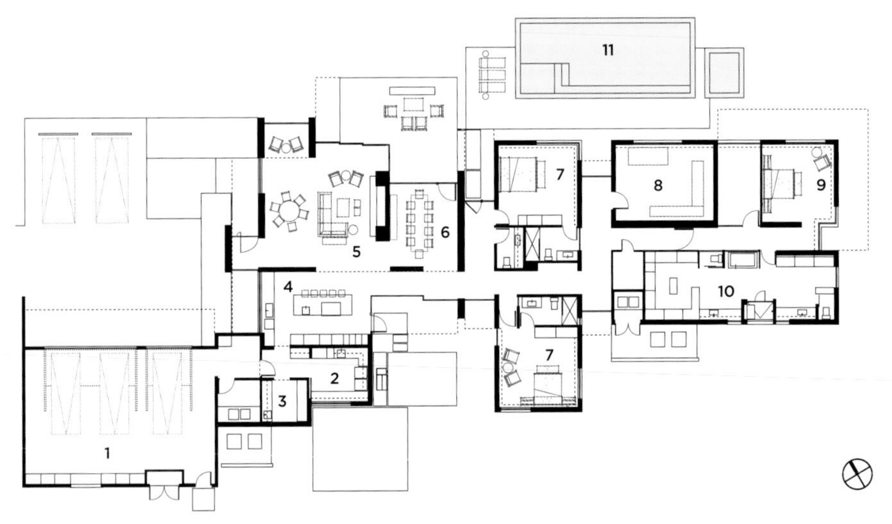


Floor plan

1. Garage
2. Laundry room
3. Wine cellar
4. Kitchen
5. Living room
6. Dining room
7. Guest bedroom
8. Studio
9. Master bedroom
10. Master bathroom
11. Pool

# DAVID HOVEY JR.

054
v

**ARIZONA COURTYARD HOUSE**

Architect and interior Designer:
David Hovey Jr., AIA
Structural Engineer:
CED Technologies, Inc.
Builder:
Optima DCHGlobal, Inc.
Photographer:
© Bill Timmerman

058
v

**RELIC ROCK**

Architect and interior Designer:
David Hovey Jr., AIA
Structural Engineer:
CED Technologies, Inc.
Builder:
Optima DCHGlobal, Inc.
Photographer:
© Bill Timmerman

www.optima.inc @optimainc

Optima DCHGlobal, Inc. designs and builds real estate projects utilizing two prefabricated modular building systems. The connector system is sustainable, multi-generational, flexible in both horizontal and vertical directions, and comprised of standardized components that could be quickly and efficiently assembled in any location, climate, or terrain. The Modular Factory-Built system (MFB) is a sustainable, multi-generational system that is produced entirely in the factory. The structural system consists of a Vierendeel truss that uses a combination of cold and hot-rolled steel shapes and is supported by concrete piers or slabs on grade. Optima DCHGlobal, Inc. is focused on innovation and efficiency and has been recognized with several national and international awards.

Optima DCHGlobal, Inc. entwirft und baut Immobilienprojekte unter Verwendung zweier vorgefertigter modularer Bausysteme. Das Stecksystem ist nachhaltig, generationenübergreifend, flexibel in horizontaler und vertikaler Richtung und besteht aus standardisierten Komponenten, die an jedem Ort, in jedem Klima und auf jedem Gelände schnell und effizient montiert werden können. Das Modulare Fabrik-Bau-System (MFB) ist ein nachhaltiges Mehrgenerationen-System, das vollständig in der Fabrik hergestellt wird. Das Tragwerkssystem besteht aus einem Vierendeel-Fachwerk, das eine Kombination aus kalt- und warmgewalzten Stahlprofilen verwendet und von Betonpfeilern oder ebenerdigen Platten getragen wird. Optima DCHGlobal, Inc. konzentriert sich auf Innovation und Effizienz und wurde bereits mit mehreren nationalen und internationalen Preisen ausgezeichnet.

Optima DCHGlobal, Inc. conçoit et construit des projets immobiliers en utilisant deux systèmes de construction modulaire préfabriqués. Le système de connecteurs est durable, multi-générationnel, flexible dans les directions horizontale et verticale, et composé d'éléments standardisés qui peuvent être assemblés rapidement et efficacement dans n'importe quel endroit, climat ou terrain. Le système modulaire fabriqué en usine (MFB) est un système durable, multigénérationnel, entièrement produit en usine. Le système structurel est constitué d'une ferme Vierendeel qui utilise une combinaison de profilés en acier laminés à froid et à chaud et est soutenu par des piliers ou des dalles en béton au sol. Optima DCHGlobal, Inc. se concentre sur l'innovation et l'efficacité et a été récompensé par plusieurs prix nationaux et internationaux.

Optima DCHGlobal, Inc. diseña y construye proyectos inmobiliarios utilizando dos sistemas de construcción modular prefabricados. El sistema de conectores es sostenible, multigeneracional, flexible en sentido horizontal y vertical, y está formado por componentes estandarizados que pueden montarse rápida y eficazmente en cualquier lugar, clima o terreno. El sistema modular construido en fábrica (MFB) es un sistema sostenible y multigeneracional que se produce íntegramente en la fábrica y que consiste en una celosía Vierendeel que utiliza una combinación de formas de acero laminado en frío y en caliente y se apoya en pilares de hormigón o losas sobre el terreno. Optima DCHGlobal, Inc. se centra en la innovación y la eficiencia y ha sido reconocida con varios premios nacionales e internacionales.

## ARIZONA COURTYARD HOUSE

Paradise Valley, Arizona, United States // Lot area: 48,660 sq ft; building area: 5,000 sq ft

The Arizona Courtyard House was built utilizing the Optima DCHGlobal modular connector system, creating a pavilion constructed with a system of standardized steel structural components and set on a base of concrete rising above terrain level. The grid of beams overhead defines the ceiling inside and flows beyond the glass enclosure to outdoor rooms in the courtyard, interconnecting inside and out. The project includes Corten steel for its sustainable characteristics and aesthetics, as its weathering steel is complementary to the colors of the desert. Roof panels of perforated Corten and press-formed louvers layered in front of the glass enclosures provide for shade and privacy wherever needed. Utilizing the modular housing system, Arizona Courtyard House was built in under five months.

L'Arizona Courtyard House a été construite à l'aide du système de connecteurs modulaire d'Optima DCHGlobal, créant un pavillon construit à l'aide d'un système d'éléments structurels en acier standardisés et posé sur une base en béton s'élevant au-dessus du niveau du terrain. La grille de poutres suspendues définit le plafond à l'intérieur et s'étend au-delà de l'enceinte vitrée jusqu'aux pièces extérieures de la cour, reliant l'intérieur et l'extérieur. Le projet comprend de l'acier Corten pour ses caractéristiques durables et son esthétique, car cet acier résistant aux intempéries est complémentaire des couleurs du désert. Les panneaux de toit en Corten perforé et les persiennes formées à la presse placées devant les enceintes en verre permettent de créer de l'ombre et de l'intimité là où c'est nécessaire. Grâce au système de logement modulaire, l'Arizona Courtyard House a été construite en moins de cinq mois.

Das Arizona Courtyard House wurde mit dem modularen Verbindersystems von Optima DCHGlobal gebaut. Es handelt sich dabei um einen Pavillon, der aus standardisierten Stahlbauteilen besteht und auf einem Betonsockel steht, der über das Geländeniveau hinausragt. Das Raster der Dachbalken definiert die Decke im Inneren des Pavillons und fließt über die Glasüberdachung hinaus in die Außenräume im Innenhof und verbindet Innen und Außen miteinander. Für das Projekt wurde Cortenstahl aufgrund seiner nachhaltigen Eigenschaften und seiner Ästhetik verwendet, da dieser verwitterungsbeständige Stahl die Farben der Wüste ergänzt. Dachpaneele aus perforiertem Cortenstahl und gepresste Lamellen, die vor die Glaswände geschichtet wurden, sorgen für Schatten und Privatsphäre, wo immer dies erforderlich ist. Das Arizona Courtyard House wurde in weniger als fünf Monaten mit Hilfe des modularen Gehäusesystems gebaut.

La Arizona Courtyard House se construyó utilizando el sistema de conectores modulares de Optima DCHGlobal, creando un pabellón construido con un sistema de componentes estructurales de acero estandarizados y asentado sobre una base de hormigón que se eleva por encima del nivel del terreno. La retícula de vigas superior define el techo en el interior y fluye más allá del recinto acristalado hacia las habitaciones exteriores en el patio, interconectando el interior y el exterior. El proyecto incluye acero corten por sus características sostenibles y su estética, ya que su acero resistente a la intemperie complementa los colores del desierto. Los paneles del tejado de acero corten perforado y las lamas moldeadas a presión colocadas delante de los cerramientos de cristal proporcionan sombra e intimidad allí donde sea necesario. Utilizando el sistema de viviendas modulares, la Arizona Courtyard House se construyó en menos de cinco meses.

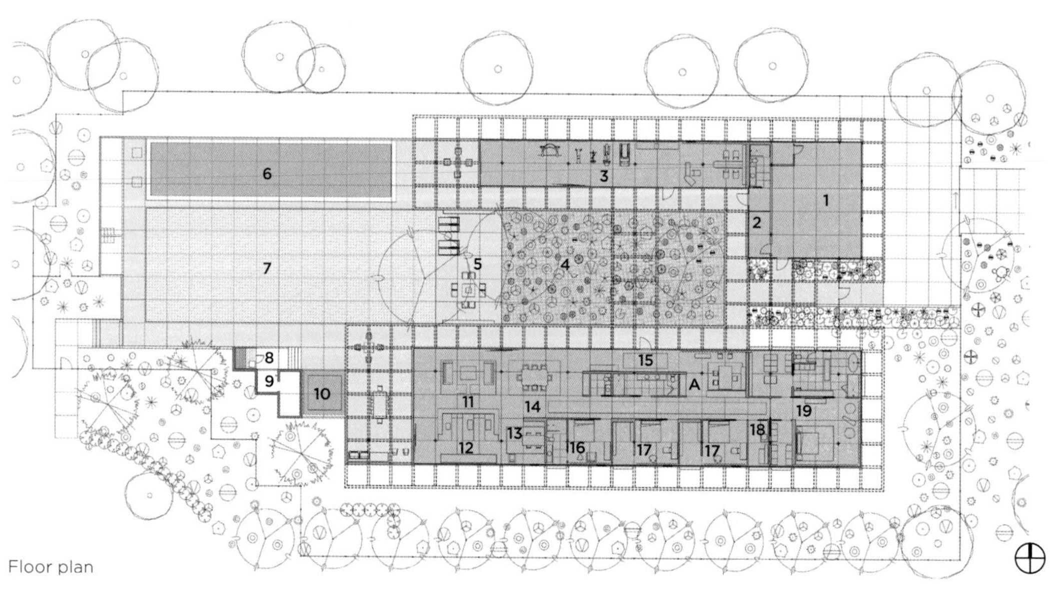


Floor plan

1. Garage
2. Storage
3. Fitness room
4. Landscaped courtyard
5. Fire pit
6. Lap pool
7. Indigenous grass
8. Sauna
9. Cold plunge
10. Spa
11. Great room
12. Kitchen
13. Study
14. Dining area
15. Entry/gallery
16. Guest room
17. Bedroom
18. Laundry room
19. Master bedroom

## RELIC ROCK

Scottsdale, Arizona, United States // Lot area: 128,016 sq ft; building area: 7,000 sq ft

As the prototype for the Optima DCHGlobal modular connector system, Relic Rock uses a flexible and sustainable building system, adaptable to a broad range of different climates and terrains. The site falls in three directions and is bordered by two deep arroyos that flood with water during monsoon season. The building sits lightly on a sloping ridge, with cantilevered floors that minimize site disruption and connect to the surrounding nature through the flow of interior and exterior space. The entire exposed structure is comprised of Corten steel, which is a 99% recycled and maintenance-free material. Natural lighting is abundant in every room of Relic Rock, reducing the need for electricity, which is reinforced by a photovoltaic system integrated into the roofing system.

En tant que prototype du système de connecteurs modulaires Optima DCHGlobal, Relic Rock utilise un système de construction flexible et durable, adaptable à un large éventail de climats et de terrains différents. Le site tombe dans trois directions et est bordé par deux arroyos profonds qui débordent d'eau pendant la mousson. Le bâtiment repose légèrement sur une crête en pente, avec des planchers en porte-à-faux qui minimisent la perturbation du site et se connectent à la nature environnante par le biais du flux d'espace intérieur et extérieur. Toute la structure exposée est constituée d'acier Corten, un matériau recyclé à 99 % et sans entretien. L'éclairage naturel est abondant dans chaque pièce de Relic Rock, réduisant ainsi les besoins en électricité, qui sont renforcés par un système photovoltaïque intégré au système de toiture.

Als Prototyp für das modulare Steckverbindersystem Optima DCHGlobal verwendet Relick Rock ein flexibles und nachhaltiges Bausystem, das sich an ein breites Spektrum unterschiedlicher Klimazonen und Geländeformen anpassen lässt. Das Gelände fällt in drei Richtungen ab und wird von zwei tiefen Arroyos begrenzt, die während der Monsunzeit überschwemmt werden. Das Gebäude liegt leicht auf einem abfallenden Bergrücken und verfügt über auskragende Böden, die die Beeinträchtigung des Geländes auf ein Minimum reduzieren und durch den Fluss der Innen- und Außenräume eine Verbindung zur umgebenden Natur herstellen. Die gesamte freiliegende Struktur besteht aus Cortenstahl, einem zu 99 % recycelten und wartungsfreien Material. Jeder Raum des Relic Rock wird von natürlichem Licht durchflutet, was den Strombedarf reduziert, der durch eine in das Dachsystem integrierte Photovoltaikanlage noch verstärkt wird.

Como prototipo del sistema de conectores modulares Optima DCHGlobal, Relic Rock utiliza un programa de construcción flexible y sostenible, adaptable a una amplia gama de climas y terrenos diferentes. El terreno cae en tres direcciones y está bordeado por dos profundos arroyos que se inundan de agua durante la temporada de monzones. El edificio se asienta ligeramente en una cresta inclinada, con pisos en voladizo que minimizan la alteración del lugar y conectan con la naturaleza circundante a través del flujo del espacio interior y exterior. Toda la estructura expuesta está compuesta por acero corten, que es un material reciclado en un 99% y que no necesita mantenimiento. La iluminación natural es abundante en todas las habitaciones, lo que reduce la necesidad de electricidad, que se ve reforzada por un sistema fotovoltaico integrado en el sistema de la cubierta.

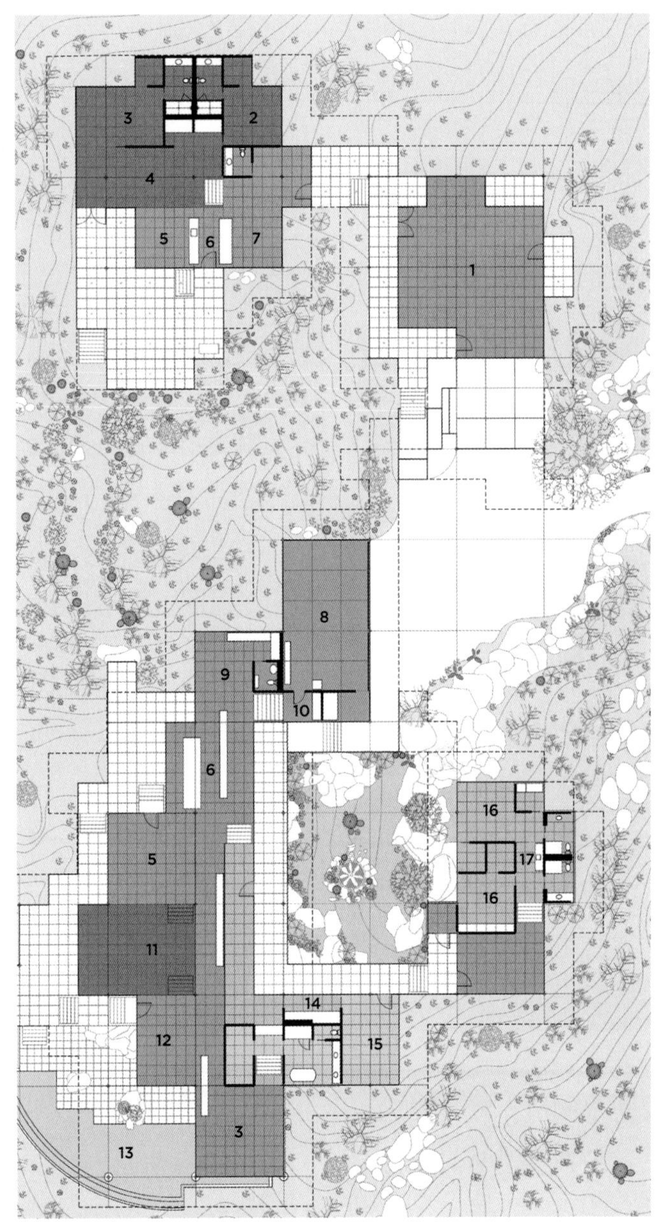

Floor plan

1. Gallery
2. Bedroom
3. Master bedroom
4. Great room
5. Dining area
6. Kitchen
7. Study
8. Garage
9. Office
10. Foyer
11. Living area
12. Recreation room
13. Pool
14. Laundry room
15. Studio
16. Guest bedroom
17. Guest kitchen

# DAVID HOVEY

066
v

**CLOUD CHASER**

Architect and Interior Designer:
David Hovey, FAIA
Structural Engineer:
Thornton Thomasetti Engineers
Builder:
Optima, Inc
Photographer:
© Bill Timmerman

070
v

**SHADOW CASTER**

Architect and Interior Designer:
David Hovey, FAIA
Structural Engineer:
Thornton Thomasetti Engineer
Builder:
Optima, Inc
Photographer:
© Bill Timmerman

074
v

**STERLING RIDGE**

Architect and Interior Designer:
David Hovey, FAIA
Structural Engineer:
Landa & Associates, Inc.
Builder:
Optima, Inc
Photographer:
© Bill Timmerman

www.optima.inc @optimainc

David Hovey, FAIA

David Hovey leads a privately held, design-driven real estate development firm with offices in Illinois and Arizona. For more than forty years, David Hovey has been developing, designing, building, marketing and managing striking urban and suburban luxury residential communities. From the beginning, David Hovey aimed to reinvent housing by integrating the functions involved in new construction within one company. David Hovey controls and executes every aspect of the process in-house—development, design, construction, sales, and management—for a dynamic system that offers greater focus and fluidity. David Hovey is committed to delivering extraordinary living through design, innovation, sustainability, and management. The result has been the creation of over forty communities in Arizona and Illinois, while being nationally recognized with over seventy-five prestigious awards.

David Hovey leitet ein privates, designorientiertes Immobilienentwicklungsunternehmen mit Niederlassungen in Illinois und Arizona. Seit mehr als vierzig Jahren entwickelt, entwirft, baut, vermarktet und verwaltet David Hovey markante städtische und vorstädtische Luxuswohnanlagen. Von Anfang an war es das Ziel von David Hovey, den Wohnungsbau neu zu erfinden, indem alle Funktionen, die mit dem Bau neuer Wohnungen zu tun haben, in einem Unternehmen zusammengeführt werden. David Hovey kontrolliert und führt jeden Aspekt des Prozesses im eigenen Haus aus - Entwicklung, Design, Bau, Verkauf und Management - und schafft so ein dynamisches System, das eine größere Konzentration und Flexibilität ermöglicht. David Hovey hat es sich zur Aufgabe gemacht, durch Design, Innovation, Nachhaltigkeit und Management außergewöhnlichen Wohnraum zu schaffen. Das Ergebnis sind mehr als vierzig Wohnanlagen in Arizona und Illinois, die landesweit mit mehr als fünfundsiebzig prestigeträchtigen Preisen ausgezeichnet wurden.

David Hovey dirige une société privée de développement immobilier axée sur la conception, avec des bureaux dans l'Illinois et en Arizona. Depuis plus de quarante ans, David Hovey développe, conçoit, construit, commercialise et gère des communautés résidentielles de luxe urbaines et suburbaines. David Hovey contrôle et exécute chaque aspect du processus en interne - développement, conception, construction, ventes et gestion - pour un système dynamique qui offre une plus grande concentration et fluidité. David Hovey s'engage à offrir un mode de vie extraordinaire grâce à la conception, l'innovation, la durabilité et la gestion. Le résultat a été la création de plus de quarante communautés en Arizona et en Illinois, tout en étant reconnu au niveau national avec plus de soixante-quinze prix prestigieux.

David Hovey dirige una empresa privada de desarrollo inmobiliario basado en el diseño, con oficinas en Illinois y Arizona. Durante más de cuarenta años, David Hovey ha desarrollado, diseñado, construido, comercializado y gestionado llamativas comunidades residenciales de lujo urbanas y suburbanas.
Desde el inicio, David Hovey controla y ejecuta todos los aspectos del proceso en la propia empresa: desarrollo, diseño, construcción, ventas y gestión, en un sistema dinámico que ofrece mayor atención y fluidez. David Hovey se ha comprometido a ofrecer una vida extraordinaria a través del diseño, la innovación, la sostenibilidad y la gestión. El resultado ha sido la creación de más de cuarenta comunidades en Arizona e Illinois, al tiempo que ha sido reconocido a nivel nacional con más de setenta y cinco prestigiosos premios.

## CLOUD CHASER

Scottsdale, Arizona, United States // Lot area: 44,530 sq ft; building area: 7,216 sq ft

A steel frame creates large, open spaces minimally enclosed with large expanses of glass. Steel was the ideal structural material for the harsh desert climate, offering timeless durability. Other materials and finishes, including the natural stone and sandblasted colored concrete masonry exterior, were selected to blend into the desert landscape. The design was influenced by historic Native American homes. The house entry begins at the high point of the steep ravine site, with a path along a reflecting pool leading to the front door, employing the concept of the Native American courtyard. A varied roofline follows the surrounding topography. From the main level, the house features expansive views of Pinnacle Peak, a nearby mountain. On the lower level, rocks, vegetation, sand, and stone are incorporated into the terrace.

L'ossature en acier crée de grands espaces ouverts, minimalement fermés par de grandes étendues de verre. L'acier était le matériau structurel idéal pour le climat rigoureux du désert, offrant une durabilité intemporelle. D'autres matériaux et finitions, notamment la pierre naturelle et l'extérieur en maçonnerie de béton coloré sablé, ont été choisis pour se fondre dans le paysage désertique. La conception a été influencée par les maisons amérindiennes historiques. L'entrée de la maison commence au point culminant du ravin escarpé, avec un chemin le long d'un bassin réfléchissant menant à la porte d'entrée, reprenant le concept de la cour amérindienne. Une ligne de toit variée suit la topographie environnante. Depuis le niveau principal, la maison offre une vue imprenable sur Pinnacle Peak, une montagne voisine. Au niveau inférieur, des rochers, de la végétation, du sable et des pierres sont intégrés à la terrasse.

Ein Stahlrahmen schafft große, offene Räume, die nur minimal mit großen Glasflächen umschlossen sind. Stahl war das ideale Konstruktionsmaterial für das raue Wüstenklima und bietet zeitlose Haltbarkeit. Andere Materialien und Oberflächen, wie der Naturstein und das sandgestrahlte farbige Betonmauerwerk, wurden so gewählt, dass sie sich in die Wüstenlandschaft einfügen. Das Design wurde von historischen indianischen Häusern beeinflusst. Der Eingang des Hauses beginnt am höchsten Punkt der steilen Schlucht und führt über einen Weg entlang eines spiegelnden Beckens zur Eingangstür, wobei das Konzept des indianischen Innenhofs übernommen wurde. Eine abwechslungsreiche Dachlinie folgt der umgebenden Topographie. Von der Hauptebene aus bietet das Haus einen weiten Blick auf den Pinnacle Peak, einen nahe gelegenen Berg. Auf der unteren Ebene sind Felsen, Vegetation, Sand und Stein in die Terrasse integriert.

Un armazón de acero crea espacios amplios y abiertos mínimamente cerrados con grandes extensiones de vidrio. El acero era el material estructural ideal para el duro clima del desierto, ofreciendo una durabilidad intemporal. Otros materiales y acabados, como la piedra natural y la mampostería de hormigón coloreado con chorro de arena, se seleccionaron para que se integraran en el paisaje desértico. El diseño está influenciado por las casas históricas de los nativos americanos. La entrada de la casa comienza en el punto más alto del empinado barranco, con un camino a lo largo de un estanque reflectante que conduce a la puerta principal, empleando el concepto de patio de los nativos americanos. Una línea de tejado variada sigue la topografía circundante. Desde el nivel principal, la casa ofrece amplias vistas de Pinnacle Peak, una montaña cercana. En el nivel inferior, las rocas, la vegetación, la arena y la piedra se incorporan a la terraza.

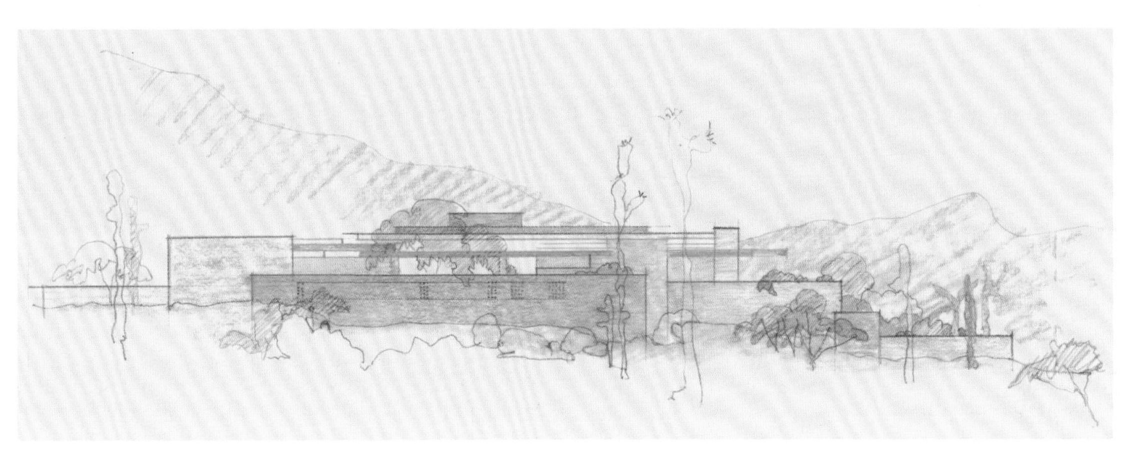

Northwest elevation

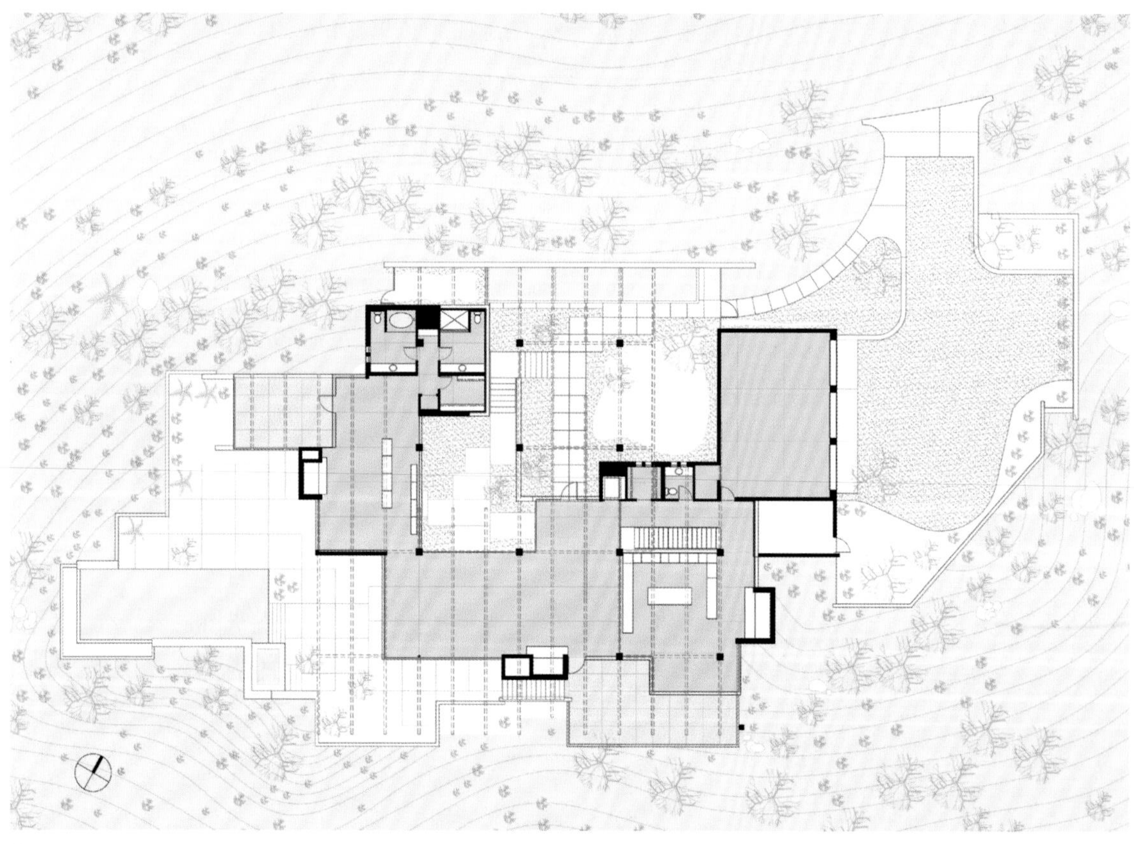

Floor plan

## SHADOW CASTER

Scottsdale, Arizona, United States // Lot area: 52,258 sq ft; building area: 6,863 sq ft

Shadow Caster was designed and built like a bridge, spanning a ravine with a series of stepped outdoor courtyards anchored to the east and west ends of opposing hills. The structure has a concrete slab foundation poured directly onto the minimally graded site. Steel beams form the horizontal supports for the bridge and the roof with enormous cantilevers spanning as far as twenty-eight feet. Steel grating projecting from the roof provides shading and beautiful patterning effects. The vertical load-bearing elements, including the walls and columns, are made of a standard concrete block tinted to match the color of the desert. Large, unframed glass planes are set directly into the routed concrete block walls and the concrete flooring, making the experience of the house inseparable from that of the landscape in which it rests.

Shadow Caster a été conçu et construit comme un pont, enjambant un ravin avec une série de cours extérieures en escalier ancrées aux extrémités est et ouest de collines opposées. La structure est constituée d'une dalle de béton coulée directement sur le site au nivellement minimal. Des poutres d'acier forment les supports horizontaux du pont et du toit, dont les énormes porte-à-faux s'étendent jusqu'à vingt-huit pieds. Les caillebotis en acier qui dépassent du toit fournissent de l'ombre et de magnifiques effets de motif. Les éléments porteurs verticaux, y compris les murs et les colonnes, sont constitués d'un bloc de béton standard teinté de la couleur du désert. De grands plans de verre non encadrés sont encastrés directement dans les murs en blocs de béton fraisés et dans le sol en béton, rendant l'expérience de la maison inséparable de celle du paysage dans lequel elle repose.

Shadow Caster wurde wie eine Brücke entworfen und gebaut, die eine Schlucht mit einer Reihe von abgestuften Außenhöfen überspannt, die an den östlichen und westlichen Enden der gegenüberliegenden Hügel verankert sind. Die Struktur besteht aus einem Betonplattenfundament, das direkt auf das minimal geneigte Gelände gegossen wurde. Stahlträger bilden die horizontalen Stützen für die Brücke und das Dach mit riesigen Auskragungen, die bis zu achtundzwanzig Fuß weit reichen. Aus dem Dach ragende Stahlgitter sorgen für Beschattung und schöne Mustereffekte. Die vertikalen tragenden Elemente, einschließlich der Wände und Säulen, bestehen aus einem Standardbetonblock, der in der Farbe der Wüste getönt ist. Große, rahmenlose Glasflächen sind direkt in die gefrästen Betonblockwände und den Betonboden eingelassen, so dass das Haus untrennbar mit der Landschaft verbunden ist, in die es eingebettet ist.

Shadow Caster se diseñó y construyó como un puente, atravesando un barranco con una serie de patios exteriores escalonados anclados en los extremos este y oeste de colinas opuestas. La estructura tiene unos cimientos de losa de hormigón vertidos directamente sobre el terreno, mínimamente nivelado. Las vigas de acero forman los soportes horizontales del puente y la cubierta, con enormes voladizos que alcanzan los veintiocho pies. Las rejillas de acero que sobresalen del tejado proporcionan sombra y un bello efecto de patrón. Los elementos portantes verticales, incluidos los muros y las columnas, están hechos de un bloque de hormigón estándar tintado para que coincida con el color del desierto. Los grandes planos de cristal sin marco se han colocado directamente en los muros de bloque y en el suelo, ambos de hormigón, lo que hace que la experiencia de la casa sea inseparable de la del paisaje en el que descansa.

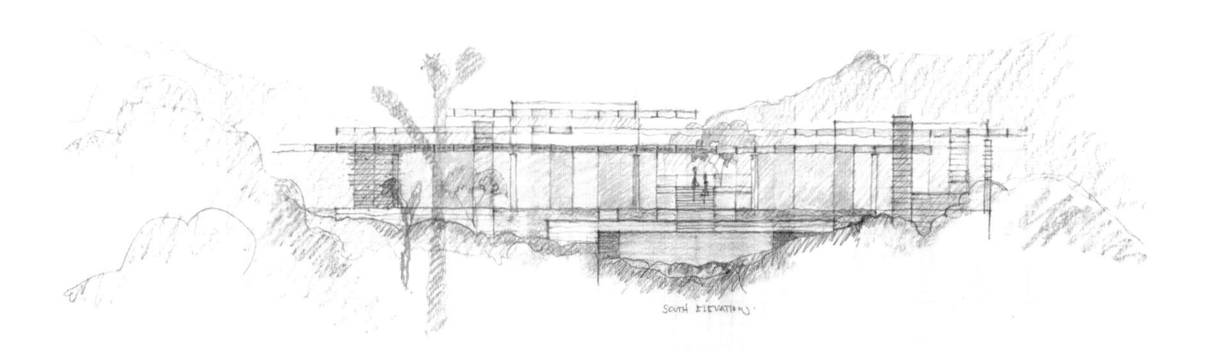


South elevation

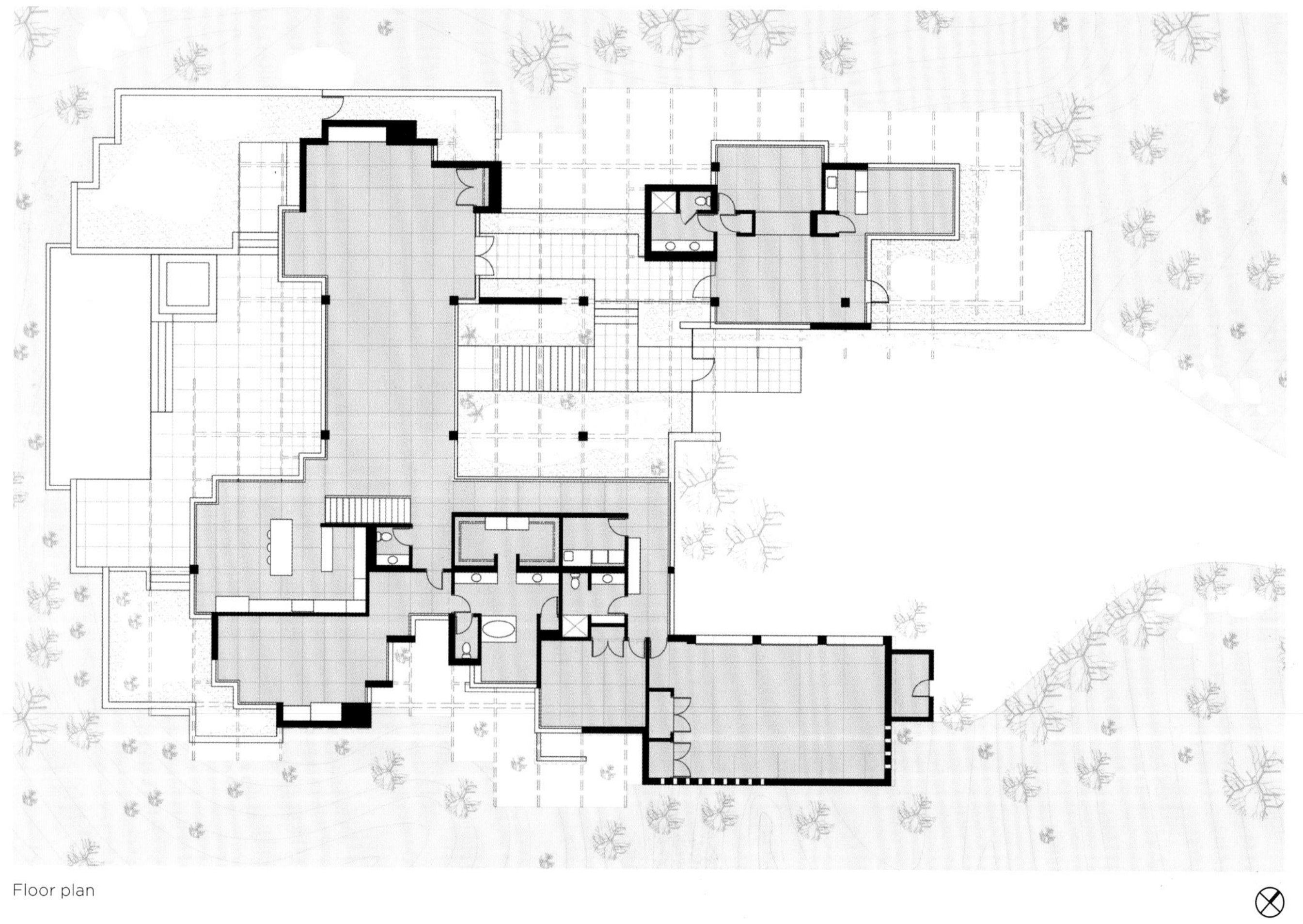

Floor plan

## STERLING RIDGE

Scottsdale, Arizona, United States // Lot area: 119,846 sq ft; building area: 11,760 sq ft

The fundamental idea is one of raw simplicity in character, composition, and assembly of materials. Concrete walls blend with the earth and the power of natural boulder outcropping, while steel beams reflect the accent colors of the vibrant desert vegetation. Transparency, antithetical to the desert's extreme heat and light, is achieved through technical innovation and large overhangs with photovoltaics that shade the desert sun while generating electricity to power the home. The boundary between interior and exterior is dissolved, creating direct, personal, and human-scale relationships to the landscape. Constructed on a seven-foot module with twenty-one-foot square bays, Sterling Ridge is experienced as an assembly of buildings containing a series of asymmetric spaces that reflect the mountainous terrain just beyond the house's walls.

L'idée fondamentale est celle d'une simplicité brute dans le caractère, la composition et l'assemblage des matériaux. Les murs en béton se mêlent à la terre et à la puissance des affleurements rocheux naturels, tandis que les poutres en acier reflètent les couleurs d'accentuation de la végétation vibrante du désert. La transparence, qui s'oppose à la chaleur et à la lumière extrêmes du désert, est obtenue grâce à l'innovation technique et à de grands surplombs équipés de panneaux photovoltaïques qui font de l'ombre au soleil du désert tout en produisant de l'électricité pour alimenter la maison. pour alimenter la maison. La frontière entre l'intérieur et l'extérieur est dissoute, créant des relations directes, personnelles et à échelle humaine avec le paysage. Construit sur un module de sept pieds avec des baies carrées de vingt et un pieds, Sterling Ridge est vécu comme un ensemble de bâtiments contenant une série d'espaces asymétriques qui reflètent le terrain montagneux juste au-delà des murs de la maison.

Shadow Caster wurde wie eine Brücke entworfen und gebaut, die eine Schlucht mit einer Reihe von abgestuften Außenhöfen überspannt, die an den östlichen und westlichen Enden der gegenüberliegenden Hügel verankert sind. Die Struktur besteht aus einem Betonplattenfundament, das direkt auf das minimal geneigte Gelände gegossen wurde. Stahlträger bilden die horizontalen Stützen für die Brücke und das Dach mit riesigen Auskragungen, die bis zu achtundzwanzig Fuß weit reichen. Aus dem Dach ragende Stahlgitter sorgen für Beschattung und schöne Mustereffekte. Die vertikalen tragenden Elemente, einschließlich der Wände und Säulen, bestehen aus einem Standardbetonblock, der in der Farbe der Wüste getönt ist. Große, rahmenlose Glasflächen sind direkt in die gefrästen Betonblockwände und den Betonboden eingelassen, so dass das Haus untrennbar mit der Landschaft verbunden ist, in die es eingebettet ist.

La idea fundamental es la de la simplicidad bruta en el carácter, la composición y el ensamblaje de los materiales. Los muros de hormigón se funden con la tierra y la fuerza de los afloramientos naturales de rocas, mientras que las vigas de acero reflejan los colores de la vibrante vegetación del desierto. La transparencia, contraria al calor y la luz extremos del desierto, se consigue mediante la innovación técnica y los grandes voladizos con energía fotovoltaica que consiguen sombra mientras generan electricidad para alimentar la casa. El límite entre el interior y el exterior se disuelve, creando relaciones directas, personales y a escala humana con el paisaje. Construida sobre un módulo de 640 m2, Sterling Ridge se experimenta como un conjunto de edificios que contienen una serie de espacios asiméticos que reflejan el terreno montañoso más allá de las paredes de la casa.

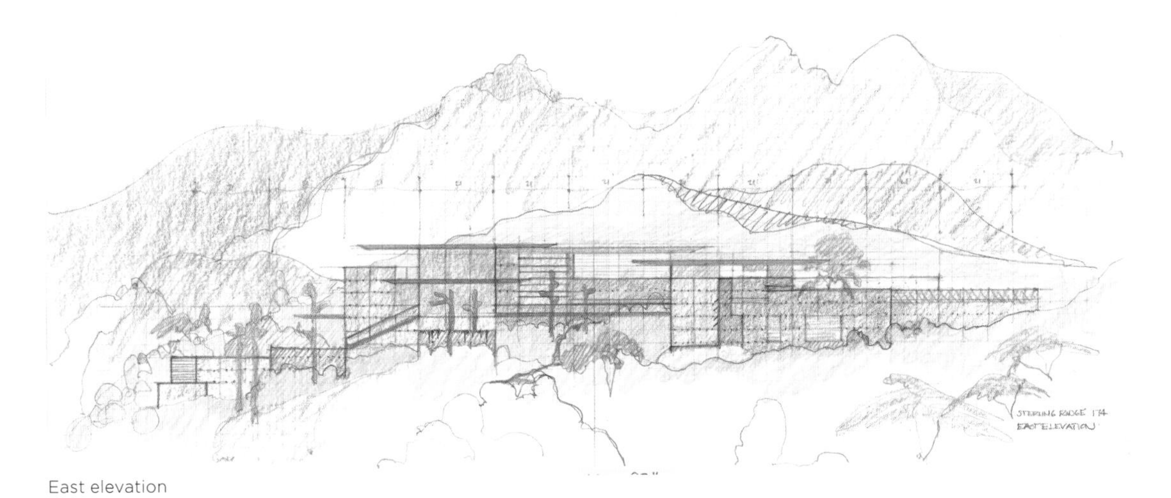


East elevation

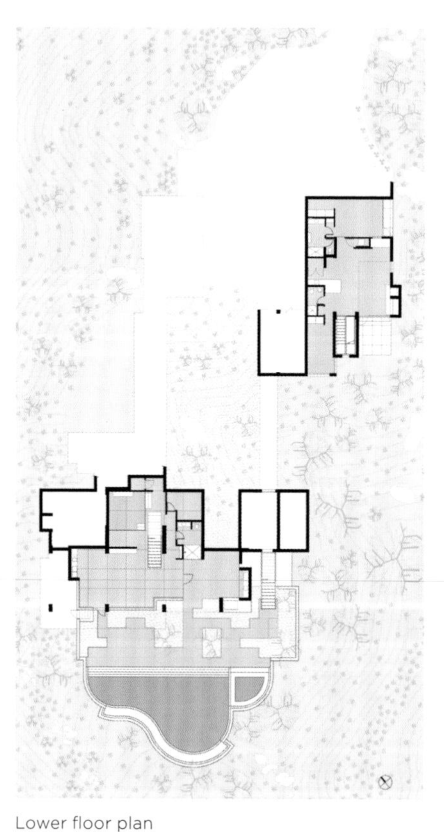

Lower floor plan

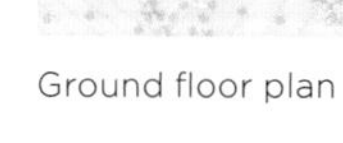

Ground floor plan

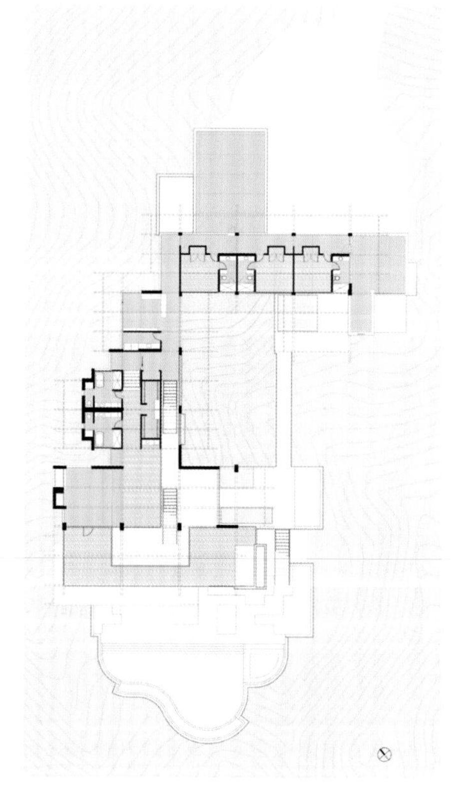

Upper floor plan

# VICTOR SIDY
# ARCHITECT

080
v

**TUCSON HILLSIDE RESIDENCE**

Architect of Record:
Victor Sidy, AIA
Design Collaborator:
Nick Mancusi, AIA
Structural Engineer:
Schneider Structural Engineers
Builder:
Repp+Mclain Design and Construction
Photographer:
© Bill Timmerman

084
v

**MOD.FAB**

Architect of Record:
Victor Sidy, AIA
Design Collaborator:
Michael P. Johnson (faculty member) and students
Builder:
Students at the Frank Lloyd Wright School of architecture
Photographer:
© Bill Timmerman

088
v

**CLEARWATER HILLS MOUNTAIN HOUSE**

Architect:
Victor Sidy, AIA
Design Collaborator:
Robert Murray (client)
Images:
© Victor Sidy Architect

www.victorsidy.com @vsidy

Victor Sidy Architect is a full-service architectural practice for specialized building and planning projects. The practice—initiated in 2000 through collaborative work with artists, architects, engineers, contractors, and developers—celebrates the act of making as the departure point for design. From 2005 to 2015, Sidy served as dean of the Frank Lloyd Wright School of Architecture. The practice expanded to include projects with students and faculty, including the prototype Mod.Fab project. As the practice has grown in recent years, the collaborative culture remains core to the work. The work tells stories of the natural beauty of the project sites, the visionary ideas of the project clients, the practical issues the designs solve, the history of the communities they serve, and the craftspeople building the structures.

Victor Sidy Architect ist ein Architekturbüro mit umfassendem Service für spezielle Bau- und Planungsprojekte. Das Büro, das im Jahr 2000 durch die Zusammenarbeit mit Künstlern, Architekten, Ingenieuren, Bauunternehmern und Entwicklern gegründet wurde, feiert den Akt des Machens als Ausgangspunkt für das Design. Von 2005 bis 2015 fungierte Sidy als Dekan der Frank Lloyd Wright School of Architecture. Das Büro wurde um Projekte mit Studenten und Dozenten erweitert, darunter das Prototyp-Projekt Mod. Fab. Auch wenn das Büro in den letzten Jahren gewachsen ist, bleibt die Kultur der Zusammenarbeit der Kern der Arbeit. Die Arbeiten erzählen Geschichten über die natürliche Schönheit der Projektstandorte, die visionären Ideen der Projektkunden, die praktischen Probleme, die die Entwürfe lösen, die Geschichte der Gemeinden, denen sie dienen, und die Handwerker, die die Strukturen bauen.

Victor Sidy Architect est un cabinet d'architecture à service complet pour des projets de construction et de planification spécialisés. La pratique - initiée en 2000 par un travail de collaboration avec des artistes, des architectes, des ingénieurs, des entrepreneurs et des promoteurs - célèbre l'acte de faire comme point de départ de la conception. De 2005 à 2015, Sidy a été le doyen de l'école d'architecture Frank Lloyd Wright. Le cabinet s'est développé pour inclure des projets avec des étudiants et des professeurs, notamment le projet prototype Mod.Fab. Alors que le cabinet s'est développé ces dernières années, la culture collaborative reste au cœur du travail. Les travaux racontent la beauté naturelle des sites des projets, les idées visionnaires des clients, les problèmes pratiques que les conceptions résolvent, l'histoire des communautés qu'elles servent et les artisans qui construisent les structures.

Victor Sidy Architect es un estudio de arquitectura llaves en mano para proyectos especializados de construcción y planificación. El estudio, iniciado en el año 2000 mediante la colaboración con artistas, arquitectos, ingenieros, contratistas y promotores, celebra el trabajo como punto de partida para el diseño. De 2005 a 2015, Sidy fue decano de la Escuela de Arquitectura Frank Lloyd Wright. El estudio se amplió para incluir proyectos con estudiantes y profesores, incluido el proyecto prototipo Mod.Fab. Aunque el estudio ha crecido en los últimos años, la cultura de colaboración sigue siendo el núcleo del trabajo. El trabajo cuenta historias de la belleza natural de los lugares de los proyectos, las ideas visionarias de los clientes de los proyectos, los problemas prácticos que resuelven los diseños, la historia de las comunidades a las que sirven y los artesanos que construyen las estructuras.

## TUCSON HILLSIDE RESIDENCE

Tucson, Arizona, United States // Lot area: 4.2 acres; building area: 2,700 sq ft

Set on a prominent ridge in the Tucson Mountains foothills, this home is a lens through which the clients can experience the magic of the Sonoran Desert. Two rectangular blocks intersecting at an oblique angle and positioned just below the ridgeline of the hill define the plan. The first block runs parallel to the contours of the land and houses the carport, workshop, and study. The second block—containing the main house—is aligned with the view of a salient butte nearby. The home is clad with mill-finished steel sheets intended to match the patinated quality of the local stones. The main concrete site wall is patterned by vertical indents activating shadows as the sun travels through the day. In contrast to the roughly-wrought exterior, the interior of the house is clean and white, a spare frame housing the life of the residents within.

Située sur une crête proéminente dans les contreforts des Tucson Mountains, cette maison est un objectif à travers lequel les clients peuvent découvrir la magie du désert de Sonoran. Deux blocs rectangulaires se croisant à un angle oblique et positionnés juste en dessous de la ligne de crête de la colline définissent le plan. Le premier bloc est parallèle aux contours du terrain et abrite l'abri à voitures, l'atelier et le bureau. Le second bloc, qui contient la maison principale, est aligné sur la vue d'une butte saillante située à proximité. La maison est revêtue de tôles d'acier finies en usine, afin de s'harmoniser avec la qualité patinée des pierres locales. Le mur principal du site en béton est structuré par des indentations verticales qui activent les ombres au fur et à mesure que le soleil se déplace dans la journée. En contraste avec l'extérieur brut, l'intérieur de la maison est propre et blanc, un cadre dépouillé abritant la vie des résidents.

Dieses auf einem markanten Bergrücken in den Ausläufern der Tucson Mountains gelegene Haus ist ein Objektiv, durch das die Bauherren die Magie der Sonoran-Wüste erleben können. Zwei rechteckige Blöcke, die sich in einem schrägen Winkel schneiden und knapp unterhalb der Kammlinie des Hügels liegen, bestimmen den Grundriss. Der erste Block verläuft parallel zu den Konturen des Grundstücks und beherbergt den Carport, die Werkstatt und das Arbeitszimmer. Der zweite Block, in dem sich das Haupthaus befindet, orientiert sich an der Aussicht auf einen nahe gelegenen, markanten Felsvorsprung. Das Haus ist mit gewalzten Stahlblechen verkleidet, die der patinierten Qualität der örtlichen Steine entsprechen sollen. Die Hauptmauer aus Beton ist mit vertikalen Einkerbungen versehen, die im Laufe des Tages Schatten werfen. Im Gegensatz zu dem grob bearbeiteten Äußeren ist das Innere des Hauses sauber und weiß, ein sparsamer Rahmen, der das Leben der Bewohner in sich aufnimmt.

Situada en una cresta prominente en las estribaciones de las montañas de Tucson, esta casa es una lente a través de la cual los clientes pueden experimentar la magia del desierto de Sonora. Dos bloques rectangulares que se cruzan en un ángulo oblicuo y se sitúan justo debajo de la línea de cresta de la colina definen el plan. El primer bloque corre paralelo a las curvas de nivel del terreno y alberga la cochera, el taller y el estudio. El segundo bloque -que contiene la casa principal- está alineado con la vista de un saliente cercano. La casa está revestida con láminas de acero con acabado de molino que pretenden combinar con la calidad patinada de las piedras locales. El muro principal de hormigón tiene un patrón de hendiduras verticales que activan las sombras a medida que el sol se desplaza a lo largo del día. En contraste con el exterior, el interior de la casa es limpio y blanco, una estructura libre que alberga la vida de los residentes.

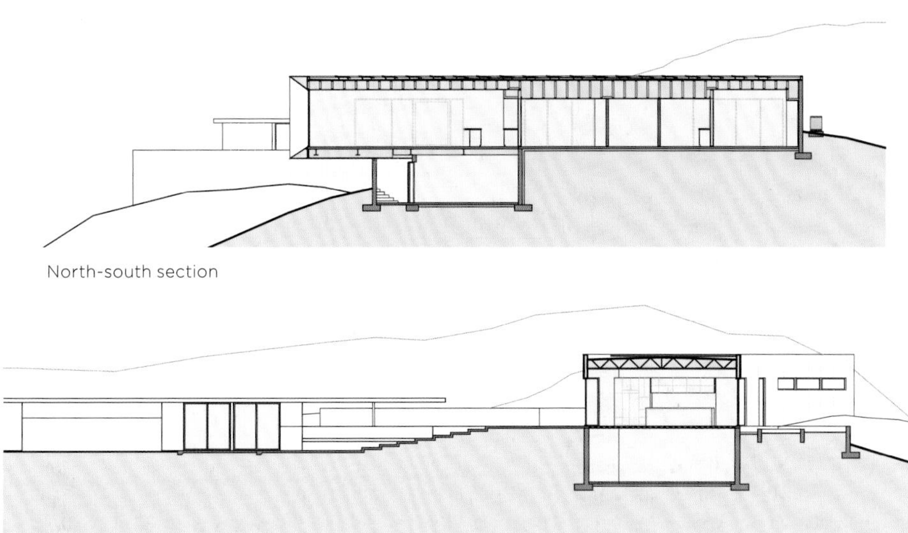

North-south section

East-west section

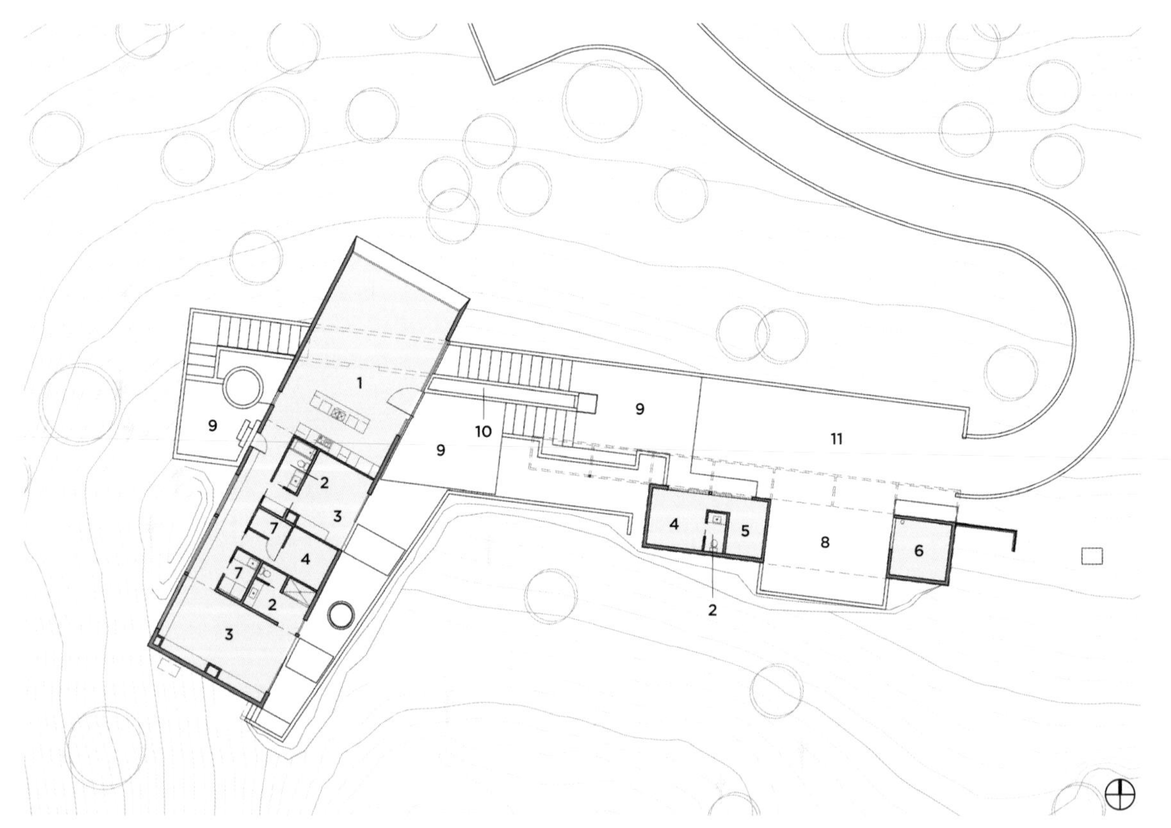


1. Living/dining/kitchen
2. Bathroom
3. Bedroom
4. Study
5. Fitness room
6. Workshop
7. Utility room
8. Carport
9. Patio/terrace
10. Fountain
11. Driveway

Floor plan

## MOD.FAB

Scottsdale, Arizona, United States // Building area: 450 sq ft

The Mod.Fab is an example of simple, elegant, and sustainable living on a small scale. The one-bedroom prototype residence relies on panelized construction to allow for speed and economy on site or in a factory and is transportable via roadway. Its chassis rests on the ground at only six points, allowing it to conform to non-level sites. The prototype was built at the Frank Lloyd Wright School of Architecture's Taliesin West campus in the Sonoran Desert, and since its completion, the design has been produced for various locations throughout the US and Canada. The Mod.Fab uses a combination of passive and active environmental control systems, including low-consumption fixtures, rainwater harvesting, greywater reuse, natural ventilation, solar orientation, and photovoltaics. The Mod.Fab was recognized as « Green Architecture Project of the Year » by *Time* magazine.

Mod.Fab est un exemple de vie simple, élégante et durable à petite échelle. La résidence prototype d'une chambre à coucher repose sur une construction en panneaux pour permettre une rapidité et une économie sur le site ou dans une usine et est transportable par la route. Son châssis ne repose sur le sol qu'en six points, ce qui lui permet de s'adapter aux sites non nivelés. Le prototype a été construit sur le campus Taliesin West de l'école d'architecture Frank Lloyd Wright, dans le désert de Sonoran, et depuis son achèvement, le concept a été produit pour divers sites à travers les États-Unis et le Canada. Mod.Fab utilise des systèmes de contrôle environnemental passifs et actifs, notamment des appareils à faible consommation, la collecte des eaux de pluie, la réutilisation des eaux grises, la ventilation naturelle, l'orientation solaire et l'énergie photovoltaïque. Mod.Fab a été reconnu comme "Projet d'architecture verte de l'année" par le magazine *Time*.

Die Mod.Fab ist ein Beispiel für einfaches, elegantes und nachhaltiges Wohnen in kleinem Maßstab. Der Prototyp des Ein-Zimmer-Wohnhauses basiert auf einer Plattenbauweise, die eine schnelle und kostengünstige Fertigung auf der Baustelle oder in einer Fabrik ermöglicht und auf der Straße transportiert werden kann. Sein Fahrgestell ruht an nur sechs Punkten auf dem Boden, so dass es sich an nicht ebene Grundstücke anpassen kann. Der Prototyp wurde auf dem Taliesin-West-Campus der Frank Lloyd Wright School of Architecture in der Sonoran-Wüste gebaut, und seit seiner Fertigstellung wurde das Design für verschiedene Standorte in den USA und Kanada produziert. Mod.Fab verwendet passive und aktive Umweltkontrollsysteme, darunter verbrauchsarme Leuchten, Regenwassernutzung, Grauwasserwiederverwendung, natürliche Belüftung, Solarorientierung und Photovoltaik. Die Mod.Fab wurde von der Zeitschrift *Time* als „Green Architecture Project of the Year" ausgezeichnet.

Mod.Fab es un ejemplo de vida sencilla, elegante y sostenible a pequeña escala. El prototipo de residencia de un dormitorio se basa en la construcción con paneles para permitir la rapidez y la economía al ser construido bien sobre el terreno o en fábrica y ser, por tanto, transportable. Su chasis se apoya en el suelo en sólo seis puntos, lo que le permite adaptarse a lugares no llanos. El prototipo se construyó en el campus Taliesin West de la Escuela de Arquitectura Frank Lloyd Wright, en el desierto de Sonora, y desde su finalización, el diseño se ha producido para varios lugares de Estados Unidos y Canadá. Mod.Fab utiliza sistemas de control ambiental pasivos y activos, incluyendo accesorios de bajo consumo, recogida de aguas pluviales, re utilización de aguas grises, ventilación natural, orientación solar y energía fotovoltaica. Mod.Fab fue reconocido como «Proyecto de Arquitectura Verde del Año» por la revista *Time*.

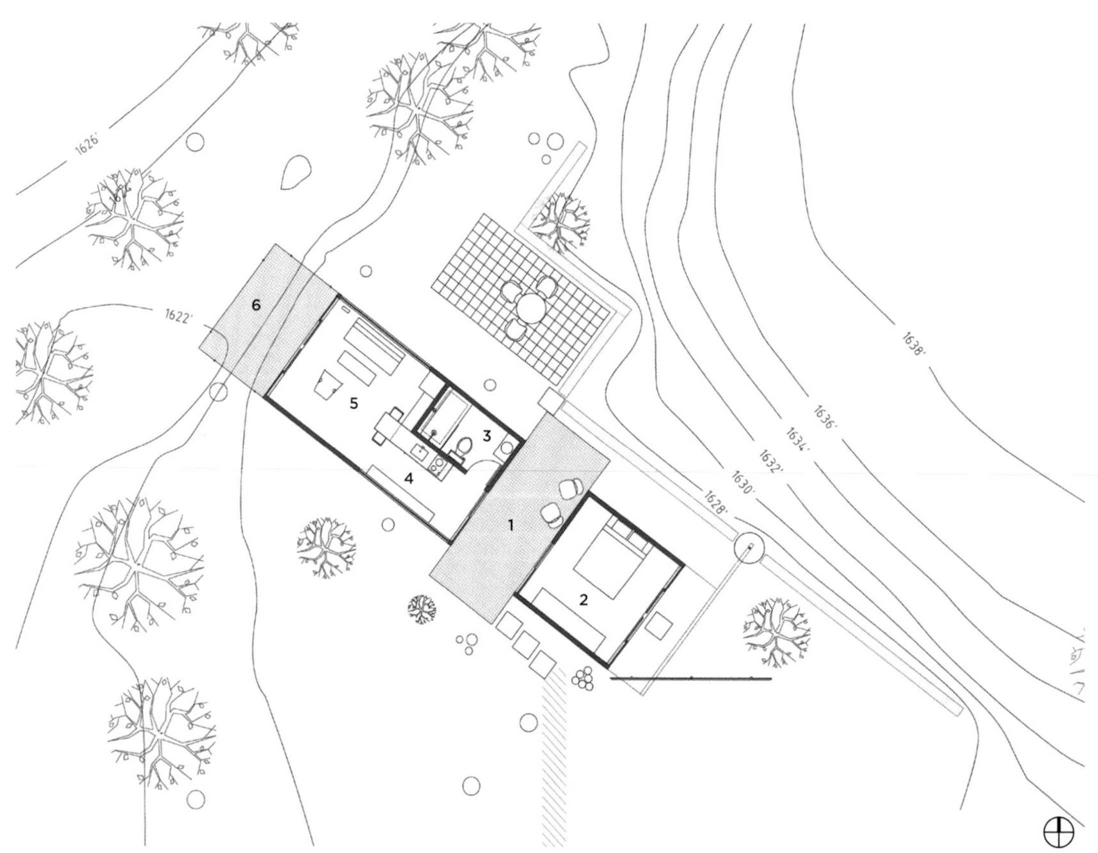


1. Breezeway
2. Bedroom
3. Bathroom
4. Kitchen
5. Living area
6. Balcony

Floor plan

## CLEARWATER HILLS MOUNTAIN HOUSE

Paradise Valley, Arizona, United States // Lot area: 3.4 acres; building area: 6,120 sq ft

The residence—currently in its pre-construction phase—is designed to adapt to the challenging topography of a steep mountain face. The design takes advantage of commanding views of Phoenix and its iconic Camelback Mountain and is situated to allow the builder to stage construction in sectors, allowing minimal additional intrusion into the natural landscape. The home is oriented in alignment with the site's rocky outcrops so as to appear to grow from the geology of its surroundings, and yet its smooth geometric forms stand in contrast to the surrounding environment. As a result, the residence becomes a series of apertures through which changing views of the desert can be experienced.

La résidence - actuellement dans sa phase de pré-construction - est conçue pour s'adapter à la topographie difficile d'une paroi montagneuse abrupte. La conception tire parti de la vue imprenable sur Phoenix et son emblématique Camelback Mountain et est située de manière à permettre au constructeur d'organiser la construction par secteurs, en minimisant l'intrusion supplémentaire dans le paysage naturel. La maison est orientée de manière à s'aligner sur les affleurements rocheux du site, de sorte qu'elle semble naître de la géologie des environs, tandis que ses formes géométriques lisses contrastent avec l'environnement. En conséquence, la résidence devient une série d'ouvertures à travers lesquelles on peut découvrir des vues changeantes du désert.

Das Wohnhaus, das sich derzeit in der Vorbauphase befindet, ist so konzipiert, dass es sich an die schwierige Topografie eines steilen Berghangs anpasst. Der Entwurf macht sich die herrliche Aussicht auf Phoenix und den ikonischen Camelback Mountain zunutze und ist so angelegt, dass der Bauherr den Bau in Sektoren unterteilen kann, was einen minimalen zusätzlichen Eingriff in die natürliche Landschaft ermöglicht. Das Haus orientiert sich an den felsigen Ausläufern des Geländes, so dass es scheint, als sei es aus der Geologie der Umgebung gewachsen, und doch stehen seine glatten geometrischen Formen im Kontrast zur Umgebung. Dadurch wird das Haus zu einer Reihe von Öffnungen, durch die man wechselnde Ausblicke auf die Wüste genießen kann.

La residencia, actualmente en fase de pre-construcción, está diseñada para adaptarse a la difícil topografía de una escarpada montaña. El diseño aprovecha las vistas dominantes de Phoenix y su emblemática montaña Camelback y está situado de forma que el constructor pueda realizar la construcción por sectores, permitiendo una mínima intrusión adicional en el paisaje natural. La casa está orientada en consonancia con los afloramientos rocosos del lugar para que parezca crecer a partir de la geología de su entorno y, sin embargo, sus suaves formas geométricas contrastan con el entorno. Como resultado, la residencia se convierte en una serie de aperturas a través de las cuales se pueden experimentar vistas cambiantes del desierto.

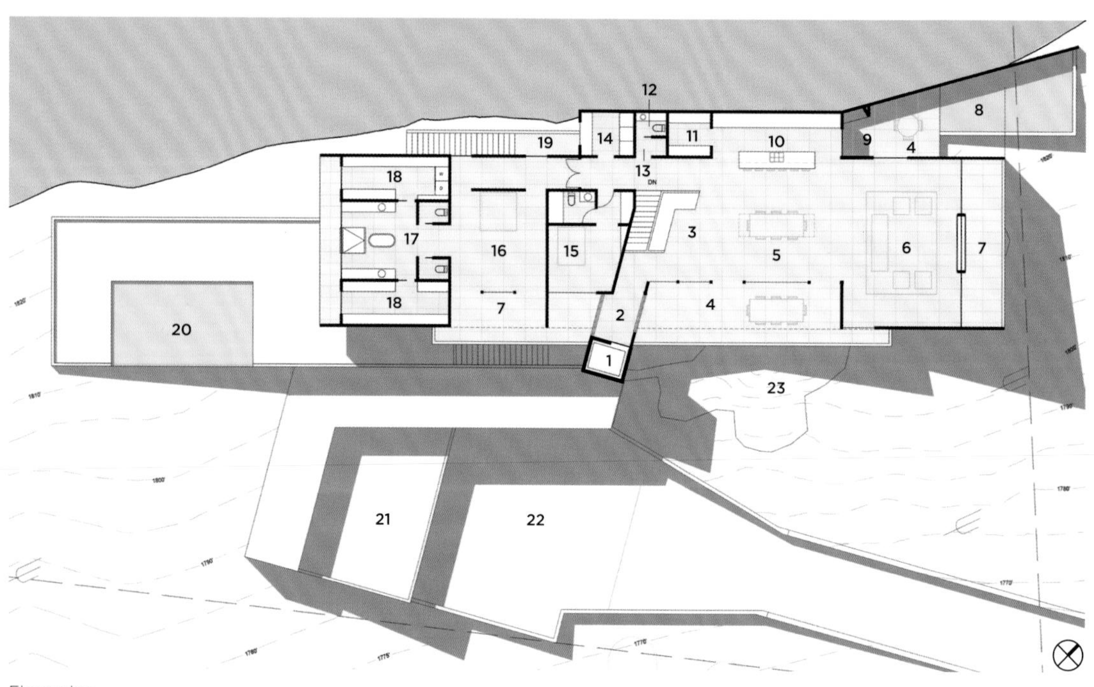

Floor plan

1. Elevator
2. Entry
3. Lounge
4. Terrace
5. Dining area
6. Living area
7. Balcony
8. Lawn
9. Barbecue area
10. Kitchen
11. Pantry
12. Powder room
13. Coat closet
14. Laundry room
15. Bedroom/study
16. Master bedroom
17. Bathroom
18. Dressing room
19. Staircase down to pool
20. Pool below
21. Terrace below
22. Car court below
23. Rock face

# LINE AND SPACE

094
v

**MARTHA COOPER LIBRARY**

Architecture Design team:
Line and Space
Landscape Architect:
McGann and Associates
Civil Engineer:
Presidio Engineering
Structural Engineer:
Turner Structural Engineering Company
Electrical Engineer:
M3 Engineering
Mechanical Engineer:
Kelly, Wright & Associates
Plumbing:
Kelly, Wright & Associates
AV:
McKay Conant Hoover
Photographer:
© Line and Space, LLC

098
v

**SAHUARITA REGIONAL LIBRARY**

Architecture Design team:
Line and Space
Landscape Architect:
McGann and Associates
Civil Engineer:
Presidio Engineering
Structural Engineer:
Turner Structural Engineering Company
Electrical Engineer:
M3 Engineering
Mechanical Engineer:
Kelly, Wright & Associates
Plumbing:
Kelly, Wright & Associates
AV:
McKay Conant Hoover
Photographer:
© Bradley Wheeler Photography

102
v

**SUL ROSS STATE UNIVERSITY CAMPUS ACCESS PROJECTS**

Architecture Design team:
Line and Space
Civil Engineer:
Maverick Engineering
Landscape Architect:
KDC Associates
Structural Engineer:
Leap!
Electrical Engineer:
Chambers Engineering
Photographer:
© Line and Space, LLC

www.lineandspace.com line.and.space

Line and Space, LLC was founded in 1978 in Tucson, Arizona, to facilitate the design and building of innovative and ecologically sound architecture. Their work throughout the Southwest is internationally known, with over 300 architectural design awards and publications.
The firm focuses on the development of creative, resource-conserving strategies that introduce users to architecture that responds to and respects each desert site. They strive for a quiet integration of structure and landscape that connects users to the natural environment, developing an interest and concern for the land. Their projects favor a deeper meaning of metaphor, entry sequence, scale, material, color, and form, all of which are important in successful architecture.

Line and Space, LLC wurde 1978 in Tucson, Arizona, gegründet, um den Entwurf und Bau innovativer und ökologisch sinnvoller Architektur zu ermöglichen. Ihre Arbeit im gesamten Südwesten ist international bekannt und wurde mit über 300 Architekturpreisen und Publikationen ausgezeichnet.
Das Büro konzentriert sich auf die Entwicklung kreativer, ressourcenschonender Strategien, die den Nutzern eine Architektur nahebringen, die auf jeden Wüstenstandort eingeht und ihn respektiert. Sie streben eine ruhige Integration von Struktur und Landschaft an, die die Nutzer mit der natürlichen Umgebung verbindet und ein Interesse und eine Sorge für das Land entwickelt. Ihre Projekte begünstigen eine tiefere Bedeutung von Metapher, Eingangssequenz, Maßstab, Material, Farbe und Form, die alle für eine erfolgreiche Architektur wichtig sind.

Line and Space, LLC a été fondé en 1978 à Tucson, en Arizona, pour faciliter la conception et la construction d'une architecture innovante et écologiquement saine. Leur travail dans le Sud-Ouest est reconnu internationalement, avec plus de 300 prix de conception architecturale et publications.
Le cabinet se concentre sur l'élaboration de stratégies créatives et respectueuses des ressources qui présentent aux utilisateurs une architecture qui répond et respecte chaque site désertique. L'agence s'efforce de réaliser une intégration discrète de la structure et du paysage qui relie les utilisateurs à l'environnement naturel, en développant un intérêt et un souci pour la terre. Leurs projets favorisent une signification plus profonde de la métaphore, de la séquence d'entrée, de l'échelle, du matériau, de la couleur et de la forme, qui sont tous importants pour une architecture réussie.

Line and Space, LLC fue fundada en 1978 en Tucson, Arizona, para facilitar el diseño y la construcción de una arquitectura innovadora y ecológica. Su trabajo en todo el suroeste es conocido internacionalmente, con más de 300 premios y publicaciones de diseño arquitectónico.
La empresa se centra en el desarrollo de estrategias creativas y de conservación de recursos que presentan a los usuarios una arquitectura que responde y respeta cada lugar del desierto. Se esfuerzan por lograr una integración discreta de la estructura y el paisaje que conecte a los usuarios con el entorno natural, desarrollando un interés y una preocupación por la tierra. Sus proyectos favorecen un significado más profundo de la metáfora, la secuencia de entrada, la escala, el material, el color y la forma, todo lo cual es importante en una arquitectura de éxito.

## MARTHA COOPER LIBRARY

Tucson, Arizona, United States // Lot area: 1.7921 acres; building area: 12,780 sq ft

The Martha Cooper Library, located in the midtown Garden District of Tucson, serves not only the surrounding neighborhood but also the city as a whole, providing improved services and a unique customer-centric experience. The project takes advantage of the existing structure's large clerestory and north-facing fenestration to provide daylighting in the children's collection and story areas and staff workspace. The Library design embraces the Garden District through exterior patios open toward landscape native to the Sonoran Desert, providing quiet and relaxing spaces to read or contemplate. Large overhangs protect floor-to-ceiling glass from the direct summer sun. Materials are expressed honestly and selected for their durability and ability to withstand desert elements.

La bibliothèque Martha Cooper, située dans le quartier des jardins du centre-ville de Tucson, sert non seulement le quartier environnant mais aussi la ville dans son ensemble, en offrant des services améliorés et une expérience unique centrée sur l'usager. Le projet tire parti de la grande claire-voie de la structure existante et de la fenestration orientée vers le nord pour fournir un éclairage naturel dans la collection des enfants, les zones d'histoires et l'espace de travail du personnel. La conception de la bibliothèque s'inscrit dans le cadre du Garden District grâce à des patios extérieurs ouverts sur le paysage indigène du désert de Sonoran, offrant des espaces calmes et relaxants pour lire ou contempler. De grands porte-à-faux protègent les vitres du sol au plafond du soleil direct de l'été. Les matériaux sont exprimés honnêtement et sélectionnés pour leur durabilité et leur capacité à résister aux éléments du désert.

Die Martha Cooper Library im Midtown Garden District von Tucson dient nicht nur der umliegenden Nachbarschaft, sondern auch der Stadt als Ganzes und bietet verbesserte Dienstleistungen und ein einzigartiges, kundenorientiertes Erlebnis. Das Projekt nutzt die Vorteile des großen Oberlichts und der nach Norden ausgerichteten Fenster des bestehenden Gebäudes, um Tageslicht in den Sammlungs- und Geschichtenbereichen für Kinder sowie in den Arbeitsbereichen der Mitarbeiter zu erhalten. Das Bibliotheksdesign bezieht das Gartenviertel durch Außenterrassen ein, die sich zur Landschaft der Sonoran-Wüste hin öffnen und ruhige und entspannende Plätze zum Lesen oder Nachdenken bieten. Große Überhänge schützen die vom Boden bis zur Decke reichenden Glasflächen vor der direkten Sommersonne. Die Materialien wurden nach ihrer Haltbarkeit und Widerstandsfähigkeit gegen die Wüsteneinflüsse ausgewählt und ehrlich ausgedrückt.

La Biblioteca Martha Cooper, situada en el distrito de los jardines del centro de Tucson, sirve no sólo al vecindario sino también a la ciudad en su conjunto, proporcionando servicios mejorados y una experiencia única centrada en el usuario. El proyecto aprovecha la gran claraboya de la estructura existente y un ventanal orientada al norte que proporciona luz natural en la colección infantil y las zonas de cuentos y el espacio de trabajo del personal. El diseño de la biblioteca abraza el Distrito de los Jardines a través de patios exteriores abiertos hacia el paisaje nativo del Desierto de Sonora, proporcionando espacios tranquilos y relajantes para leer o contemplar. Los grandes voladizos protegen los cristales del suelo al techo del sol directo del verano. Los materiales se expresan con honestidad y se seleccionan por su durabilidad y capacidad para soportar los elementos del desierto.

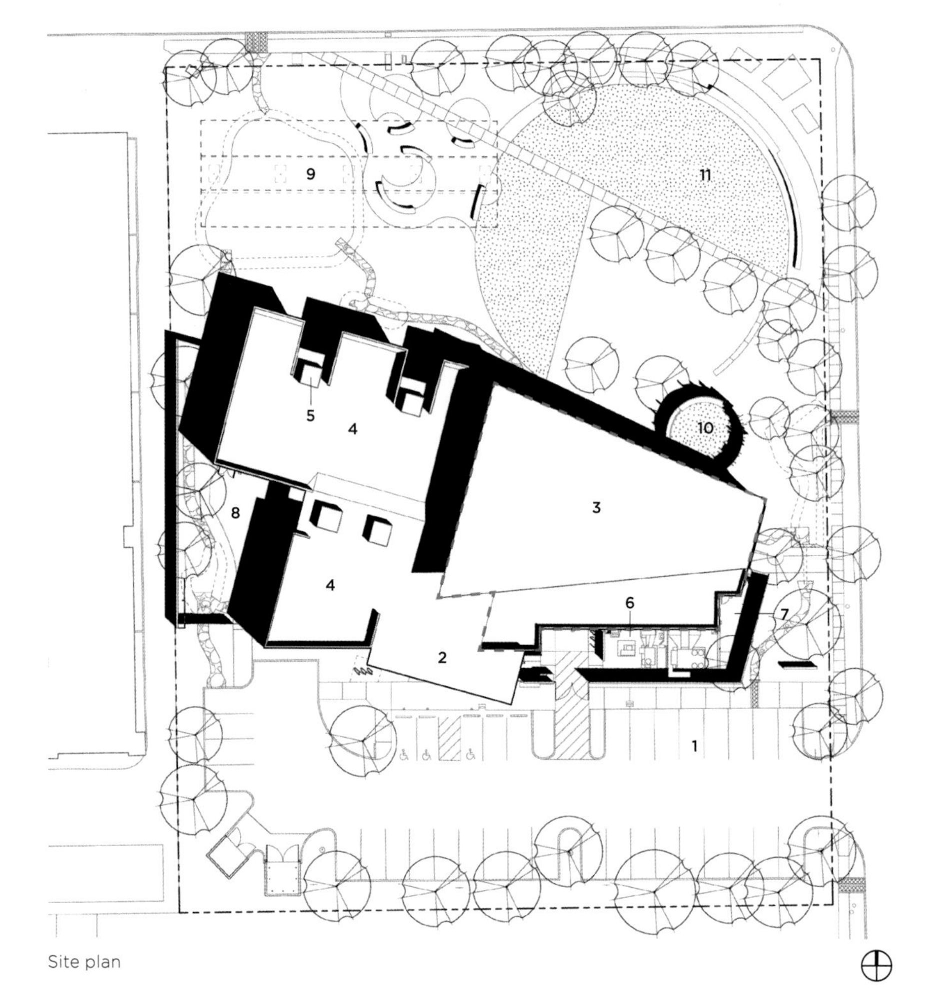

Site plan

- - - Existing building

1. Visitor parking
2. Entry plaza
3. Existing building
4. New construction
5. Skylights for daylighting
6. Mechanical yard
7. Staff patio
8. Community garden
9. Shaded gathering area (dashed line indicates photovoltaic panels above)
10. Children's outdoor play area
11. Existing landscaping

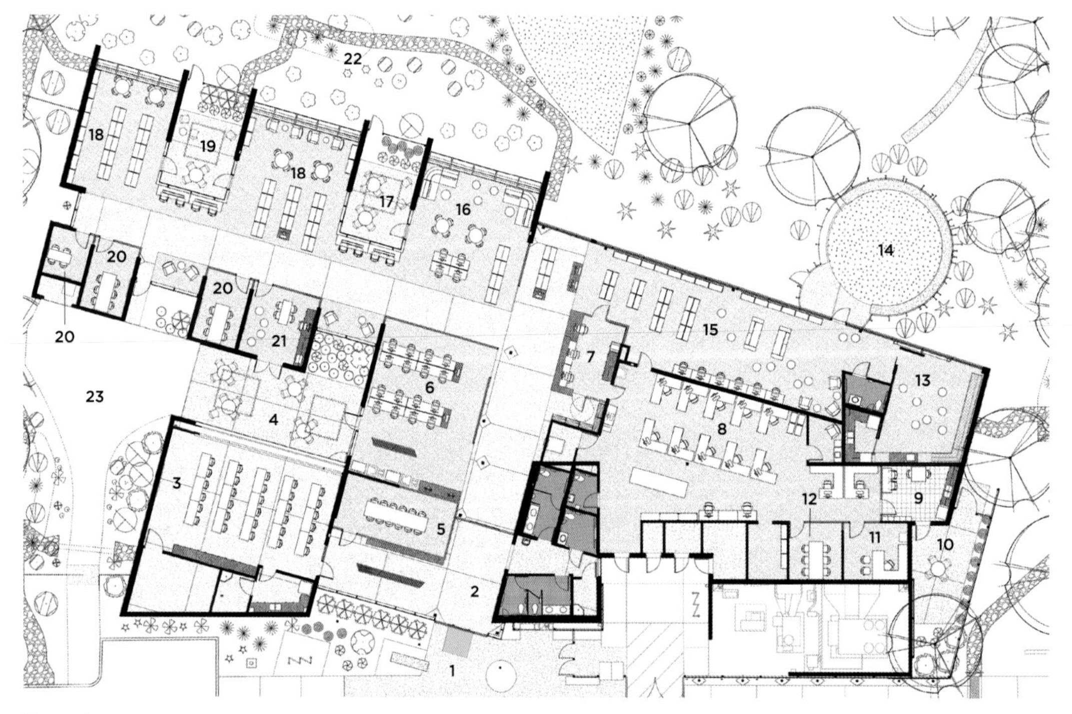

Floor plan

1. Entry plaza
2. Entry vestibule
3. Multi-purpose room (MPR)
4. Outdoor reading patio
5. Large study room
6. Computer commons
7. Service desk
8. Staff workroom
9. Staff break room
10. Staff patio
11. Manager's office
12. Staff conference room
13. Children's story time room
14. Children's outdoor play area
15. Children's collection
16. Teen collection
17. Teen's outdoor reading patio
18. Adult collection
19. Adult's outdoor reading patio
20. Study room
21. Next Big Thing room
22. Water harvesting swales and basin
23. Community garden

## SAHUARITA REGIONAL LIBRARY

Sahuarita, Arizona, United States // Lot area: 2.09476 acres; building area: 17,700 sq ft

The Sahuarita Regional Library provides spaces for children, teens, and adults to enjoy collections, access to new learning technologies, and a user-focused experience. As positive vistas are lacking from the site, the facility utilizes a low ribbon window to focus views on adjacent bioswales planted with native Sonoran Desert vegetation and irrigated with rainwater collected from the roof and hardscape. Steel shade structures, an abstraction of the area's copper mining activities, rise from the south elevation. These structures—or "shards"—allow diffused natural light into the interior spaces and define outdoor reading patios. With longevity and durability in mind, selected materials include steel cladding, glass and aluminum curtain walls, and exposed masonry.

La bibliothèque régionale de Sahuarita offre des espaces aux enfants, aux adolescents et aux adultes pour profiter des collections, de l'accès aux nouvelles technologies d'apprentissage et d'une expérience centrée sur l'utilisateur. En l'absence de points de vue positifs sur le site, l'installation utilise une fenêtre en ruban basse pour concentrer les vues sur les biodégradations adjacentes plantées de végétation indigène du désert de Sonoran et irriguées par l'eau de pluie collectée sur le toit et le paysage dur. Des structures d'ombrage en acier, une abstraction des activités minières de cuivre de la région, s'élèvent sur la façade sud. Ces structures - ou « tessons » - permettent de diffuser la lumière naturelle dans les espaces intérieurs et définissent les patios de lecture extérieurs. Dans un souci de longévité et de durabilité, les matériaux sélectionnés comprennent des revêtements en acier, des murs-rideaux en verre et en aluminium, et de la maçonnerie apparente.

Die Sahuarita Regional Library bietet Kindern, Jugendlichen und Erwachsenen Räume, in denen sie sich an den Sammlungen erfreuen können, Zugang zu neuen Lerntechnologien haben und ein benutzerorientiertes Erlebnis haben. Da es an positiven Ausblicken vom Standort aus mangelt, nutzt die Einrichtung ein niedriges Fensterband, um den Blick auf die angrenzenden Bioswales zu lenken, die mit einheimischer Sonoran-Wüstenvegetation bepflanzt sind und mit Regenwasser bewässert werden, das vom Dach und den Außenanlagen aufgefangen wird. An der Südseite erheben sich stählerne Schattenspender, die an den Kupferabbau in der Region erinnern. Diese Strukturen - oder „Scherben"- lassen diffuses natürliches Licht in die Innenräume und definieren die Leseterrassen im Freien. Im Hinblick auf Langlebigkeit und Beständigkeit wurden Materialien wie Stahlverkleidungen, Glas- und Aluminiumfassaden und Sichtmauerwerk ausgewählt.

La Biblioteca Regional Sahuarita ofrece espacios para que los niños, adolescentes y adultos disfruten de las colecciones, el acceso a las nuevas tecnologías de aprendizaje y una experiencia centrada en el usuario. Como no hay vistas interesantes desde el terreno, la instalación utiliza una ventana de cinta baja para enfocar las vistas de los canales biológicos adyacentes plantados con vegetación nativa del Desierto de Sonora y regados con agua de lluvia recolectada desde el techo y el paisaje duro. Las estructuras de sombra, acabadas en acero, una abstracción de las actividades mineras de cobre de la zona, se elevan desde la parte sur. Estas estructuras, o «fragmentos», permiten la entrada de luz natural difusa en los espacios interiores y definen los patios exteriores. Teniendo en cuenta la longevidad y la durabilidad, los materiales seleccionados incluyen revestimientos de acero, muros cortina de vidrio y aluminio, y mampostería expuesta.

670

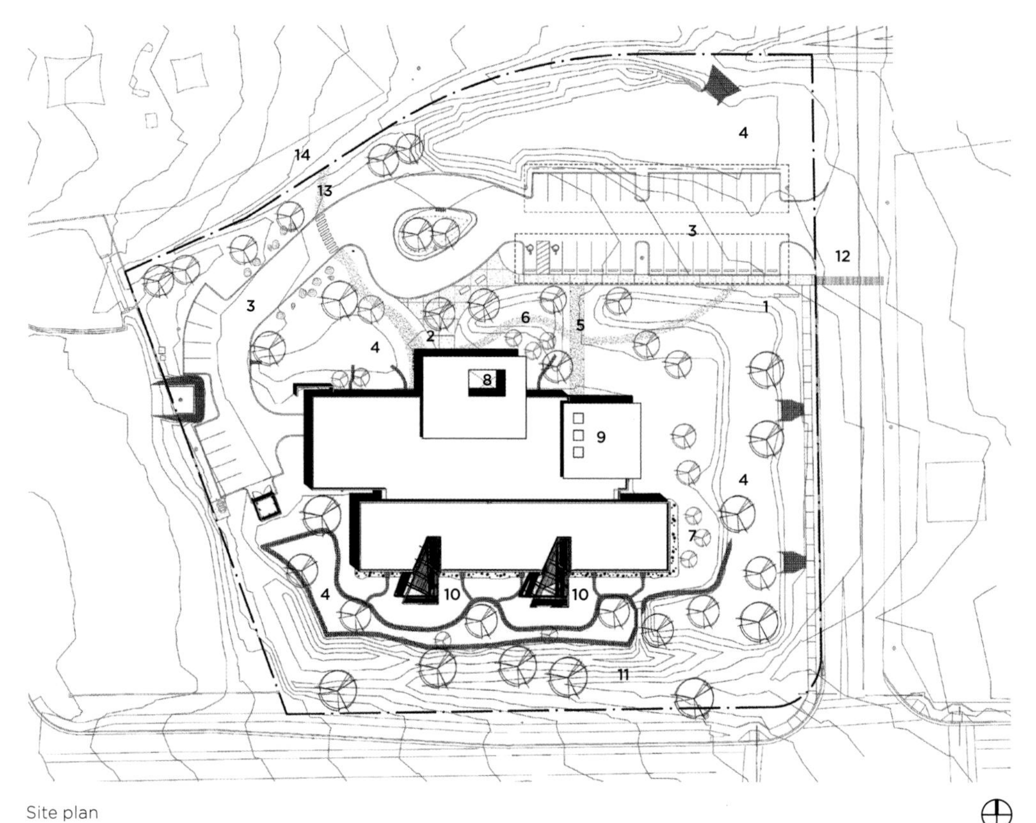

1. Entry sign
2. Entry plaza
3. Parking
4. Water harvesting basin holds water from roofs and hardscapes
5. Desert path
6. Butterfly garden
7. Perimeter cactus garden
8. Skyhole
9. Skylights
10. "Shards" (outdoor patio)
11. Desert berm mitigates noise from street
12. Crosswalk to middle and high school
13. Future path to primary school
14. Existing arroyo

Site plan

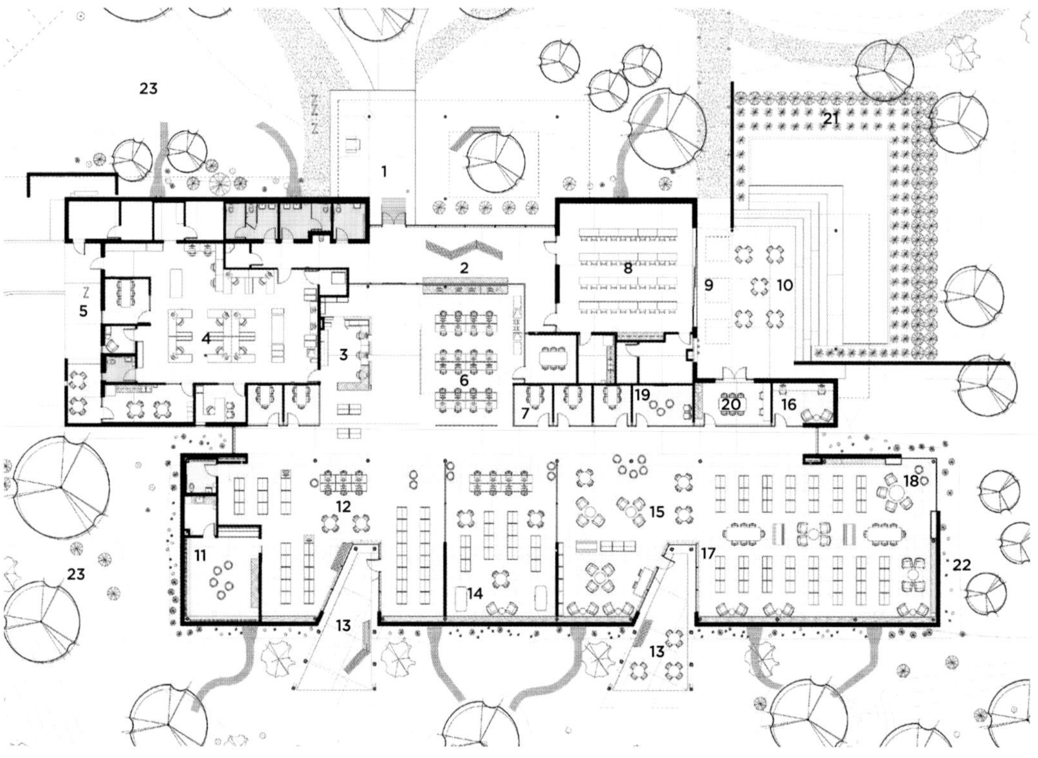

1. Entry plaza
2. Entry vestibule
3. Service desk
4. Staff work room
5. Staff patio
6. Computer commons
7. Study room
8. Multipurpose room
9. Sliding glass door
10. Performance patio with tiered seating
11. Story time room
12. Children's collection
13. "Shards" (outdoor patio)
14. Teen collection
15. Periodicals
16. Business development space
17. Adult collection
18. Reading lounge
19. Gaming center
20. "Next Big Thing" room
21. Earth berm
22. Perimeter cactus garden
23. Water harvesting basin collects water from roofs and hardscapes

Floor plan

## SUL ROSS STATE UNIVERSITY CAMPUS ACCESS PROJECTS

Alpine, Texas, United States // Lot area: 93 acres

Within the Chihuahuan Desert of West Texas, the Campus Access Projects focus on the overall quality and connectivity of outdoor spaces across Sul Ross State University's main campus. The project consists of circulation, accessibility, and wayfinding improvements, as well as the addition of outdoor performance, gathering, and teaching areas. Throughout areas of the campus, non-native landscaping is replaced with low water-use vegetation of the Big Bend area, and existing site lighting is upgraded to be dark sky compliant. Enhancing the "front yard" and entry to the University, the design creates a series of new large outdoor multi-purpose plazas, progressing to more intimate areas. The use of natural, durable materials readily available in the area include native stone from a nearby quarry combined with exposed concrete and steel.

Dans le désert de Chihuahuan de l'ouest du Texas, les projets d'accès au campus se concentrent sur la qualité globale et la connectivité des espaces extérieurs du campus principal de l'université d'État de Sul Ross. Le projet consiste en des améliorations de la circulation, de l'accessibilité et de l'orientation, ainsi qu'en l'ajout d'espaces extérieurs de représentation, de rassemblement et d'enseignement. Dans toutes les zones du campus, les aménagements paysagers non indigènes sont remplacés par une végétation à faible consommation d'eau de la région de Big Bend, et l'éclairage existant du site est mis à niveau pour être conforme au principe du ciel noir. Pour mettre en valeur la « cour avant » et l'entrée de l'université, la conception crée une série de nouvelles grandes places extérieures polyvalentes, puis des zones plus intimes. L'utilisation de matériaux naturels et durables facilement disponibles dans la région comprend de la pierre indigène provenant d'une carrière voisine, combinée à du béton apparent et de l'acier.

In der Chihuahuan-Wüste im Westen von Texas konzentrieren sich die Campus Access Projects auf die Qualität und Konnektivität von Außenbereichen auf dem Hauptcampus der Sul Ross State University. Das Projekt umfasst Verbesserungen der Verkehrsführung, der Zugänglichkeit und der Wegeführung sowie die Einrichtung von Spiel-, Versammlungs- und Lehrbereichen im Freien. Auf dem gesamten Campus wird die nicht einheimische Landschaftsgestaltung durch Vegetation mit geringem Wasserverbrauch des Big Bend-Gebiets ersetzt, und die vorhandene Standortbeleuchtung wird so aufgerüstet, dass sie mit dunklem Himmel kompatibel ist. Zur Aufwertung des „Vorgartens" und des Eingangs zur Universität sieht der Entwurf eine Reihe großer Mehrzweckplätze im Freien vor, die sich zu intimeren Bereichen entwickeln. Die Verwendung natürlicher, langlebiger Materialien, die in der Gegend leicht verfügbar sind, umfasst einheimischen Stein aus einem nahe gelegenen Steinbruch in Kombination mit Sichtbeton und Stahl.

En el desierto chihuahuense del oeste de Texas, los proyectos de acceso al campus se centran en la calidad general y la conectividad de los espacios exteriores del campus principal de la Universidad Estatal Sul Ross. El proyecto consiste en la mejora de la circulación, la accesibilidad y la orientación, así como en la adición de áreas de actuación, reunión y enseñanza al aire libre. En todas las zonas del campus, se ha sustituido la jardinería no autóctona por vegetación de bajo consumo de agua de la zona de Big Bend, y se ha mejorado el alumbrado existente para que sea compatible con el cielo oscuro. Para mejorar el «patio delantero»y la entrada a la Universidad, el diseño crea una serie de grandes plazas polivalentes al aire libre, que progresan hacia zonas más íntimas. El uso de materiales naturales y duraderos fácilmente disponibles en la zona incluye la piedra autóctona de una cantera cercana combinada con el hormigón visto y el acero.

Before

# AMD ARCHITECTURE

108
v

**MOUNTAIN SANCTUARY**

Architecture Design team: Angela Dean/ AMD Architecture
Structural Engineer: Canyons Consulting
Wall System: Faswall ICF
Interior Wall Finish: American Clay
Exterior Wall Finish: Zinc and reclaimed cedar
Mechanical: Rais stove, Radiant floors, ERV ventilation
Renewable Energy: Photovoltaic electric system, Solar hot water collection
Photographer: © Chris Talvy and Ian Matteson

112
v

**DWELLING IN THE TREES**

Architecture Design team:Angela Dean and Brandon Jenkins/AMD Architecture
Structural Engineer: Bearghost Inc.
Builder: Owner
Windows: Sierra Pacific Windows and Doors
Mechanical: Thermal Engineering - Radiant floors, ERV ventilation, ductless mini-split heat pumps, tankless on-demand hot water
Renewable Energy: Photovoltaic electric system
Exterior stone: Local Browns Canyon Stone
Exterior siding: Cambria, Thermally Modified Poplar T&G
Custom Millwork: Scherr's Cabinet and Doors
Tile: Venetian Tile and Stone
Photographer: © Brandon Jenkins

116
v

**SKI LODGE**

Architecture Design team:
Valerio Campi, Massimiliano Brugia, and Lucia Catenacci/OBICUA; Angela Dean and Danielle Clark/AMD Architecture
Structural Engineer: Epic Engineering
Builder: Benchmark Modern
Interior Plaster: La Fucina
Interior/exterior wood: Reclaimed cedar and teak
Exterior Metal: MBCI Steel
Custom Millwork: Andrea Mellare
Mechanical: Radiant floors, ERV ventilation, tankless on-demand hot water
Lighting: Flos
Green Roof: Greengrid
Windows: Reynaers
Photographer: © Luigi Filetici

www.amdarchitecture.com amdarchitecture

Angela Dean, AIA, LEED, AP

While in graduate school, Angela Dean spent her summers running rivers, exploring the desert southwest, and discovering Ancestral Puebloan dwellings that generated deep respect for a culture attuned to nature's cycles. The timeless methods of working with climate and natural forces were embedded in her professional ethos. She launched AMD Architecture in 1997 to pursue her commitment to sustainable design and passion for creating places where people thrive. Along with talented and dedicated staff, AMD has maintained an architectural practice committed to those goals. Angela credits the success of AMD's projects to their clients, who bring their passions and personal ethos to the process. From owner-built, off-grid, straw-bale homes to retail spaces for a global company, AMD attracts clients who strive to walk the talk. They believe that the design process is a journey, not a destination and that our buildings shape us as we shape them.

Während ihres Studiums verbrachte Angela Dean ihre Sommer damit, die Flüsse hinunterzulaufen, den Wüstensüdwesten zu erkunden und die Behausungen der Puebloaner der Vorfahren zu entdecken, die ihr einen tiefen Respekt für eine Kultur im Einklang mit den Zyklen der Natur verliehen. Die zeitlosen Methoden der Arbeit mit dem Klima und den natürlichen Kräften wurden in ihr Berufsethos eingebettet. 1997 gründete sie AMD Architecture, um ihrem Engagement für nachhaltiges Design und ihrer Leidenschaft für die Schaffung von Orten, an denen sich Menschen wohlfühlen, nachzugehen. Zusammen mit talentierten und engagierten Mitarbeitern hat AMD ein Architekturbüro aufgebaut, das sich diesen Zielen verschrieben hat. Angela führt den Erfolg der AMD-Projekte auf die Kunden zurück, die ihre Leidenschaften und ihr persönliches Ethos in den Prozess einbringen, was zu äußerst lohnenswerten Arbeiten und Ergebnissen führt. Von in Eigenregie gebauten, netzunabhängigen Strohballenhäusern bis hin zu Einzelhandelsflächen für ein weltweit tätiges Unternehmen ziehen AMD Kunden an, die sich bemühen, ihren Worten Taten folgen zu lassen. Sie glauben, dass der Designprozess eine Reise und kein Ziel ist und dass unsere Gebäude uns formen, während wir sie formen.

Pendant ses études, Angela Dean a passé ses étés à descendre les rivières, à explorer le désert du Sud-Ouest et à découvrir des maisons d'Indiens Pueblos ancestrales qui lui ont donné un profond respect pour une culture en phase avec les cycles de la nature. Les méthodes intemporelles de travail avec le climat et les forces naturelles font partie intégrante de son éthique professionnelle. Elle a lancé AMD Architecture en 1997 poursuivant son engagement en faveur de la conception durable et sa passion pour la création de lieux où les gens s'épanouissent. Avec un personnel talentueux et dévoué, AMD a maintenu une pratique architecturale engagée dans ces objectifs. Angela attribue le succès des projets d'AMD à ses clients, qui apportent leurs passions et leur éthique personnelle au processus. Qu'il s'agisse de maisons en bottes de paille hors réseau construites par le propriétaire ou d'espaces de vente au détail pour une entreprise internationale, AMD attire des clients qui s'efforcent de joindre le geste à la parole. Ils estiment que le processus de conception est un voyage, et non une destination, et que nos bâtiments nous façonnent comme nous les façonnons.

Mientras estudiaba, Angela Dean pasaba los veranos corriendo por los ríos, explorando el desierto del suroeste y descubriendo viviendas de Indios Pueblo ancestrales que le generó un profundo respeto por una cultura en sintonía con los ciclos de la naturaleza. Los métodos intemporales de trabajo con el clima y las fuerzas naturales se integraron en su ética profesional. En 1997, fundó AMD Architecture para llevar a cabo su compromiso con el diseño sostenible y su pasión por crear lugares en los que las personas prosperen. Junto con un personal de gran talento y dedicación, AMD ha mantenido un estudio de arquitectura comprometido con esos objetivos. Angela atribuye el éxito de los proyectos de AMD a sus clientes, que aportan sus pasiones y su ética personal al proceso, lo que conduce a un trabajo y unos resultados sumamente gratificantes. Desde casas de balas de paja construidas por el propietario hasta espacios comerciales para una empresa global, AMD atrae a clientes que se esfuerzan por cumplir con lo que dicen. Creen que el proceso de diseño es un viaje, no un destino, y que nuestros edificios nos dan forma a nosotros y nosotros a ellos.

## MOUNTAIN SANCTUARY

Park City, Utah, United States // Lot area: 22,000 sq ft; building area: 2,080 sq ft

Passive, natural, healthy, and simple were the design basis for this mountain home, whose staggered box form creates flexible interior spaces and sheltered outdoor areas while addressing passive solar control, natural ventilation, and snow management. The concept of sustainability materialized in a system of breathable walls made with pre-formed blocks that regulates energy, humidity, sound, and comfort, while exposed concrete floors provide a durable, low-maintenance finish and serve as a heat sink. An attached greenhouse not only provides fresh vegetables through an extended growing season but also serves as a solar heat collector for warmth during the depths of winter. Outside, the landscape has been revegetated with native shrubs and wildflowers, which require no supplemental watering while serving as a spectacular show of color from all spaces in the home.

Une conception passive, naturelle, saine et simple définit cette maison de montagne, dont la forme décalée crée des espaces intérieurs flexibles et des zones extérieures protégées, tout en assurant un contrôle solaire passif, une ventilation naturelle et une gestion des chutes de neige. Le concept de durabilité s'est concrétisé dans un système de murs respirants constitué de blocs préformés qui régulent l'énergie, l'humidité, le son et le confort, tandis que les sols en béton apparent offrent une finition durable nécessitant peu d'entretien et servent de dissipateur de chaleur. Une serre attenante fournit non seulement des légumes frais pour une longue saison de croissance, mais sert également de collecteur de chaleur solaire pour le chauffage en hiver. À l'extérieur, l'aménagement paysager a été replanté d'arbustes et de fleurs sauvages indigènes, qui ne nécessitent aucune irrigation supplémentaire et offrent un spectacle de couleurs visible de n'importe où dans la maison.

Ein passives, natürliches, gesundes und einfaches Design definiert dieses Berghaus, dessen gestaffelte Form flexible Innenräume und geschützte Außenzonen schafft und gleichzeitig passiven Sonnenschutz, natürliche Belüftung und Schneefallmanagement bietet. Das Konzept der Nachhaltigkeit verwirklichte sich in einem System atmungsaktiver Wände aus vorgeformten Blöcken, die Energie, Feuchtigkeit, Schall und Komfort regulieren, während Sichtbetonböden eine dauerhafte, pflegeleichte Oberfläche bieten und als Wärmesenke dienen. Ein angeschlossenes Gewächshaus sorgt nicht nur für frisches Gemüse für eine lange Vegetationsperiode, sondern dient auch als Solarwärmekollektor für die Winterheizung. Draußen wurde die Landschaftsgestaltung mit einheimischen Sträuchern und Wildblumen neu bepflanzt, die keine zusätzliche Bewässerung benötigen und ein Farbspektakel bieten, das von überall im Haus gesehen werden kann.

Un diseño pasivo, natural, saludable y sencillo define esta casa de montaña, cuya forma escalonada crea espacios interiores flexibles y zonas exterior protegidas, a la vez que proporciona control solar pasivo, ventilación natural y una gestión de la caída de nieve. El concepto de sostenibilidad se materializo en un sistema de muros transpirables realizados con bloques preformados que regulan la energía, la humedad, el sonido y el confort, mientras que suelos de hormigón visto brindan un acabado duradero y de bajo mantenimiento a la vez que sirven como disipadores térmicos. Un invernadero adjunto no sólo proporciona hortalizas frescas durante una larga temporada de cultivo, sino que también sirve como colector de calor solar para calentarse en invierno. En el exterior, el paisaje se ha replantado con arbustos y flores silvestres autóctonas, que no requieren riego suplementario y ofrecen un espectáculo de color que puede apreciarse desde cualquier espacio de la casa.

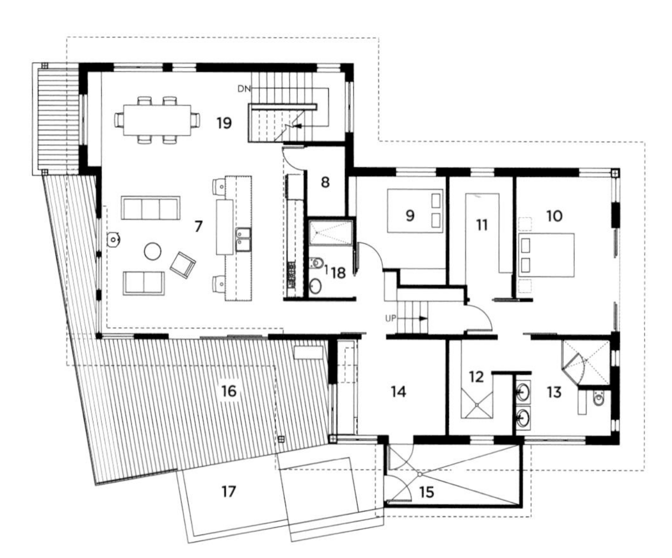


Main floor plan

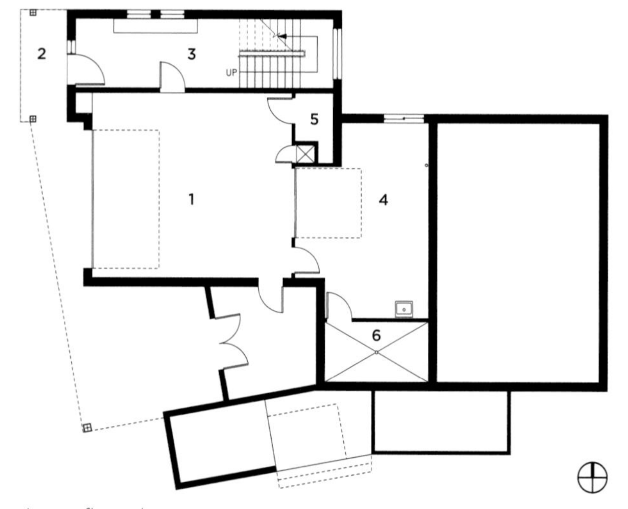


Lower floor plan

1. Garage
2. Covered entry
3. Mud room
4. Shop
5. Storage
6. Mechanical room
7. Living area
8. Pantry
9. Guest bedroom
10. Primary bedroom
11. Primary closet
12. Laundry room
13. Primary bathroom
14. Office
15. Greenhouse
16. Deck
17. Planting area
18. Guest bathroom
19. Dining area

## DWELLING IN THE TREES

Park City, Utah, United States // Lot area: 37,000 sq ft; building area: 3,375 sq ft

The owners fell in love with this site in a secluded and dense mature forest with access to mountain recreation from their doorstep. They directed AMD Architecture to design an open-plan home suitable to showcase their art collection and accommodate their extended family. The result is a sculpted form throughout the forest, providing unique views while maintaining privacy, all without sacrificing any of their beloved trees on the site. Living spaces along the south optimize passive solar strategies, and covered patios and balconies surrounding the home strengthen the indoor-outdoor connection. The construction of this home was a labor of love involving the whole family in its creation. The homeowners brought their eye for interior design and craftsmanship skills to the project from the foundation through the finishing touches.

Les propriétaires sont tombés amoureux de ce site situé dans une forêt mature, dense et isolée, avec un accès aux loisirs de montagne depuis leur porte. Ils ont demandé à AMD Architecture de concevoir une maison à aire ouverte capable de mettre en valeur leur collection d'art et d'accueillir leur famille élargie. Le résultat est une forme sculptée dans la forêt, offrant des vues uniques tout en préservant l'intimité, le tout sans sacrifier aucun de leurs arbres bien-aimés sur le site. Les espaces de vie situés au sud optimisent les stratégies solaires passives, et les patios et balcons couverts qui entourent la maison renforcent le lien entre l'intérieur et l'extérieur. La construction de cette maison a été un travail d'amour impliquant toute la famille dans sa création. Les propriétaires ont apporté leur sens de la décoration intérieure et leurs compétences artisanales au projet, de la fondation aux finitions.

Die Eigentümer verliebten sich in dieses Grundstück in einem abgelegenen und dichten Wald mit Zugang zu den Bergen vor ihrer Haustür. Sie beauftragten AMD Architecture mit dem Entwurf eines Hauses mit offenem Grundriss, in dem sie ihre Kunstsammlung ausstellen und ihre Großfamilie unterbringen konnten. Das Ergebnis ist eine geformte Form im gesamten Wald, die einzigartige Ausblicke bietet und gleichzeitig die Privatsphäre bewahrt, ohne einen ihrer geliebten Bäume auf dem Gelände zu opfern. Die Wohnräume entlang der Südseite optimieren die passive Sonneneinstrahlung, und die überdachten Terrassen und Balkone, die das Haus umgeben, verstärken die Verbindung zwischen Innen und Außen. Der Bau dieses Hauses war ein Werk der Liebe, an dem die ganze Familie beteiligt war. Die Hausbesitzer brachten ihr Auge für Innenarchitektur und ihr handwerkliches Geschick in das Projekt ein - vom Fundament bis zum letzten Schliff.

Los propietarios se enamoraron de este emplazamiento en un bosque maduro, aislado y denso, con acceso a las actividades recreativas de la montaña desde su misma puerta. Encargaron a AMD Architecture el diseño de una casa de planta abierta adecuada para exhibir su colección de arte y dar cabida a su extensa familia. El resultado es una forma esculpida a lo largo del bosque, proporcionando vistas únicas mientras se mantiene la privacidad, todo ello sin sacrificar ninguno de sus queridos árboles. Los espacios habitables a lo largo del sur optimizan las estrategias solares pasivas, y los patios y balcones cubiertos que rodean la casa refuerzan la conexión entre el interior y el exterior. La construcción de esta casa fue un trabajo de amor en el que participó toda la familia. Los propietarios aportaron su ojo para el diseño de interiores y sus habilidades artesanales al proyecto, desde los cimientos hasta los toques finales.

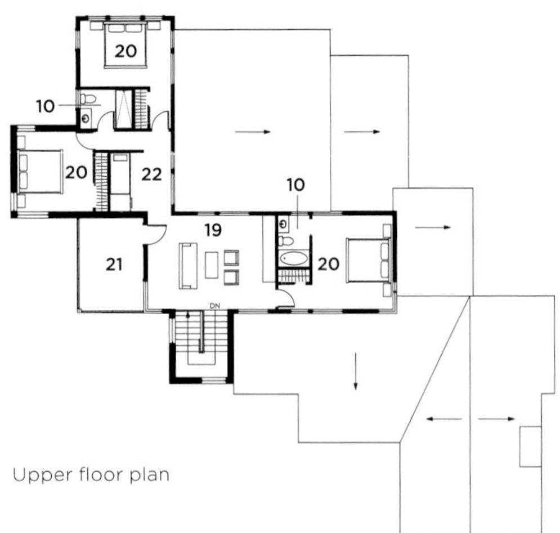


Upper floor plan

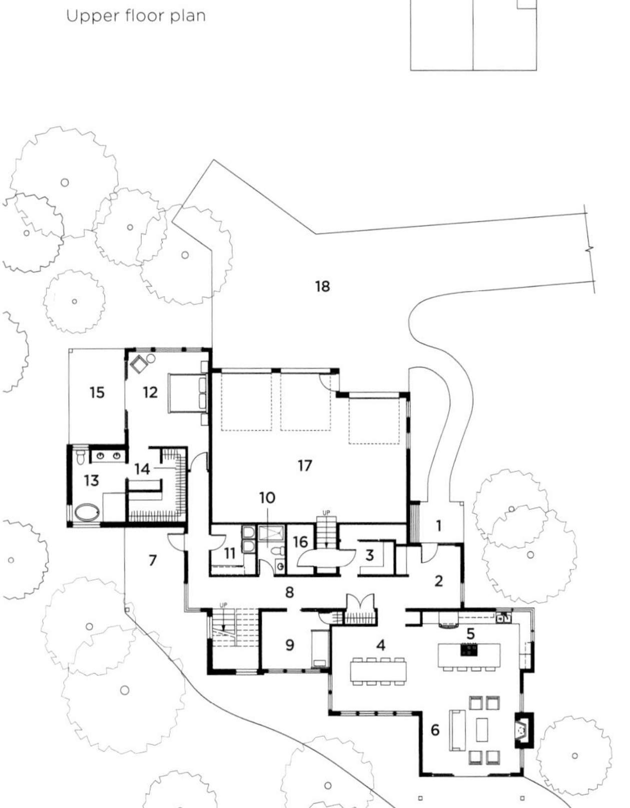

Main floor plan

1. Covered porch
2. Entry
3. Mud room
4. Sunroom/ dining
5. Kitchen
6. Living room
7. Patio
8. Gallery
9. Study
10. Bathroom
11. Laundry room
12. Master bedroom
13. Master bathroom
14. Walk-in closet
15. West patio
16. Mechanical room
17. Garage
18. Driveway
19. Loft
20. Bedroom
21. Deck
22. Bunk alcove

## SKI LODGE

Eden, Utah, United States // Lot area: 42,000 sq ft; building area: 4,500 sq ft

The Ski Lodge is a modern interpretation of a mountain retreat integrating timeless ecological building practices with the latest technologies. The efficient design of the lodge responds to extreme weather conditions while capitalizing on the incredible beauty of the site at 8,000 feet above sea level on Powder Mountain. The house is divided into two blocks—one for guests and kids, the other for the owners—linked vertically through a double-height space serving as the entry and core circulation. South-facing balconies provide sheltered expansion of living spaces to the outdoors while controlling passive solar gain. The Ski Lodge was designed to achieve LEED® Gold standards by minimizing the construction impact on resources, conserving energy and water, optimizing occupant health, and reducing long-term operational energy use.

Le chalet de ski est une interprétation moderne d'une retraite en montagne intégrant des pratiques de construction écologiques intemporelles et les dernières technologies. La conception efficace du pavillon répond aux conditions météorologiques extrêmes tout en tirant parti de l'incroyable beauté du site, à 8 000 pieds d'altitude sur Powder Mountain. La maison est divisée en deux blocs - un pour les invités et les enfants, l'autre pour les propriétaires - reliés verticalement par un espace à double hauteur servant d'entrée et de circulation centrale. Des balcons orientés au sud permettent d'étendre les espaces de vie vers l'extérieur tout en contrôlant les apports solaires passifs. Le Ski Lodge a été conçu pour atteindre lla qualification LEED® Or en minimisant l'impact de la construction sur les ressources, en conservant l'énergie et l'eau, en optimisant la santé des occupants et en réduisant la consommation d'énergie opérationnelle à long terme.

Die Ski Lodge ist eine moderne Interpretation eines Rückzugsortes in den Bergen, die zeitlose ökologische Baupraktiken mit den neuesten Technologien verbindet. Das effiziente Design der Lodge reagiert auf extreme Wetterbedingungen und nutzt gleichzeitig die unglaubliche Schönheit des Standorts auf 8.000 Fuß über dem Meeresspiegel am Powder Mountain. Das Haus ist in zwei Blöcke unterteilt - einer für Gäste und Kinder, der andere für die Eigentümer -, die vertikal durch einen Raum mit doppelter Höhe verbunden sind, der als Eingangsbereich und Kernzirkulation dient. Die nach Süden ausgerichteten Balkone bieten eine geschützte Erweiterung der Wohnräume nach außen und kontrollieren gleichzeitig die passive Sonneneinstrahlung. Die Ski Lodge wurde entwickelt, um die LEED® Gold-Standards zu erreichen, indem die Auswirkungen des Baus auf Ressourcen minimiert, Energie und Wasser gespart, die Gesundheit der Bewohner optimiert und der langfristige Energieverbrauch im Betrieb reduziert werden.

El Ski Lodge es una interpretación moderna de un refugio de montaña que integra prácticas de construcción ecológicas atemporales con las últimas tecnologías. El eficiente diseño de la casa responde a las condiciones climáticas extremas, a la vez que aprovecha la increíble belleza del lugar, situado a 8.000 pies sobre el nivel del mar en Powder Mountain. La casa está dividida en dos bloques -uno para los huéspedes y los niños, y otro para los propietarios- unidos verticalmente a través de un espacio de doble altura que sirve de entrada y circulación central. Los balcones orientados al sur ofrecen una expansión protegida de los espacios habitables hacia el exterior, al tiempo que controlan la ganancia solar pasiva. El Ski Lodge fue diseñado para lograr la calificación LEED® Gold al minimizar el impacto de la construcción en los recursos, conservar energía y agua, optimizar la salud de los ocupantes y reducir el uso de energía operativa a largo plazo.

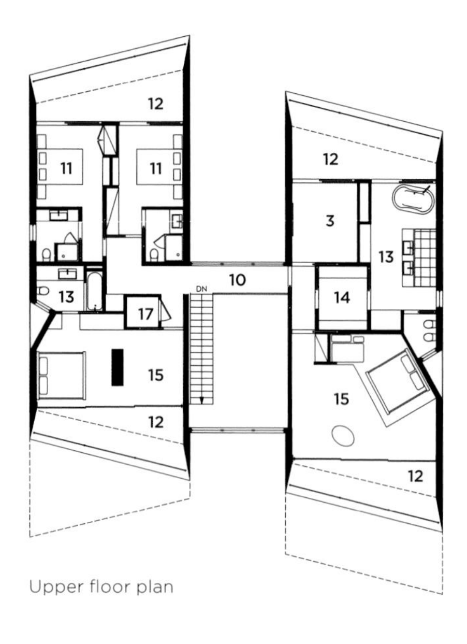


Upper floor plan

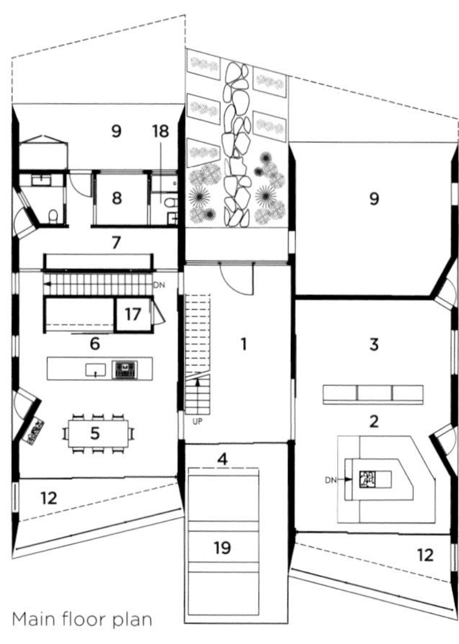


Main floor plan

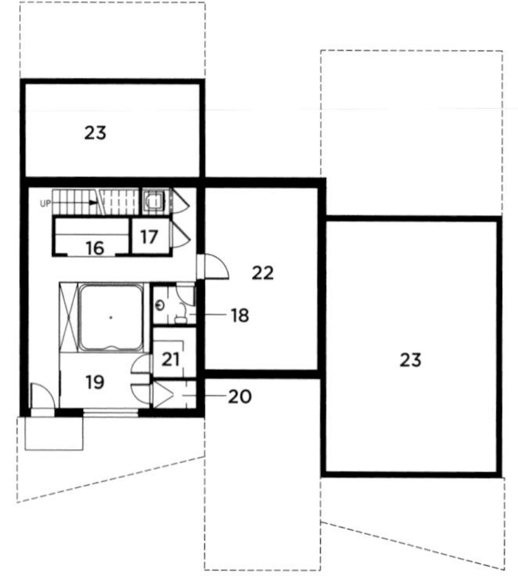


Lower floor plan

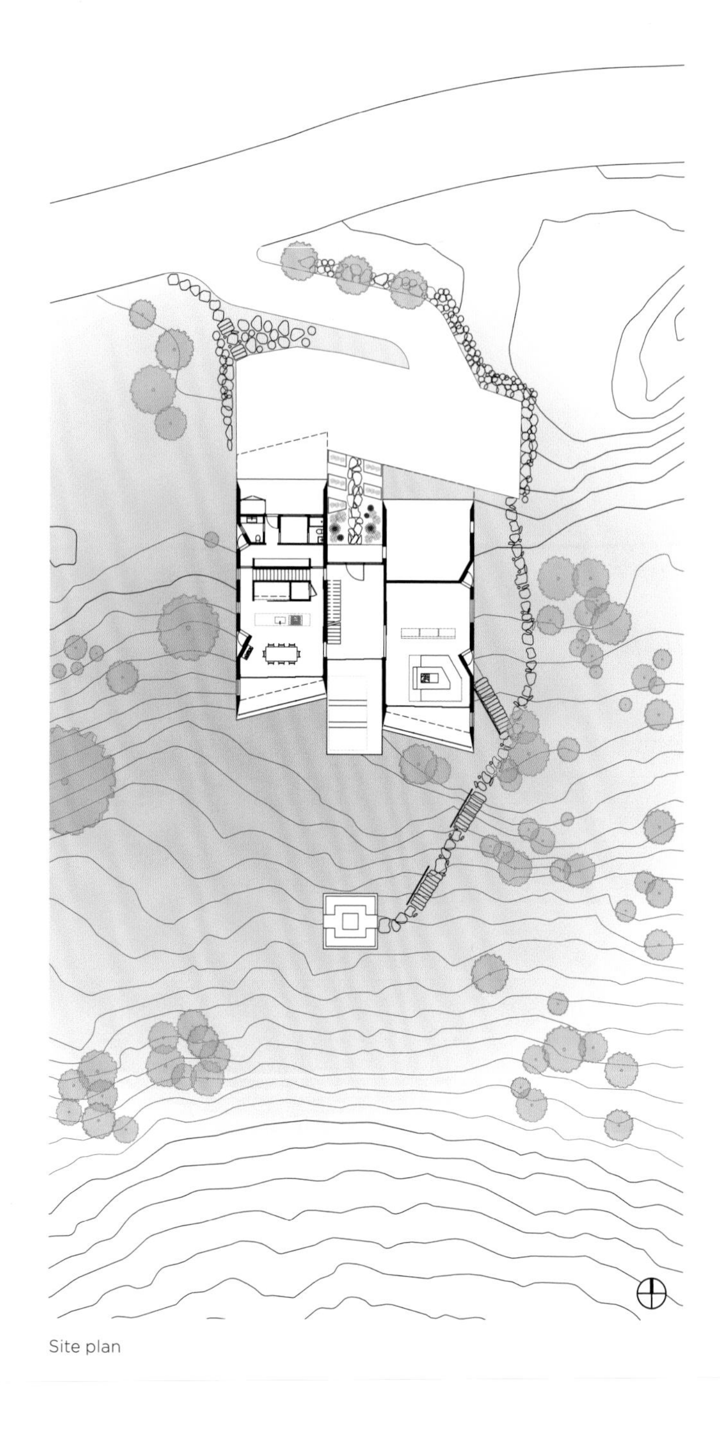

Site plan

1. Entry
2. Recessed conversation lounge
3. Sitting room
4. Patio
5. Dining room
6. Kitchen
7. Mud room
8. Service room
9. Carport
10. Bridge
11. Bedroom
12. Balcony
13. Primary bathroom
14. Primary closet
15. Primary bedroom
16. Ski storage
17. Elevator
18. Powder room
19. Hot tub
20. Shower
21. Sauna
22. Mechanical room
23. Crawl space

# KELLY & STONE ARCHITECTS

124
v

**HINMAN CREEK**

Architect:
Kelly & Stone Architects
Interior Designer:
Kelly & Stone Architects
Cabinetry/casework:
Fedewa Custom Works
Timber:
Spearhead
Builder:
Dover Development and Construction
Photographer:
© Tim Stone Photography

128
v

**PEARL STREET**

Architect:
Kelly & Stone Architects
Interior Designer:
Kelly & Stone Architects
Builder:
Tim Stone
Key Subcontractors:
New Mountain Builders, Vaussa, and High Point Roofing
Photographer:
© Tim Stone Photography

132
v

**SWIFTS STATION 20**

Architect:
Kelly & Stone Architects
Interior Designer:
Kelly & Stone Architects
Builder:
NSM
Photographer:
© Paul Dyer Photography

www.kellyandstone.com kellyandstonearch

At Kelly & Stone, architecture isn't about expressing our egos or individual design preferences. It's an opportunity to collaborate with clients as we translate their goals and aspirations into timeless living environments that serve their occupants. We understand that designing and building a custom home is a significant—and often emotional—experience for our clients, and we are dedicated to making that experience as positive, transparent, and successful as possible. Sustainability guides all of our work. We are committed to minimizing our environmental impact by prioritizing energy efficiency, integrating responsible materials, and advancing building science. As designers, it's our responsibility to create spaces that honor the sites, landscapes, and climates where they reside while supporting the lifestyle of their occupants and connecting them to the natural world.

Bei Kelly & Stone geht es bei der Architektur nicht darum, unser Ego oder unsere individuellen Designvorlieben zum Ausdruck zu bringen. Es ist eine Gelegenheit, mit den Kunden zusammenzuarbeiten und ihre Ziele und Wünsche in zeitlose Lebensumgebungen zu übersetzen, die ihren Bewohnern dienen. Wir wissen, dass die Planung und der Bau eines Hauses nach Maß für unsere Kunden eine bedeutende - und oft emotionale - Erfahrung ist, und wir sind bestrebt, diese Erfahrung so positiv, transparent und erfolgreich wie möglich zu gestalten. Nachhaltigkeit ist der Leitfaden für unsere gesamte Arbeit. Wir sind bestrebt, die Auswirkungen auf die Umwelt so gering wie möglich zu halten, indem wir der Energieeffizienz den Vorrang geben, verantwortungsbewusste Materialien verwenden und die Bauwissenschaft voranbringen. Als Designer ist es unsere Aufgabe, Räume zu schaffen, die den Standorten, Landschaften und dem Klima, in dem sie sich befinden, gerecht werden und gleichzeitig den Lebensstil ihrer Bewohner unterstützen und sie mit der natürlichen Welt verbinden.

Chez Kelly & Stone, l'architecture ne consiste pas à exprimer notre ego ou nos préférences individuelles en matière de design. C'est une occasion de collaborer avec les clients en traduisant leurs objectifs et leurs aspirations en environnements de vie intemporels qui servent leurs occupants. Nous comprenons que la conception et la construction d'une maison personnalisée est une expérience significative - et souvent émotionnelle - pour nos clients, et nous nous engageons à rendre cette expérience aussi positive, transparente et réussie que possible. Le développement durable guide l'ensemble de notre travail. Nous nous engageons à minimiser notre impact sur l'environnement en privilégiant l'efficacité énergétique, en intégrant des matériaux responsables et en faisant progresser la science du bâtiment. En tant que concepteurs, il est de notre responsabilité de créer des espaces qui honorent les sites, les paysages et les climats où ils se trouvent, tout en soutenant le mode de vie de leurs occupants et en les reliant au monde naturel.

En Kelly & Stone, la arquitectura no consiste en expresar nuestros egos o preferencias de diseño individuales. Es una oportunidad para colaborar con los clientes a medida que traducimos sus objetivos y aspiraciones en entornos de vida atemporales que sirven a sus ocupantes. Entendemos que el diseño y la construcción de una casa a medida es una experiencia significativa -y a menudo emocional- para nuestros clientes, y nos dedicamos a hacer que esa experiencia sea lo más positiva, transparente y exitosa posible. La sostenibilidad guía todo nuestro trabajo. Nos comprometemos a minimizar nuestro impacto medioambiental dando prioridad a la eficiencia energética, integrando materiales responsables y avanzando en la ciencia de la construcción. Como diseñadores, es nuestra responsabilidad crear espacios que honren los lugares, los paisajes y los climas donde residen, al tiempo que apoyan el estilo de vida de sus ocupantes y los conectan con el mundo natural.

## HINMAN CREEK

Clark, Colorado, United States // Lot area: 70 acres; main house:7,500 sq ft; wine cave: 600 sq ft; barn: 3,600 sq ft; arena: 14,000 sq ft

Located at the foot of Big Agnes and Mount Farwell in the Mount Zirkel Wilderness Area, this ranch-style house engages its environment by taking in wide views of the peaks. The expansive house is conceived as a series of pavilions that balance the need for shelter and privacy with the desire to pull in light, views, and landscape. Its arched configuration allows for the creation of multiple outdoor spaces articulated by the pavilions. Inside, a timber frame and exposed steelwork create human-scaled spaces that are warm and inviting. The Kelly & Stone team oversaw all architecture and interior design and commissioned artwork for the wine cellar.

Située au pied de Big Agnes et du mont Farwell, dans la zone de nature sauvage du mont Zirkel, cette maison de style ranch s'intègre à son environnement en offrant de larges vues sur les sommets. La maison expansive est conçue comme une série de pavillons qui équilibrent le besoin d'abri et d'intimité avec le désir d'attirer la lumière, les vues et le paysage. Sa configuration en arc permet la création de multiples espaces extérieurs articulés par les pavillons. À l'intérieur, l'ossature en bois et la charpente métallique apparente créent des espaces à taille humaine, chaleureux et accueillants. L'équipe de Kelly & Stone a supervisé l'ensemble de l'architecture et de la décoration intérieure et a commandé des œuvres d'art pour la cave à vin.

Am Fuße von Big Agnes und Mount Farwell in der Mount Zirkel Wilderness Area gelegen, bezieht dieses Haus im Ranch-Stil seine Umgebung ein, indem es weite Ausblicke auf die Gipfel bietet. Das weitläufige Haus ist als eine Reihe von Pavillons konzipiert, die ein Gleichgewicht zwischen dem Bedürfnis nach Schutz und Privatsphäre und dem Wunsch nach Licht, Aussicht und Landschaft schaffen. Die bogenförmige Konfiguration ermöglicht die Schaffung mehrerer Außenräume, die durch die Pavillons gegliedert werden. Im Inneren schaffen ein Holzrahmen und freiliegende Stahlkonstruktionen Räume mit menschlichem Maß, die warm und einladend sind. Das Team von Kelly & Stone überwachte die gesamte Architektur und Inneneinrichtung und gab Kunstwerke für den Weinkeller in Auftrag.

Situada a los pies de Big Agnes y Mount Farwell, en la zona salvaje de Mount Zirkel, esta casa de estilo rancho se integra en su entorno con amplias vistas de las cumbres. La amplia casa está concebida como una serie de pabellones que equilibran la necesidad de refugio y privacidad con el deseo de atraer la luz, las vistas y el paisaje. Su configuración en arco permite crear múltiples espacios exteriores articulados por los pabellones. En el interior, la estructura de madera y la estructura de acero expuesta crean espacios a escala humana que son cálidos y acogedores. El equipo de Kelly & Stone supervisó toda la arquitectura y el diseño interior y encargó obras de arte para la bodega.

West elevation

Southwest elevation

East elevation

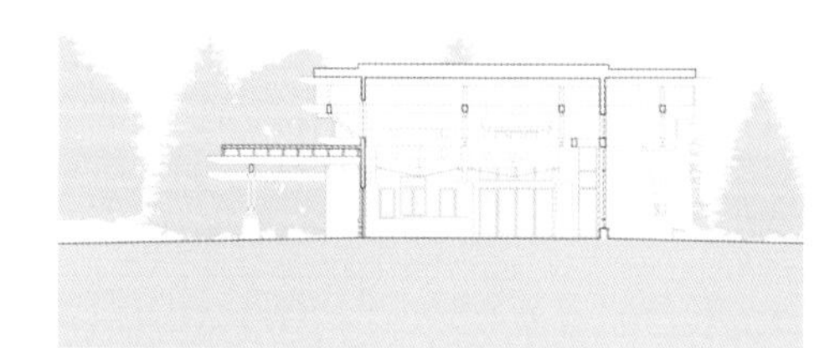

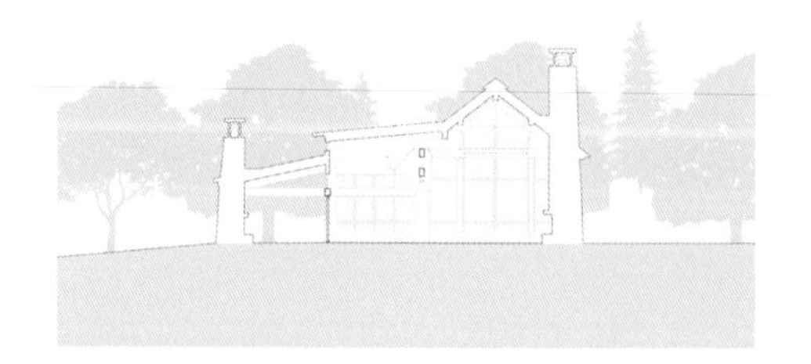

Sections

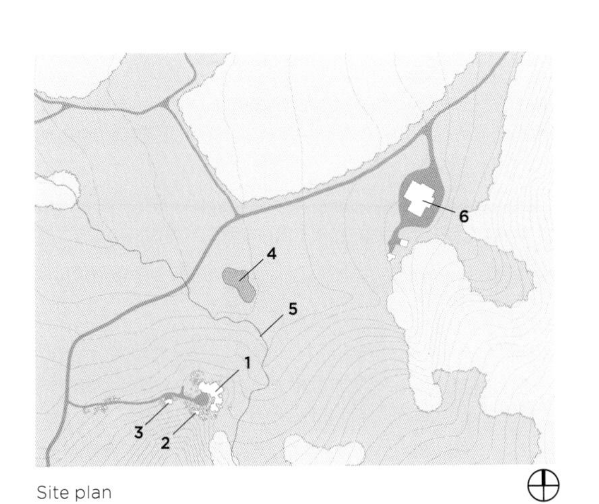


Site plan

1. Main house
2. Wine cellar
3. Guest house
4. Lake
5. Stream
6. Riding arena

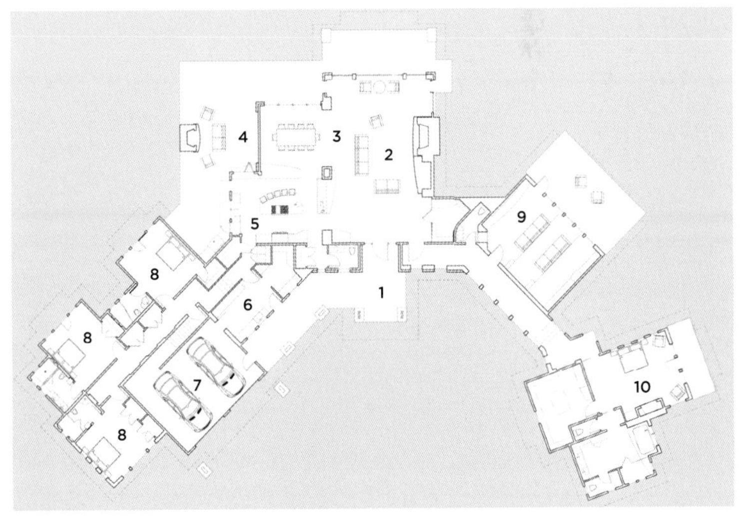


Main house floor plan

1. Entry
2. Great room
3. Dining area
4. Outdoor fireplace
5. Kitchen
6. Mud room
7. Garage
8. Suite
9. Theater
10. Master suite

## PEARL STREET

Steam Boat Springs, Colorado, United States // Lot area: 7,000 sq ft; main house area: 1,950 sq ft; ADU area: 650 sq ft

Kelly & Stone Architects' partner Tim Stone designed this home for his own family on a property that also includes a two-bedroom accessory dwelling unit (ADU). The house captures the views of Emerald Mountain and Mount Werner, while eastern and western decks optimize outdoor living. Simple gable forms and a generous use of timber reflect the old town mountain vernacular. Designed with thermal efficiency in mind, the ventilation of the house is achieved with a heat recovery ventilator that pumps fresh air into the interiors, avoiding the use of an air conditioning system. Triple-glazed windows and continuous insulation minimize energy usage. In line with the green building principles, the building's exterior is clad with reclaimed corral fencing, a sustainable building material that requires no maintenance.

Tim Stone, partenaire de Kelly & Stone Architects, a conçu cette maison pour sa propre famille sur une propriété qui comprend également un logement accessoire (ADU) de deux chambres. La maison profite des vues sur Emerald Mountain et Mount Werner, tandis que les terrasses est et ouest optimisent la vie en plein air. Les formes simples des pignons et l'utilisation généreuse du bois reflètent le vernaculaire des vieilles villes de montagne. Conçue dans un souci d'efficacité thermique, la ventilation de la maison est assurée par un ventilateur à récupération de chaleur qui pompe l'air frais dans les intérieurs, évitant ainsi l'utilisation d'un système de climatisation. Des fenêtres à triple vitrage et une isolation continue minimisent la consommation d'énergie. Conformément aux principes de la construction écologique, l'extérieur du bâtiment est revêtu de clôtures de corral récupérées, un matériau de construction durable qui ne nécessite aucun entretien.

Tim Stone, Partner von Kelly & Stone Architects, entwarf dieses Haus für seine eigene Familie auf einem Grundstück, zu dem auch eine zusätzliche Wohneinheit (ADU) mit zwei Schlafzimmern gehört. Das Haus fängt die Aussicht auf Emerald Mountain und Mount Werner ein, während die Ost- und Westterrasse das Leben im Freien optimieren. Einfache Giebelformen und die großzügige Verwendung von Holz spiegeln die Tradition der alten Bergstadt wider. Die Belüftung des Hauses erfolgt über einen Wärmerückgewinnungslüfter, der Frischluft in die Innenräume pumpt und so den Einsatz einer Klimaanlage überflüssig macht. Dreifach verglaste Fenster und eine durchgehende Isolierung minimieren den Energieverbrauch. Im Einklang mit den Grundsätzen des grünen Bauens ist das Äußere des Gebäudes mit einem wiederverwendeten Korralzaun verkleidet, einem nachhaltigen Baumaterial, das keine Wartung erfordert.

Tim Stone, socio de Kelly & Stone Architects, diseñó esta casa para su propia familia en una propiedad que también incluye una unidad de vivienda accesoria (ADU) de dos dormitorios. La casa capta las vistas de Emerald Mountain y Mount Werner, mientras que las cubiertas oriental y occidental optimizan la vida al aire libre. Las formas sencillas de los hastiales y el generoso uso de la madera reflejan el estilo vernáculo de la vieja ciudad de montaña. Diseñada pensando en la eficiencia térmica, la ventilación de la casa se consigue con un ventilador de recuperación de calor que bombea aire fresco a los interiores, evitando el uso de un sistema de aire acondicionado. Las ventanas de triple acristalamiento y el aislamiento continuo minimizan el uso de energía. En consonancia con los principios de la construcción ecológica, el exterior del edificio está revestido con vallas de corral recuperadas, un material de construcción sostenible que no requiere mantenimiento.

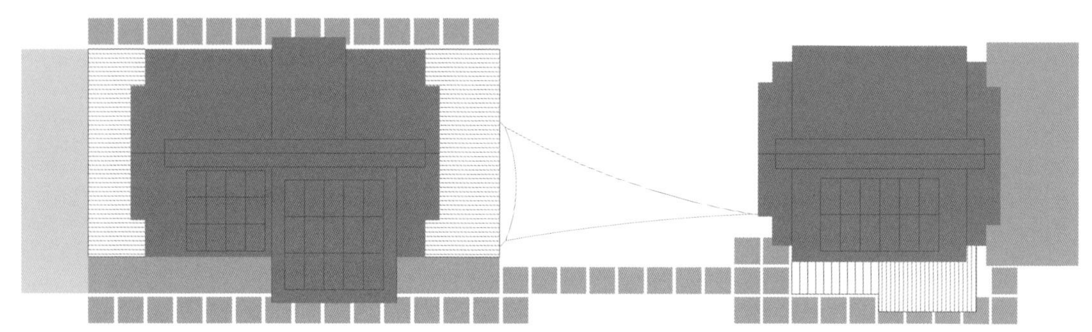

Site plan

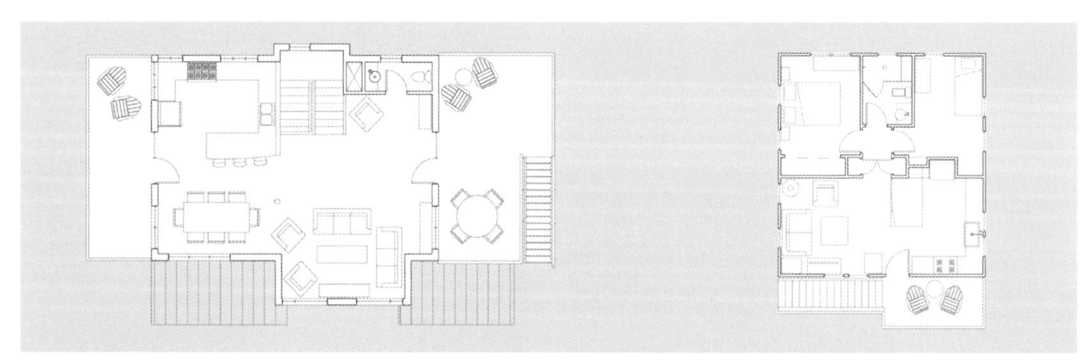

Upper floor plan

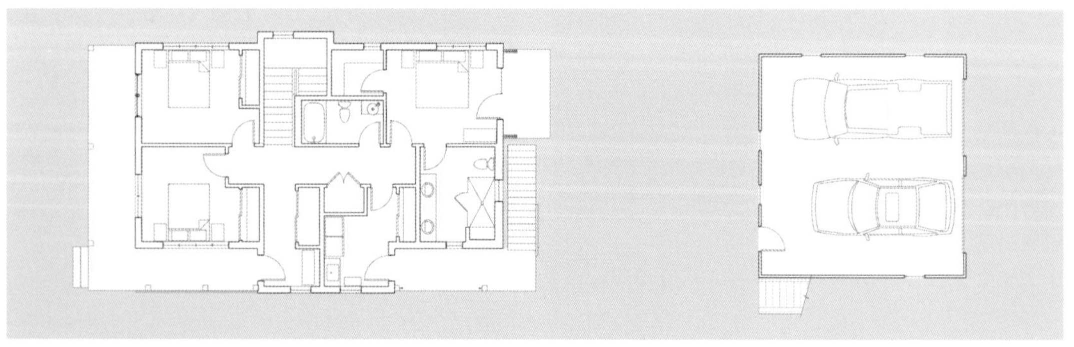

Lower floor plan

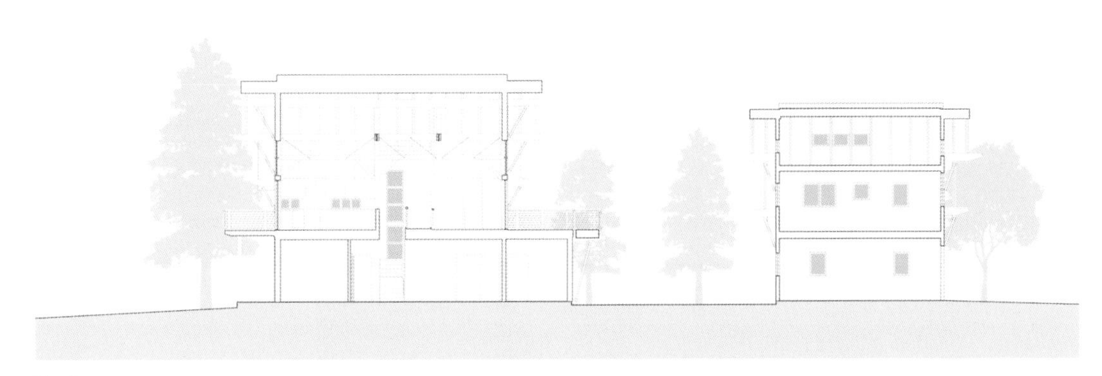

Section

Elevations

## SWIFTS STATION 20

Carson City, Nevada, United States // Lot area: 5 acres; building area: 7,000 sq ft

Undulating metal roofs echo the morphology of the mountains to the west and south. This striking design feature makes this mountain contemporary home very visible from the road. Walls of cedar and natural stone relate the house with its breathtaking surroundings in a new Clear Creek Tahoe development. The interior features open-plan living spaces capitalizing on the views of the Carson Valley and surrounding mountains. Floor-to-ceiling glass panels throughout let in abundant daylight and minimize the boundaries between the interior and the exterior. To that end, outdoor living spaces take full advantage of the mild climate and contribute to the integration of the construction into the natural setting.

Les toits métalliques ondulés font écho à la morphologie des montagnes à l'ouest et au sud. Cet élément de conception frappant rend cette maison contemporaine de montagne très visible depuis la route. Des murs en cèdre et en pierre naturelle relient la maison à son environnement époustouflant dans un nouveau lotissement de Clear Creek Tahoe. L'intérieur comprend des espaces de vie ouverts qui tirent parti de la vue sur la vallée de Carson et les montagnes environnantes. Des panneaux vitrés du sol au plafond laissent entrer une lumière naturelle abondante et minimisent les frontières entre l'intérieur et l'extérieur. À cette fin, les espaces de vie extérieurs profitent pleinement de la douceur du climat et contribuent à l'intégration de la construction dans le cadre naturel.

Die gewellten Metalldächer spiegeln die Morphologie der Berge im Westen und Süden wider. Dieses auffällige Designmerkmal macht dieses moderne Haus in den Bergen von der Straße aus gut sichtbar. Wände aus Zedernholz und Naturstein verbinden das Haus mit seiner atemberaubenden Umgebung in einem neuen Baugebiet in Clear Creek Tahoe. Das Innere bietet offene Wohnräume, die den Blick auf das Carson Valley und die umliegenden Berge optimal nutzen. Vom Boden bis zur Decke reichende Glaspaneele lassen reichlich Tageslicht herein und minimieren die Grenzen zwischen Innen und Außen. Die Außenbereiche nutzen das milde Klima voll aus und tragen zur Integration des Gebäudes in die natürliche Umgebung bei.

Los tejados metálicos ondulados se hacen eco de la morfología de las montañas situadas al oeste y al sur. Esta llamativa característica de diseño hace que esta casa contemporánea de montaña sea muy visible desde la carretera. Las paredes de cedro y piedra natural relacionan la casa con su impresionante entorno en una nueva urbanización de Clear Creek Tahoe. El interior cuenta con espacios abiertos que aprovechan las vistas del valle de Carson y las montañas circundantes. Los paneles de cristal que van del suelo al techo dejan pasar abundante luz natural y minimizan los límites entre el interior y el exterior. Para ello, los espacios exteriores aprovechan al máximo el clima templado y contribuyen a la integración de la construcción en el entorno natural.

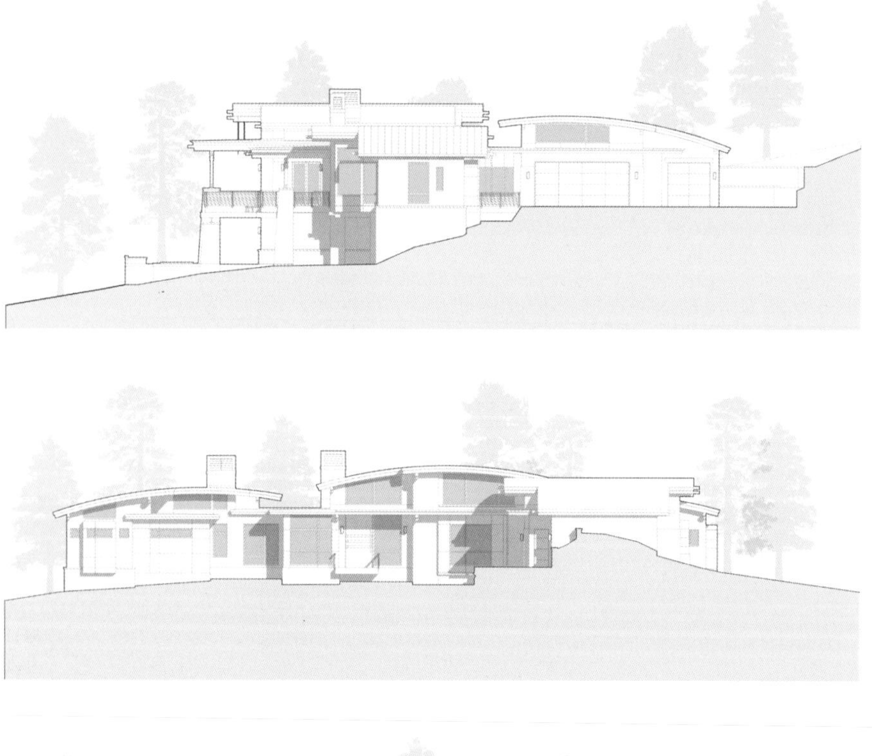

Elevations

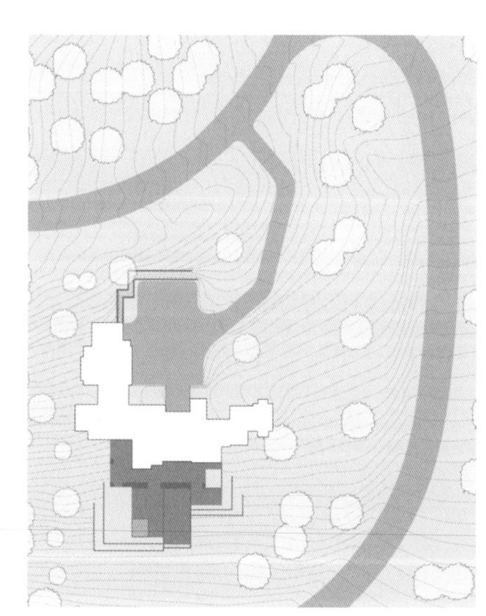

Site plan

# EWERS ARCHITECTURE

138
v

**ROMAN RESTREPO RESIDENCE**

Architect:
Ewers Architecture
Interior Designer:
Jill Pfeiffer Design
Kitchen Designer:
New Mountain Design
Structural Engineer:
Malouff Engineering
Sustainability Consultant:
BrightSense
Builder:
Terra Firma Custom Homes
Photographer:
© Emily Minton Redfield

142
v

**BARTON RESIDENCE**

Architect:
Ewers Architecture
Structural Engineer:
The Engineering Loft
Builder:
Kinsman Construction
Photographer:
© Joe Thompson

146
v

**COMPASS MONTESSORI SCHOOL**

Architect:
Ewers Architecture
Landscape Architect:
Susan Saarinen
Civil Engineer:
R&R Engineers
Structural Engineer:
KL&A
Mechanical and Electrical Engineer:
Priest Engineering
Sustainability Consultant:
Lightly Treading
Builder:
Pirnack Walters
Photographer:
© Jerry Walters and Peter Ewers

www.ewersarchitecture.com @ewersarch

Peter Ewers founded Ewers Architecture in 1998 in Golden, Colorado, as a small firm focused on "creating beautiful architecture that respects our natural environment." The firm designs residential and commercial projects with an emphasis on sustainability, and they currently design only all-electric buildings with a Net Zero Energy goal. Each project develops the style and aesthetics from the client's desires, the site location, and a response to the environment. Ewers Architecture has limited the firm's size to five employees so that Peter Ewers can be intimately involved in every project. Their office is a renovated 1866 schoolhouse in historic downtown Golden and is within walking distance of Peter's home. Their project locations are limited to the state of Colorado to ensure regionalism and intimate knowledge of the climate. Every project strives for spaces that allow for connection with the outdoors, envelopes that far surpass code-required insulation and air tightness, and architecture that delights all our senses.

Peter Ewers gründete Ewers Architecture 1998 in Golden, Colorado, als kleines Büro mit dem Ziel, „schöne Architektur zu schaffen, die unsere natürliche Umwelt respektiert". Das Büro entwirft Wohn- und Gewerbeprojekte mit Schwerpunkt auf Nachhaltigkeit. Derzeit werden ausschließlich vollelektrische Gebäude mit einem Netto-Null-Energieziel entworfen. Der Stil und die Ästhetik eines jeden Projekts ergeben sich aus den Wünschen des Kunden, der Lage des Standorts und der Reaktion auf die Umwelt. Ewers Architecture hat die Größe des Büros auf fünf Mitarbeiter begrenzt, damit Peter Ewers an jedem Projekt mitwirken kann. Das Büro befindet sich in einem renovierten Schulhaus aus dem Jahr 1866 in der historischen Innenstadt von Golden und ist nur wenige Gehminuten von Peter Ewers' Wohnung entfernt. Die Projektstandorte beschränken sich auf den Bundesstaat Colorado, um Regionalität und genaue Kenntnis des Klimas zu gewährleisten. Bei jedem Projekt streben sie nach Räumen, die eine Verbindung mit der Natur ermöglichen, nach Gebäudehüllen, die weit über die gesetzlich vorgeschriebene Isolierung und Luftdichtheit hinausgehen, und nach einer Architektur, die alle unsere Sinne erfreut.

Peter Ewers a fondé Ewers Architecture en 1998 à Golden, dans le Colorado, en tant que petite entreprise axée sur « la création d'une belle architecture qui respecte notre environnement naturel ». Le cabinet conçoit des projets résidentiels et commerciaux en mettant l'accent sur la durabilité, et il ne conçoit actuellement que des bâtiments entièrement électriques avec un objectif d'énergie nette zéro. Chaque projet développe son style et son esthétique à partir des désirs du client, de l'emplacement du site et d'une réponse à l'environnement. Ewers Architecture a limité la taille de l'entreprise à cinq employés afin que Peter Ewers puisse être impliqué dans chaque projet. Le bureaux est situé dans une école rénovée de 1866 dans le centre-ville historique de Golden, à quelques pas de la maison de Peter. La localisation de leurs projets est limitée à l'État du Colorado afin de garantir le régionalisme et une connaissance profonde du climat. Chaque projet vise à créer des espaces qui permettent une connexion avec l'extérieur, des enveloppes qui surpassent de loin l'isolation et l'étanchéité à l'air requises par le code, et une architecture qui ravit tous nos sens.

Peter Ewers fundó Ewers Architecture en 1998 en Golden, Colorado, como una pequeña empresa centrada en «crear una bella arquitectura que respete nuestro entorno natural». La firma diseña proyectos residenciales y comerciales con énfasis en la sostenibilidad, y actualmente sólo diseñan edificios totalmente eléctricos con un objetivo de energía neta cero. Cada proyecto desarrolla el estilo y la estética a partir de los deseos del cliente, la ubicación del lugar y una respuesta al entorno. Ewers Architecture ha limitado el tamaño de la empresa a cinco empleados para que Peter Ewers pueda estar íntimamente involucrado en cada proyecto. Su oficina es una escuela renovada de 1866 en el centro histórico de Golden y está a poca distancia de la casa de Peter. La ubicación de sus proyectos se limita al estado de Colorado para garantizar el regionalismo y el conocimiento íntimo del clima. Cada proyecto se esfuerza por conseguir espacios que permitan la conexión con el exterior, envolturas que superen con creces el aislamiento y la estanqueidad al aire requeridos por la normativa, y una arquitectura que deleite todos nuestros sentidos.

## ROMAN RESTREPO RESIDENCE

Fraser, Colorado, United States // Lot area: 2.5 acres; building area: 3,300-sq ft house + 550-sq ft garage

Nestled in the Rockies, about ninety minutes from downtown Denver, this home invites its expansive surroundings inside by opening to the outside. The natural views are enjoyed from every location in the home through all the seasons. The main floor features all living spaces plus the master suite and equal guest suite for the adults, with additional bedrooms and a recreational room on the lower floor for the kids. The tuck-under garage takes advantage of the gently sloping site and minimizes the building footprint. Natural building materials inside and out help the house blend in with the surroundings, and in-floor radiant heating with a double-stud wall, tight construction ensures the home is comfortable all year round. This ski getaway is the perfect place for the owners to relax with their family and friends.

Nichée dans les Rocheuses, à environ quatre-vingt-dix minutes du centre-ville de Denver, cette maison invite son vaste environnement à l'intérieur en s'ouvrant sur l'extérieur. Les vues naturelles sont appréciées de tous les endroits de la maison au fil des saisons. Le rez-de-chaussée comprend tous les espaces de vie, ainsi que la suite parentale et une suite d'invités égale pour les adultes, avec des chambres supplémentaires et une salle de loisirs à l'étage inférieur pour les enfants. Le garage encastré tire parti du site en pente douce et minimise l'empreinte du bâtiment. Les matériaux de construction naturels à l'intérieur et à l'extérieur aident la maison à se fondre dans l'environnement, et le chauffage radiant au sol avec une construction étanche à double paroi garantit le confort de la maison toute l'année. Cette escapade au ski est l'endroit idéal pour que les propriétaires se détendent avec leur famille et leurs amis.

Eingebettet in die Rocky Mountains, etwa neunzig Minuten vom Stadtzentrum Denvers entfernt, lädt dieses Haus seine weitläufige Umgebung nach innen ein, indem es sich nach außen hin öffnet. Die Aussicht auf die Natur kann man von jedem Ort des Hauses aus zu jeder Jahreszeit genießen. Im Hauptgeschoss befinden sich alle Wohnräume sowie das Hauptschlafzimmer und ein Gästezimmer für die Erwachsenen, während sich im Untergeschoss weitere Schlafzimmer und ein Freizeitraum für die Kinder befinden. Die unterfahrbare Garage nutzt die Vorteile des sanft abfallenden Grundstücks und minimiert die Grundfläche des Gebäudes. Natürliche Baumaterialien im Innen- und Außenbereich tragen dazu bei, dass sich das Haus in die Umgebung einfügt, und eine Fußbodenheizung mit doppelwandiger, dichter Konstruktion sorgt dafür, dass das Haus das ganze Jahr über komfortabel ist. Dieses Skigebiet ist der perfekte Ort für die Eigentümer, um mit ihrer Familie und ihren Freunden zu entspannen.

Enclavada en las Montañas Rocosas, a unos noventa minutos del centro de Denver, esta casa invita a su amplio entorno a entrar abriéndose al exterior. Las vistas naturales se disfrutan desde todos los lugares de la casa en todas las estaciones. La planta principal cuenta con todos los espacios de vida, además de la suite principal y la suite de invitados iguales para los adultos, con dormitorios adicionales y una sala de recreo en la planta baja para los niños. El garaje, situado debajo de la casa, aprovecha la suave inclinación del terreno y minimiza la huella del edificio. Los materiales de construcción naturales, tanto en el interior como en el exterior, ayudan a que la casa se integre en el entorno. Un sistema de calefacción por suelo radiante, con una pared de doble tachuela y una construcción hermética, garantizan el confort de la casa durante todo el año. Esta escapada de esquí es el lugar perfecto para que los propietarios se relajen con su familia y amigos.

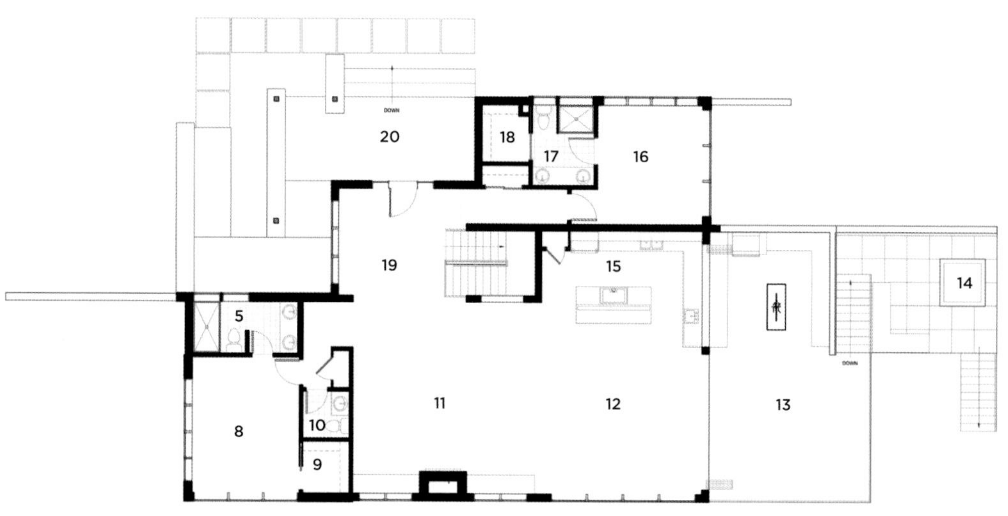


Main floor plan

Lower floor plan

1. Patio
2. Two-car garage
3. Recreational room
4. Bedroom
5. Bathroom
6. Mechanical room
7. Mud/laundry room
8. Guest room
9. Walk-in closet
10. Powder room
11. Living area
12. Dining area
13. Deck
14. Hot tub
15. Kitchen
16. Master bedroom
17. Master bathroom
18. Master closet
19. Foyer
20. Porch

## BARTON RESIDENCE

Golden, Colorado, United States // Lot area: 10,000 sq ft; building area: 2,800-sq ft house + 550-sq ft garage

This modern home sits on the cusp of North Table Mountain, overlooking historic Golden, Colorado, and the Rocky Mountain foothills. The large south-facing windows maximize the views and provide warmth from the winter sun, while large overhangs and shading devices provide shade during the summer months. Due to the steep slope of the lot, a lower-level patio is built into the hill, while the main floor deck extends over the flat roof of the lower floor. A smaller north deck offers a cool outdoor space for the summer months. The double-stud wall construction provides ample wall depth for large amounts of continuous insulation between the staggered studs. Photovoltaic roof panels that clip cleanly to the standing seam metal roof provide power to offset all electricity used in the home.

Cette maison moderne se trouve sur le sommet de North Table Mountain, avec vue sur la ville historique de Golden, dans le Colorado, et sur les contreforts des Rocheuses. Les grandes fenêtres orientées au sud permettent d'optimiser la vue et de se réchauffer au soleil d'hiver, tandis que les grands porte-à-faux et les dispositifs d'ombrage fournissent de l'ombre pendant les mois d'été. En raison de la forte pente du terrain, un patio au niveau inférieur est construit dans la colline, tandis que la terrasse de l'étage principal s'étend au-dessus du toit plat de l'étage inférieur. Une terrasse nord plus petite offre un espace extérieur frais pour les mois d'été. La construction des murs à deux montants offre une grande profondeur de mur pour de grandes quantités d'isolation continue entre les montants décalés. Les panneaux photovoltaïques du toit, qui s'accrochent proprement au toit métallique à joints debout, fournissent l'énergie nécessaire pour compenser la totalité de la consommation électrique de la maison.

Dieses moderne Haus liegt auf der Spitze des North Table Mountain mit Blick auf das historische Golden, Colorado, und die Ausläufer der Rocky Mountains. Die großen, nach Süden ausgerichteten Fenster maximieren die Aussicht und spenden Wärme von der Wintersonne, während große Überhänge und Beschattungsvorrichtungen in den Sommermonaten Schatten spenden. Aufgrund der steilen Hanglage des Grundstücks ist eine untere Terrasse in den Hügel eingebaut, während sich das Hauptgeschossdeck über das Flachdach des Untergeschosses erstreckt. Ein kleineres Norddeck bietet einen kühlen Platz im Freien für die Sommermonate. Die Doppelständerwandkonstruktion bietet ausreichend Wandtiefe für eine große Menge an durchgehender Isolierung zwischen den versetzten Ständern. Photovoltaik-Dachpaneele, die sauber auf dem Stehfalz-Metalldach befestigt werden, liefern Strom, der den gesamten Stromverbrauch des Hauses ausgleicht.

Esta moderna casa se encuentra en la cúspide de North Table Mountain, con vistas al histórico Golden, Colorado, y a las estribaciones de las Montañas Rocosas. Los grandes ventanales orientados al sur maximizan las vistas y proporcionan calor del sol de invierno, mientras que los grandes voladizos y los dispositivos de sombreado proporcionan sombra durante los meses de verano. Debido a la pronunciada pendiente del terreno, un patio en el nivel inferior está construido en la misma colina, mientras que la terraza de la planta principal se extiende sobre el tejado plano de la planta inferior. Una cubierta norte más pequeña ofrece un espacio exterior para los meses de verano. La construcción de paredes de doble montante proporciona una amplia profundidad para grandes cantidades de aislamiento continuo entre los montantes escalonados. Los paneles fotovoltaicos del tejado, que se sujetan limpiamente a él a través de una costura de pie, proporcionan energía para compensar toda la electricidad utilizada en la casa.

414

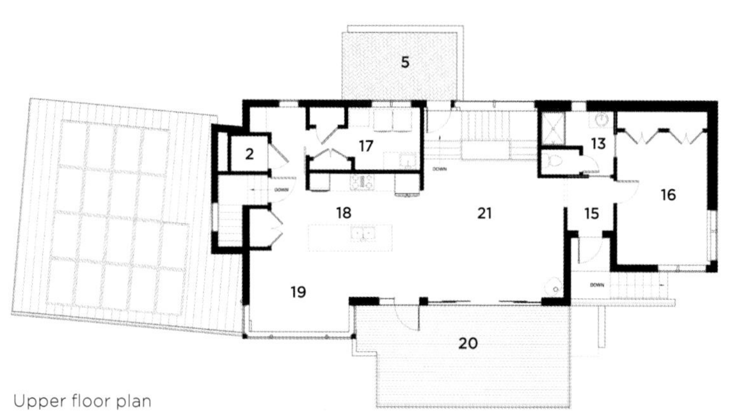

Upper floor plan

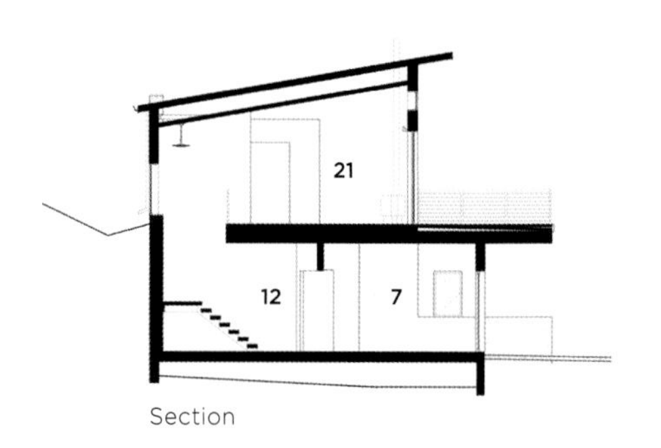

Section

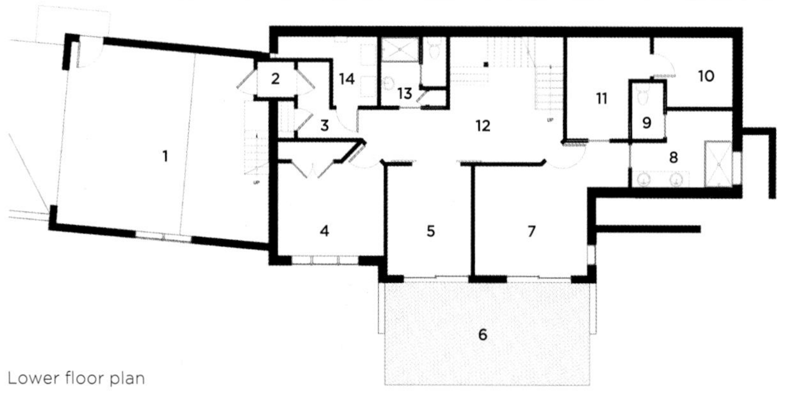

Lower floor plan

1. Garage
2. Elevator
3. Hall
4. Guest room
5. Office
6. Patio
7. Master bedroom
8. Master bathroom
9. Toilet room
10. Storage
11. Closet
12. Sitting area
13. Bathroom
14. Mechanical room
15. Foyer
16. Studio
17. Laundry/ mud room
18. Kitchen
19. Dining area
20. Deck
21. Living area

## COMPASS MONTESSORI SCHOOL

Golden, Colorado, United States // Lot area: 8 acres; building area: 31,000 sq ft

This new charter school campus was designed for 7th through 12th grades but was quickly modified for K-12. The middle school building is a farm school where the students raise livestock and crops while receiving classroom instruction. Despite a tight budget and a short schedule, the overall feel of the buildings and campus was not compromised. The metal building structure saved both time and cost, but replacing the steel with wood trusses in the main hall satisfied the desired aesthetics plus revealed the workings of the building as a learning tool. Stone, reclaimed barn wood siding, various metal claddings, and shapes found in traditional mountain west architecture define the project, which has received several design awards and has been used by a local university as an example of vernacular Colorado architecture.

Ce nouveau campus d'école à charte a été conçu pour les classes de la 7e à la 12e année, mais a été rapidement modifié pour la maternelle à la 12e année. Le bâtiment du collège est une ferme-école où les enfants élèvent du bétail et des cultures tout en recevant un enseignement en classe. Malgré un budget serré et un calendrier court, l'aspect général des bâtiments et du campus n'a pas été compromis. La structure métallique du bâtiment a permis de gagner du temps et de l'argent, mais le remplacement de l'acier par des fermes en bois dans le hall principal a permis d'obtenir l'esthétique souhaitée et de révéler le fonctionnement du bâtiment en tant qu'outil d'apprentissage. La pierre, le bardage en bois de grange récupéré, divers revêtements métalliques et les formes que l'on retrouve dans l'architecture traditionnelle de l'ouest des montagnes définissent le projet, qui a reçu plusieurs prix de design et a été utilisé par une université locale comme exemple d'architecture vernaculaire du Colorado.

Dieser neue Schulcampus war ursprünglich für die 7. bis 12. Klasse vorgesehen, wurde aber schnell für die Klassen K-12 umgebaut. Das Gebäude der Mittelstufe ist eine Landwirtschaftsschule, in der die Schüler während des Unterrichts Vieh züchten und Feldfrüchte anbauen. Trotz eines knappen Budgets und eines engen Zeitplans wurde das Gesamtbild der Gebäude und des Geländes nicht beeinträchtigt. Die Metallkonstruktion sparte sowohl Zeit als auch Kosten, aber der Ersatz des Stahls durch Holzbinder in der Haupthalle entsprach der gewünschten Ästhetik und machte die Funktionsweise des Gebäudes als Lernmittel sichtbar. Stein, wiederverwendetes Scheunenholz, verschiedene Metallverkleidungen und Formen, die in der traditionellen Architektur des Bergwestens zu finden sind, prägen das Projekt, das mehrere Designpreise erhalten hat und von einer örtlichen Universität als Beispiel für die traditionelle Architektur Colorados verwendet wird.

Este nuevo campus escolar concertado se diseñó originariamente para albergar alumnos de educación primaria, pero se modificó rápidamente para albergar espacio de guardería . El edificio de la escuela intermedia es una granja escuela donde los estudiantes crían ganado y cultivos mientras reciben instrucción en el aula. A pesar de lo ajustado del presupuesto y calendario, la sensación general de los edificios y del campus no se vio comprometida. La estructura metálica del edificio permitió ahorrar tiempo y costes, pero la sustitución del acero por cerchas de madera en el vestíbulo principal satisfizo la estética deseada y reveló el funcionamiento del edificio como herramienta de aprendizaje. La piedra, el revestimiento de madera de granero recuperada, varios revestimientos metálicos y las formas de la arquitectura tradicional del oeste de la montaña definen el proyecto, que ha recibido varios premios de diseño y ha sido utilizado por una universidad local como ejemplo de la arquitectura vernácula de Colorado.

COMPASS MONTESSORI SCHOOL

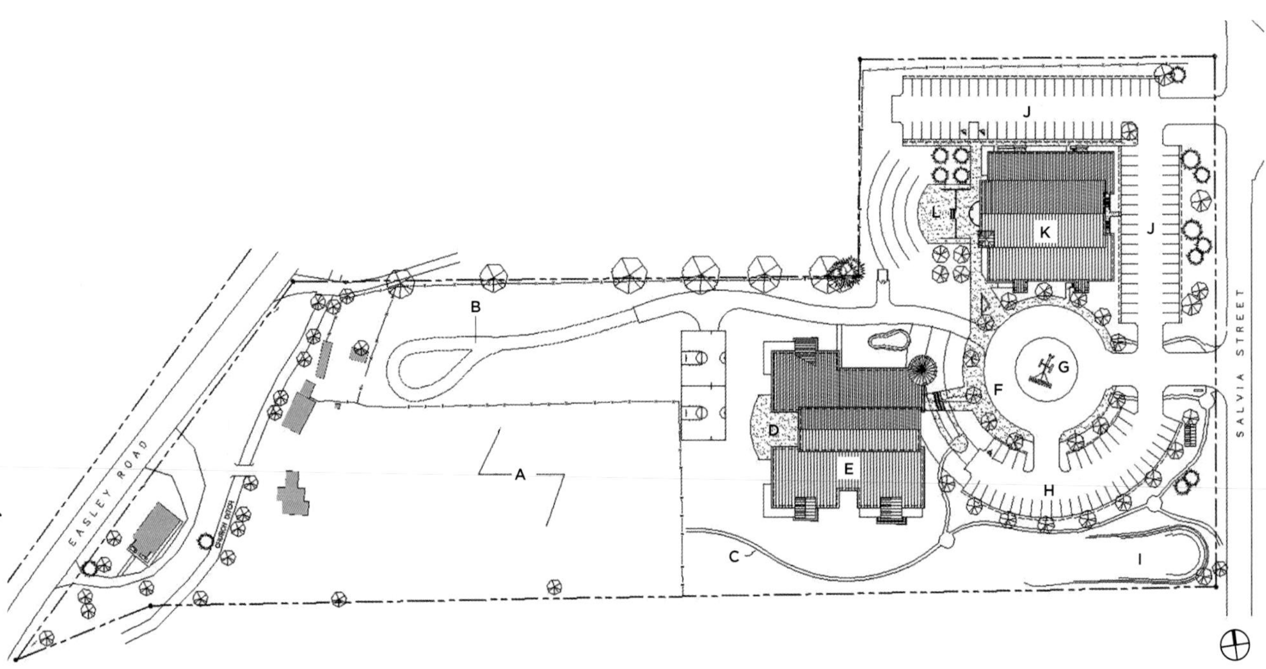


Campus site plan

| | |
|---|---|
| A. Existing farm | G. Farm relic |
| B. Farm delivery road | H. Teacher parking |
| C. Trail | I. Detention pond |
| D. Dining court | J. Student parking |
| E. Middle school | K. High school |
| F. Drop-off | L. Student plaza |

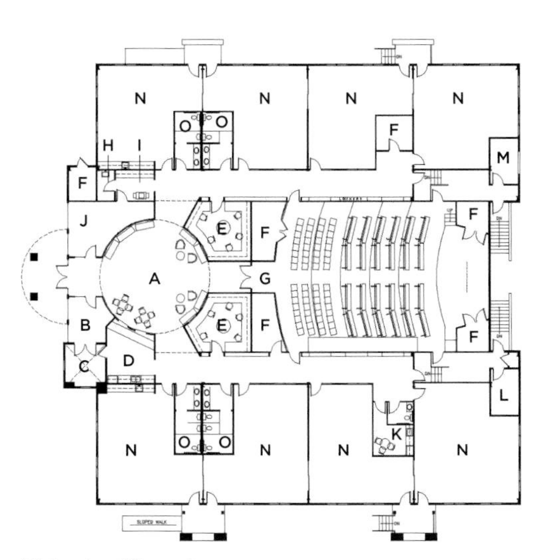

High school floor plan

A. The Commons
B. Administration
C. Conference room
D. Kitchen
E. Teachers room
F. Storage
G. Auditorium
H. Janitor's room
I. Copy room
J. Media room
K. Break room
L. Electrical room
M. Boiler room
N. Classrooms
O. Toilet room

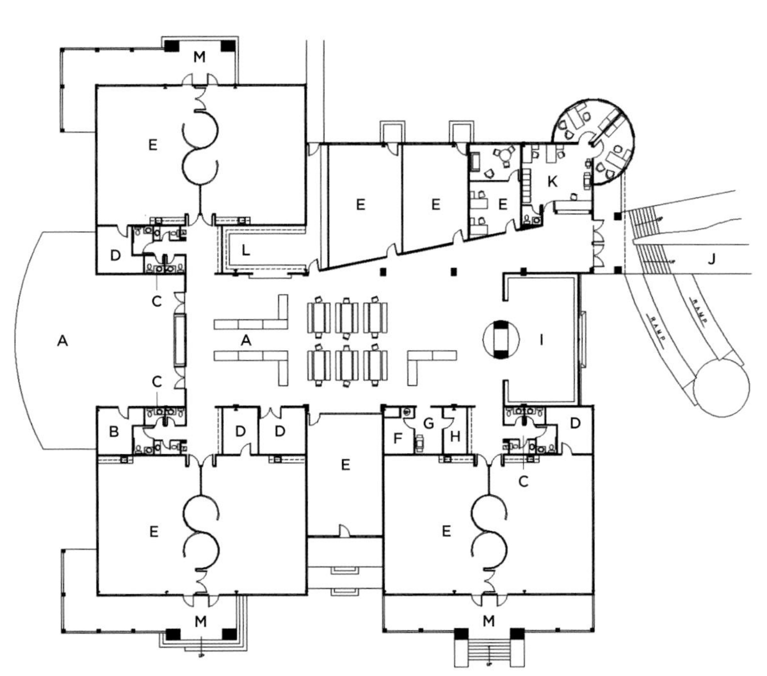

Middle school floor plan

A. Dining court
B. Mechanical room
C. Toilet room
D. Storage
E. Classroom
F. Janitor's room
G. Copy room
H. Electrical room
I. Library
J. Entrance court
K. Administration
L. Kitchen
M. Back porch

# KA DESIGNWORKS

152
v

**EDGEWOOD CREEK RESIDENCE**

Architect:
KA DesignWorks
Landscape Architecture:
Aceto Landscape Architecture
Structural Enginner:
Riverstone Structural
Builder:
Janckila Construction
Photographer:
© Dallas & Harris Photography

156
v

**GUGGENHILL RESIDENCE**

Architect:
KA DesignWorks
Landscape Architecture:
RCLA
Furnishings:
Malibu Market and Design
Builder:
Janckila Construction
Photographer:
© Dallas & Harris Photography

160
v

**WHITEHORSE SPRINGS RESIDENCE**

Architect:
KA DesignWorks
Landscape Architecture:
RCLA
Structural Enginner:
Riverstone Structural
Builder:
Janckila Construction and
Whitecap Deveopement
Photographer:
© Dallas & Harris Photography

www.ka-designworks.com @kadesignworks

Kenneth Adler, AIA

Founded by Kenneth Adler, AIA, in 2006, we are a young and growing architecture and interiors company based in the Roaring Fork Valley, just outside Aspen, Colorado. With over twenty years of experience in the AEC industry, Ken has an extensive background in residential, hospitality, and commercial design. With dozens of new homes and remodel projects running the entire spectrum of scope and budget, we have a wealth of experience in guiding the client through the design, permitting, and construction process. Successful client relationships have been our foundation, with a majority of work resulting from word of mouth referrals and repeat customers. We relish the opportunity to be your "architect for life."

Wir wurden 2006 von Kenneth Adler, AIA, gegründet und sind ein junges und wachsendes Architektur- und Innenarchitekturbüro mit Sitz im Roaring Fork Valley, in der Nähe von Aspen, Colorado. Mit mehr als swanzig Jahren Erfahrung in der AEC-Branche verfügt Ken Adler über einen umfangreichen Hintergrund in den Bereichen Wohnungsbau, Gastgewerbe und kommerzielles Design. Mit Dutzenden von neuen Häusern und Umbauprojekten, die das gesamte Spektrum an Umfang und Budget abdecken, verfügen wir über einen reichen Erfahrungsschatz bei der Begleitung des Kunden durch den Entwurfs-, Genehmigungs- und Bauprozess. Erfolgreiche Kundenbeziehungen sind unsere Grundlage, wobei ein Großteil der Aufträge durch Mundpropaganda und Wiederholungskunden zustande kommt. Wir freuen uns auf die Gelegenheit, Ihr „Architekt fürs Leben" zu sein.

Fondée par Kenneth Adler, AIA, en 2006, nous sommes une jeune entreprise d'architecture et d'aménagement intérieur en pleine croissance, basée dans la vallée de Roaring Fork, juste à côté d'Aspen, dans le Colorado. Avec plus de vingt ans d'expérience dans le secteur de l'architecture, de l'ingénierie et de la construction (AEC), Ken possède une vaste expérience en matière de conception résidentielle, hôtelière et commerciale. Avec des dizaines de maisons neuves et de projets de rénovation couvrant tout le spectre de la portée et du budget, nous avons une grande expérience pour guider le client à travers le processus de conception, d'autorisation et de construction. Des relations fructueuses avec nos clients ont été notre fondement, la majorité de notre travail résultant de références de bouche à oreille et de clients réguliers. Nous sommes heureux d'avoir l'opportunité d'être votre « architecte pour la vie ».

Fundada por Kenneth Adler, AIA, en 2006, somos una joven y creciente empresa de arquitectura e interiores con sede en el valle de Roaring Fork, a las afueras de Aspen, Colorado. Con más de veinte años de experiencia en la industria AEC, Ken tiene una amplia experiencia en el diseño residencial, la hospitalidad, y comercial. Con docenas de casas nuevas y proyectos de remodelación que abarcan todo el espectro de alcance y presupuesto, tenemos una gran experiencia en guiar al cliente a través del proceso de diseño, permisos y construcción. El éxito de las relaciones con los clientes ha sido nuestra base, con una mayoría de trabajo resultante de la palabra de referencias de boca en boca y los clientes de la repetición. Nos encanta la oportunidad de ser su «arquitecto de por vida».

## EDGEWOOD CREEK RESIDENCE

Snowmass Village, Colorado, United States // Lot area: 75,000 sq ft; building area: 6,700 sq ft

The Edgewood Creek Residence sits on a ski-in/ski-out property in Snowmass Village. Its design originated as a unique glass-and-timber bridge that crosses a small stream. The homeowners, a husband and wife from Chicago, had been coming to Snowmass for over thirty years, and they wanted a home that would bring them and their four grown children together for ski vacations. The couple was interested in the idea of "mountain modern," a place that fits well with the environment. Adler started with a simple gable form complemented by heavy, warm-wood timber trusses, metal bracing, and exposed fasteners, adding a contemporary, industrial spin. The windows provide the true artwork of the home: the views. To that end, the landscape design by Richard Camp Landscape Architecture is equally impressive.

La résidence Edgewood Creek se trouve sur une propriété accessible par les pistes de ski à Snowmass Village. Elle a été conçue à partir d'un pont unique en verre et en bois qui traverse un petit ruisseau. Les propriétaires, un mari et une femme de Chicago, venaient à Snowmass depuis plus de trente ans et souhaitaient une maison qui les réunirait, eux et leurs quatre enfants adultes, pour les vacances de ski. Le couple était intéressé par l'idée de « modernité montagnarde », un lieu qui s'intègre bien à l'environnement. Adler a commencé par une forme de pignon simple, complétée par de lourdes fermes en bois chaud, des contreventements métalliques et des fixations apparentes, ajoutant une touche contemporaine et industrielle. Les fenêtres constituent la véritable œuvre d'art de la maison : les vues. À cet effet, l'aménagement paysager réalisé par Richard Camp Landscape Architecture est tout aussi impressionnant.

Die Edgewood Creek Residence befindet sich auf einem Ski-in/Ski-out Grundstück in Snowmass Village. Ihr Design entstand aus einer einzigartigen Brücke aus Glas und Holz, die über einen kleinen Bach führt. Die Hausbesitzer, ein Ehepaar aus Chicago, kommen seit über dreißig Jahren nach Snowmass und wollten ein Haus, in dem sie und ihre vier erwachsenen Kinder gemeinsam Skiurlaub machen können. Das Ehepaar interessierte sich für die Idee des „Mountain Modern", eines Hauses, das sich gut in die Umgebung einfügt. Adler begann mit einer einfachen Giebelform, die durch schwere Holzbinder aus warmem Holz, Metallverstrebungen und freiliegende Befestigungselemente ergänzt wurde, was dem Ganzen einen modernen, industriellen Touch verlieh. Die Fenster sind das wahre Kunstwerk des Hauses: die Aussicht. Ebenso beeindruckend ist die von Richard Camp Landscape Architecture entworfene Landschaft.

Edgewood Creek Residence se encuentra en una propiedad con acceso directo a las pistas de esquí en Snowmass Village. Su diseño se originó como un puente único de vidrio y madera que cruza un pequeño arroyo. Los propietarios, un matrimonio de Chicago, llevaban más de treinta años viniendo a Snowmass y querían una casa que les reuniera a ellos y a sus cuatro hijos mayores para las vacaciones de esquí. La pareja estaba interesada en la idea de lo «moderno de montaña», un lugar que encajara bien con el entorno. Adler comenzó con una forma sencilla de frontón complementada por cerchas pesadas de madera cálida, tirantes metálicos y sujetadores expuestos, añadiendo un giro contemporáneo e industrial. Las ventanas son la verdadera obra de arte de la casa: las vistas. En este sentido, el diseño paisajístico de Richard Camp Landscape Architecture es igualmente impresionante.

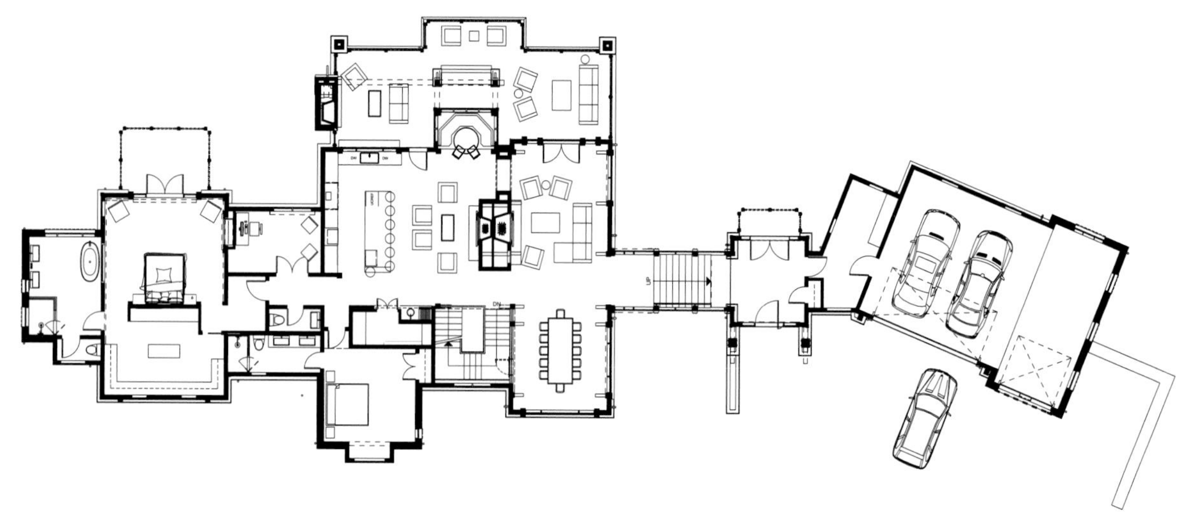

Main level floor plan

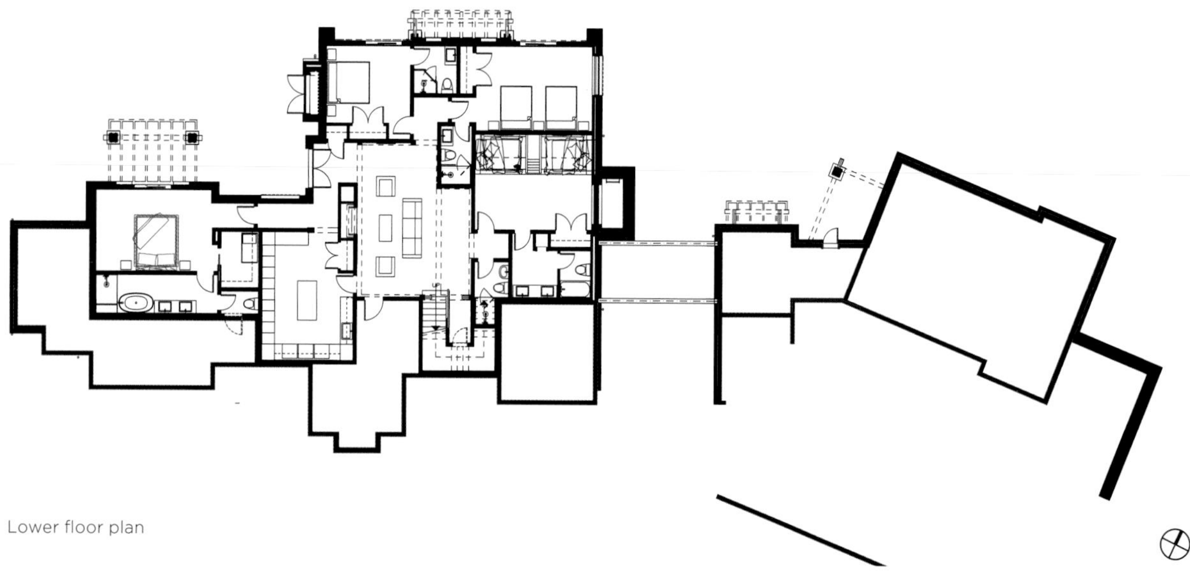

Lower floor plan

## GUGGENHILL RESIDENCE

Snowmass Village, Colorado, United States // Lot area: 30,000 sq ft; building area: 5,000 sq ft

This home lies at the magical intersection of modern and historic, perched at the top of a private ski run called Guggenhill, named after the famous Guggenheims who built the first single-family home in Snowmass at this very site. The original home the Guggenheims built in the 1960s appeared dated on the site that was begging for something more contemporary. Adler replaced the old house with a new, relatively modest two-level home adapting to the steep topography. The design evolved from his previous work, traditional to mid-century modern, to what Adler calls "mountain modern." Generous fenestration capitalizes on the views and the indoor-outdoor connection without compromising privacy and allowing for cozy interiors.

Cette maison se trouve à l'intersection magique du moderne et de l'historique, perchée au sommet d'une piste de ski privée appelée Guggenhill, du nom des célèbres Guggenheim qui ont construit la première maison unifamiliale à Snowmass à cet endroit précis. La maison originale construite par les Guggenheims dans les années 1960 paraissait dépassée sur le site qui demandait quelque chose de plus contemporain. Adler a remplacé l'ancienne maison par une nouvelle, relativement modeste, à deux niveaux, s'adaptant à la topographie escarpée. Le design a évolué à partir de son travail précédent, traditionnel et moderne du milieu du siècle, vers ce qu'Adler appelle « modernité montagnarde ». La fenestration généreuse tire parti des vues et du lien entre l'intérieur et l'extérieur sans compromettre l'intimité et en permettant des intérieurs confortables.

Dieses Haus liegt an der magischen Schnittstelle zwischen Modernem und Historischem, an der Spitze einer privaten Skipiste namens Guggenhill, benannt nach den berühmten Guggenheims, die an dieser Stelle das erste Einfamilienhaus in Snowmass bauten. Das ursprüngliche Haus, das die Guggenheims in den 1960er Jahren errichteten, wirkte an diesem Ort, der nach etwas Zeitgemäßem schrie, veraltet. Adler ersetzte das alte Haus durch ein neues, relativ bescheidenes zweistöckiges Haus, das sich an die steile Topografie anpasst. Das Design entwickelte sich von seiner früheren Arbeit, die von der Tradition bis zur Mitte des Jahrhunderts reichte, zu dem, was Adler als „Mountain Modern" bezeichnet. Die großzügigen Fenster machen sich die Aussicht und die Verbindung zwischen Innen- und Außenbereich zunutze, ohne die Privatsphäre zu beeinträchtigen und gemütliche Innenräume zu schaffen.

Esta casa se encuentra en la mágica intersección de lo moderno y lo histórico, encaramada en la cima de una pista de esquí privada llamada Guggenhill, que lleva el nombre de los famosos Guggenheims que construyeron la primera casa unifamiliar en Snowmass en este mismo lugar. La casa original que los Guggenheims construyeron en la década de 1960 parecía anticuada en un lugar que pedía algo más contemporáneo. Adler sustituyó la antigua casa por una nueva y relativamente modesta de dos niveles que se adapta a la escarpada topografía. El diseño evolucionó de su trabajo anterior, tradicional a moderno de mediados de siglo, a lo que Adler llama «moderno de montaña». La generosa zona de ventanales aprovecha las vistas y la conexión entre el interior y el exterior sin comprometer la privacidad y permitiendo unos interiores acogedores.

Guggenhill
Do Not
Park
Between
Signs

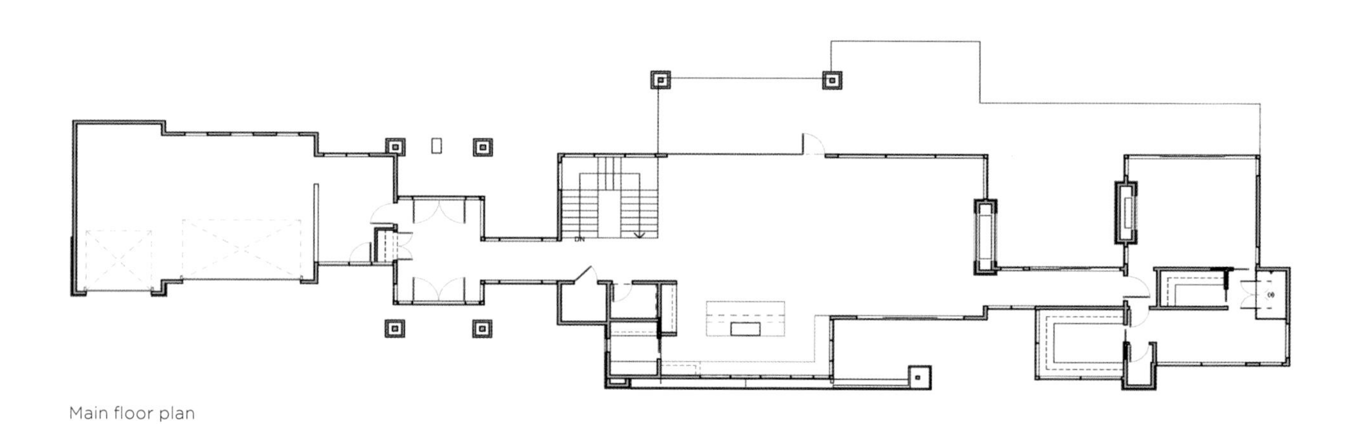

Main floor plan

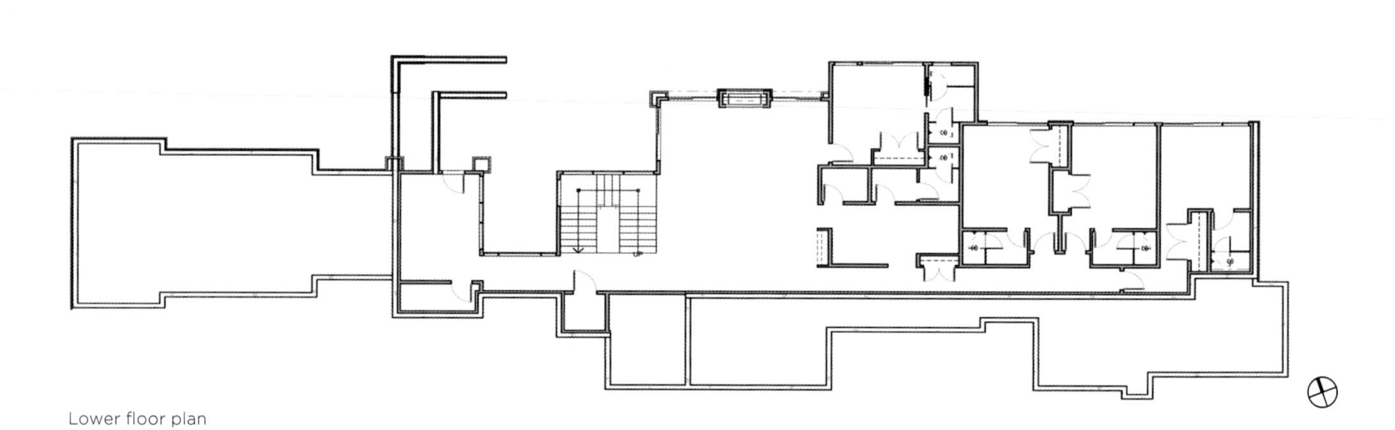

Lower floor plan

## WHITEHORSE SPRINGS RESIDENCE

Aspen, Colorado, United States // Lot area: 5.5 acres; building area: 11,500 sq ft

Whitehorse enjoys the benefits of rural ranch living with a sophisticated modern design. The original house, designed in the 1980s in the Ricardo Legorreta style, stood out for its unique foreign architecture and distinctive pink color. Its structure had interesting features, including multiple exterior rooms formed by the various wings but seemed out of place in both context and time, inspiring the remodel of the home. The design focused on three main goals: open the house to the impressive mountain views, strengthen the connection with its context through natural materials, and enhance the outdoor spaces to increase the home's effective area. All three goals were mainly achieved through the use of large motorized glass sliding doors that dematerialize the edge of the building, extending the house to the outdoors.

Whitehorse bénéficie des avantages de la vie de ranch rural avec un design moderne sophistiqué. La maison d'origine, conçue dans les années 1980 dans le style de Ricardo Legorreta, se distinguait par son architecture étrangère unique et sa couleur rose distinctive. Sa structure présentait des caractéristiques intéressantes, notamment de multiples pièces extérieures formées par les différentes ailes, mais elle semblait déplacée à la fois dans le contexte et dans le temps, ce qui a inspiré la rénovation de la maison. La conception s'est concentrée sur trois objectifs principaux : ouvrir la maison sur la vue impressionnante des montagnes, renforcer le lien avec son contexte grâce à des matériaux naturels, et améliorer les espaces extérieurs pour augmenter la surface effective de la maison. Ces trois objectifs ont été principalement atteints grâce à l'utilisation de grandes portes coulissantes en verre motorisées qui dématérialisent le bord du bâtiment, étendant la maison vers l'extérieur.

Whitehorse genießt die Vorteile des Lebens auf einer ländlichen Ranch mit einem anspruchsvollen modernen Design. Das ursprüngliche Haus, das in den 1980er Jahren im Stil von Ricardo Legorreta entworfen wurde, zeichnete sich durch seine einzigartige fremdländische Architektur und seine auffällige rosa Farbe aus. Seine Struktur wies interessante Merkmale auf, darunter mehrere Außenräume, die von den verschiedenen Flügeln gebildet wurden, wirkte aber sowohl im Kontext als auch in der Zeit fehl am Platz, was den Umbau des Hauses inspirierte. Das Design konzentrierte sich auf drei Hauptziele: das Haus für die beeindruckende Aussicht auf die Berge zu öffnen, die Verbindung mit der Umgebung durch natürliche Materialien zu stärken und die Außenbereiche zu verbessern, um die Nutzfläche des Hauses zu vergrößern. Alle drei Ziele wurden vor allem durch den Einsatz großer motorisierter Glasschiebetüren erreicht, die den Rand des Gebäudes entmaterialisieren und das Haus nach außen hin erweitern.

Whitehorse disfruta de las ventajas de la vida en un rancho rural con un sofisticado diseño moderno. La casa original, diseñada en la década de 1980 en el estilo de Ricardo Legorreta, destacaba por su singular arquitectura foránea y su distintivo color rosa. La estructura tenía características interesantes, como las múltiples habitaciones exteriores formadas por las distintas alas, pero parecía fuera de lugar tanto en el contexto como en el tiempo, lo que inspiró la remodelación de la casa. El diseño se centró en tres objetivos principales: abrir la casa a las impresionantes vistas de la montaña, reforzar la conexión con su contexto a través de materiales naturales y mejorar los espacios exteriores para aumentar la superficie efectiva de la vivienda. Los tres objetivos se lograron principalmente mediante el uso de grandes puertas correderas de cristal motorizadas que desmaterializan el borde del edificio, extendiendo la casa hacia el exterior.

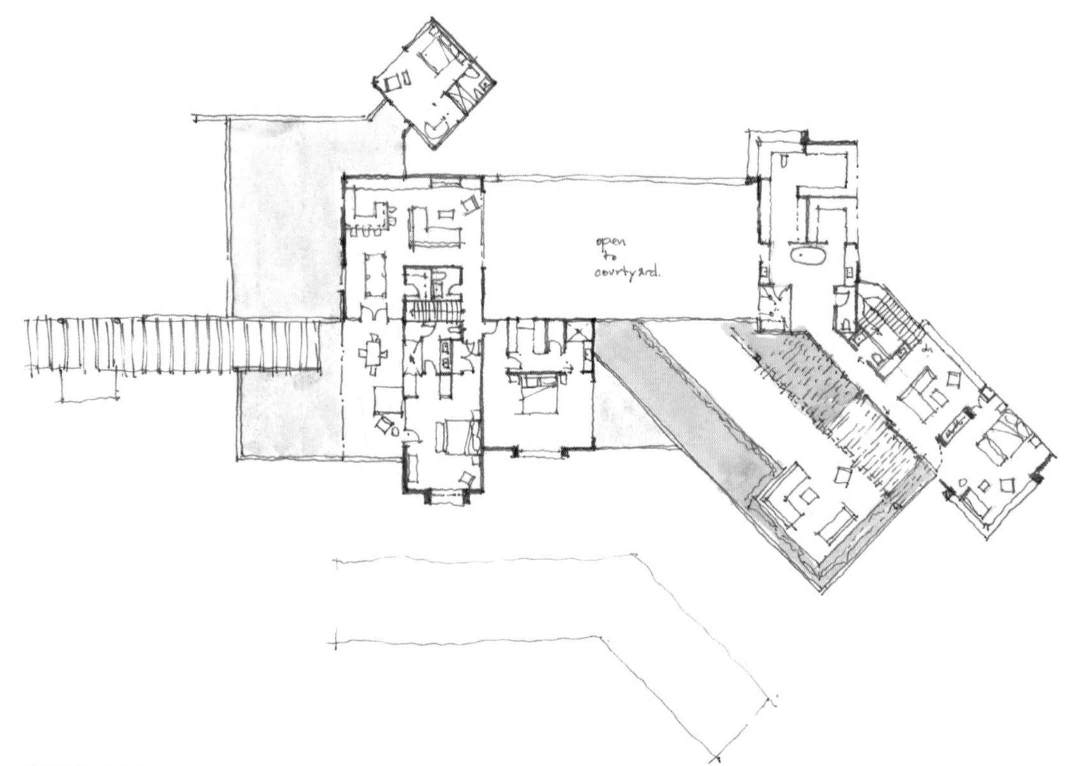


Upper floor plan

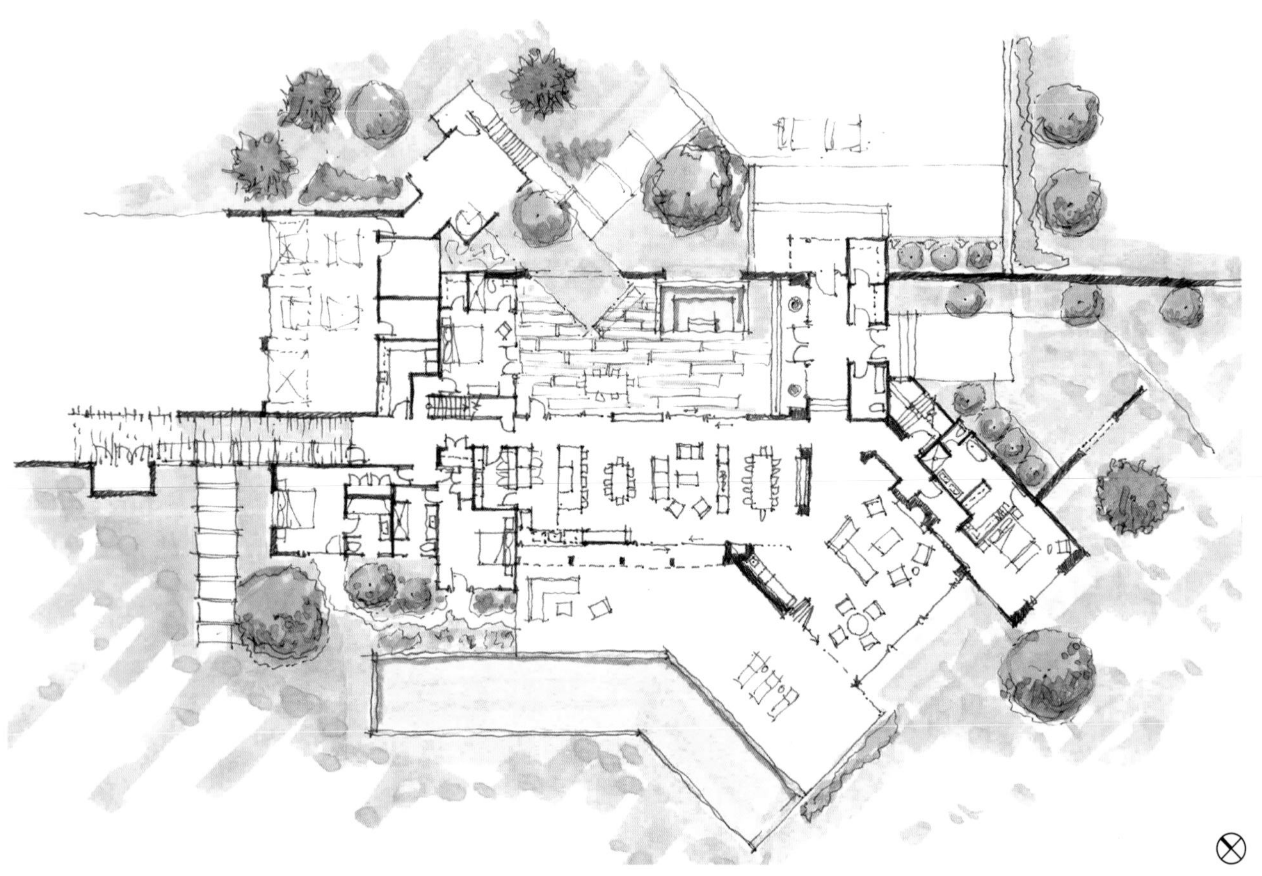

Lower floor plan

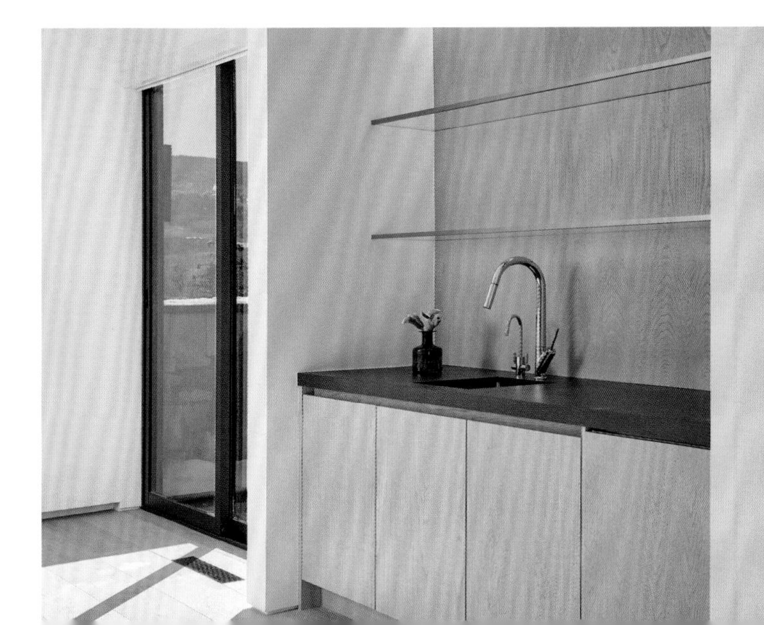

# MARPA

166
v

**ARAPAHOE HILL**

Landscape Design and Construction:
Marpa
House Architect:
Studio B
House Builder:
Treeline Homes
Civil Engineer:
Sanitas Civil Engineering
Swimming Pool Construction:
Mr. Pool
Spa and Cold Plunge Fabrication:
TWO Create Fabrication
Photographers:
© Logan Manaker and Bodie Hultin

170
v

**BLACK BEAR**

Landscape Design and Construction:
Marpa
House Architect:
Surround Architecture
House Builder:
Treeline Homes
Swimming Pool Construction:
Integrity Pool Builders
Photographers:
© Logan Manaker and Bodie Hultin

174
v

**CALCAIRE**

Landscape Design and Construction:
Marpa
House Architect:
Surround Architecture
House Builder:
Harrington Stanko
Steel Fence Fabrication:
TWO Create Fabrication and Metal Craft
Photographers:
© Logan Manaker and Bodie Hultin

www.marpa.com @marpalandscapes

Marpa is a Landscape Architecture and Construction firm based in Boulder, Colorado. For more than forty years, they have been creating meaningful spaces that are deeply in tune with their clients and their land. The firm was founded in 1974 by Martin Mosko, who trained extensively in Japanese garden design. Applying this approach to the Rocky Mountain region of Colorado, Marpa's creative process has evolved into a practice of Contemplative Design: a thoughtful process that aligns the energy and natural characteristics of the landscape with the goals and values of the client. The firm works closely with the project team to provide unique outdoor spaces that enhance the surrounding architecture and amplify the functionality of the landscape. Marpa's work spans scales, from small home gardens to large private estates, botanical gardens to religious retreats, and mixed-use developments to educational campuses. Ultimately, Marpa believes that a well-designed, responsive space can connect us to the environment, our histories, and our communities.

Marpa ist ein Landschaftsarchitektur- und Bauunternehmen mit Sitz in Boulder, Colorado. Seit mehr als vierzig Jahren schaffen sie bedeutungsvolle Räume, die in enger Verbindung mit ihren Kunden und ihrem Land stehen. Die Firma wurde 1974 von Martin Mosko gegründet, der eine umfassende Ausbildung in japanischer Gartengestaltung absolvierte. Durch die Anwendung dieses Ansatzes in der Rocky Mountain Region von Colorado hat sich der kreative Prozess von Marpa zu einer Praxis des kontemplativen Designs entwickelt: ein durchdachter Prozess, der die Energie und die natürlichen Eigenschaften der Landschaft mit den Zielen und Werten des Kunden in Einklang bringt. Das Unternehmen arbeitet eng mit dem Projektteam zusammen, um einzigartige Außenräume zu schaffen, die die umgebende Architektur aufwerten und die Funktionalität der Landschaft verstärken. Marpas Arbeit reicht von kleinen Hausgärten bis hin zu großen privaten Anwesen, von botanischen Gärten bis hin zu religiösen Rückzugsorten und von gemischt genutzten Projekten bis hin zu Bildungseinrichtungen. Letztendlich glauben wir, dass ein gut gestalteter, ansprechend gestalteter Raum uns mit der Umwelt, unserer Geschichte und unseren Gemeinschaften verbinden kann.

Marpa est un bureau d'architecture paysagère et de construction basé à Boulder, dans le Colorado. Depuis plus de quarante ans, ils créent des espaces significatifs qui sont profondément en phase avec leurs clients et leur terre. Le bureau a été fondé en 1974 par Martin Mosko, qui a suivi une formation en conception de jardins japonais. Appliquant cette approche à la région des Rocheuses du Colorado, le processus créatif de Marpa a évolué vers une pratique de conception contemplative : un processus réfléchi qui aligne l'énergie et les traits naturels du paysage avec les objectifs et les valeurs du client. Le bureau travaille en collaboration avec l'équipe du projet pour créer des espaces extérieurs uniques qui mettent en valeur l'architecture environnante et amplifient la fonctionnalité du paysage. Le travail de Marpa s'étend sur plusieurs échelles, des petits jardins de maison aux grands domaines privés, des jardins botaniques aux retraites religieuses, et des développements à usage mixte aux campus éducatifs. En fin de compte, nous pensons qu'un espace bien conçu et adapté peut nous relier à l'environnement, à notre histoire et à nos communautés.

Marpa es un estudio de arquitectura paisajística y construcción con sede en Boulder, Colorado. Durante más de cuarenta años, han creado espacios significativos que están en sintonía con sus clientes y sus tierras. El estudio fue fundado en 1974 por Martin Mosko, quien se formó en el diseño de jardines japoneses. Aplicando este enfoque a la región de las Montañas Rocosas de Colorado, el proceso creativo de Marpa ha evolucionado hasta convertirse en una práctica de Diseño Contemplativo: un proceso reflexivo que alinea la energía y las características naturales del paisaje con los objetivos y valores del cliente. El estudio colabora con el equipo del proyecto para proporcionar espacios exteriores únicos que realzan la arquitectura circundante y amplían la funcionalidad del paisaje. El trabajo de Marpa abarca desde pequeños jardines domésticos hasta grandes fincas privadas, desde jardines botánicos hasta retiros religiosos, y desde desarrollos de uso mixto hasta centros educativos. En definitiva, creemos que un espacio bien diseñado y con adaptabilidad puede conectarnos con el medio ambiente, nuestras historias y nuestras comunidades.

## ARAPAHOE HILL

Boulder, Colorado, United States // Lot area: 124,983 sq ft

Arapahoe Hill is situated in a unique transitional zone between the short grass prairie of the plains and the Rocky Mountains. Severe flooding in 2013 caused significant erosion and damage to the hillside above the main house. The design team's objective was to create a stable environment within a delicate ecology that sees snow, drought, intense surface runoff, and dramatic temperature swings. The landscape plan included a range of systems that allow for a degree of self-sufficiency and ecological protection. A series of boulder retaining walls with interwoven plantings were carefully set to create a terraced, usable yard. Adjacent agricultural fields and a greenhouse produce food throughout the year, while a living roof helps reduce energy costs. The landscape also has well-programmed spaces for play, relaxation, and gathering.

Arapahoe Hill est situé dans une zone de transition unique entre la prairie d'herbe courte des plaines et les montagnes Rocheuses. De graves flooding en 2013 ont causé une érosion et des dommages significants au flanc de la colline au-dessus de la maison principale. L'objectif de l'équipe de conception était de créer un environnement stable au sein d'une écologie délicate qui voit la neige, la sécheresse, le ruissellement de surface intense et des variations de température dramatiques. Le plan d'aménagement paysager comprenait une gamme de systèmes permettant un degré d'autosuffisance et de protection écologique. Une série de murs de soutènement en blocs rocheux avec des plantations entrelacées ont été soigneusement placés pour créer une cour utilisable en terrasse. Les fields agricoles adjacents et une serre produisent des aliments tout au long de l'année, tandis qu'un toit vivant permet de réduire les coûts énergétiques. Le paysage comporte également des espaces bien programmés pour le jeu, la relaxation et le rassemblement.

Arapahoe Hill liegt in einer einzigartigen Übergangszone zwischen der Kurzgras-Prärie der Prärie und den Rocky Mountains. Schwere Überschwemmungen im Jahr 2013 verursachten erhebliche Erosionen und Schäden an den Hängen oberhalb des Haupthauses. Das Ziel des Planungsteams war es, eine stabile Umgebung in einer empfindlichen Ökologie zu schaffen, die von Schnee, Trockenheit, starkem Oberflächenabfluss und dramatischen Temperaturschwankungen geprägt ist. Der Landschaftsplan umfasste eine Reihe von Systemen, die ein gewisses Maß an Autarkie und ökologischem Schutz ermöglichen. Eine Reihe von bepflanzten Felswänden wurde sorgfältig platziert, um einen nutzbaren Terrassenhof zu schaffen. Angrenzende landwirtschaftliche Felder und ein Gewächshaus produzieren das ganze Jahr über Lebensmittel, während ein lebendiges Dach zur Senkung der Energiekosten beiträgt. Die Landschaft bietet außerdem gut gestaltete Bereiche zum Spielen, Entspannen und Zusammenkommen.

Arapahoe Hill está situada en una zona de transición única entre las llanuras de hierba corta y las Montañas Rocosas. Las graves inundaciones de 2013 provocaron una importante erosión y daños en la ladera por encima de la casa principal. El objetivo del equipo de diseño fue crear un entorno estable en el contexto de una ecología delicada en la que se producen nevadas, sequías, evacuaciones superficiales intensas y cambios drásticos de temperatura. El plan de paisajismo incluyó una serie de sistemas que permiten un grado de autosuficiencia y protección ecológica. Una serie de muros de rocas con plantaciones se colocaron cuidadosamente para crear un patio utilizable en terrazas. Los campos agrícolas adyacentes y un invernadero producen alimentos durante todo el año, mientras que un techo vivo ayuda a reducir los costes de energía. El paisaje también cuenta con espacios bien programados para jugar, relajarse y reunirse.

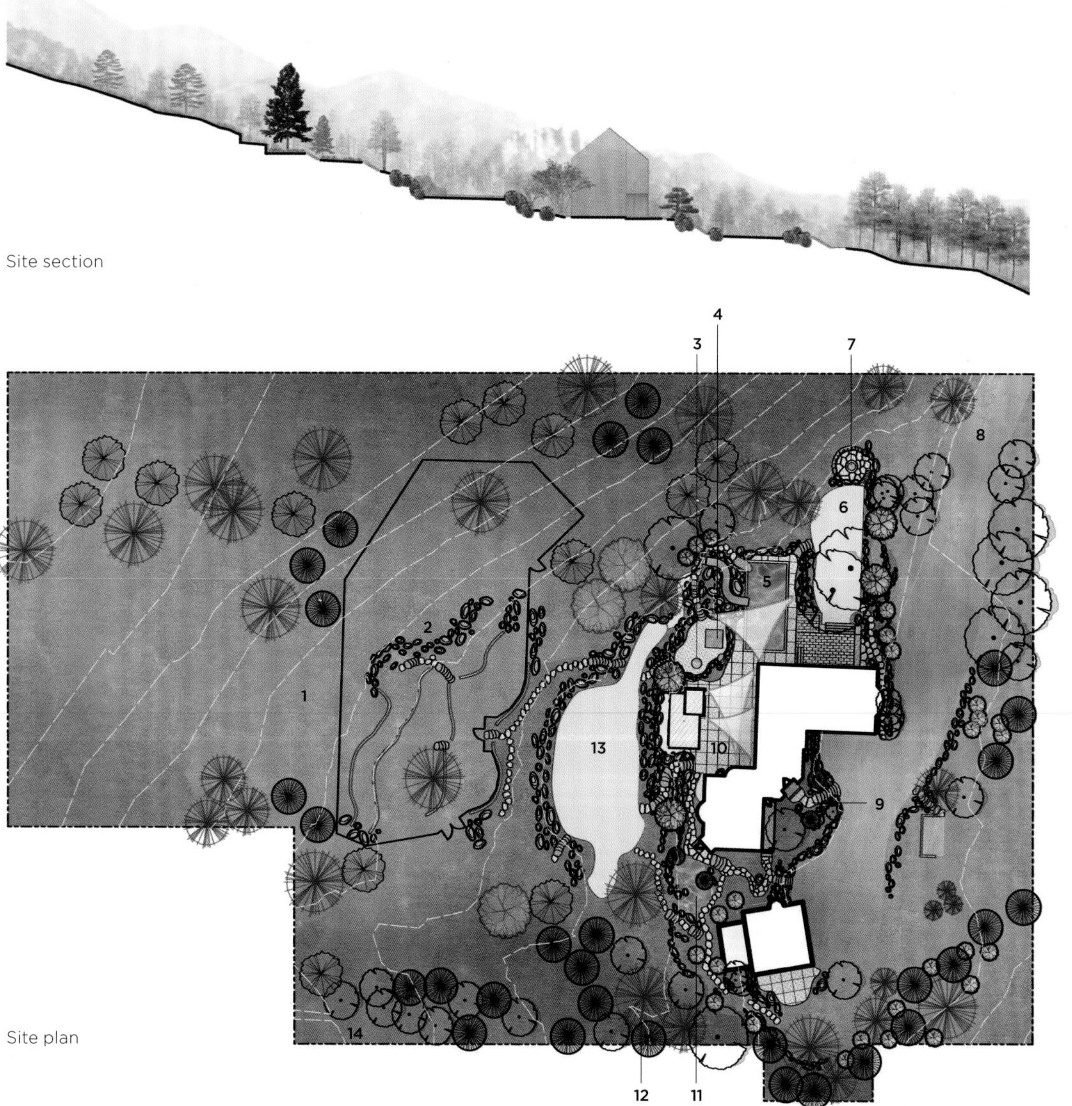

Site section

Site plan

1. Upper hillside lavender fields
2. Terraced cultivated gardens
3. Custom cold plunge
4. Custom spa
5. Pool with custom slide and jump rock
6. Lawn
7. Grotto with fire feature
8. Driveway
9. Entrance gardens
10. Main terrace
11. Koi pond
12. Riparian drainage corridor
13. Play lawn
14. Mixed forest

## BLACK BEAR

Boulder, Colorado, United States // Lot area: 17,478 sq ft

Backing up to the foothills of the Rocky Mountains, the steep slopes of Black Bear showcase an articulated progression of steps, outdoor rooms and microclimates that combine clean surfaces and rich plantings. At the site's entrance, a progression of boulder steppers leads to a staggered concrete staircase nestled between dense plantings and ornamental boulders that end at a formal staircase to the front door. A swimming pool intersects the back courtyard, which sits adjacent to a naturalized hillside with a boulder staircase that moves through Aspen trees and swaths of shade-tolerant plants. By treating the site's challenging terrain as an opportunity, the design team was able to maximize the potential of the landscape by creating spaces of profound beauty while acknowledging the natural environment in which it resides.

Adossées aux contreforts des Rocheuses, les pentes abruptes de Black Bear présentent une progression articulée de marches, de salles extérieures et de microclimats qui combinent des surfaces nettes et des plantations riches. À l'entrée du site, une progression de marches en blocs rocheux mène à un escalier en béton échelonné, niché entre des plantations denses et des blocs rocheux ornementaux, qui se termine par un escalier formel menant à la porte d'entrée. Une piscine traverse la cour arrière, qui est adjacente à une colline naturalisée avec un escalier de blocs rocheux qui se déplace entre des trembles et des bandes de plantes tolérantes à l'ombre. En traitant le terrain difficile du site comme une opportunité, l'équipe de conception a pu maximiser le potentiel du paysage en créant des espaces d'une profonde beauté tout en reconnaissant l'environnement naturel dans lequel il se trouve.

Die steilen Hänge von Black Bear, die sich bis zu den Ausläufern der Rocky Mountains erstrecken, weisen eine gegliederte Abfolge von Stufen, Außenräumen und Mikroklimata auf, die saubere Oberflächen und üppige Bepflanzungen miteinander verbinden. Am Eingang des Geländes führt eine Reihe von Steinstufen zu einer gestaffelten Betontreppe, die zwischen dichten Bepflanzungen und Zierblöcken eingebettet ist und in einer formellen Treppe zur Eingangstür endet. Ein Swimmingpool durchschneidet den hinteren Hof, der an einen naturbelassenen Hang mit einer Gerölltreppe angrenzt, die sich zwischen Espen und schattentoleranten Pflanzen bewegt. Indem das Designteam das schwierige Gelände als Chance betrachtete, konnte es das Potenzial der Landschaft maximieren, indem es Räume von tiefer Schönheit schuf und gleichzeitig die natürliche Umgebung, in der sie sich befindet, berücksichtigte.

Con vistas a las estribaciones de las Montañas Rocosas, las empinadas laderas de Black Bear muestran una progresión articulada de escalones, salas exteriores y microclimas que combinan superficies limpias y ricas plantaciones. En la entrada del lugar, una progresión de escalones de piedra conduce a una escalera de hormigón escalonada entre densas plantaciones y rocas ornamentales que terminan en una escalera formal hacia la puerta principal. Una piscina se cruza con el patio trasero, que se encuentra junto a una ladera naturalizada con una escalera de cantos rodados que se mueve entre álamos y franjas de plantas tolerantes a la sombra. Al tratar el terreno desafiante como una oportunidad, el equipo de diseño pudo maximizar el potencial del paisaje al crear espacios de profunda belleza al tiempo que reconoce el entorno natural en el que reside.

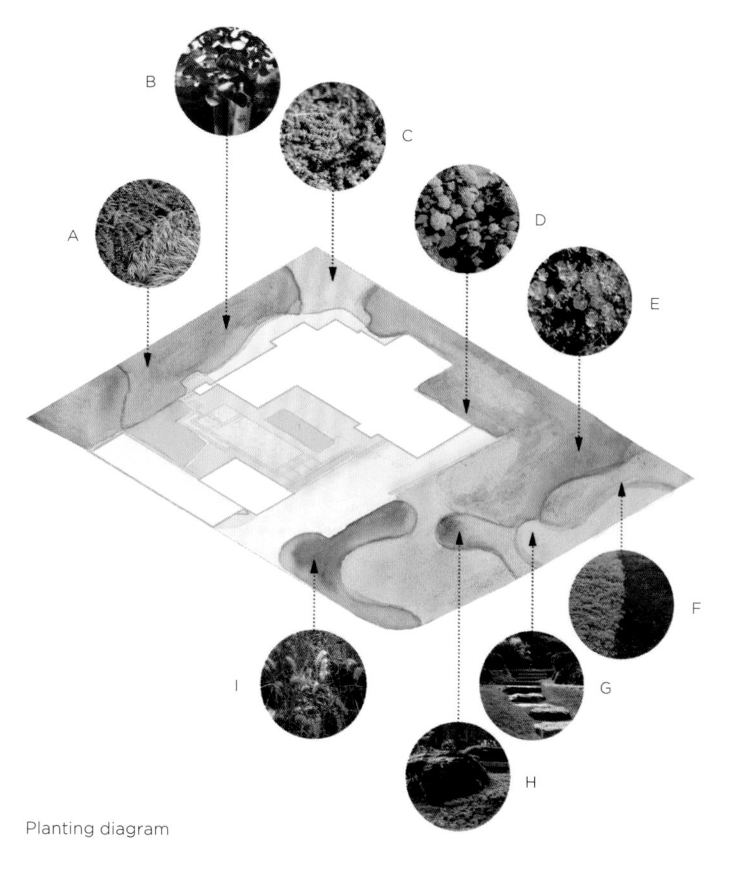


Planting diagram

A. Modern woodland
B. Aspen grove
C. Sunny pollinator hill
D. Planted rock wall
E. Dappled edge
F. Ground cover border
G. Contrasting threshold
H. Refined rock terrace
I. Large grasses

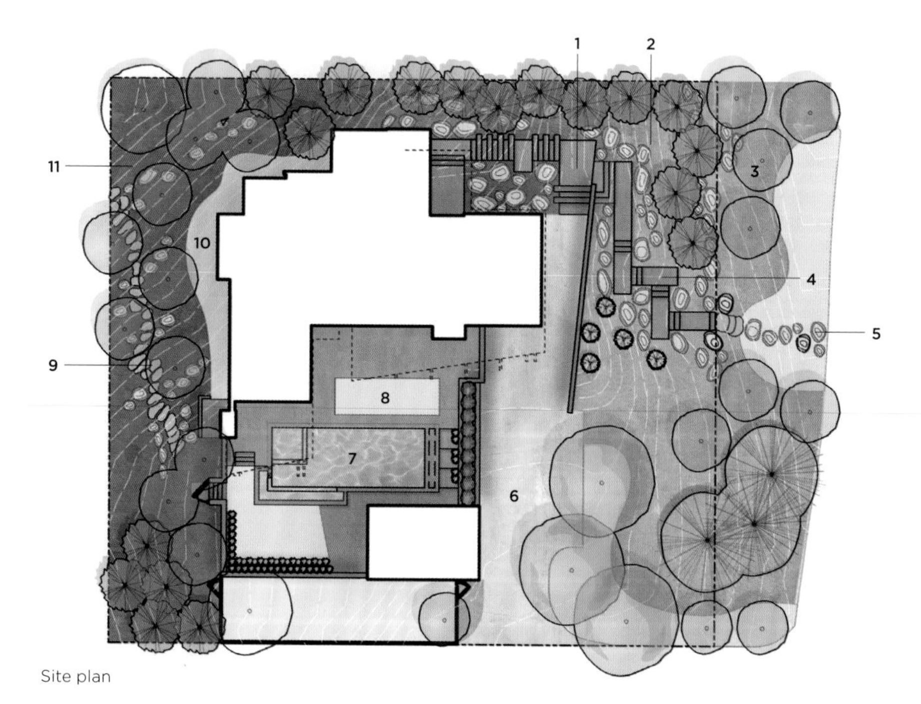


Site plan

1. Formal staircase to front door
2. Front hillside gardens
3. Fruit tree grove
4. Staggered concrete staircase
5. Entrance boulder steppers
6. Driveway
7. Pool and spa
8. Lawn terrace
9. Rear boulder staircase
10. Dry stream swale
11. Hillside woodland garden

## CALCAIRE

Boulder, Colorado, United States // Lot area: 270,573 sq ft

Water serves as a focal point at Calcaire, a six-acre estate located in the heart of Boulder, Colorado. A vibrant planted pond near the home's entrance, a circuitous farmer's ditch winding through the site, and a cobbled channel directing water from the neighboring property through the middle of the site and collecting in the pond are some of the features implemented into the design for their practical and aesthetic values. Also notable are a walking path circulating the entirety of the property and a custom gabion wall on the northern edge of the property serving as both a visual and sound barrier from a busy street beyond. A lush shade garden and curved water feature at the owner's suite create a calming retreat, while the main courtyard provides space for gathering with a custom fire pit, bocce court and uninterrupted views to the Flatirons.

L'eau est le point central de Calcaire, un domaine de six acres situé au cœur de Boulder, dans le Colorado. Un étang éclatant près de l'entrée de la maison, un fossé de fermier qui serpente à travers le site, et un canal pavé qui dirige l'eau de la propriété voisine à travers le milieu du site et la collecte dans l'étang sont quelques-unes des caractéristiques mises en œuvre dans la conception pour leurs valeurs pratiques et esthétiques. On notera également la présence d'un sentier pédestre qui circule sur l'ensemble de la propriété et d'un mur de gabions personnalisé sur le bord nord de la propriété, qui sert à la fois de barrière visuelle et sonore par rapport à une rue très fréquentée. Un jardin d'ombre luxuriant et une fontaine incurvée à la suite du propriétaire créent une retraite apaisante, tandis que la cour principale offre un espace de rassemblement avec une fosse à fire personnalisée, un terrain de pétanque et des vues ininterrompues sur les Flatirons.

Wasser ist ein zentraler Punkt in Calcaire, einem sechs Acre großen Anwesen im Herzen von Boulder, Colorado. Ein lebendig bepflanzter Teich in der Nähe des Hauseingangs, ein umlaufender Landwirtschaftsgraben, der sich durch das Grundstück schlängelt, und ein gepflasterter Kanal, der das Wasser vom Nachbargrundstück durch die Mitte des Grundstücks leitet und im Teich sammelt, sind einige der Merkmale, die aufgrund ihres praktischen und ästhetischen Werts in den Entwurf integriert wurden. Bemerkenswert sind auch ein Wanderweg, der das gesamte Grundstück umläuft, und eine speziell angefertigte Gabionenwand am nördlichen Rand des Grundstücks, die sowohl als Sicht- als auch als Lärmschutzwand gegenüber einer stark befahrenen Straße dient. Ein üppiger schattiger Garten und ein geschwungenes Wasserspiel an der Suite des Eigentümers schaffen einen beruhigenden Rückzugsort, während der Haupthof mit einer maßgefertigten Feuerstelle, einem Boccia-Platz und einem ungehinderten Blick auf die Flatirons Raum für Zusammenkünfte bietet.

El agua es el punto central de Calcaire, una finca de seis acres situada en el corazón de Boulder, Colorado. Un brillante estanque cerca de la entrada de la casa, una sinuosa zanja agrícola que atraviesa el terreno y un canal empedrado que dirige el agua de la propiedad vecina a través del terreno y se acumula en el estanque son algunas de las características implementadas en el diseño por sus valores prácticos y estéticos. También cabe destacar un sendero que recorre toda la propiedad y un muro de gaviones hecho a medida en el extremo norte de la propiedad que sirve de barrera visual y acústica frente a una calle muy transitada. Un exuberante jardín de sombra y una fuente curvada en la suite del propietario crean un refugio relajante, mientras que el patio principal ofrece un espacio para reunirse con un pozo de fuego personalizado, una pista de bochas y vistas ininterrumpidas a los Flatirons.

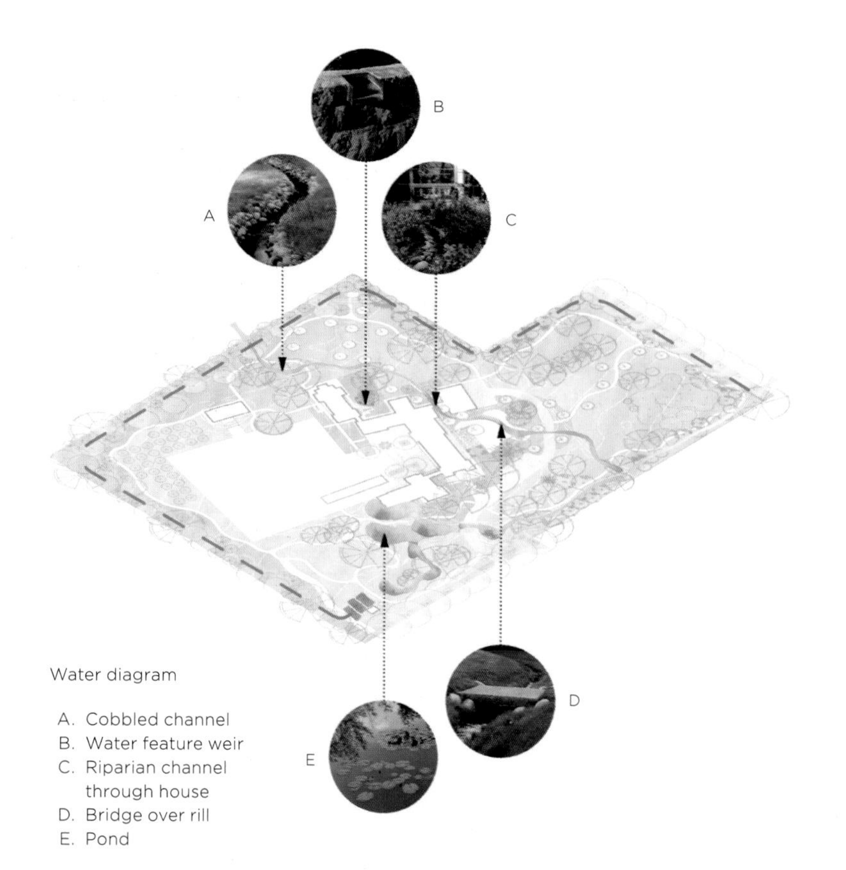


Water diagram

A. Cobbled channel
B. Water feature weir
C. Riparian channel through house
D. Bridge over rill
E. Pond

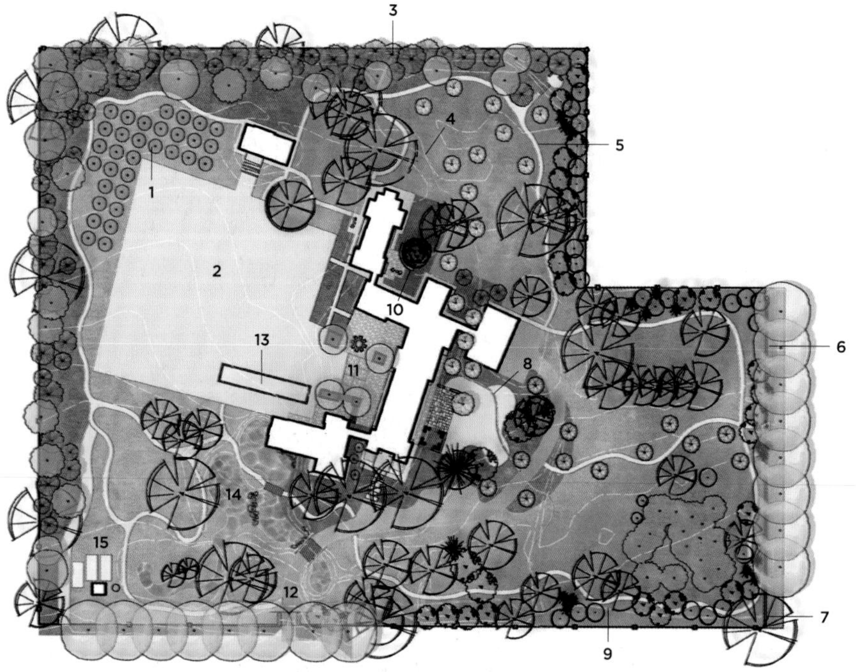

Site plan

1. Orchard
2. Sports field
3. Water entry point
4. Cobbled channel through riparian zone
5. Walking trail
6. Gabion wall
7. Water exit point
8. Grass-lined rill
9. Woodland stream
10. Courtyard water feature
11. Main courtyard
12. Driveway
13. Bocce court
14. Pond + stream system
15. Pump house and cisterns

# DICK CLARK + ASSOCIATES

180
v

**BELLVILLE**

Architect:
Kevin Gallaugher, AIA
Landscape Architect:
Ten Eyck Landscape Architects
Structural Engineer:
StructuresPE
Builder:
Mark Goodrich
Photographer:
© Dror Baldinger

184
v

**LIVE OAK**

Architect:
Kim Power, AIA
Structural Engineer:
Steinman Luevano Structures, L.L.P.
Builder:
Jon Luce Builder
Photographer:
© Paul Bardagjy

188
v

**SKYBOX**

Architect:
Kristopher White, AIA
Structural Engineer:
Feldt Consulting Engineers
Builder:
Vinson Radke Homes
Photographer:
© Dror Baldinger

www.dcarch.com  dc_architecture

Kim Power

Kristopher White

Kevin Gallaugher

Dick Clark + Associates was founded in 1979 as a full-service architecture and interior design firm based in Austin. The firm believes in the ability of great design to create a sense of place, represent an individual's or organization's values, and enhance the lives of its inhabitants. To this end, the firm is deeply engaged in the community, participating in the shaping of the city, Central Texas, and beyond. As a full-service architecture and interior design firm, DC+A's work covers a wide range of project types, from high-end custom residential to boutique commercial and hospitality projects. The firm balances high-quality, professional work with a welcoming, laid-back office environment where ideas flow and collaboration is constant. DC+A prides themselves on creating memorable landmark projects and inspirational spaces that capture Austin's unique quality and lifestyle.

Dick Clark + Associates wurde 1979 als ein Architektur- und Innenarchitekturbüro mit Sitz in Austin gegründet. Das Unternehmen glaubt an die Fähigkeit von großartigem Design, ein Gefühl für einen Ort zu schaffen, die Werte einer Person oder eines Unternehmens zu repräsentieren und das Leben seiner Bewohner zu verbessern. Zu diesem Zweck engagiert sich das Unternehmen stark in der Gemeinschaft und nimmt an der Gestaltung der Stadt, von Zentraltexas und darüber hinaus teil. Als Full-Service-Architektur- und Innenarchitekturbüro deckt die Arbeit von DC+A ein breites Spektrum an Projekttypen ab, von hochwertigen, individuell gestalteten Wohngebäuden bis hin zu kommerziellen Boutique- und Gastgewerbeprojekten. Das Unternehmen verbindet hochwertige, professionelle Arbeit mit einer einladenden, entspannten Büroumgebung, in der Ideen fließen und die Zusammenarbeit konstant ist. DC+A ist stolz darauf, denkwürdige Projekte und inspirierende Räume zu schaffen, die die einzigartige Qualität und den Lebensstil von Austin einfangen.

Dick Clark + Associates a été fondé en 1979 en tant que cabinet d'architecture et de décoration intérieure à service complet basé à Austin. Le cabinet croit en la capacité d'un grand design à créer un sens du lieu, à représenter les valeurs d'un individu ou d'une organisation et à améliorer la vie de ses habitants. À cette fin, le cabinet est profondément engagé dans la communauté, participant au façonnement de la ville, du centre du Texas et au-delà. En tant que cabinet d'architecture et de décoration d'intérieur à service complet, le travail de DC+A couvre un large éventail de types de projets, des résidences personnalisées haut de gamme aux projets commerciaux et d'accueil. Le cabinet concilie un travail professionnel de haute qualité avec un environnement de bureau accueillant et décontracté où les idées fusent et où la collaboration est constante. DC+A s'enorgueillit de créer des projets mémorables et des espaces inspirants qui reflètent la qualité et le style de vie uniques d'Austin.

Dick Clark + Associates se fundó en 1979 como una empresa de servicios completos de arquitectura y diseño de interiores con sede en Austin. La empresa cree en la capacidad de un gran diseño para crear un sentido de lugar, representar los valores de una persona u organización y mejorar la vida de sus habitantes. Para ello, la empresa está profundamente comprometida con la comunidad, participando en la configuración de la ciudad, el centro de Texas y más allá. Como empresa de servicios integrales de arquitectura y diseño de interiores, el trabajo de DC+A abarca una amplia gama de tipos de proyectos, desde proyectos residenciales de alta gama hasta proyectos comerciales y de hostelería. La empresa equilibra un trabajo profesional de alta calidad con un entorno de oficina acogedor y relajado en el que las ideas fluyen y la colaboración es constante. DC+A se enorgullece de crear proyectos memorables y espacios inspiradores que capturan la calidad y el estilo de vida únicos de Austin.

## BELLVILLE

Belleville, Texas, United States // Guest house 1 area: 1,857 sq ft; guest house 2 area: 1,218 sq ft; and central pavilion area: 3,237 sq ft

The Bellville Project is a communal ranch formed by two private residences and a shared pavilion. The design team visualized the pavilion as accessible from the two residences, but the true challenge was to create custom homes that individually addressed the couples' different aesthetics and wish lists while ensuring a unified design. The pavilion is distinctly contemporary, with cues taken from traditional farmhouse design and a decidedly Texas aesthetic thanks to the knotty Post oak found throughout the structure. The homes open up to the idyllic landscape with a series of outdoor rooms accentuating the indoor/outdoor relationship. The smaller of the two residences is built next to the property's original 150-year-old farmhouse and designed to be compatible with the farmhouse vernacular.

Le projet Bellville est un ranch communal formé par deux résidences privées et un pavillon partagé. L'équipe de conception a imaginé que le pavillon serait accessible à partir des deux résidences, mais le véritable défi consistait à créer des maisons personnalisées qui répondaient individuellement aux différentes esthétiques et listes de souhaits des couples, tout en assurant un design unifié. Le pavillon est résolument contemporain, avec des touches inspirées du design traditionnel des fermes et une esthétique typiquement texane grâce au chêne noueux de Post que l'on retrouve dans toute la structure. Les maisons s'ouvrent sur le paysage idyllique avec une série de pièces extérieures accentuant la relation intérieur/extérieur. La plus petite des deux résidences est construite à côté de la ferme originale de la propriété, vieille de 150 ans, et conçue pour être compatible avec le style de la ferme.

Das Bellville-Projekt ist eine gemeinschaftliche Ranch, die aus zwei privaten Wohnhäusern und einem gemeinsamen Pavillon besteht. Das Designteam stellte sich vor, dass der gemeinsame Pavillon von den beiden Residenzen aus zugänglich sein sollte. Die eigentliche Herausforderung bestand jedoch darin, maßgeschneiderte Häuser zu schaffen, die den unterschiedlichen ästhetischen Vorstellungen und Wünschen der Paare gerecht werden und gleichzeitig ein einheitliches Design gewährleisten. Der Pavillon ist eindeutig zeitgenössisch, mit Anklängen an das traditionelle Bauernhausdesign und einer entschieden texanischen Ästhetik dank der knorrigen Post-Eiche, die überall in der Struktur zu finden ist. Die Häuser öffnen sich zur idyllischen Landschaft mit einer Reihe von Außenräumen, die die Beziehung zwischen Innen- und Außenbereich betonen. Das kleinere der beiden Häuser wurde neben dem 150 Jahre alten ursprünglichen Bauernhaus des Anwesens gebaut und so gestaltet, dass es mit der typischen Bauweise eines Bauernhauses kompatibel ist.

El proyecto Bellville es un rancho comunal formado por dos residencias privadas y un pabellón compartido. El equipo de diseño visualizó el pabellón como accesible desde las dos residencias, pero el verdadero reto era crear casas personalizadas que abordaran individualmente las diferentes estéticas y listas de deseos de las parejas, al tiempo que se garantizaba un diseño unificado. El pabellón es claramente contemporáneo, con elementos tomados del diseño tradicional de las granjas y una estética decididamente tejana gracias al roble nudoso de Post que se encuentra en toda la estructura. Las viviendas se abren al idílico paisaje con una serie de habitaciones exteriores que acentúan la relación entre el interior y el exterior. La más pequeña de las dos residencias se ha construido junto a la granja original de 150 años de antigüedad y se ha diseñado para que sea compatible con el estilo de la granja.

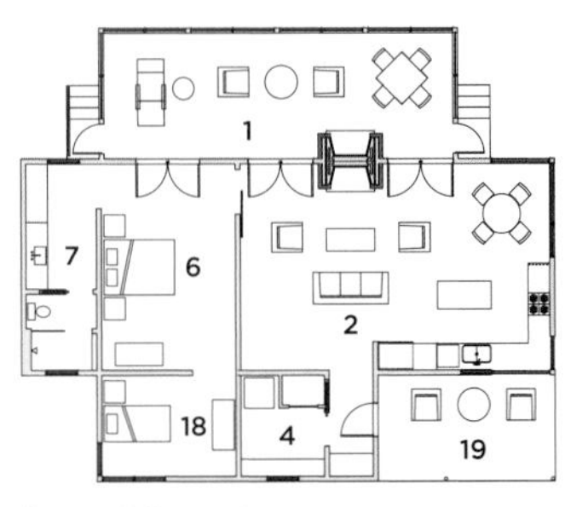

House 2 floor plan

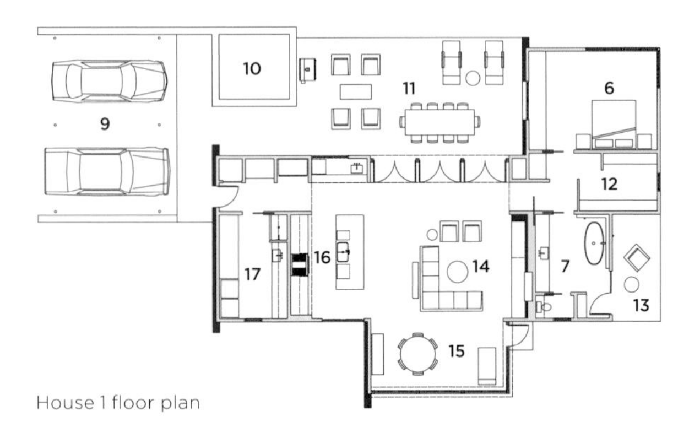

House 1 floor plan

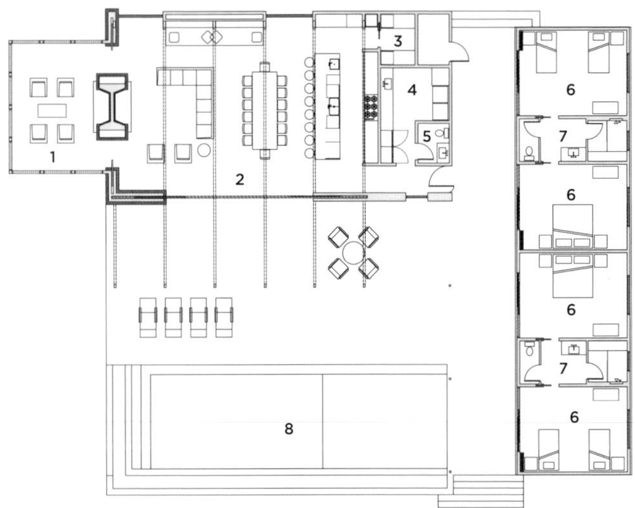

Central pavilion floor plan

1. Screened porch
2. Living/dining/kitchen area
3. Pantry
4. Utility room
5. Powder room
6. Bedroom
7. Bathroom
8. Pool
9. Covered parking
10. Planter
11. Patio
12. Closet
13. Private patio
14. Living area
15. Dining area
16. Kitchen
17. Mud room
18. Office/sleeping room
19. Covered porch

## LIVE OAK

Austin, Texas, United States // Lot area: 63,369 sq ft; building area: 7,400 sq ft

The modern exterior of this stunning home is composed of a series of layers, unfolding behind a dense tree cover of mature live oak trees. Reserved and serene from a distance, close attention to detail and careful selection of materials create a unique and strikingly modern home that complements the existing neighborhood fabric. A thin, linear form stretches along the contours of the steeply sloping hillside. The living spaces on the main floor transition from grounded in the site to completely transparent, floating over the lower level in a breathtaking cantilever. This composition results in an elegantly articulated series of indoor and outdoor spaces that make the most of the striking hill-country views.

L'extérieur moderne de cette maison étonnante est composé d'une série de couches, se déployant derrière une couverture arborée dense de chênes vivants matures. Réservée et sereine de loin, l'attention portée aux détails et la sélection minutieuse des matériaux créent une maison unique et étonnamment moderne qui s'intègre au tissu existant du quartier. Une forme mince et linéaire s'étire le long des contours de la colline en pente raide. Les espaces de vie du rez-de-chaussée passent de l'ancrage dans le site à la transparence totale, flottant au-dessus du niveau inférieur dans un cantilever à couper le souffle. Cette composition donne lieu à une série d'espaces intérieurs et extérieurs élégamment articulés qui tirent le meilleur parti des vues saisissantes sur la colline.

Das moderne Äußere dieses atemberaubenden Hauses besteht aus einer Reihe von Schichten, die sich hinter einem dichten Baumbestand aus alten Eichen entfalten. Aus der Ferne wirkt es zurückhaltend und ruhig, doch die Liebe zum Detail und die sorgfältige Auswahl der Materialien schaffen ein einzigartiges und auffallend modernes Haus, das sich in die bestehende Nachbarschaft einfügt. Eine schlanke, lineare Form erstreckt sich entlang der Konturen des steil abfallenden Hangs. Die Wohnräume im Hauptgeschoss gehen von der Bodenhaftung in völlige Transparenz über und schweben in einer atemberaubenden Auskragung über der unteren Ebene. Diese Komposition ergibt eine elegant gegliederte Reihe von Innen- und Außenräumen, die das Beste aus der beeindruckenden Aussicht auf die Hügel machen.

El moderno exterior de esta impresionante casa se compone de una serie de capas, que se despliegan detrás de una densa cubierta de robles vivos maduros. Reservada y serena desde la distancia, la atención a los detalles y la cuidadosa selección de materiales crean una casa única y sorprendentemente moderna que complementa el tejido existente en el vecindario. Una forma delgada y lineal se extiende a lo largo de los contornos de la ladera de fuerte pendiente. Los espacios habitables de la planta principal pasan de estar anclados en el lugar a ser completamente transparentes, flotando sobre el nivel inferior en un impresionante voladizo. Esta composición da lugar a una serie de espacios interiores y exteriores elegantemente articulados que aprovechan al máximo las impresionantes vistas de la colina.

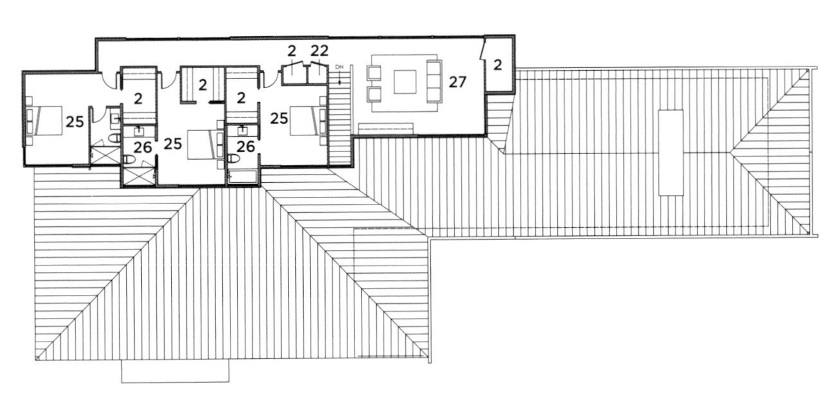

Upper floor plan

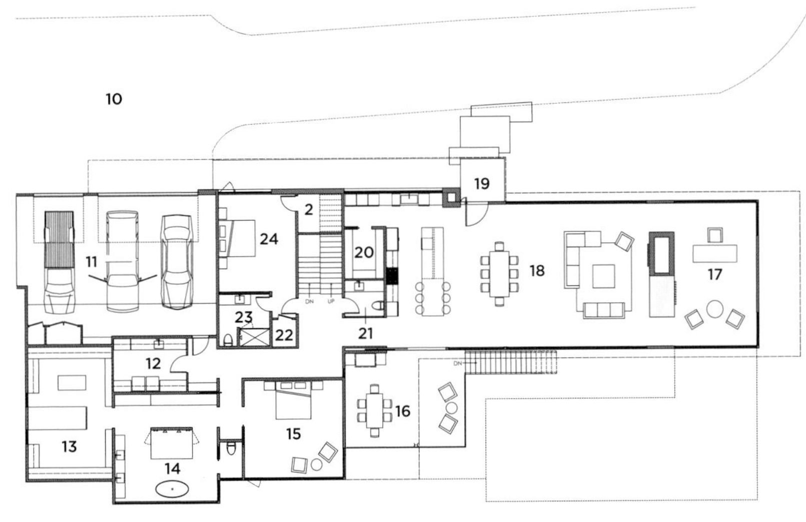

Main floor plan

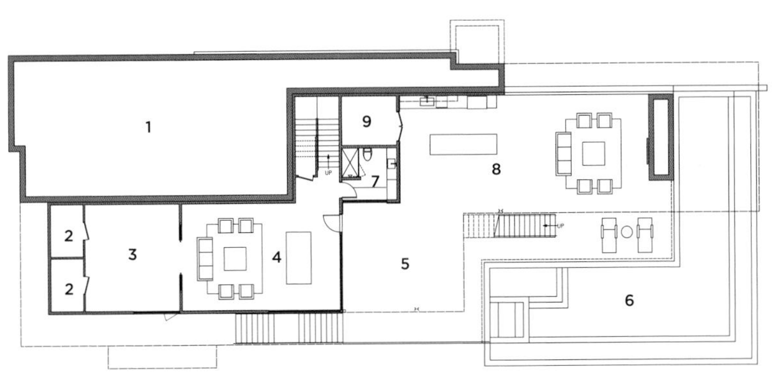

Lower floor plan

1. Foundation above
2. Closet
3. Studio
4. Game room/cabana
5. Pool deck
6. Pool
7. Pool bathroom
8. Outdoor living space
9. Storage
10. Driveway/turnaround
11. Garage
12. Utility room
13. Master closet
14. Master bathroom
15. Master bedroom
16. Deck
17. Study
18. Kitchen/dining/living
19. Front entry
20. Pantry
21. Powder room
22. Mechanical room
23. Guest bathroom
24. Guest bedroom
25. Bedroom
26. Bathroom
27. Lounge

## SKYBOX

Austin, Texas, United States // Lot area: 8,071 sq ft; building area: 4,556 sq ft

This speculative home originated as a conversation about how most new houses in Austin seemed forced and without real design thought. Coming from the custom residential mindset, the Skybox embodies the challenge to create a house that raises the overall quality of a home and the quality of life for residents whom we may never meet. Skybox is composed of two simple and elegant forms complemented with a sense of discovery, from the entry sequence that engages visitors in a visual and tactile experience to the floor plan that opens up to the landscape. Doors and windows are strategically placed to bring in comforting natural light and frame views above the neighboring homes without sacrificing privacy. The result is a home with the design aspects that everyone appreciates in custom residential projects yet reformulated to become suitable for any homeowner.

Cette maison spéculative est née d'une conversation sur le fait que la plupart des nouvelles maisons à Austin semblaient forcées et sans réelle réflexion sur le design. Issue de l'esprit des résidences personnalisées, la Skybox incarne le défi de créer une maison qui améliore la qualité globale d'une habitation et la qualité de vie de résidents que nous ne rencontrerons peut-être jamais. Skybox se compose de deux formes simples et élégantes complétées par un sens de la découverte, de la séquence d'entrée qui engage les visiteurs dans une expérience visuelle et tactile au plan d'étage qui s'ouvre sur le paysage. Les portes et les fenêtres sont placées stratégiquement pour faire entrer une lumière naturelle réconfortante et encadrer les vues sur les maisons voisines sans sacrifier l'intimité. Le résultat est une maison avec les aspects de conception que tout le monde apprécie dans les projets résidentiels personnalisés, mais reformulée pour convenir à tout propriétaire.

Dieses Haus entstand als Gespräch darüber, wie die meisten neuen Häuser in Austin gezwungen und gedankenlos wirken. Skybox kommt aus dem Bereich des individuellen Wohnungsbaus und verkörpert die Herausforderung, ein Haus zu schaffen, das die Gesamtqualität eines Hauses und die Lebensqualität der Bewohner erhöht, die wir vielleicht nie kennenlernen. Die Skybox besteht aus zwei einfachen und eleganten Formen, die durch einen Sinn für Entdeckungen ergänzt werden, von der Eingangssequenz, die den Besucher zu einem visuellen und taktilen Erlebnis einlädt, bis hin zum Grundriss, der sich zur Landschaft hin öffnet. Türen und Fenster sind strategisch so platziert, dass sie angenehmes natürliches Licht hereinlassen und den Blick auf die benachbarten Häuser freigeben, ohne die Privatsphäre zu beeinträchtigen. Das Ergebnis ist ein Haus mit den Designaspekten, die jeder an maßgeschneiderten Wohnprojekten schätzt, das jedoch so umgestaltet wurde, dass es sich für jeden Hausbesitzer eignet.

Esta casa se originó como una conversación sobre cómo la mayoría de las casas nuevas en Austin parecían forzadas y sin una verdadera reflexion sobre el diseño. Procedente de la mentalidad residencial personalizada, la Skybox encarna el reto de crear una casa que eleve la calidad de un hogar y la calidad de vida de los residentes a los que quizá nunca conozcamos. Skybox se compone de dos formas sencillas y elegantes que se complementan con una sensación de descubrimiento, desde la secuencia de entrada que involucra a los visitantes en una experiencia visual y táctil hasta la planta que se abre al paisaje. Las puertas y ventanas están colocadas estratégicamente para que entre una luz natural reconfortante y enmarquen las vistas sobre las casas vecinas sin sacrificar la privacidad. El resultado es una casa con los aspectos de diseño que todo el mundo aprecia en los proyectos residenciales a medida, pero reformulada para que se adapte a cualquier propietario.

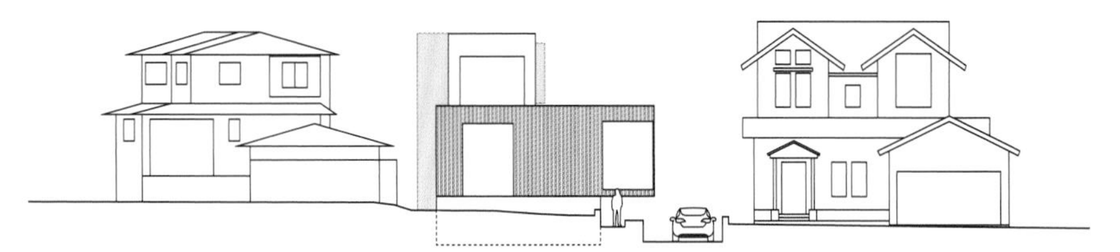

Street context elevation

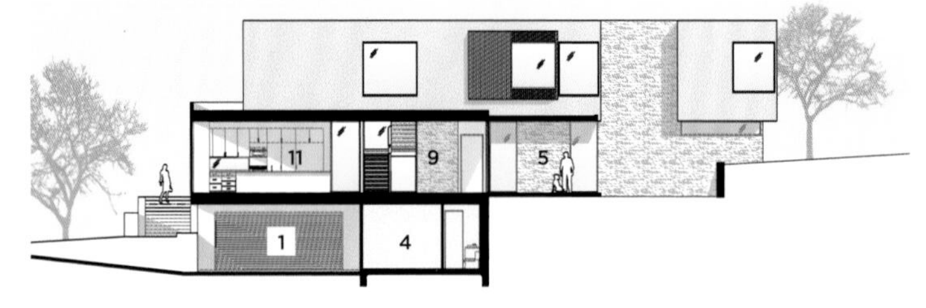


Section

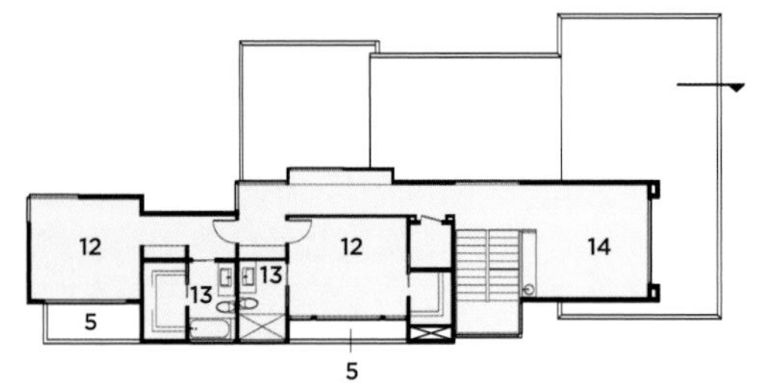


Second floor plan

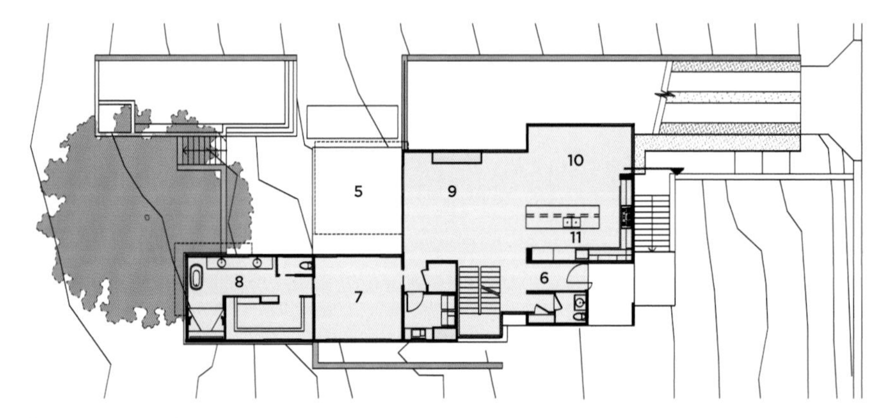


Site and ground floor plan

1. Driveway
2. Garage
3. Storage
4. Basement
5. Patio
6. Entry
7. Master bedroom
8. Master bathroom
9. Living area
10. Dining area
11. Kitchen
12. Bedroom
13. Bathroom
14. Flex. space

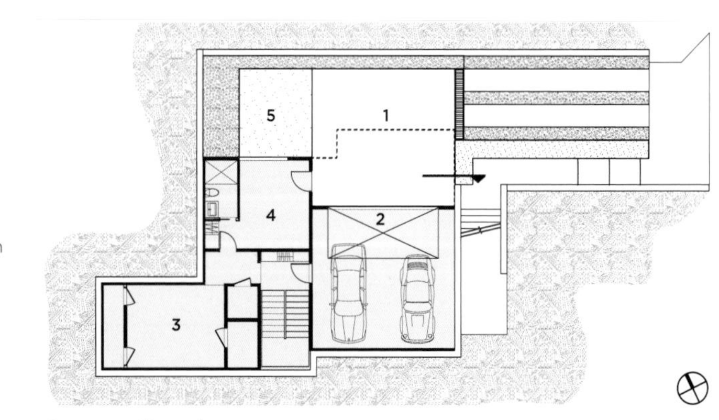


Basement floor plan

# A. GRUPPO

194
v

**ALDWICK RESIDENCE**

Architecture Design team:
A.GRUPPO
Photographer:
© Charles Davis Smith, FAIA

198
v

**RIVERBEND RESIDENCE**

Architecture Design team:
A.GRUPPO
Photographer:
© Dror Baldinger, AIA

202
v

**16 VANGUARD**

Architecture Design team:
A.GRUPPO
Photographer:
© Thad Reeves, AIA

www.agruppo.com a_gruppo_architects

Andrew Nance

Thad Reeves

Andrew Nance and Thad Reeves founded A Gruppo in 2005, and their steady growth has led the studio to run offices in San Marcos and Dallas. They both share a passion for teaching—Nance at UT Arlington and currently at Texas State University and Reeves at UT Arlington—a passion they see as an opportunity to offer and hear critique, incubate ideas, and maintain a sense of exploration in every project. The name A Gruppo signifies not only a group of people but also a group effort. In this context, Nance and Reeves collaborate with professionals—and on occasions with their students—to draw on their expertise. A Gruppo specializes in residential and small commercial projects, each project building on its predecessor in the matter of material exploration or construction technology. With a growing list of Central Texas projects that have received wide acclaim, A Gruppo have developed a distinctly modern Hill Country vernacular informed by the building traditions of the region.

Andrew Nance und Thad Reeves gründeten A Gruppo im Jahr 2005, und ihr stetiges Wachstum hat das Studio dazu veranlasst, Büros in San Marcos und Dallas zu betreiben. Beide teilen eine Leidenschaft für das Unterrichten - Nance an der UT Arlington und derzeit an der Texas State University und Reeves an der UT Arlington - eine Leidenschaft, die sie als Gelegenheit sehen, Kritik zu äußern und anzuhören, Ideen zu inkubieren und bei jedem Projekt ein Gefühl der Erforschung zu bewahren. Der Name A Gruppo steht nicht nur für eine Gruppe von Menschen, sondern auch für eine Gruppenleistung. In diesem Zusammenhang arbeiten Nance und Reeves mit Fachleuten - und gelegentlich mit ihren Studenten - zusammen, um auf deren Fachwissen zurückzugreifen. A Gruppo ist spezialisiert auf Wohn- und kleine Gewerbeprojekte, wobei jedes Projekt in Sachen Materialexploration oder Bautechnologie auf seinem Vorgänger aufbaut. Mit einer wachsenden Liste von Projekten in Zentraltexas, die breite Anerkennung gefunden haben, hat A Gruppo eine ausgesprochen moderne Umgangssprache des Hill Country entwickelt, die von den Bautraditionen der Region geprägt ist.

Andrew Nance et Thad Reeves ont fondé A Gruppo en 2005, et leur croissance constante a conduit le studio à gérer des bureaux à San Marcos et à Dallas. Ils partagent tous deux une passion pour l'enseignement - Nance à UT Arlington et actuellement à la Texas State University et Reeves à UT Arlington - une passion qu'ils considèrent comme une opportunité d'offrir et d'entendre des critiques, d'incuber des idées et de maintenir un sens de l'exploration dans chaque projet. Le nom A Gruppo signifie non seulement un groupe de personnes mais aussi un effort de groupe. Dans ce contexte, Nance et Reeves collaborent avec des professionnels - et parfois avec leurs étudiants - pour tirer parti de leur expertise. A Gruppo se spécialise dans les projets résidentiels et les petits projets commerciaux, chaque projet s'appuyant sur son prédécesseur en matière d'exploration de matériaux ou de technologie de construction. Avec une liste croissante de projets du centre du Texas qui ont reçu un large succès, A Gruppo a développé une langue vernaculaire Hill Country résolument moderne informée par les traditions de construction de la région.

Andrew Nance y Thad Reeves fundaron A Gruppo en 2005 y su constante crecimiento ha llevado al estudio a tener oficinas en San Marcos y Dallas. Ambos comparten una pasión por la enseñanza: Nance en UT Arlington y actualmente en Texas State University y Reeves en UT Arlington, una pasión que ven como una oportunidad para ofrecer y escuchar críticas, incubar ideas y mantener un sentido de exploración en cada proyecto. El nombre A Gruppo significa no solo un grupo de personas sino también un esfuerzo grupal. En este contexto, Nance y Reeves colaboran con profesionales -y en ocasiones con sus alumnos- para aprovechar su experiencia. A Gruppo se especializa en proyectos residenciales y comerciales pequeños, y cada proyecto se basa en su predecesor en materia de exploración de materiales o tecnología de construcción. Con una lista creciente de proyectos del centro de Texas que han recibido un gran reconocimiento, A Gruppo ha desarrollado una lengua vernácula distintivamente moderna de Hill Country informada por las tradiciones de construcción de la región.

## ALDWICK RESIDENCE

Dallas, Texas, United States // Building area: 3,200 sq ft

To design this modern house, A. Gruppo drew inspiration from a mature oak tree in the front yard and the surrounding properties on the same street. The owners wanted a contemporary home that would not stand out but blend with the neighboring homes. To this end, the house exterior combines brick and shake siding, echoing the materials on other nearby properties. The design of the house adapts sensibly to its context, making the most of the views while providing privacy. Inside, the spaces are open and bright, spilling onto a private rear yard that invites outdoor living.

Pour concevoir cette maison moderne, A. Gruppo s'est inspiré d'un chêne mature dans la cour avant et des propriétés environnantes dans la même rue. Les propriétaires voulaient une maison contemporaine qui ne se démarquerait pas mais se fondrait avec les maisons voisines. À cette fin, l'extérieur de la maison combine un revêtement en brique et en bardeau de fente, faisant écho aux matériaux des autres propriétés voisines. La conception de la maison s'adapte judicieusement à son contexte, tirant le meilleur parti des vues tout en préservant l'intimité. À l'intérieur, les espaces sont ouverts et lumineux, débordant sur une cour arrière privée qui invite à la vie en plein air.

Um dieses moderne Haus zu entwerfen, ließ sich A. Gruppo von einer ausgewachsenen Eiche im Vorgarten und den umliegenden Grundstücken in derselben Straße inspirieren. Die Eigentümer wollten ein zeitgemäßes Haus, das nicht auffällt, sondern sich in die Nachbarhäuser einfügt. Zu diesem Zweck kombiniert das Äußere des Hauses Ziegel- und Schüttelverkleidungen und spiegelt die Materialien anderer nahe gelegener Grundstücke wider. Das Design des Hauses passt sich sinnvoll seinem Kontext an, macht das Beste aus der Aussicht und bietet gleichzeitig Privatsphäre. Im Inneren sind die Räume offen und hell und gehen auf einen privaten Hinterhof über, der zum Leben im Freien einlädt.

Para diseñar esta casa moderna, A. Gruppo se inspiró en un roble maduro en el patio delantero y las propiedades circundantes en la misma calle. Los propietarios querían una casa contemporánea que no se destacara sino que se mezclara con las casas vecinas. Con este fin, el exterior de la casa combina ladrillos y revestimientos de listones, haciéndose eco de los materiales de otras propiedades cercanas. El diseño de la casa se adapta con sensatez a su contexto, aprovechando al máximo las vistas y proporcionando privacidad. En el interior, los espacios son abiertos y luminosos, y se extienden hacia un patio trasero privado que invita a la vida al aire libre.

## RIVERBEND RESIDENCE

San Marcos, Texas, United States // Building area: 3,300 sq ft

The owners of the Riverbend Residence wanted a uniquely personal floor plan, good use of natural light, and strong connections to the outdoors. The architects designed the house as a nod to the vernacular stone buildings that might have belonged to a neighboring quarry and had recently been updated with glass and steel elements. The house plan is broken into three buildings that wrap around an existing grove of Live oaks that creates a screen between the house and the street and a sense that the house has been there for a long time. The buildings are oriented to allow breezes and the updraft from a nearby river to flow through the interiors comfortably while also managing the heat load during the summer. Various outdoor spaces at the rear of the house provide sheltered and open areas to take in views and sunsets.

Les propriétaires de la résidence Riverbend souhaitaient un plan d'étage unique et personnalisé, une bonne utilisation de la lumière naturelle et des liens étroits avec l'extérieur. Les architectes ont conçu la maison comme un clin d'œil aux bâtiments en pierre vernaculaire qui auraient pu appartenir à une carrière voisine et qui ont été récemment modernisés avec des éléments en verre et en acier. Le plan de la maison est divisé en trois bâtiments qui s'enroulent autour d'un bosquet existant de chênes verts qui crée un écran entre la maison et la rue et donne l'impression que la maison est là depuis longtemps. Les bâtiments sont orientés de manière à permettre aux brises et au courant ascendant d'une rivière voisine de circuler confortablement à l'intérieur, tout en gérant la charge thermique pendant l'été. Divers espaces extérieurs à l'arrière de la maison offrent des zones abritées et ouvertes pour profiter des vues et des couchers de soleil.

Die Eigentümer der Riverbend Residence wünschten sich einen ganz persönlichen Grundriss, eine gute Nutzung des natürlichen Lichts und eine starke Verbindung zur Außenwelt. Die Architekten entwarfen das Haus als Anspielung auf die traditionellen Steingebäude, die möglicherweise zu einem benachbarten Steinbruch gehörten und vor kurzem mit Glas- und Stahlelementen modernisiert worden waren. Das Haus ist in drei Gebäude unterteilt, die sich um einen bestehenden Hain von Traubeneichen winden, der das Haus von der Straße abschirmt und den Eindruck vermittelt, dass das Haus schon seit langem dort steht. Die Gebäude sind so ausgerichtet, dass Brisen und der Aufwind eines nahe gelegenen Flusses bequem durch die Innenräume strömen können, während gleichzeitig die Wärmebelastung in den Sommermonaten gemanagt wird. Verschiedene Außenbereiche auf der Rückseite des Hauses bieten geschützte und offene Bereiche, um die Aussicht und die Sonnenuntergänge zu genießen.

Los propietarios de la Residencia Riverbend querían una planta única y personal, un buen uso de la luz natural y fuertes conexiones con el exterior. Los arquitectos diseñaron la casa como un guiño a los edificios vernáculos de piedra que podrían haber pertenecido a una cantera vecina y que habían sido actualizados recientemente con elementos de vidrio y acero. La planta de la casa está dividida en tres edificios que rodean una arboleda de robles vivos que crea una pantalla entre la casa y la calle y una sensación de que la vivienda ha estado allí durante mucho tiempo. Los edificios están orientados para que la brisa y la corriente ascendente de un río cercano fluyan cómodamente por los interiores, al tiempo que se gestiona la carga de calor durante el verano. Varios espacios exteriores en la parte trasera de la casa ofrecen zonas protegidas y abiertas para disfrutar de las vistas y las puestas de sol.

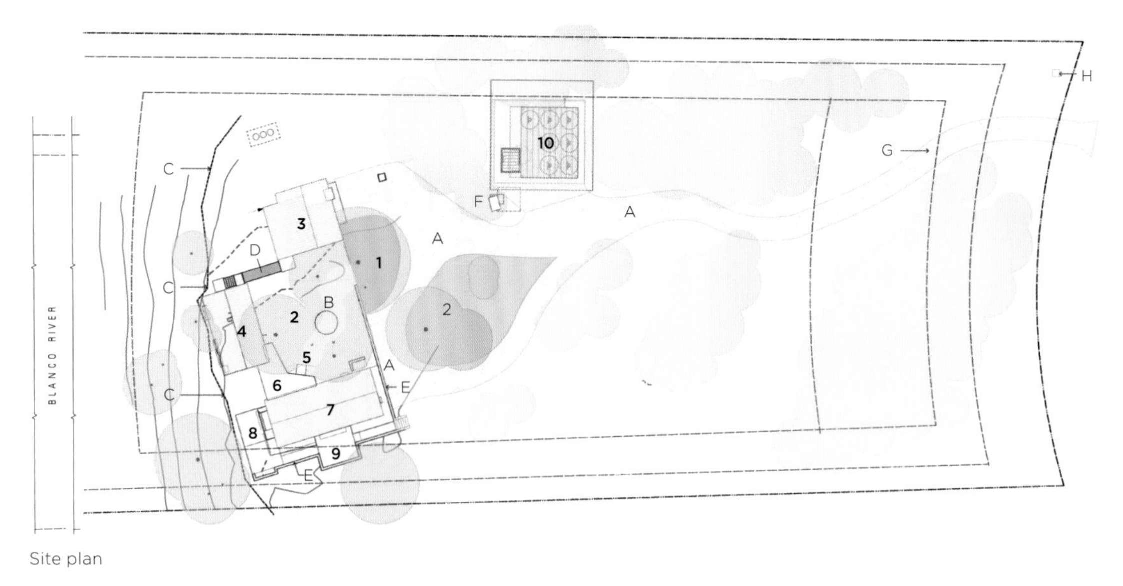


Site plan

1. Courtyard entry
2. Courtyard
3. Garage and guest room
4. Master suite
5. Front door
6. Dining room
7. Main house
8. Deck
9. Patio
10. Rainwater barn

A. Driveway
B. Protected trees with mulch base
C. Approx. edge bluff
D. Ramp
E. Retaining wall
F. Transformer
G. New driveway along existing path
H. Existing electrical transformer

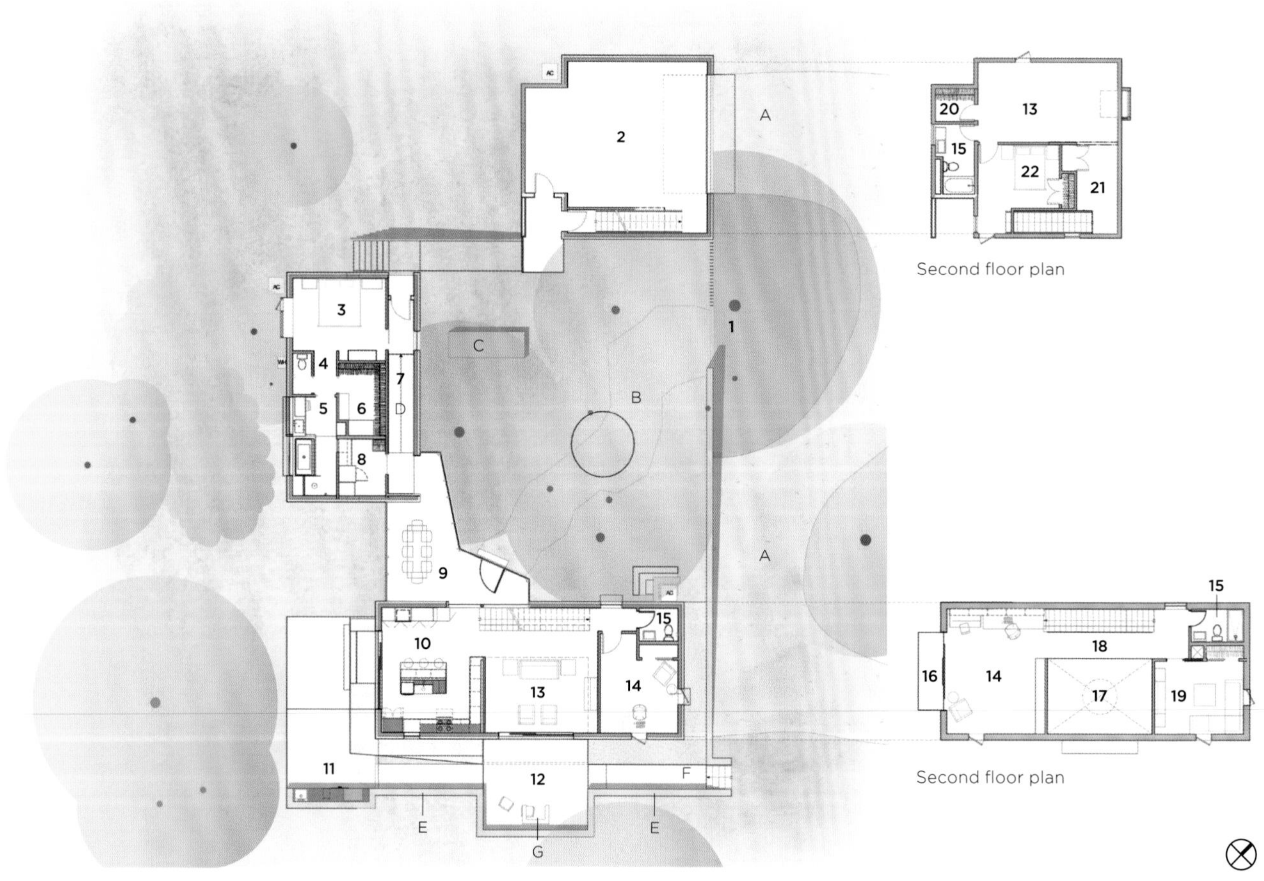

Second floor plan

Second floor plan

First floor plan

1. Courtyard entry
2. Garage
3. Master suite
4. Water closet
5. Master bathroom
6. Walk-in closet
7. Hallway
8. Laundry room
9. Dining room
10. Kitchen
11. Barbecue area
12. Living room patio
13. Living room
14. Studio
15. Bathroom
16. Balcony
17. Open to below
18. Bridge
19. TV room
20. Storage
21. Guest room
22. Loft

A. Driveway
B. Stone paver walkway
C. Steel planter
D. Ramp down
E. Retaining wall
F. Back access
G. Fire pit

## 16 VANGUARD

Dallas, Texas, United States // Building area: 2,500 sq ft

16 Vanguard Way is located at the north end of the Urban Reserve's main pond in Dallas, with the main entry facade fronting Vanguard Way to the west and the south facade looking out across the main pond.The clients desired to take advantage of the views on the site, in particular the pond. Maximizing the glass on the ground floor was a driving design. One of the main issues in dealing with the exterior design of the house was how to address the street facade and the pond facade as competing elements. As a strategy to develop more facade area, a garden wall was implemented, continuing the sense of containment started by the neighboring house. The garden wall is also a device to provide a modern take on the porch concept, offering privacy to the essentially all-glass lower level.

Le 16 Vanguard Way est situé à l'extrémité nord de l'étang principal de l'Urban Reserve à Dallas, la façade de l'entrée principale donnant sur Vanguard Way à l'ouest et la façade sud donnant sur l'étang principal. Les clients souhaitaient profiter des vues du site, en particulier de l'étang. La maximisation du verre au rez-de-chaussée a été un élément moteur de la conception. L'un des principaux problèmes de la conception extérieure de la maison était de savoir comment aborder la façade sur la rue et la façade sur l'étang comme des éléments concurrents. Afin de développer une plus grande surface de façade, un mur de jardin a été mis en place, poursuivant le sentiment de confinement initié par la maison voisine. Le mur de jardin est également un moyen de fournir une version moderne du concept de porche, offrant une certaine intimité au niveau inférieur essentiellement entièrement en verre.

16 Vanguard Way liegt am nördlichen Ende des Hauptteichs des Urban Reserve in Dallas, wobei die Haupteingangsfassade nach Westen auf den Vanguard Way und die Südfassade auf den Hauptteich ausgerichtet ist. Die Bauherren wollten die Aussicht auf das Gelände, insbesondere auf den Teich, optimal nutzen. Die Maximierung des Glasanteils im Erdgeschoss war ein wichtiger Aspekt des Entwurfs. Eine der Hauptfragen bei der Außengestaltung des Hauses war, wie die Straßenfassade und die Teichfassade als konkurrierende Elemente behandelt werden sollten. Um mehr Fassadenfläche zu gewinnen, wurde eine Gartenmauer errichtet, die das vom Nachbarhaus ausgehende Gefühl der Begrenzung fortsetzt. Die Gartenmauer ist auch eine moderne Variante des Verandakonzepts und bietet Privatsphäre für die im Wesentlichen vollständig verglaste untere Ebene.

El 16 de Vanguard Way está situado en el extremo norte del estanque principal de la Reserva Urbana de Dallas, con la fachada de entrada principal frente a Vanguard Way hacia el oeste y la fachada sur mirando hacia el estanque principal. Los clientes deseaban aprovechar las vistas del lugar, en particular del estanque. La maximización del vidrio en la planta baja fue un diseño impulsor. Uno de los principales problemas a la hora de abordar el diseño exterior era cómo abordar la fachada de la calle y la del estanque como elementos que compiten entre sí. Como estrategia para desarrollar más superficie de fachada, se implementó un muro ajardinado, continuando la sensación de contención iniciada por la casa vecina. El muro del jardín es también un dispositivo para proporcionar una versión moderna del concepto de porche, ofreciendo privacidad al nivel inferior, esencialmente de cristal.

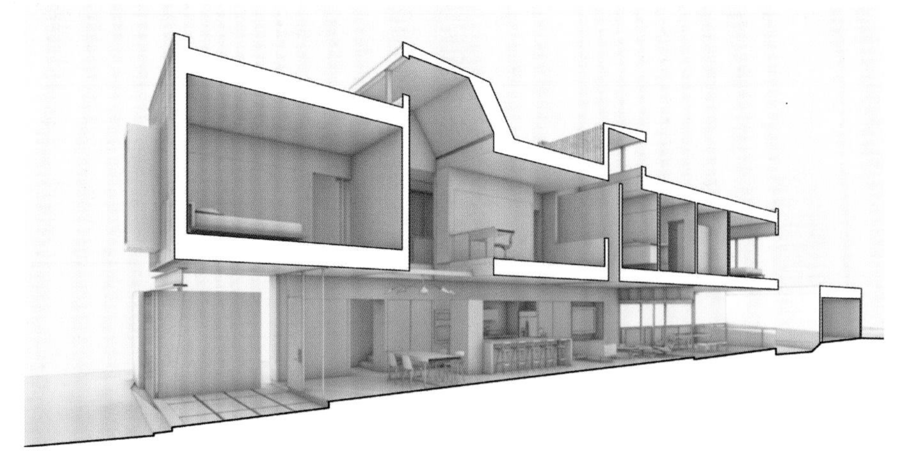

Perspective section

Building section

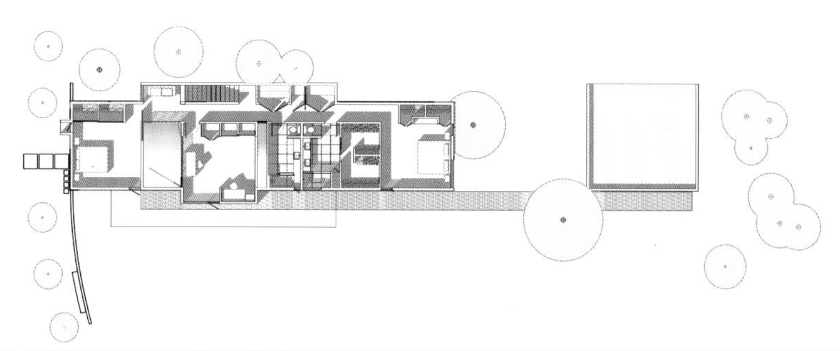

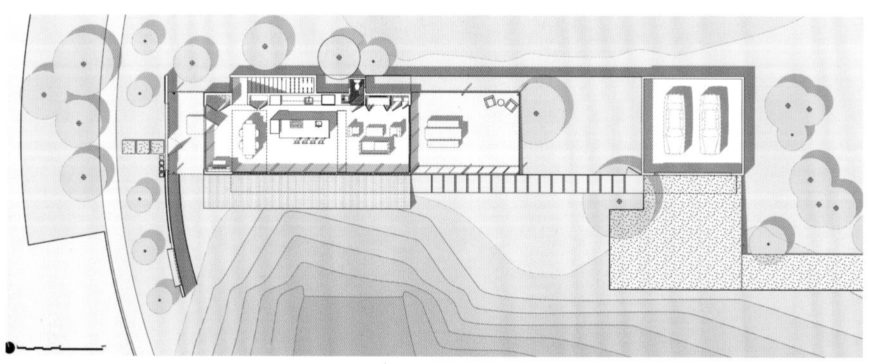

Floor plan

# BURLESON DESIGN GROUP

208
v

**RANCHO GRAN CUMBRE**

Architectural Design Team:
Rick Burleson AIA, David Costea, Tommy Horine
Structural Engineer:
Gessner Engineering
Builder:
Schmidt Custom Homes
Photographer:
© Casey Fry

212
v

**CREEK ROAD RETREAT**

Architectural Design Team:
Rick Burleson AIA, Camelo Colca
Structural Engineer:
Gessner Engineering
Builder:
Schmidt Custom Homes
Photographer:
© Casey Fry

216
v

**OAK HEIGHTS HAVEN**

Architectural Design Team:
Rick Burleson AIA, David Costea, Camelo Colca
Structural Engineer:
Gessner Engineering
Builder:
Burnette Builders
Photographer:
© Casey Fry

www.burlesondesigngroup.com

Burleson Design Group—based in Wimberley, Texas—is focused on the creation of distinctive ranch homes and family retreats throughout the Texas Hill Country since 2004. Our architectural team, along with a network of experienced contractors, interior designers, and engineers, create places that provide enjoyment to the residents and their guests for generations to come. Our design approach integrates three primary forces—Client · Climate · Land—to develop one-of-a-kind homes that respond to our clients' aspirations, are shaped for the sun and breeze, and engage with the land's natural beauty.

Die Burleson Design Group mit Sitz in Wimberley, Texas, konzentriert sich seit 2004 auf die Gestaltung von unverwechselbaren Ranchhäusern und Familienresidenzen im Texas Hill Country. Unser Architektenteam arbeitet mit einem Netzwerk von erfahrenen Bauunternehmern, Innenarchitekten und Ingenieuren zusammen, um Orte zu schaffen, die den Bewohnern und ihren Gästen über Generationen hinweg Freude bereiten. Unser Designansatz integriert drei Hauptkräfte - Kunde · Klima · Land - um einzigartige Häuser zu entwickeln, die den Wünschen unserer Kunden entsprechen, die für die Sonne und die Brise geformt sind und die die natürliche Schönheit des Landes einbeziehen.

Burleson Design Group, dont le siège se trouve à Wimberley, au Texas, se concentre depuis 2004 sur la création de ranchs et de retraites familiales distinctives dans le Texas Hill Country. Notre équipe d'architectes, ainsi qu'un réseau d'entrepreneurs, de décorateurs d'intérieur et d'ingénieurs expérimentés, créent des lieux qui procurent du plaisir aux résidents et à leurs invités pour les générations à venir. Notre approche de la conception intègre trois forces principales - Client, Climat · Terre - pour développer des maisons uniques en leur genre qui répondent aux aspirations de nos clients, qui sont façonnées pour le soleil et la brise et qui s'engagent dans la beauté naturelle de la terre.

Burleson Design Group, con sede en Wimberley, Texas, se centra en la creación de casas rancho y retiros familiares distintivos en todo el Texas Hill Country desde 2004. Nuestro equipo de arquitectos, junto con una red de experimentados contratistas, diseñadores de interiores e ingenieros, crean lugares que proporcionan disfrute a los residentes y a sus invitados durante generaciones. Nuestro enfoque de diseño integra tres fuerzas principales -Cliente · Clima · Tierra- para desarrollar casas únicas en su tipo que responden a las aspiraciones de nuestros clientes, están formadas para el sol y la brisa, y se involucran con la belleza natural del terreno.

## RANCHO GRAN CUMBRE

Central Texas, United States // Building area: 7,849 sq ft house + 550 sq ft garage

This project—more than most—required careful, artful, site-driven design. The buildings are arrayed along a U-shaped plateau, hugging the hillside and overlooking a ravine. The shifting cardinality of rooms ensures full advantage of all hilltop views and creates a sprawling effect that gives the clients their desired "room to ramble". Facing due south with the site's most rewarding vista, the great room's massive 12 x 24-inch structural glulam beams provide a ten-foot cantilevered overhang to protect the faceted window wall against the harsh Texas sun. To its side, the home brew pub opens onto a shared southern patio, edged along the view with a pool that cools entering breezes. Rainwater catchment, a solar array on the south-facing hillside, and a small vegetable garden add environmental resilience to the summit ranch.

Ce projet, plus que tout autre, a nécessité une conception soignée, artistique et adaptée au site. Les bâtiments sont disposés le long d'un plateau en U, épousant le flanc de la colline et surplombant un ravin. L'évolution de la cardinalité des pièces permet de profiter pleinement de toutes les vues sur la colline et crée un effet tentaculaire qui donne aux clients l'espace souhaité pour « divaguer ». Orientées plein sud, avec la vue la plus gratifiante du site, les poutres massives en lamellé-collé de 12 x 24 pouces de la grande salle offrent un surplomb en porte-à-faux de dix pieds pour protéger le mur de fenêtres à facettes contre le dur soleil du Texas. Sur le côté, le pub de bière artisanale s'ouvre sur un patio méridional partagé, bordé le long de la vue par une piscine qui rafraîchit les brises entrantes. La récupération des eaux de pluie, un panneau solaire sur le versant sud de la colline et un petit jardin potager ajoutent une résistance environnementale au ranch du sommet.

Dieses Projekt erforderte - mehr als die meisten anderen - ein sorgfältiges, kunstvolles und standortbezogenes Design. Die Gebäude sind entlang eines U-förmigen Plateaus angeordnet, das sich an den Hang schmiegt und eine Schlucht überblickt. Die wechselnde Kardinalität der Räume sorgt dafür, dass alle Ausblicke auf den Hügel voll genutzt werden können, und schafft einen weitläufigen Effekt, der den Bauherren den gewünschten „Raum zum Wandern" bietet. Die massiven 12 x 24-Zoll-Leimholzbalken des großen Saals, der nach Süden ausgerichtet ist und den schönsten Ausblick des Grundstücks bietet, bilden einen zehn Fuß hohen, freitragenden Überhang, der die facettierte Fensterwand vor der rauen texanischen Sonne schützt. An der Seite öffnet sich die Hausbrauerei zu einer gemeinsamen Südterrasse, die mit einem Pool eingefasst ist, der die eindringende Brise abkühlt. Eine Regenwasserauffanganlage, eine Solaranlage auf dem Südhang und ein kleiner Gemüsegarten machen die Summit Ranch umweltverträglicher.

Este proyecto —más que la mayoría— requería un diseño cuidadoso, artístico y enfocado al lugar. Los edificios están dispuestos a lo largo de una meseta en forma de U, abrazando la ladera y con vistas a un barranco. El cambio en la orientación de las habitaciones permite aprovechar al máximo todas las vistas de la colina y crea un efecto de expansión que da a los clientes su deseado «espacio para pasear». Orientado hacia el sur, con la vista más gratificante del lugar, las enormes vigas estructurales de madera laminada de 12x24 pulgadas del gran salón proporcionan un voladizo de diez piés para proteger la pared de la ventana del duro sol de Texas. A su lado, la cervecería casera se abre a un patio en la parte sur y bordeada con una refrescante piscina. La captación de agua de lluvia, un panel solar en la ladera orientada al sur y un pequeño huerto añaden resistencia medioambiental al rancho.

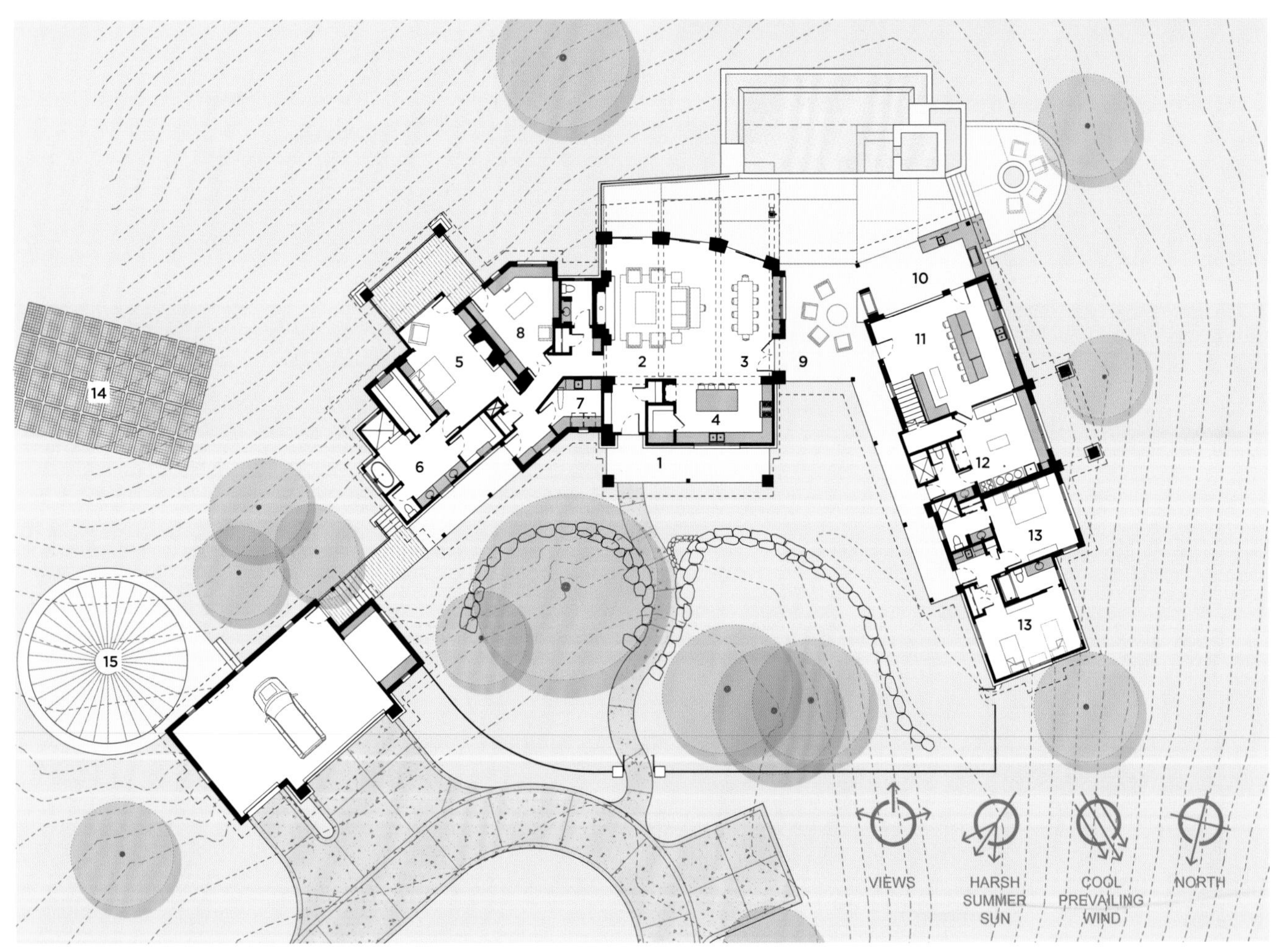


Floor plan

1. Entry porch
2. Living
3. Dining
4. Kitchen
5. Master bedroom
6. Master bathroom
7. Laundry room
8. Office
9. Dogtrot
10. Outdoor kitchen
11. Pub
12. Brew room
13. Bedroom
14. Solar panel array
15. Rainwater storage tank

## CREEK ROAD RETREAT

Centreal Texas, United States // Building area: 5,250 sq ft

Creek Road Retreat is nestled into a hillside among copses of oaks in a quiet corner of the Texas hill country. In this climate, enjoyable outdoor space must be coaxed forth with intentional design. A dogtrot separating the guest rooms from the main house funnels southern breezes over the pool and across the covered porch. The great room's floor-to-ceiling windows let in indirect light from the southwest view while protected by the porch's deep overhangs. Simple shapes and natural materials avoid an ornate feel and reflect the natural setting. Inside, the locally-sourced fossilized limestone hearth is elegant yet unfussy. It harmonizes with the client's collection of fossilized sea shells embedded into the stone columns built using a method of masonry used on existing stone ranch walls on the property.

Creek Road Retreat est niché à flanc de colline, parmi des bosquets de chênes, dans un coin tranquille de la région montagneuse du Texas. Dans ce climat, l'espace extérieur agréable doit être aménagé de manière intentionnelle. Un dogtrot séparant les chambres d'hôtes de la maison principale fait passer la brise du sud au-dessus de la piscine et sous le porche couvert. Les fenêtres du sol au plafond de la grande salle laissent entrer la lumière indirecte de la vue sur le sud-ouest tout en étant protégées par les profonds surplombs du porche. Les formes simples et les matériaux naturels évitent l'aspect ornemental et reflètent le cadre naturel. À l'intérieur, l'âtre en pierre calcaire fossilisée d'origine locale est élégant mais pas trop compliqué. Il s'harmonise avec la collection de coquillages fossilisés du client, encastrée dans les colonnes en pierre construites selon une méthode de maçonnerie utilisée sur les murs de ranch en pierre existants sur la propriété.

Das Creek Road Retreat liegt in einer ruhigen Ecke des texanischen Hügellandes inmitten von Eichenwäldern an einem Berghang. In diesem Klima muss der Außenbereich bewusst gestaltet werden, um ihn zu genießen. Ein Dogtrot, der die Gästezimmer vom Haupthaus trennt, leitet die südliche Brise über den Pool und die überdachte Veranda. Die raumhohen Fenster des großen Zimmers lassen indirektes Licht aus dem Südwesten herein, während sie von den tiefen Überhängen der Veranda geschützt werden. Einfache Formen und natürliche Materialien vermeiden eine verschnörkelte Atmosphäre und spiegeln die natürliche Umgebung wider. Im Inneren ist die Feuerstelle aus versteinertem Kalkstein aus der Region elegant und doch schlicht. Er harmoniert mit der Sammlung versteinerter Muscheln des Bauherrn, die in die Steinsäulen eingebettet sind, die nach einer Methode gemauert wurden, die bereits bei den Steinmauern der Ranch auf dem Grundstück verwendet wurde.

Creek Road Retreat está enclavado en la ladera de una colina, entre bosquecillos de robles, en un tranquilo rincón de la región montañosa de Texas. En este clima, el espacio exterior agradable debe ser provocado con un diseño intencionado. Un pasillo que separa las habitaciones de los huéspedes de la casa principal hace que las brisas del sur pasen por encima de la piscina y por el porche cubierto. Los ventanales del suelo al techo del gran salón dejan pasar la luz indirecta de la vista del suroeste mientras están protegidos por los profundos voladizos del porche. Las formas sencillas y los materiales naturales sin ornamentos reflejan el entorno natural. En el interior, la chimenea de piedra caliza fosilizada de origen local es elegante pero sin pretensiones. Armoniza con la colección del cliente de conchas marinas fosilizadas incrustadas en las columnas de piedra construidas con un método de albañilería utilizado en los muros de piedra existentes en la propiedad.

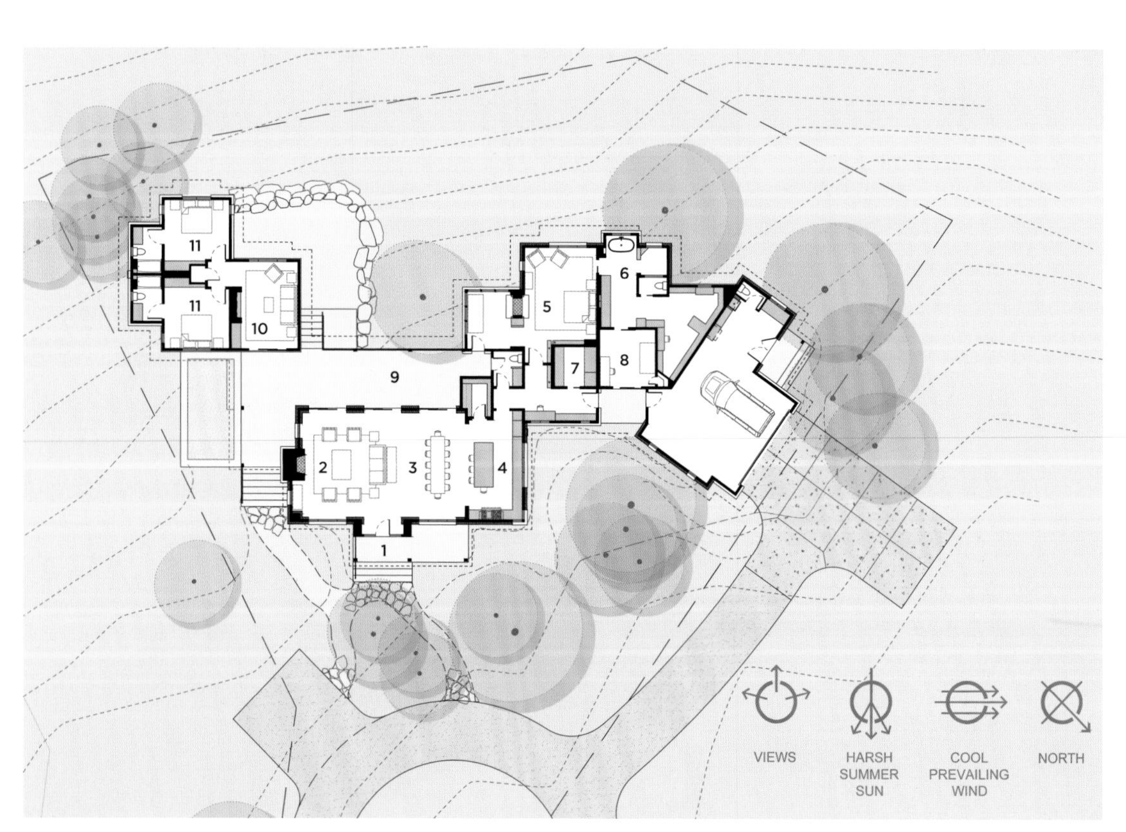


1. Entry porch
2. Living
3. Dining
4. Kitchen
5. Master bedroom
6. Master bathroom
7. Laundry room
8. Office
9. Covered porch
10. Den
11. Bedroom

Floor plan

## OAK HEIGHTS HAVEN

Central Texas, United States // Building area: 2,837 sq ft

This retreat rests on a wooded site that gently slopes towards the Blanco River valley. The faceted window wall of the great room traces the slight curve of the ridgeline, capturing views and light. Two guest suites flank the great room as distinct buildings, with covered dogtrots between providing privacy and separation. By funneling prevailing breezes from the river valley, the porches can moderate temperature and thus be a pleasant place to enjoy a sunrise or sunset. The main entertainment building mass playfully leans back and into the earth, allowing the design to get away from the traditional idea of a roof differentiated from a wall. The exterior top and sides are clad in aged corrugated metal, which then wraps with its pristine counterpart onto the interior walls to define and unify.

Cette retraite repose sur un site boisé qui descend en pente douce vers la vallée de la rivière Blanco. Le mur de fenêtres à facettes de la grande salle suit la légère courbe de la ligne de crête, capturant les vues et la lumière. Deux suites d'invités flanquent la grande salle comme des bâtiments distincts, avec des passerelles couvertes entre les deux pour assurer l'intimité et la séparation. En canalisant les brises dominantes de la vallée de la rivière, les porches peuvent modérer la température et ainsi être un endroit agréable pour profiter du lever ou du coucher du soleil. La masse du bâtiment principal de divertissement s'incline de manière ludique vers l'arrière et dans la terre, permettant à la conception de s'éloigner de l'idée traditionnelle d'un toit différencié d'un mur. Le toit et les côtés extérieurs sont revêtus de métal ondulé vieilli, qui s'enroule ensuite avec son homologue immaculé sur les murs intérieurs pour définir et unifier.

Dieser Rückzugsort befindet sich auf einem bewaldeten Grundstück, das sanft zum Tal des Blanco River hin abfällt. Die facettierte Fensterwand des großen Raums folgt der leichten Kurve des Bergrückens und fängt die Aussicht und das Licht ein. Zwei Gästesuiten flankieren den großen Raum als getrennte Gebäude, mit überdachten Dogtrots dazwischen, die für Privatsphäre und Abgrenzung sorgen. Da die Veranden die vorherrschende Brise aus dem Flusstal ableiten, können sie die Temperatur mäßigen und sind somit ein angenehmer Ort, um den Sonnenaufgang oder den Sonnenuntergang zu genießen. Die Hauptmasse des Unterhaltungsgebäudes lehnt sich spielerisch zurück und in die Erde hinein, was es dem Entwurf ermöglicht, sich von der traditionellen Vorstellung eines von der Wand abgehobenen Dachs zu lösen. Die äußere Oberseite und die Seiten sind mit gealtertem Wellblech verkleidet, das sich dann mit seinem ursprünglichen Gegenstück an den Innenwänden umhüllt, um diese zu definieren und zu vereinheitlichen.

Este refugio se encuentra en un terreno boscoso suavemente inclinado hacia el valle del Río Blanco. La pared acristaladas de la gran sala traza la ligera curva de la cresta del volumen, capturando las vistas y la luz. Dos suites de invitados flanquean el gran salón como edificios distintos, con patios cubiertos entre ellos que proporcionan privacidad y separación. Al canalizar las brisas predominantes del valle, los porches pueden moderar la temperatura y ser así un lugar agradable para disfrutar de un amanecer o una puesta de sol. La masa principal del edificio de ocio se inclina hacia atrás y hacia el terreno, lo que permite que el diseño se aleje de la idea tradicional de un techo diferenciado de una pared. La parte superior y los laterales exteriores están revestidos de chapa corrugada envejecida, doblando la esquina con su contraparte prístina en las paredes interiores para definir y unificar.

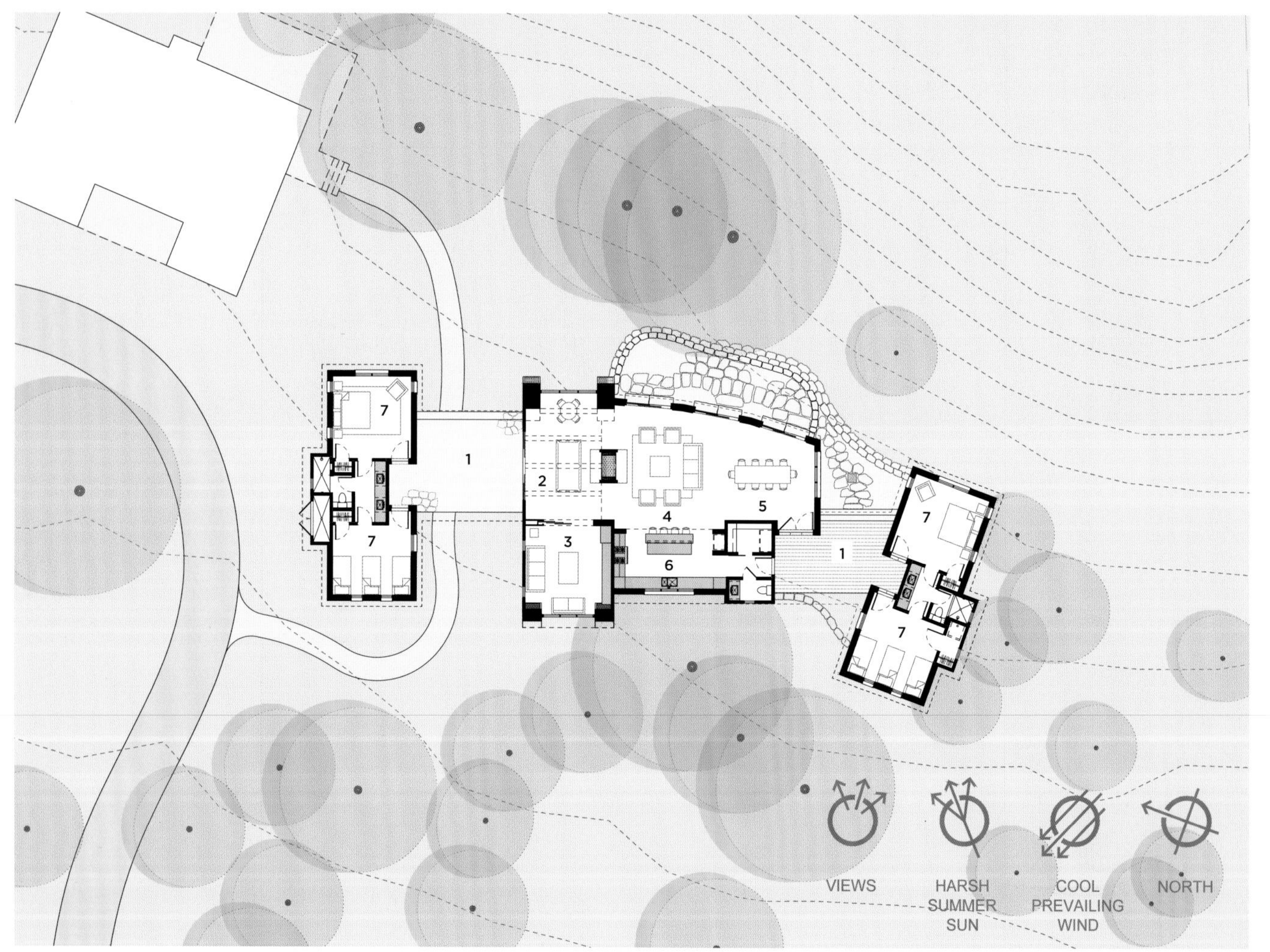


Floor plan

1. Dogtrot
2. Game room
3. Media room
4. Living
5. Dining
6. Kitchen
7. Bedroom

# DAVEY McEATHRON ARCHITECTURE

222
v

**KENWOOD RESIDENCE**

Architecture Design team:
Davey McEathron, AIA and Natalia Sanchez.
Structural Engineer: GreenEarth Engineering
Landscape Architect: Courtney Tarver, LA
Builder: South Austin Development Group
Arborist: Davey Tree
Handmade tiles: Zia Tile
Countertops: Austin Granite Direct
Stucco: Legend Plaster and Stucco
Masonry: Serafin Juarez
Roofing: E&G Roofing
Windows: Martel Windows and Doors
Photographer: © Leonid Furmansky

226
v

**THE PEDERNALES HOUSE**

Architecture Design team:
Davey McEathron, AIA and Bailey Craighead.
Structural Engineer: SEC Solutions
Builder: AVision General Contractors
Arborist: Davey Tree
Handmade tiles: Clay Imports
Roofing: R&L Roofing
Cabinets: Sunset Carpentry
Windows: Accolade Exteriors
Photographer: © Leonid Furmansky

230
v

**SOUTH FOURTH HOUSE AND ADU**

Architecture Design team:
Davey McEathron, AIA; Hunter Tipps, AIA, Natalia Sanchez; and Eric Dethamphaivan.
Structural Engineer: GreenEarth Engineering
Civil Engineer: Servant Engineering
Landscape Architect: Philip Koske, LA
Builder: Urban ATX
Arborist: Davey Tree
Handmade tiles: Clay Imports
Custom Steel Fabrication: Azmitia
Countertops: Austin Granite Direct
Stucco: Legend Plaster and Stucco
Roofing: R&L Roofing
Windows: Accolade Exteriors
Photographer: © Leonid Furmansky

www.daveymarchitecture.com davey.mceathron.architecture

In the summer of 2014, Davey McEathron Architecture was founded upon the idea of the architect as an artist, collaborator, and craftsperson. With an equal amount of space dedicated to a design studio and a fabrication studio, DMA positions itself in a unique location between design, testing, and realization.
After working from a home-based studio for five years, DMA created their new office in the North Loop neighborhood of Austin, Texas—an area known for being paradoxically both laid back and colorful. Starting with an existing building, DMA tore it back to the studs and reimagined both the shell and interior of the structure to reflect the design ethos of the firm and the character of the neighborhood.
DMA takes pride in unique solutions and fine detailing—always perfecting, learning, and reinventing. The firm has become well known for its vibrant interiors, creative geometries, and elegant use of raw materials that exemplify the hand of the craftsperson and speak to the unique culture found in Central Texas.

Im Sommer 2014 wurde Davey McEathron Architecture auf der Grundlage der Idee des Architekten als Künstler, Kollaborateur und Handwerker gegründet. Mit einer gleich großen Fläche, die einem Designstudio und einem Fertigungsstudio gewidmet ist, positioniert sich DMA an einem einzigartigen Ort zwischen Design, Prüfung und Realisierung.
Nachdem DMA fünf Jahre lang von einem Heimstudio aus gearbeitet hatte, richtete das Unternehmen sein neues Büro im Viertel North Loop in Austin, Texas, ein - paradoxerweise - für seine entspannte und farbenfrohe Atmosphäre bekanntes Gebiet ein. DMA begann mit einem bestehenden Gebäude, riss es bis auf die Grundmauern ab und gestaltete sowohl die Hülle als auch das Innere des Gebäudes neu, um das Designethos des Unternehmens und den Charakter des Viertels widerzuspiegeln.
DMA ist stolz auf seine einzigartigen Lösungen und feinen Details - sie perfektionieren, lernen und erfinden sich immer wieder neu. Das Unternehmen ist bekannt für seine lebendigen Innenräume, kreativen Geometrien und die elegante Verwendung von Rohmaterialien, die die Hand des Handwerkers widerspiegeln und die einzigartige Kultur von Zentraltexas widerspiegeln.

Au cours de l'été 2014, Davey McEathron Architecture a été fondé sur l'idée que l'architecte est un artiste, un collaborateur et un artisan. Avec une quantité égale d'espace dédié à un studio de conception et un studio de fabrication, DMA se positionne dans un endroit unique entre la conception, les essais et la réalisation.
Après avoir travaillé dans un studio à domicile pendant cinq ans, DMA a créé son nouveau bureau dans le quartier North Loop d'Austin, au Texas - un quartier connu pour être paradoxalement à la fois décontracté et coloré. Partant d'un bâtiment existant, DMA l'a remis en état et a réimaginé l'enveloppe et l'intérieur de la structure afin de refléter l'esprit de design de l'entreprise et le caractère du quartier.
DMA est fier de ses solutions uniques et de la finesse de ses détails - toujours en train de se perfectionner, d'apprendre et de réinventer. L'entreprise est connue pour ses intérieurs dynamiques, ses géométries créatives et son utilisation élégante de matériaux bruts qui illustrent la main de l'artisan et témoignent de la culture unique du centre du Texas.

En el verano de 2014, Davey McEathron Architecture se fundó sobre la idea del arquitecto como artista, colaborador y artesano. Con una cantidad igual de espacio dedicado a un estudio de diseño y un estudio de fabricación, DMA se posiciona en una ubicación única entre el diseño, la prueba y la realización.
Después de trabajar en un estudio en casa durante cinco años, DMA creó su nueva oficina en el barrio de North Loop de Austin (Texas), una zona conocida por ser paradójicamente relajada y colorida. Partiendo de un edificio ya existente, DMA lo rediseñó hasta los cimientos y re imaginó tanto el armazón como el interior de la estructura para reflejar el espíritu de diseño de la empresa y el carácter del barrio.
DMA se enorgullece de sus soluciones únicas y sus detalles, siempre perfeccionando, aprendiendo y reinventando. La empresa es conocida por sus vibrantes interiores, sus geometrías creativas y el elegante uso de materias primas que ejemplifican la mano del artesano y hablan de la cultura única del centro de Texas.

## KENWOOD RESIDENCE

Austin, Texas, United States // Lot area: 10,469 sq ft; building area: 3,594 sq ft

The Kenwood Residence is a short distance south of Austin's bustling downtown, seeking a feeling of tranquility among winding roads, gentle hills, and beautiful, mature, live oaks. Taking cues from the neighboring mid-century homes, long linear massing and asymmetrical, low-pitched roofs form an L-shape plan around a sunken courtyard merging with the sloping terrain. Inside, the spaces are separated through screens and transition areas, creating a sense of openness reinforced by the blending of indoors and outdoors. Graphic textures and select pops of color echo the colors of the surrounding landscape. Seeking to revamp the design and organization of mid-century modernism, the Kenwood Residence shirks the conventional understanding of an urban neighborhood house while delivering a unique and familiar home.

La résidence Kenwood se trouve à une courte distance au sud du centre-ville animé d'Austin, à la recherche d'un sentiment de tranquillité parmi des routes sinueuses, des collines douces et de magnifiques chênes verts adultes. S'inspirant des maisons voisines du milieu du siècle, la masse linéaire et les toits asymétriques à faible pente forment un plan en forme de L autour d'une cour creuse qui se fond dans le terrain en pente. À l'intérieur, les espaces sont séparés par des écrans et des zones de transition, créant un sentiment d'ouverture renforcé par le mélange de l'intérieur et de l'extérieur. Les textures graphiques et les touches de couleur choisies font écho aux couleurs du paysage environnant. Cherchant à rénover la conception et l'organisation du modernisme du milieu du siècle, la résidence Kenwood fait fi de la conception conventionnelle d'une maison de quartier urbain tout en offrant une maison unique et familière.

Die Kenwood Residence liegt nur wenige Kilometer südlich des geschäftigen Stadtzentrums von Austin und vermittelt ein Gefühl der Ruhe zwischen kurvenreichen Straßen, sanften Hügeln und wunderschönen, alten Eichen. In Anlehnung an die benachbarten Häuser aus der Mitte des Jahrhunderts bilden lange, geradlinige Baukörper und asymmetrische, flach geneigte Dächer einen L-förmigen Grundriss um einen versenkten Innenhof, der mit dem abfallenden Gelände verschmilzt. Im Inneren sind die Räume durch Trennwände und Übergangszonen getrennt, wodurch ein Gefühl der Offenheit und Verbindung nach außen entsteht. Grafische Texturen und ausgewählte Farbtupfer greifen die Farben der umgebenden Landschaft auf. Die Kenwood Residence versucht, das Design und die Organisation des Modernismus aus der Mitte des Jahrhunderts neu zu gestalten, und entzieht sich dem konventionellen Verständnis eines Hauses in der städtischen Nachbarschaft, während sie ein einzigartiges und vertrautes Zuhause schafft.

La Residencia Kenwood se encuentra a poca distancia al sur del bullicioso centro de Austin, buscando una sensación de tranquilidad entre carreteras sinuosas, suaves colinas y hermosos robles vivos maduros. Tomando como referencia las casas vecinas de mediados de siglo, la masa lineal larga y los tejados asimétricos de leve inclinación forman una planta en forma de L alrededor de un patio hundido que se funde con el terreno en pendiente. En el interior, los espacios se separan mediante pantallas y zonas de transición, creando una sensación de apertura y conexión con el exterior. Las texturas gráficas y las selecciones de color se hacen eco de los colores del paisaje. Buscando renovar el diseño y la organización del modernismo de mediados de siglo, la Residencia Kenwood elude la concepción convencional de una casa urbana de barrio, a la vez que ofrece un hogar único y familiar.

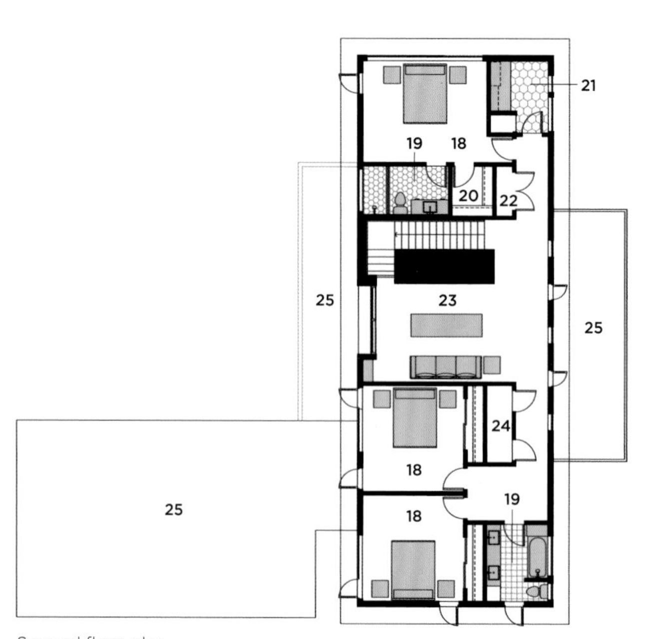


Second floor plan

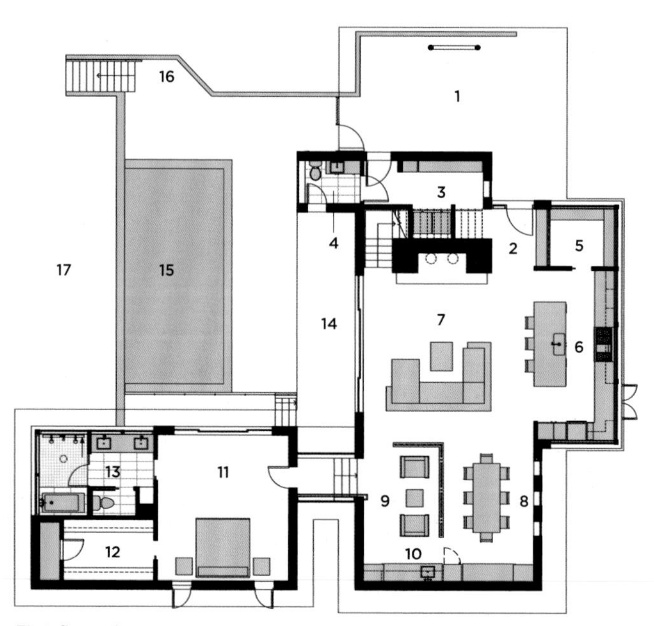


First floor plan

1. Carport
2. Entry
3. Mud room
4. Powder room
5. Pantry
6. Kitchen
7. Living area
8. Dining area
9. Reading nook
10. Wet bar
11. Primary bedroom
12. Primary closet
13. Primary bath
14. Covered patio
15. Pool
16. Stair to upper yard + garage
17. Upper yard
18. Bedroom
19. Bathroom
20. Closet
21. Utility room
22. Storage
23. Den
24. Mechanical room
25. Roof below

## THE PEDERNALES HOUSE

Austin, Texas, United States // Lot area: 3,450 sq ft; building area: 1,380 sq ft

The Pedernales House is tailored to its location in every single way. The project started with a very small lot, heavily developed in the last century by the previous owners. To make the lot even more challenging, a 33-inch diameter pecan tree in the middle of the buildable area needed to be preserved per city regulations. The resulting design maximizes the site's buildable area, and the tree, once seen as dead weight, became the project's highlight, bestowing a treehouse-like atmosphere. The tree forces a natural demarcation and divides the house into two separate volumes connected by a two-story glass tendon. Large glass doors in the open concept living and kitchen spaces blur the lines between interior and exterior and allow the living room to extend outside, under the tree canopy, and onto the private interior courtyard.

La Pedernales House est adaptée à son emplacement à tous points de vue. Le projet a débuté avec un très petit terrain, fortement développé au siècle dernier par les propriétaires précédents. Pour rendre le terrain encore plus difficile, un pacanier de 33 pouces de diamètre situé au milieu de la zone constructible devait être préservé conformément aux réglementations de la ville. La conception qui en résulte maximise la zone constructible du site, et l'arbre, autrefois considéré comme un poids mort, est devenu le point fort du projet, conférant une atmosphère de cabane dans les arbres. L'arbre force une démarcation naturelle et divise la maison en deux volumes distincts reliés par un tendon en verre de deux étages. De grandes portes vitrées dans les espaces ouverts du salon et de la cuisine estompent les lignes entre l'intérieur et l'extérieur et permettent au salon de s'étendre à l'extérieur, sous l'auvent de l'arbre, et sur la cour intérieure privée.

Das Pedernales-Haus ist in jeder Hinsicht auf seinen Standort zugeschnitten. Das Projekt begann mit einem sehr kleinen Grundstück, das im letzten Jahrhundert von den Vorbesitzern stark bebaut wurde. Erschwerend kam hinzu, dass ein Pekannussbaum mit einem Durchmesser von 33 Zentimetern in der Mitte des bebaubaren Bereichs gemäß den städtischen Vorschriften erhalten werden musste. Der daraus resultierende Entwurf maximiert die bebaubare Fläche des Grundstücks, und der Baum, der einst als totes Gewicht galt, wurde zum Highlight des Projekts, das eine baumhausähnliche Atmosphäre vermittelt. Der Baum erzwingt eine natürliche Abgrenzung und teilt das Haus in zwei getrennte Volumen, die durch eine zweistöckige Glasspange verbunden sind. Große Glastüren in den offen gestalteten Wohn- und Küchenräumen lassen die Grenzen zwischen Innen und Außen verschwimmen und ermöglichen es dem Wohnzimmer, sich unter der Baumkrone nach draußen und in den privaten Innenhof zu erstrecken.

La Casa Pedernales está adaptada a su ubicación en todos los sentidos. El proyecto comenzó con un terreno muy pequeño, muy urbanizado en el siglo pasado por los anteriores propietarios. Para hacer el terreno aún más difícil, y según las normas de la ciudad, era necesario preservar un árbol Pacana de 83 cm. de diámetro en el centro de la zona edificable. El diseño resultante aprovecha al máximo la superficie edificable del solar, y el árbol, que antes se consideraba un peso muerto, se convirtió en el punto culminante del proyecto, confiriendo una atmósfera de casa-árbol. El tronco fuerza una demarcación natural y divide la casa en dos volúmenes separados conectados por un tendido de vidrio de dos pisos. Las grandes puertas de cristal de los espacios abiertos de la sala de estar y la cocina desdibujan las líneas entre el interior y el exterior y permiten que el salón se extienda al exterior, bajo la copa del árbol, y al patio interior privado.

Massing and programatic diagrams

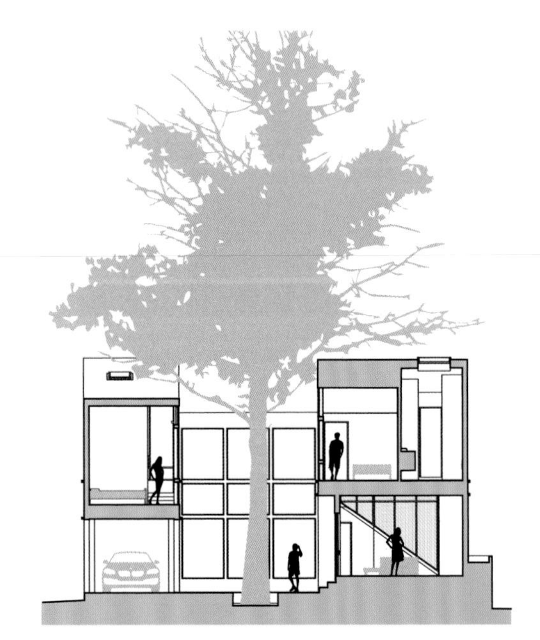

Building section

STREET

STREET

Site plan

1. Drive to ground floor carport
2. Guest parking
3. House
4. Tree courtyard

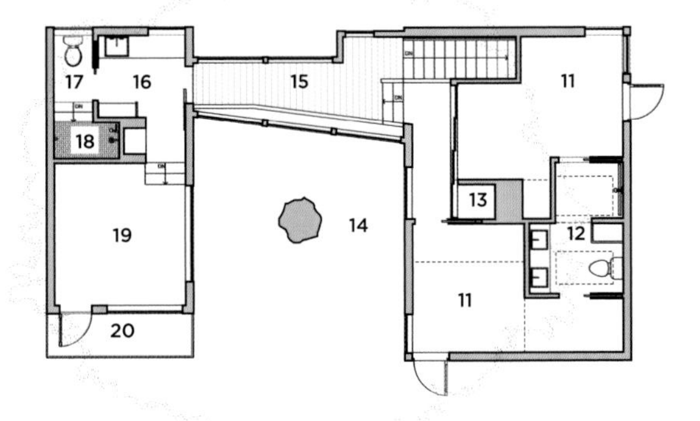

Second floor plan

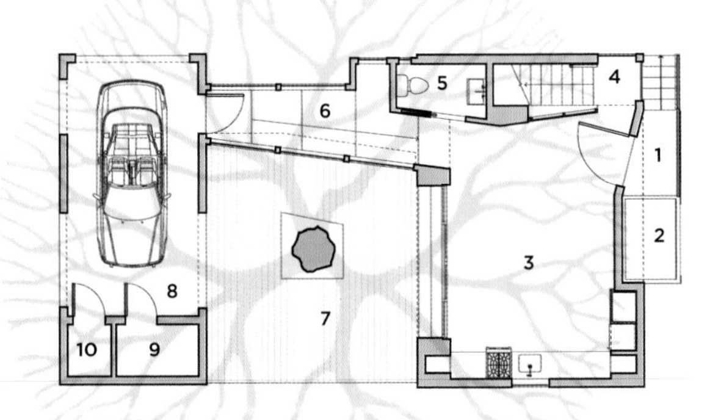

Ground floor plan

1. Entry porch
2. Planter box
3. Kitchen and living area
4. Stairs
5. Powder room
6. Connector
7. Tree courtyard
8. Garage
9. Storage
10. HVAC
11. Bedroom
12. Bathroom
13. Laundry closet
14. Courtyard below
15. Bridge connection
16. Open dressing area
17. Water closet
18. Sunken bath
19. Primary bedroom
20. Balcony

## SOUTH FOURTH HOUSE AND ADU

Austin, Texas, United States // Lot area: 12,901 sq ft; house area: 3,462 sq ft; ADU area: 1,100 sq ft

The South 4th House and ADU represent an architecture that capitalizes on its unique urban infill lot in South Austin and takes full advantage of the city of Austin's zoning code, which allows for an 1,100-square-foot accessory dwelling unit (ADU) to share a lot with a primary residence. The buildings are carved into a steeply sloped lot with a series of stacked boxes in rich wood, glass, and burnished stucco that afford views of the horizon above the neighboring homes. For this lot, the architects were gifted with a street at the site's front and a private alley at the rear, allowing each unit to have separate driveways, parking, and entrances on opposite ends of the property. The resulting design orients the buildings in a manner that allows for a sense of separation while keeping a shared design language.

La South 4th House et l'ADU représentent une architecture qui tire parti d'un terrain intercalaire urbain unique dans le sud d'Austin et tire pleinement parti du code de zonage de la ville d'Austin, qui permet à une unité d'habitation accessoire (ADU) de 1 100 pieds carrés de partager un terrain avec une résidence principale. Les bâtiments sont taillés dans un terrain en pente raide avec une série de boîtes empilées en bois riche, en verre et en stuc bruni qui offrent des vues sur l'horizon au-dessus des maisons voisines. Pour ce terrain, les architectes ont eu le privilège de disposer d'une rue à l'avant du site et d'une allée privée à l'arrière, ce qui a permis à chaque unité de disposer d'allées, de parkings et d'entrées séparés aux extrémités opposées de la propriété. La conception qui en résulte oriente les bâtiments de manière à donner un sentiment de séparation tout en conservant un langage de conception commun.

Das South 4th House und die ADU stellen eine Architektur dar, die aus dem einzigartigen Grundstück in South Austin Kapital schlägt und die Bauvorschriften der Stadt Austin voll ausschöpft, die es erlauben, dass sich eine 1.100 Quadratmeter große Wohneinheit (ADU) ein Grundstück mit einem Hauptwohnsitz teilt. Die Gebäude sind in ein steil abfallendes Grundstück mit einer Reihe von gestapelten Boxen aus reichem Holz, Glas und poliertem Stuck eingepasst, die den Blick auf den Horizont über den benachbarten Häusern freigeben. Für dieses Grundstück wurde den Architekten eine Straße an der Vorderseite und eine private Gasse an der Rückseite zur Verfügung gestellt, so dass jede Einheit über separate Zufahrten, Parkplätze und Eingänge an den gegenüberliegenden Enden des Grundstücks verfügt. Das Ergebnis ist ein Entwurf, der die Gebäude so ausrichtet, dass ein Gefühl der Trennung entsteht und gleichzeitig eine gemeinsame Formensprache beibehalten wird.

La South 4th House y la ADU representan una arquitectura que saca provecho de su parcela urbana única en el sur de Austin y aprovecha al máximo el código de zonificación de la ciudad, que permite que una unidad de vivienda accesoria (ADU) de 1.000m2 comparta una parcela con una residencia principal. Los edificios están tallados en un terreno de gran pendiente con una serie de cajas apiladas de rica madera, vidrio y estuco bruñido que permiten ver el horizonte por encima de las casas vecinas. Para esta parcela, los arquitectos contaron con una calle en la parte delantera y un callejón privado en la parte trasera, lo que permitió que cada unidad tuviera accesos, aparcamientos y entradas independientes en extremos opuestos de la propiedad. El diseño resultante orienta los edificios de tal manera que permite una sensación de separación al tiempo que mantiene un lenguaje de diseño compartido.

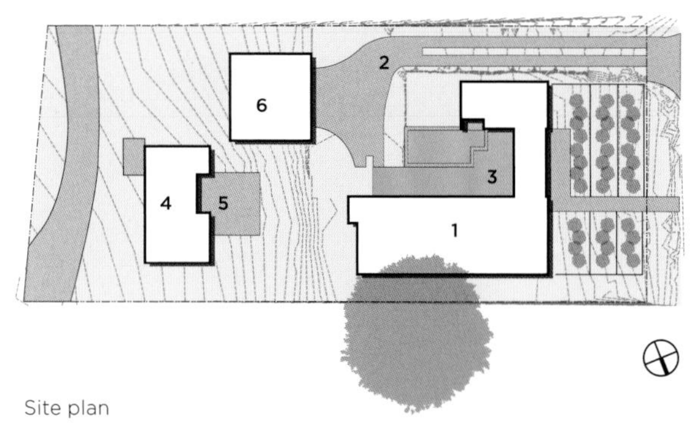


Site plan

1. Main house
2. Main house drive
3. Main house deck + pool
4. ADU
5. ADU porch
6. Main house garage

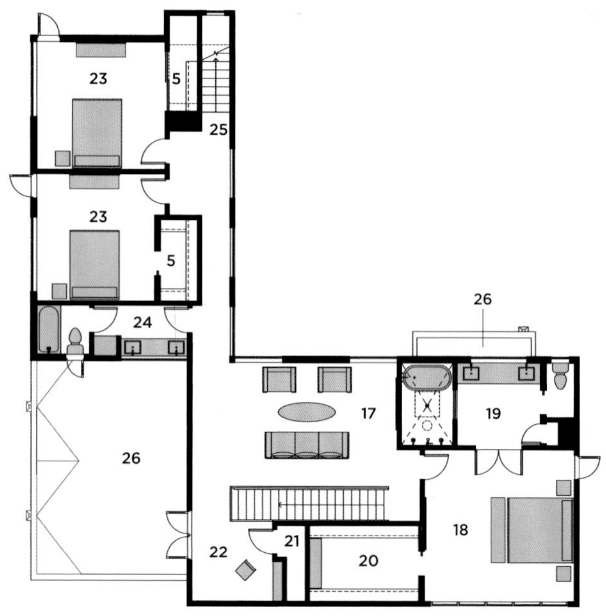


Main house second floor plan

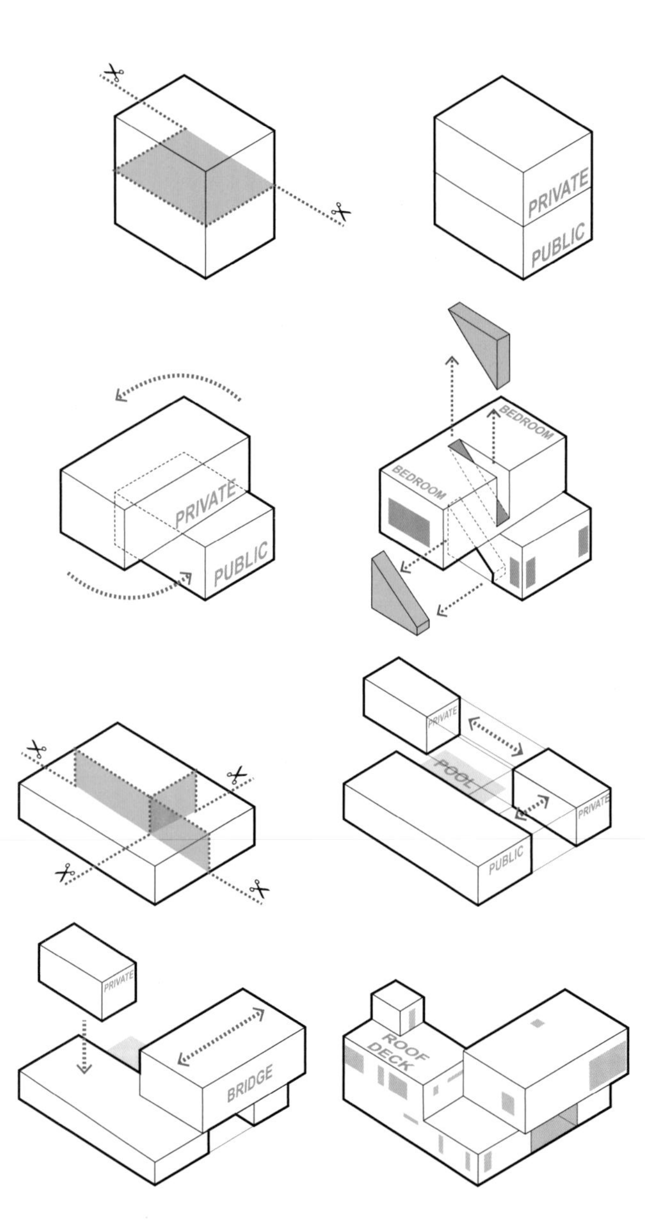


Massing and programatic diagrams

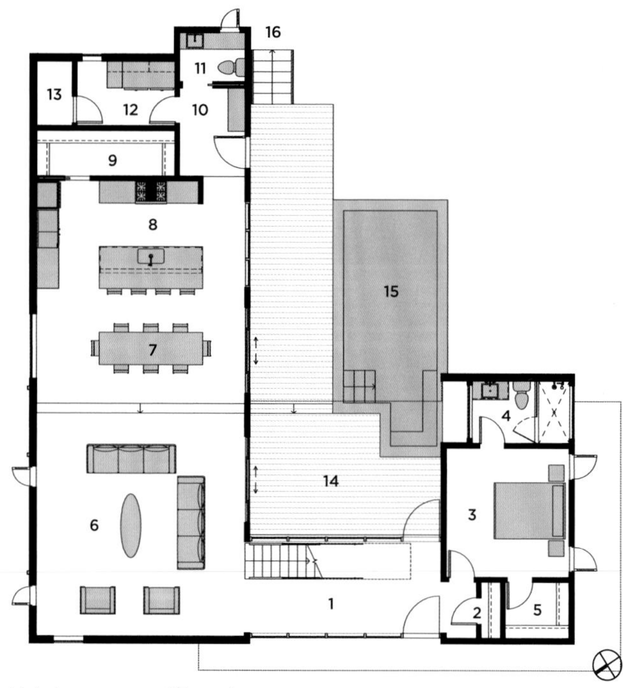


Main house ground floor plan

1. Entry
2. Coat closet
3. Guest suite
4. Bathroom
5. Closet
6. Living room
7. Dining room
8. Kitchen
9. Pantry
10. Mud room
11. Powder room
12. Utility room
13. HVAC
14. Patio
15. Pool
16. Stair to upper yard + ADU
17. Play room
18. Primary bedroom
19. Primary bathroom
20. Primary closet
21. Mechanical room
22. Study
23. Bedroom
24. Bathroom
25. Stairs to third floor roof deck
26. Roof below

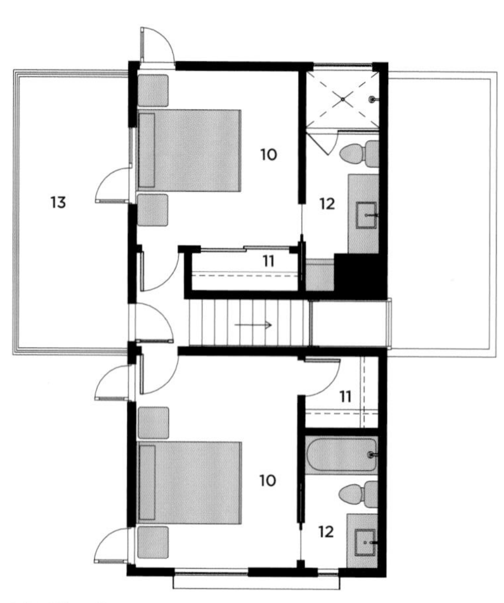


ADU first floor plan

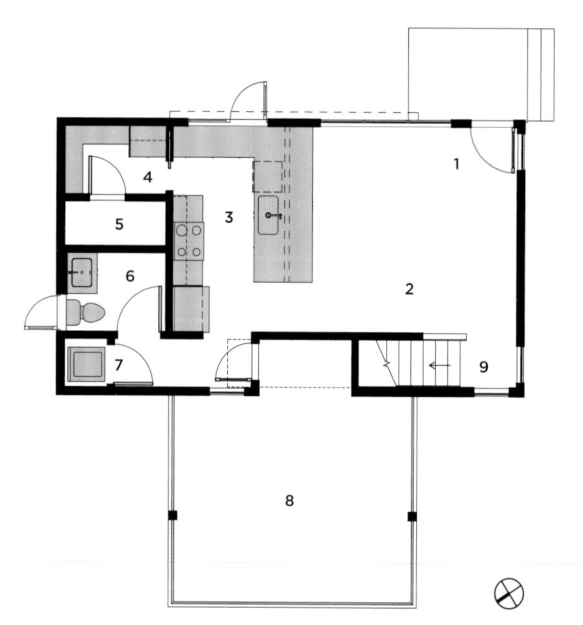


ADU ground floor plan

1. Entry
2. Living room
3. Kitchen
4. Pantry
5. Mechanical room
6. Powder room
7. Utility room
8. Covered patio
9. Stairs to second floor
10. Bedroom
11. Closet
12. Bathroom
13. Roof deck

# HOLLENBECK ARCHITECTS

238
v

**BARBARA LANE**

Architecture Design team:
Brad Hollenbeck, AIA and Karen Brenner
Interior Designer:
Christine Ho Interiors
Builder:
Levitt Builders
Photographer:
© Ben Hill

242
v

**BELLAIRE BOULEVARD**

Architecture Design team:
Brad Hollenbeck, AIA; Paulina Diaz; and Karen Brenner
Interior Designer:
Marie Flannigan Interiors
Contractor:
Bentley Custom Homes
Photographer:
© Ben Hill and Julie Soefer

246
v

**HIBURY RESIDENCE**

Architecture Design team:
Brad Hollenbeck, AIA; Paulina Diaz; and Maurice Marroquin
Interior Designer:
HAI
Contractor:
Legion Custom Homes
Photographer:
© Ben Hill

www.hollenbeckarchitects.com @hollenbeckarchitects

Hollenbeck Architects is an award-winning, leading residential design firm led by founding partner Brad Hollenbeck, AIA. With a talented team of designers, the firm is recognized for its diverse architectural styles and dedication to its client's program and site design. Our company, a Houston-based architecture firm, has been serving the Greater Houston Area for twenty-four years, creating high-quality homes that respond to the clients' specific wants, needs, and tastes. We want these homes to be appropriate to their setting while, at the same time, achieving the goal of functionality and sustainability. The style of our buildings is as unique as our clients and timeless. Our precision and passion shine through in our work.

Hollenbeck Architects ist ein preisgekröntes, führendes Architekturbüro für Wohnhäuser unter der Leitung des Gründungspartners Brad Hollenbeck, AIA. Mit einem talentierten Team von Designern ist das Unternehmen für seine vielfältigen architektonischen Stile und sein Engagement für das Programm und den Standort seiner Kunden bekannt. Unser Unternehmen, ein in Houston ansässiges Architekturbüro, ist seit vierundzwanzig Jahren im Großraum Houston tätig und entwirft hochwertige Häuser, die den spezifischen Wünschen, Bedürfnissen und dem Geschmack der Kunden entsprechen. Wir wollen, dass diese Häuser ihrer Umgebung angemessen sind und gleichzeitig das Ziel der Funktionalität und Nachhaltigkeit erreichen. Der Stil unserer Gebäude ist so einzigartig wie unsere Kunden und zeitlos. Unsere Präzision und Leidenschaft spiegeln sich in unserer Arbeit wider.

Hollenbeck Architects est un cabinet de conception résidentielle primé et de premier plan, dirigé par l'associé fondateur Brad Hollenbeck, AIA. Avec une équipe de concepteurs talentueux, le cabinet est reconnu pour ses divers styles architecturaux et son dévouement au programme de ses clients et à la conception du site. Notre société, un cabinet d'architecture basé à Houston, dessert la région du Grand Houston depuis vingt-quatre ans, créant des maisons de haute qualité qui répondent aux désirs, aux besoins et aux goûts spécifiques des clients. Nous voulons que ces maisons soient adaptées à leur environnement tout en atteignant l'objectif de fonctionnalité et de durabilité. Le style de nos bâtiments est aussi unique que nos clients et intemporel. Notre précision et notre passion transparaissent dans notre travail.

Hollenbeck Architects es una empresa de diseño residencial líder y galardonada, dirigida por el socio fundador Brad Hollenbeck, AIA. Con un talentoso equipo de diseñadores, la firma es reconocida por sus diversos estilos arquitectónicos y su dedicación al programa de sus clientes. Nuestra empresa, una firma de arquitectura con sede en Houston, ha estado sirviendo el área metropolitana de Houston durante veinticuatro años, la creación de viviendas de alta calidad que responden a los deseos específicos de los clientes, las necesidades y gustos. Queremos que estas viviendas sean adecuadas a su entorno y que, al mismo tiempo, alcancen el objetivo de funcionalidad y sostenibilidad. El estilo de nuestros edificios es tan único como el de nuestros clientes y es intemporal. Nuestra precisión y pasión brillan en nuestro trabajo.

## BARBARA LANE

West University Place, Texas, United States // Lot area: 21,256 acres; building area: 5,745 sq ft

The use of clean lines and natural materials set the mood for this modern yet warm Houston Residence. The butterfly roof design covers intersecting volumes, where the different materials and movement bring to life the composition of the house. The large pivot front door opens up to the two-story entry space, where the floating stairs and thick porcelain-clad wall give privacy to the rest of the home. Large format porcelain tile flooring transitions from one room to the next, creating a sense of spaciousness perfect for entertaining. A decorative custom metal screen in the living room enhances the room's visual appeal. Large ten-foot-tall sliding doors and butt-glass corner windows provide a sense of openness to the exterior, allowing abundant natural light in and offering a view of a quiet backyard retreat.

L'utilisation de lignes épurées et de matériaux naturels crée l'ambiance de cette résidence moderne mais chaleureuse de Houston. La conception du toit papillon couvre des volumes qui se croisent, où les différents matériaux et le mouvement donnent vie à la composition de la maison. La grande porte d'entrée pivotante s'ouvre sur l'espace d'entrée à deux étages, où les escaliers flottants et le mur plus épais revêtu de porcelaine donnent de l'intimité au reste de la maison. Les revêtements de sol en carreaux de porcelaine grand format passent d'une pièce à l'autre, créant une sensation d'espace parfaite pour les réceptions. Dans le salon, un écran métallique décoratif personnalisé rehausse l'attrait visuel de la pièce. Les grandes portes coulissantes de trois mètres de haut et les fenêtres d'angle en verre donnent un sentiment d'ouverture sur l'extérieur, laissant entrer une abondante lumière naturelle et offrant une vue sur un jardin tranquille.

Die Verwendung klarer Linien und natürlicher Materialien prägen die Stimmung dieses modernen und doch warmen Wohnhauses in Houston. Das Schmetterlingsdach deckt die sich überschneidenden Volumen ab, wobei die verschiedenen Materialien und Bewegungen die Komposition des Hauses zum Leben erwecken. Die große, schwenkbare Eingangstür führt in den zweistöckigen Eingangsbereich, in dem die schwebende Treppe und die dickere, mit Porzellan verkleidete Wand dem Rest des Hauses Privatsphäre verleihen. Großformatige Feinsteinzeugfliesen gehen von einem Raum zum nächsten über und schaffen ein Gefühl von Geräumigkeit, das sich perfekt für Gäste eignen. Ein dekorativer kundenspezifischer Metallschirm im Wohnzimmer erhöht die visuelle Attraktivität des Raums. Große, drei Meter hohe Schiebetüren und Eckfenster aus Stumpfglas vermitteln ein Gefühl der Offenheit nach außen, lassen viel natürliches Licht herein und bieten einen Blick auf einen ruhigen Hinterhof.

El uso de líneas limpias y de materiales naturales crea el ambiente de esta moderna pero cálida residencia de Houston. El tejado mariposa cubre unos volúmenes que se cruzan, donde los diferentes materiales y el movimiento dan vida a la composición de la casa. La gran puerta principal pivotante se abre al espacio de entrada de dos niveles, donde la escalera flotante y la pared revestida de porcelana dan privacidad al resto de la casa. Los suelos de baldosas de porcelana de gran formato crean una transición perfecta de una habitación a otra, creando una sensación de amplitud perfecta para el entretenimiento. Una mampara metálica personalizada en el salón realza el atractivo visual de la habitación. Las grandes puertas correderas de tres metros. de altura y las ventanas esquineras de cristal a tope proporcionan una sensación de apertura hacia el exterior, permitiendo la entrada de abundante luz natural y ofreciendo vistas a un tranquilo patio trasero.

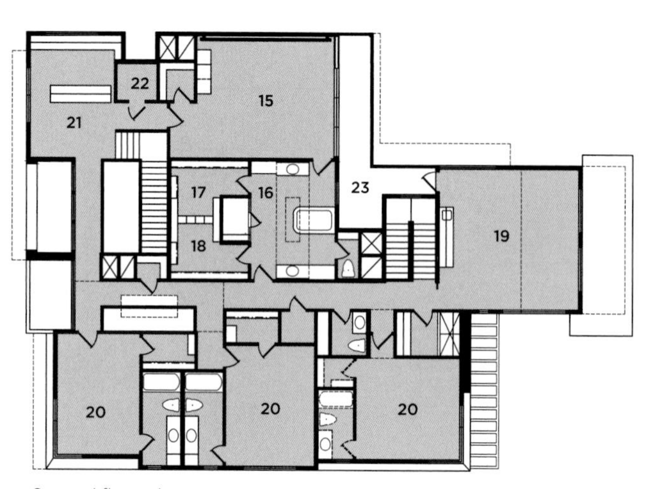

Second floor plan

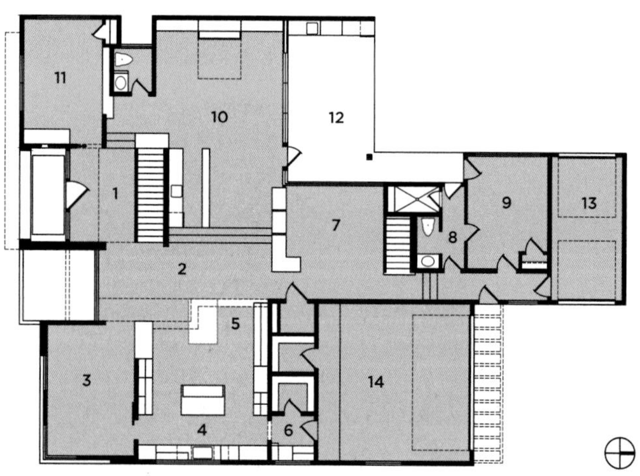

Ground floor plan

1. Entry
2. Gallery
3. Dining area
4. Kitchen
5. Breakfast
6. Mud room
7. Play room
8. Cabana
9. Guest bedroom
10. Living area
11. Study
12. Veranda
13. One-car garage
14. Two-car garage
15. Master bedroom
16. Master bathroom
17. Her closet
18. His closet
19. Game room
20. Bedroom
21. Office
22. Mechanical room
23. Balcony

## BELLAIRE BOULEVARD

West University Place, Texas, United States // Lot area: 40,940 acres; building area: 8,100 sq ft

This home, designed to meet the needs of an active young family, pushes and pulls stucco volumes strategically around a tennis court, swimming pool, and outdoor living spaces to create a family oasis from the surrounding bustling city streets of Houston, Texas. Large gables with smooth cedar rafters and heavy tiles create an inviting modern Spanish colonial architectural palette accented with large windows set deep into thick plaster walls. When entering through the glass front doors into the arched gallery, the house reveals its modern open spaces organized around a three-story wood stair. Past the stairs, the house opens up to a double-wide indoor-outdoor living space with glass window walls and wood ceilings. Above the first-floor gallery, a second-floor gallery provides easy access to bedrooms.

Cette maison, conçue pour répondre aux besoins d'une jeune famille active, pousse et tire des volumes en stuc de manière stratégique autour d'un court de tennis, d'une piscine et d'espaces de vie extérieurs pour créer une oasis familiale loin des rues animées de Houston, au Texas. De grands pignons avec des chevrons en cèdre lisse et de lourdes tuiles créent une palette architecturale coloniale espagnole moderne et accueillante, accentuée par de grandes fenêtres encastrées dans d'épais murs en plâtre. En entrant par les portes d'entrée vitrées dans la galerie arquée, la maison révèle ses espaces ouverts modernes organisés autour d'un escalier en bois de trois étages. Passé l'escalier, la maison s'ouvre sur un espace de vie intérieur-extérieur à double largeur avec des murs vitrés et des plafonds en bois. Au-dessus de la galerie du premier étage, une galerie du deuxième étage permet d'accéder facilement aux chambres.

Dieses Haus, das für die Bedürfnisse einer aktiven jungen Familie entworfen wurde, schiebt und zieht Stuckvolumen strategisch um einen Tennisplatz, einen Swimmingpool und Außenwohnbereiche, um eine Familienoase von den umliegenden geschäftigen Straßen von Houston, Texas, zu schaffen. Große Giebel mit glatten Zedernsparren und schweren Ziegeln schaffen eine einladende moderne spanische Kolonialarchitektur, die durch große, tief in die dicken Gipswände eingelassene Fenster akzentuiert wird. Wenn man durch die gläsernen Eingangstüren in die gewölbte Galerie eintritt, offenbart das Haus seine modernen, offenen Räume, die um eine dreistöckige Holztreppe herum angeordnet sind. Hinter der Treppe öffnet sich das Haus zu einem doppelbreiten Innen- und Außenwohnbereich mit Glasfensterwänden und Holzdecken. Über der Galerie im ersten Stock bietet eine Galerie im zweiten Stock einfachen Zugang zu den Schlafzimmern.

Esta casa, diseñada para satisfacer las necesidades de una familia joven y activa, empuja y tira de los volúmenes de estuco estratégicamente alrededor de una pista de tenis, piscina y espacios de vida al aire libre para crear un oasis familiar en las bulliciosas calles de la ciudad de Houston, Texas. Los grandes hastiales con vigas de cedro lisas y las pesadas tejas crean un acogedor conjunto arquitectónico moderno de estilo colonial español acentuado con grandes ventanales encajados en gruesas paredes de yeso. Al entrar por las puertas acristaladas en una galería arqueada, la casa revela sus modernos espacios abiertos organizados en torno a una escalera de madera de tres niveles. Pasada la escalera, la casa se abre a un espacio interior-exterior de doble ancho con paredes acristaladas y techos de madera. al igual que en el primer piso, otra galería en el segundo piso facilita el acceso a los dormitorios.

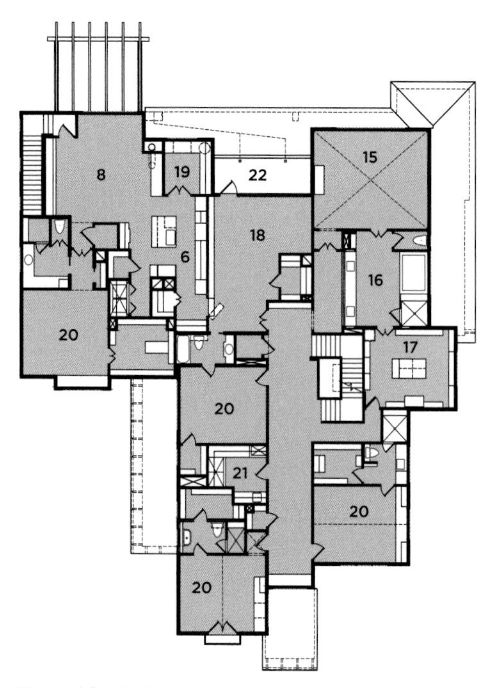

Second floor plan

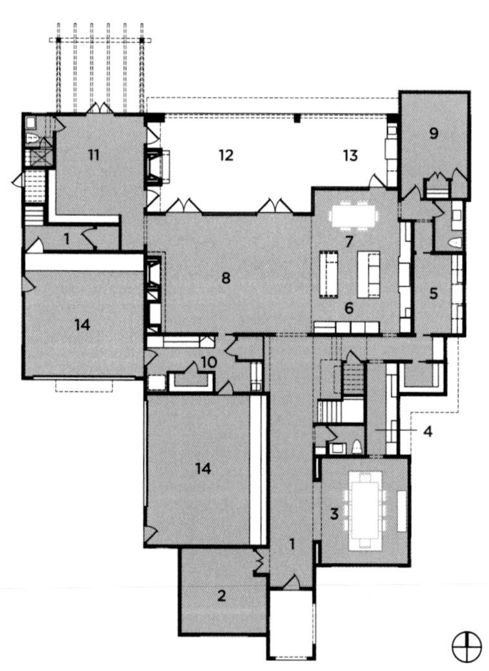

Ground floor plan

1. Entry
2. Study
3. Dining area
4. Butler's pantry
5. Project room
6. Kitchen
7. Breakfast nook
8. Living area
9. Gymnasium
10. Mud room
11. Pool room
12. Veranda
13. Summer kitchen
14. Two-car garage
15. Master bedroom
16. Master bathroom
17. Master closet
18. Game room
19. Office
20. Bedroom
21. Balcony

## HIBURY RESIDENCE

Houston, Texas, United States // Lot area: 21,000 sq ft; building area: 6,400 sq ft

The existing mature trees on the property inspired the design of spaces that feel open to the outside while maintaining privacy. A two-story entry and living room that bridges the outside and the inside with floor-to-ceiling windows and pivot doors create a welcoming sense of entry. A stone wall cuts through the house, creating two wings connected by a bridge floating through the two-story living room and entry. The kitchen and breakfast on the ground floor wrap around the veranda to take full advantage of the backyard view. The mix of earth tones in the stone, stucco, and wood creates a happy marriage with its natural surroundings. For sustainability of design, the windows are double glazed and have a Low-E coating for energy efficiency, while a two-story covered porch contributes to the control of energy use on the west side.

Les arbres matures existant sur la propriété ont inspiré la conception d'espaces ouverts sur l'extérieur tout en préservant l'intimité. Une entrée et un salon à deux étages qui relient l'extérieur et l'intérieur grâce à des fenêtres du sol au plafond et des portes pivotantes créent un effet d'entrée accueillant. Un mur en pierre traverse la maison créaent des ailes reliées par un pont flottant à travers le salon et l'entrée à deux étages. La cuisine et le coin repas s'enroulent autour de la véranda pour profiter pleinement de la vue sur l'arrière-cour. Le mélange de tons de terre dans la pierre, le stuc et le bois crée un mariage plaisant avec son environnement naturel. Dans un souci de conception durable, les fenêtres sont dotées d'un revêtement Low-E et d'un double vitrage pour une meilleure efficacité énergétique, tandis qu'un porche couvert de deux étages permet de contrôler la consommation d'énergie du côté ouest.

Die vorhandenen alten Bäume auf dem Grundstück inspirierten die Gestaltung von Räumen, die sich nach außen offen anfühlen und gleichzeitig die Privatsphäre wahren. Ein zweistöckiges Eingangs- und Wohnzimmer, das mit raumhohen Fenstern und Drehtüren eine Brücke zwischen Außen und Innen schlägt, schafft ein einladendes Gefühl des Betretens. Eine Steinmauer durchschneidet das Haus und schafft zwei Flügel, die durch eine Brücke verbunden sind, die durch das zweistöckige Wohnzimmer und den Eingang schwebt. Die Küche und Frühstücksraum im Erdgeschoss umschließen die Veranda, um den Blick auf den Hinterhof voll auszunutzen. Die Mischung aus Erdtönen in Stein, Stuck und Holz schafft eine glückliche Verbindung mit der natürlichen Umgebung. Für ein nachhaltiges Design sind die Fenster doppelt verglast und haben eine Low-E-Beschichtung für Energieeffizienz, während eine zweistöckige überdachte Veranda zur Kontrolle des Energieverbrauchs auf der Westseite beiträgt.

Los árboles maduros existentes en la propiedad inspiraron el diseño de espacios abiertos al exterior manteniendo la privacidad. Una gran entrada de dos pisos y una sala de estar que une el exterior y el interior con ventanas del suelo al techo y puertas pivotantes crean una acogedora sensación de entrada. Un muro de piedra atraviesa la casa, creando dos alas conectados por un puente que atraviesa el salón y la entrada de dos niveles. En la primera planta, la cocina y la zona de desayuno envuelven el porche para aprovechar al máximo las vistas del patio trasero. La mezcla de tonos tierra en la piedra, el estuco y la madera crea una unión armoniosa con su entorno natural. En aras de la sostenibilidad del diseño, las ventanas son de doble acristalamiento y tienen un revestimiento de baja emisividad para lograr la eficiencia energética, mientras que un porche cubierto de dos niveles sirve para controlar el uso de la energía en el lado oeste.

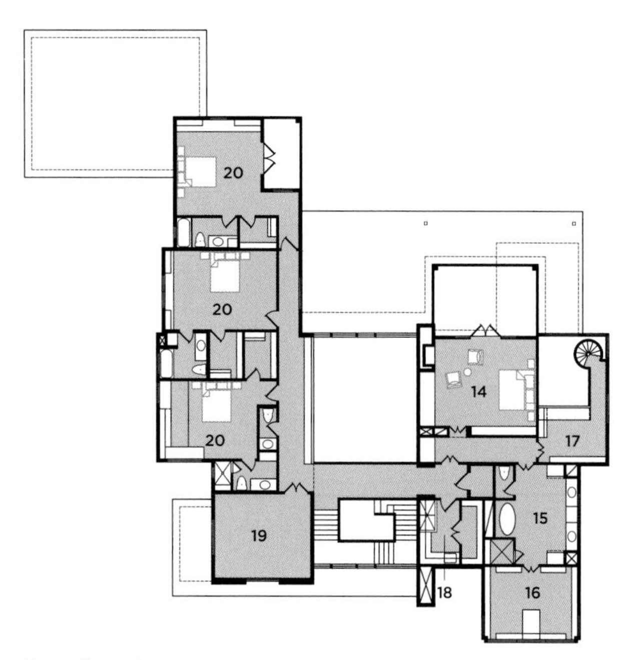


Upper floor plan

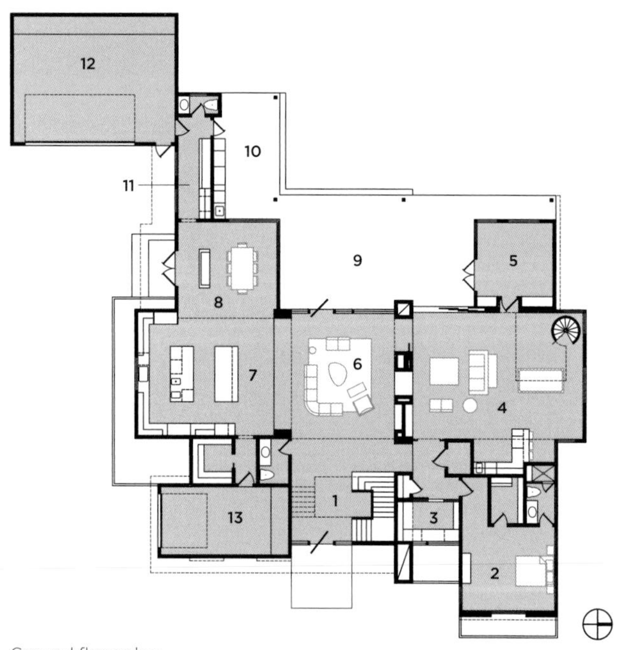


Ground floor plan

1. Entry
2. Guest room
3. Office
4. Game room
5. Exercise room
6. Family room
7. Kitchen
8. Breakfast
9. Veranda
10. Summer kitchen
11. Mud room
12. Two-car garage
13. One-car garage
14. Master bedroom
15. Master bathroom
16. Master closet
17. Study
18. Utility room
19. Play room
20. Bedroom

# IGNACIO SALAS-HUMARA ARCHITECT

252
v

**THE GOAT SHEDS**

Architecture Design:
Ignacio Salas-Humara, AIA
Owners:
David Hddle and Alysia Juracek;
Jeff and Carol (original).
Builder:
Cody Doyle
Photographer:
© Ignacio Salas-Humara

256
v

**ALTA LUZ**

Architecture Design:
Ignacio Salas-Humara, AIA
Owners:
Bill Fore and Joe Loose
Builder:
Koviak Built
Photographer:
© Ignacio Salas-Humara unless otherwise noted ©Bill Fore

260
v

**THE OUTPOST**

Architecture Design:
Ignacio Salas-Humara, AIA
Owners:
Steve Gelinske and Wendy Reiner
Builder:
Koviak Built
Photographer:
© Ignacio Salas-Humara

www.isharchitect.com @isharchitect

Ignacio Salas-Humara, AIA

Every project we do is of the landscape it inhabits. Each is a product of and responds to the special qualities of its site: landscape in which to nestle and with which to interact, trees for shade, prevailing breezes for cooling, the changing direction and intensity of light from the sun as it arcs across the sky, local history, and local building traditions and materials. We strive for elegant simplicity, a harmonious collection of details and materiality that together impart a sense of comfort, security, and belonging. There is a subconscious undercurrent of romantic imagery—ancient ruins, forest campsites, farmsteads in black-and-white movies, castles, childhood memories. There is an interplay of the modern and the primitive; of technology and craftsmanship. The clients are our inspiration. Collaboration is the driver. Each project is an adventure with the client riding shotgun. Our goal is for the process of developing a new house design from the initial idea to the finished product to be exciting and rewarding for all involved. Why else do it?

Jedes Projekt, das wir realisieren, ist ein Teil der Landschaft, in der es steht. Jedes Projekt ist ein Produkt der besonderen Qualitäten seines Standorts und reagiert auf diese: die Landschaft, in die es sich einfügt und mit der es interagiert, die Bäume, die Schatten spenden, die vorherrschende Brise, die für Abkühlung sorgt, die wechselnde Richtung und Intensität des Sonnenlichts, das sich über den Himmel wölbt, die lokale Geschichte sowie die lokalen Bautraditionen und Materialien. Wir streben nach eleganter Einfachheit, einer harmonischen Zusammenstellung von Details und Materialien, die zusammen ein Gefühl von Komfort, Sicherheit und Zugehörigkeit vermitteln. Es gibt eine unterbewusste Unterströmung romantischer Bilder - antike Ruinen, Waldcampingplätze, Bauernhöfe in Schwarz-Weiß-Filmen, Schlösser, Kindheitserinnerungen. Es gibt ein Zusammenspiel von Modernem und Primitivem, von Technologie und Handwerkskunst. Die Kunden sind unsere Inspiration. Die Zusammenarbeit ist der Motor. Jedes Projekt ist ein Abenteuer mit dem Kunden als Beifahrer. Unser Ziel ist es, dass der Prozess der Entwicklung eines neuen Hausentwurfs von der ersten Idee bis zum fertigen Produkt für alle Beteiligten spannend, lohnend und erfüllend ist. Warum sollte man es sonst tun?

Chaque projet que nous réalisons est issu du paysage qu'il habite, devenant le produit des qualités particulières et une réponse à son site : le paysage dans lequel il se niche et avec lequel il interagit, les arbres ombrageux, les brises dominantes pour le rafraîchissement, la direction et l'intensité changeantes de la lumière du soleil lorsqu'il arque le ciel, l'histoire locale, ainsi que les traditions et les matériaux de construction locaux. Nous recherchons une simplicité élégante, une collection harmonieuse de détails et de matériaux qui transmettent un sentiment de confort, de sécurité et d'appartenance. Il existe un courant subconscient d'images romantiques - ruines anciennes, campings en forêt, fermes dans les films en noir et blanc, châteaux, souvenirs d'enfance. Il y a une interaction entre le moderne et le primitif, entre la technologie et l'artisanat. Les clients sont notre inspiration. La collaboration est notre moteur. Chaque projet est une aventure avec le client comme passager. Notre objectif est de faire en sorte que le processus de conception d'une nouvelle maison, de l'idée initiale au produit fini, soit passionnant et gratifiant pour toutes les personnes concernées. Pourquoi le faire autrement ?

Cada proyecto que hacemos es del paisaje que habita. Cada uno de ellos es un producto y responde a las cualidades especiales de su emplazamiento: el paisaje en el que anidar y con el que interactuar, los árboles para dar sombra, las brisas predominantes para refrescarse, la dirección e intensidad cambiante de la luz del sol cuando se arquea por el cielo, la historia local y las tradiciones y materiales de construcción locales. Nos esforzamos por lograr una simplicidad elegante, un conjunto armonioso de detalles y materiales que transmiten una sensación de confort, seguridad y pertenencia. Hay un trasfondo subconsciente de imágenes románticas: ruinas antiguas, campamentos en el bosque, granjas en películas en blanco y negro, castillos, recuerdos de la infancia. Hay una interacción entre lo moderno y lo primitivo, entre la tecnología y la artesanía. Los clientes son nuestra inspiración. La colaboración es el motor. Cada proyecto es una aventura en la que el cliente va de copiloto. Nuestro objetivo es que el proceso de desarrollo de un nuevo diseño de casa, desde la idea inicial hasta el producto final, sea emocionante y gratificante para todos los implicados. ¿Por qué hacerlo si no?

## THE GOAT SHEDS

Medina, Texas, United States // Lot area: 375 acres; building area: 5,555 sq ft; 950 sq ft garage; and 1,150 sq ft porches

The Goat Sheds is a new residence on an inherited parcel of a family goat ranch. The husband worked on the ranch as a young adult when it was owned by his future wife's parents. The wife spent memorable summers on this very ranch as a child when it was still her grandparents'. The architect was given a box of vintage photos of the goat ranch. One photo of galvanized tin goat sheds connected by cedar branch fences inspired the design concept. At once primitive and modern, the new house pays homage to the ranching vernacular of the area and honors her childhood memories of her grandparents' goat ranch. The structure is a series of limestone walls, like scattered ruins, with galvanized steel sheds built onto them. At the rear, the sheds have sliding glass walls that open to the natural landscape and spectacular views of the valleys where the wife hiked and camped as a youngster.

The Goat Sheds est une nouvelle résidence sur une parcelle héritée d'un ranch de chèvres familial. Le mari a travaillé dans ce ranch lorsqu'il était jeune adulte, à l'époque où il appartenait aux parents de sa future épouse. La femme a passé des étés mémorables dans ce même ranch lorsqu'elle était enfant et qu'il appartenait encore à ses grands-parents. L'architecte a reçu une boîte de photos anciennes de l'élevage de chèvres. Une photo montrant des chèvreries en tôle galvanisée reliées par des clôtures en branches de cèdre a inspiré le concept de design. À la fois primitive et moderne, la nouvelle maison rend hommage à la tradition d'élevage de la région et honore les souvenirs d'enfance de ses grands-parents dans la chèvrerie. La structure est une série de murs en pierre calcaire, comme des ruines éparses, sur lesquels sont construits des hangars en acier galvanisé. À l'arrière, les hangars sont dotés de parois vitrées coulissantes qui s'ouvrent sur le paysage naturel et offrent des vues spectaculaires sur les vallées où l'épouse faisait de la randonnée et du camping lorsqu'elle était jeune.

The Goat Sheds ist ein neues Wohnhaus auf einer geerbten Parzelle einer Ziegenfarm der Familie. Der Ehemann arbeitete als junger Erwachsener auf der Ranch, als sie noch den Eltern seiner zukünftigen Frau gehörte. Die Ehefrau verbrachte als Kind unvergessliche Sommer auf dieser Ranch, die noch ihren Großeltern gehörte. Der Architekt erhielt eine Schachtel mit alten Fotos von der Ziegenfarm. Ein Foto, auf dem verzinkte Ziegenställe aus Blech zu sehen sind, die durch Zedernholzzäune verbunden sind, inspirierte ihn zu seinem Entwurfskonzept. Das neue Haus, das gleichzeitig primitiv und modern ist, ist eine Hommage an die Ranchkultur der Region und erinnert an die Kindheitserinnerungen an die Ziegenfarm ihrer Großeltern. Das Gebäude besteht aus einer Reihe von Kalksteinmauern, die wie verstreute Ruinen aussehen, an die verzinkte Stahlschuppen angebaut sind. Auf der Rückseite sind die Schuppen mit Glasschiebewänden versehen, die den Blick auf die natürliche Landschaft und die spektakuläre Aussicht auf die Täler freigeben, in denen die Frau als Jugendliche wanderte und zeltete.

The Goat Sheds es una nueva residencia en una propiedad heredada de un rancho de cabras familiar. El marido trabajó en el rancho de joven cuando pertenecía a los padres de su futura esposa. La mujer pasó veranos memorables en este mismo rancho de niña, cuando aún era de sus abuelos. El arquitecto recibió una caja de fotos antiguas del rancho y una foto de cobertizos de chapa galvanizada unidos por vallas de ramas de cedro inspiró el diseño. La nueva casa, primitiva y moderna a la vez, homenajea la tradición ganadera de la zona y los recuerdos de infancia en el rancho de los abuelos. La estructura es una serie de muros de piedra caliza, como ruinas dispersas, con cobertizos de acero galvanizado construidos sobre ellos. En la parte trasera, los cobertizos tienen paredes correderas de cristal que se abren al paisaje y a las espectaculares vistas de los valles en los que la mujer, de joven, hacía senderismo y acampaba.

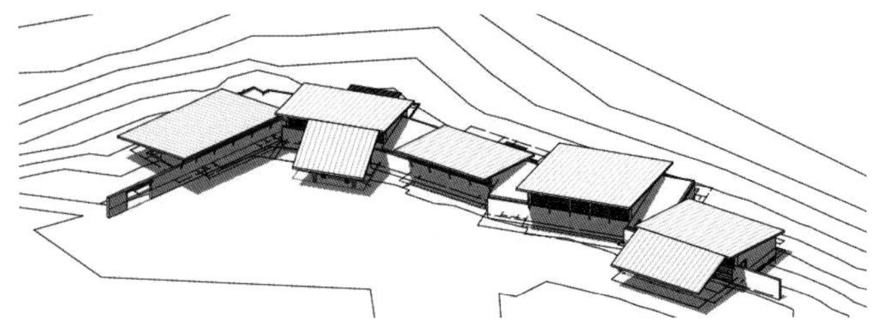

Shadow study, June 22, 3 p. m.

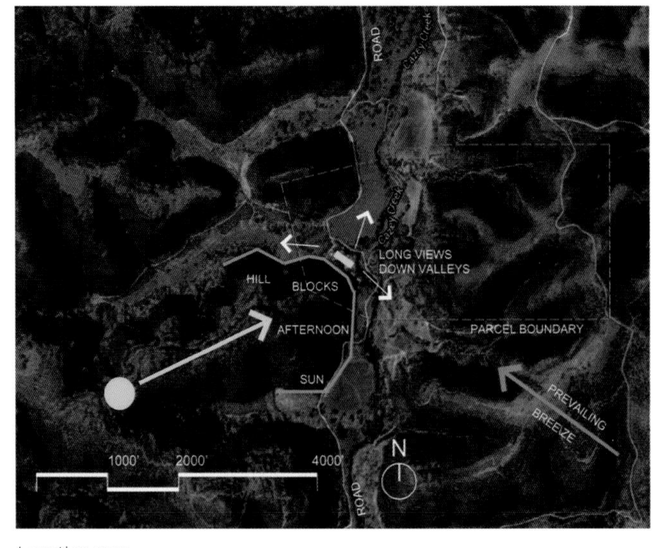



Location map

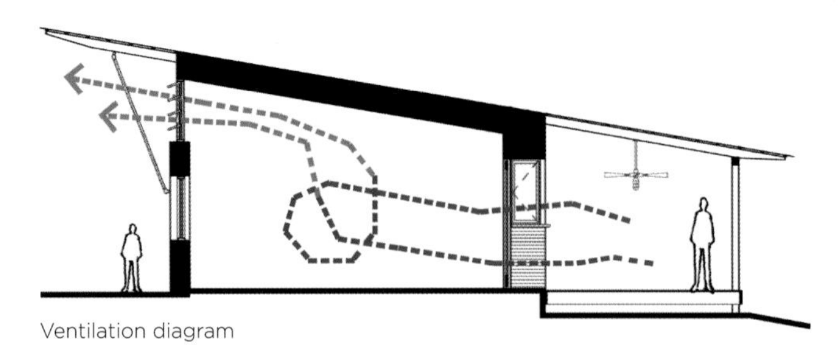

Ventilation diagram

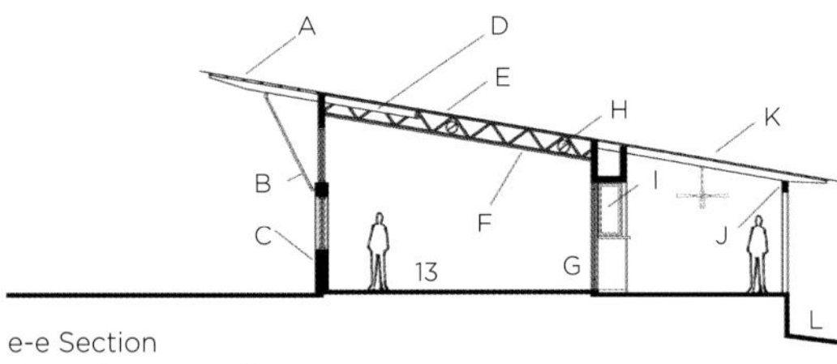

e-e Section
at great room pod

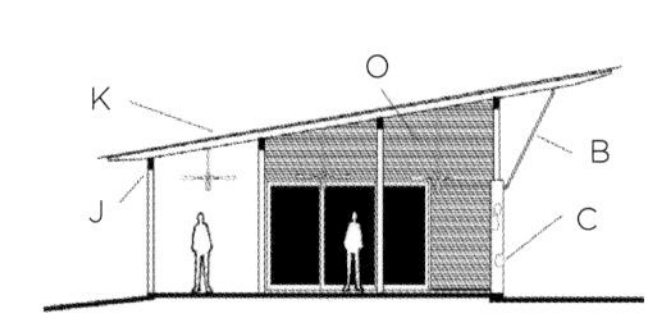

Section
at master suite pod

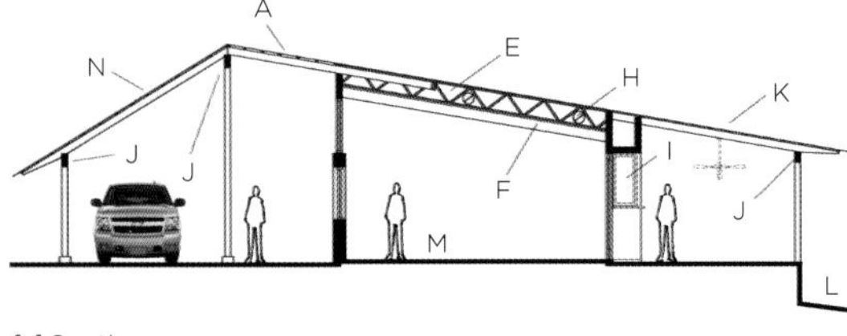

f-f Section
at great room pod

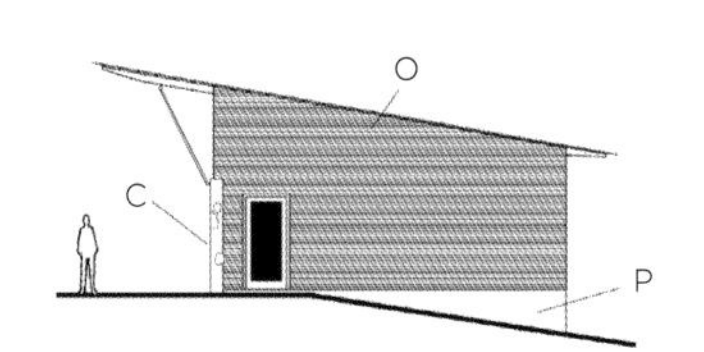

Exterior elevation
at garage pod (end)

A. Typical front overhang: corrugated galvanized. steel over 2x4 runners, over exposed 2x8 wood rafters
B. 1-1/4" I.D. galvanized steel support brackets
C. 8"-high stone veneer wall
D. 2x8 wood rafters anchored to wood trusses and to double 2x8 wood blocking between trusses
E. Engineered wood trusses
F. Ceiling options: Sheetrock/1x6 wood/ 1/2" wood veneer plywood
G. Sliding glass door
H. HVAC duct system
I. Kitchen window beyond
J. 6x10 wood beam over 6x6 wood post
K. Typical porch roof: Corrugated galvanized steel over 2x4 runners, over exposed 2x8 wood rafters
L. Existing grade
M. Stained concrete floor
N. Porte cochere roof is same as front overhang
O. Corrugated steel siding
P. Poured concrete foundation

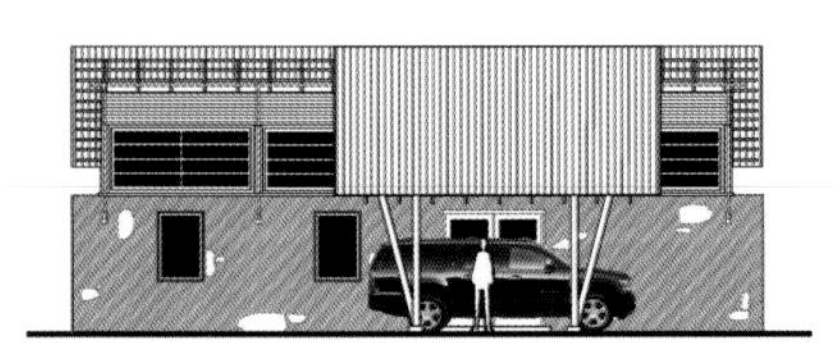

Exterior elevation at great room pod (front)

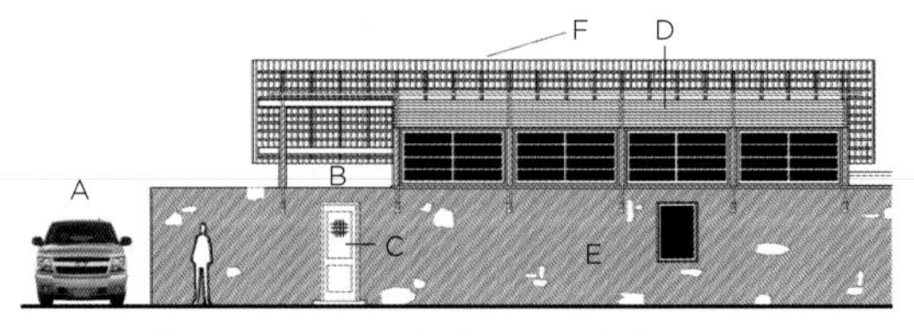

Exterior elevation at master bedroom pod (front)

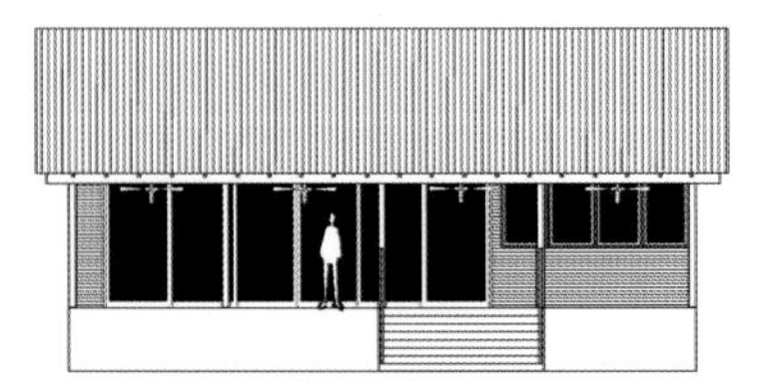

Exterior elevation at great room pod (rear)

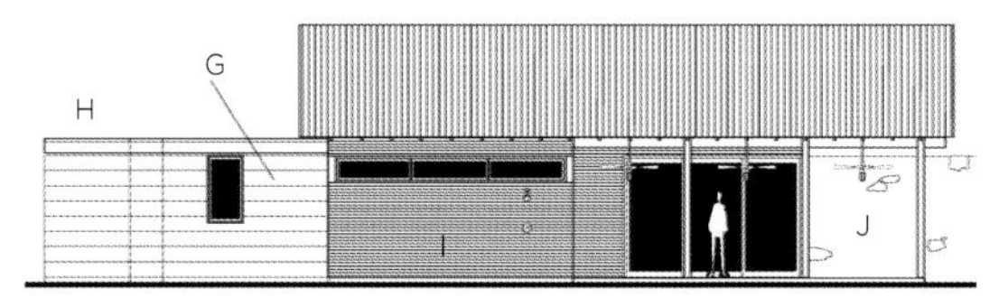

Exterior elevation at master bedroom pod (rear)

A. Gateway to compound
B. Porch beyond
C. Antique wood door to porch
D. Rusted corrugated steel
E. Stone wall
F. Corrugated galvanized overhang and porch roof
G. Painted hardiboard siding—run in 12"-wide horizontal planks
H. Flat-roofed connector: laundry room and mud room
I. Rusted corrugated steel siding installed horizontally
J. Stone wall beyond

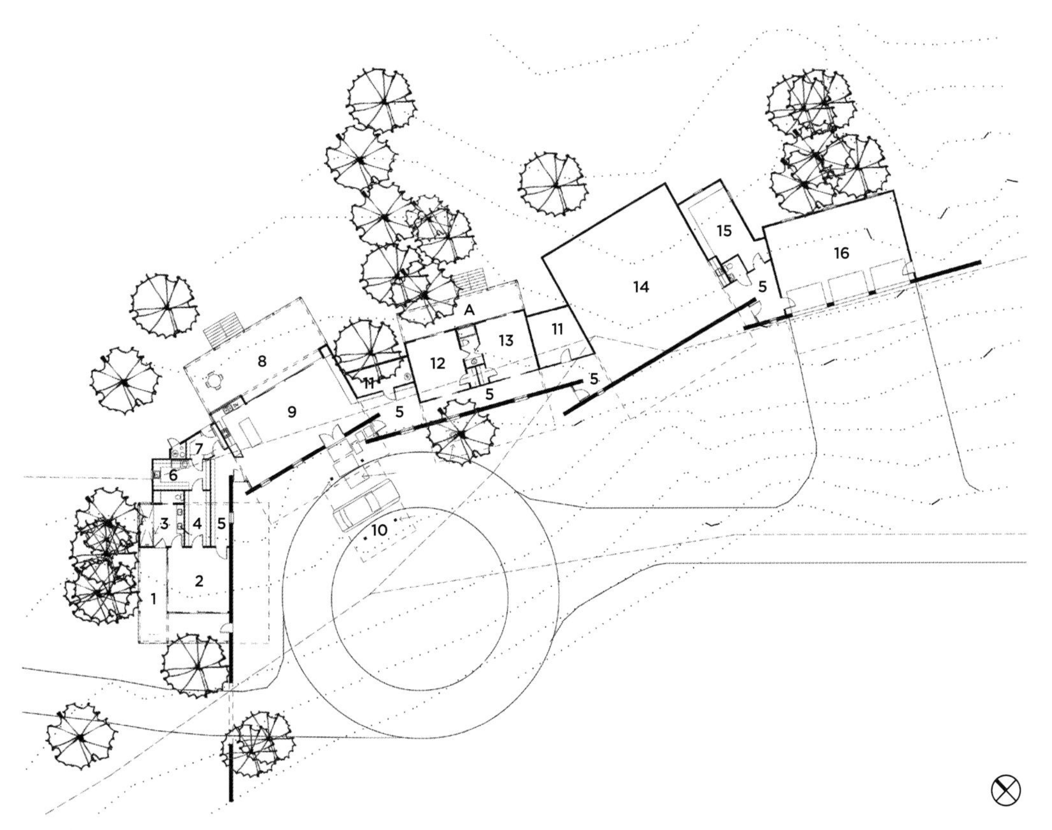


1. 8'-Deep covered porch
2. Master bedroom
3. Master bathroom
4. Closet
5. Gallery
6. Laundry room
7. Mud room and pantry
8. 12'-14'-deep covered porch
9. Great room
10. Porte cochere
11. Storage
12. Study
13. Bedroom
14. Train room
15. Shop and storage
16. Three-car garage

Site plan

## ALTA LUZ

Kendall County, Texas, United States // Lot area: 5 acres; building area: 816 sq ft

Alta Luz is a small, one-bedroom house on a hill overlooking the Guadalupe River in the Texas Hill Country. The site is thick with juniper bushes and cedar trees, obscuring the house from the street as well as from the driveway to the house. Freestanding walls in the landscape were used to keep the house obscured and direct the visitor through a procession of outdoor and indoor rooms and a series of "reveals". One of these walls forms the parking area. It hides the house from view as it guides the visitor by foot to a gate that reveals an outdoor space that reveals another wall in the landscape, long, blank and mysterious. This "freestanding wall" is the house itself. One of the wall's sixteen identical wall panels pushes open to reveal a light-filled indoor volume, which in turn, reveals the broad valley view framed by selectively placed window walls.

Alta Luz est une petite maison d'une chambre à coucher située sur une colline surplombant la rivière Guadalupe, dans le Texas Hill Country. Le site est couvert de buissons de genévrier et de cèdres, ce qui masque la maison depuis la rue et depuis l'allée qui y mène. Des murs autoportants dans le paysage ont été utilisés pour maintenir la maison cachée et diriger le visiteur à travers une procession de pièces extérieures et intérieures et une série de « révélations ». L'un de ces murs forme l'aire de stationnement. Il cache la maison à la vue tout en guidant le visiteur à pied vers une porte qui révèle un espace extérieur qui révèle un autre mur dans le paysage, long, vide et mystérieux. Ce « mur autoportant » est la maison elle-même. L'un des seize panneaux muraux identiques du mur s'ouvre pour révéler un volume intérieur lumineux qui, à son tour, révèle la large vue sur la vallée encadrée par des murs de fenêtres placées de manière sélective.

Alta Luz ist ein kleines Haus mit einem Schlafzimmer auf einem Hügel mit Blick auf den Guadalupe River im Texas Hill Country. Das Grundstück ist dicht mit Wacholderbüschen und Zedern bewachsen, so dass das Haus sowohl von der Straße als auch von der Zufahrt aus nicht zu sehen ist. Freistehende Mauern in der Landschaft wurden verwendet, um das Haus zu verbergen und den Besucher durch eine Reihe von Außen- und Innenräumen und eine Reihe von „Enthüllungen" zu führen. Eine dieser Mauern bildet den Parkbereich. Sie verbirgt das Haus, während sie den Besucher zu Fuß zu einem Tor führt, das einen Außenraum freigibt, der eine weitere lange, leere und geheimnisvolle Mauer in der Landschaft offenbart. Diese „freistehende Wand" ist das Haus selbst. Eine der sechzehn identischen Wandpaneele lässt sich aufschieben und gibt einen lichtdurchfluteten Innenraum frei, der wiederum den Blick auf das weite Tal freigibt, das von gezielt platzierten Fensterwänden eingerahmt wird.

Alta Luz es una pequeña casa de un dormitorio situada en una colina con vistas al río Guadalupe, en la región de las colinas de Texas. El lugar está repleto de arbustos de enebro y cedros, que ocultan la casa tanto desde la calle como desde el camino de entrada a la casa. Se utilizaron muros independientes en el paisaje para mantener la casa oculta y dirigir al visitante a través de una procesión de habitaciones exteriores e interiores y una serie de «revelaciones». Uno de estos muros forma la zona de aparcamiento. Oculta la casa a la vista mientras guía al visitante a pie hasta una puerta que revela un espacio exterior que deja ver otro muro en el paisaje, largo, blanco y misterioso. Este «muro independiente» es la propia casa. Uno de los dieciséis paneles idénticos del muro se abre para revelar un volumen interior lleno de luz que, a su vez, deja ver la amplia vista del valle enmarcada por paredes de ventanas colocadas selectivamente.

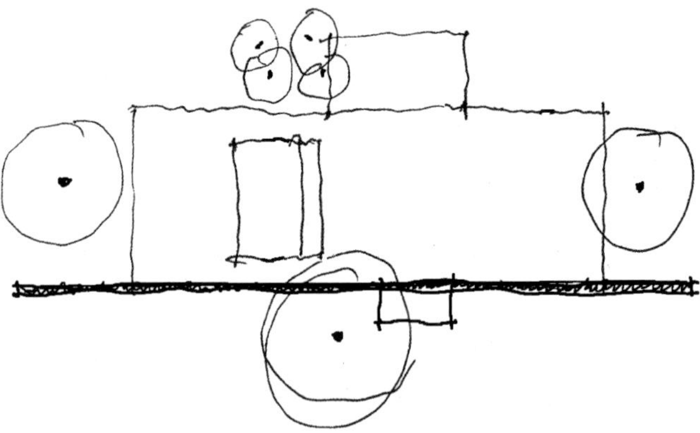

Conceptual design

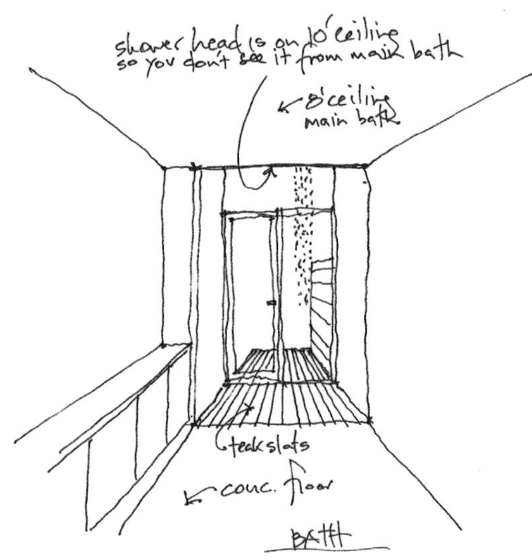


Bathroom sketch

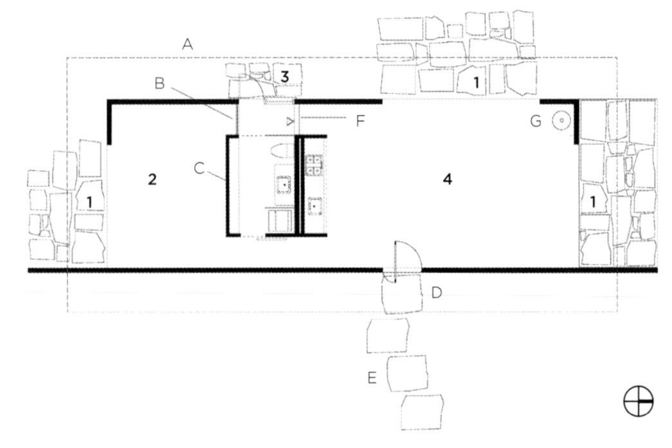


Floor plan

1. Flagstone patio
2. Bedroom
3. Outdoor shower
4. Living area

A. 48" roof overhang above
B. Sandblasted glass panel instead of gypsum wall
C. Walnut paneling on all four sides
D. 4'x8' pivot panel
E. Large flagstones
F. 8'-foot partition
G. Wood stove

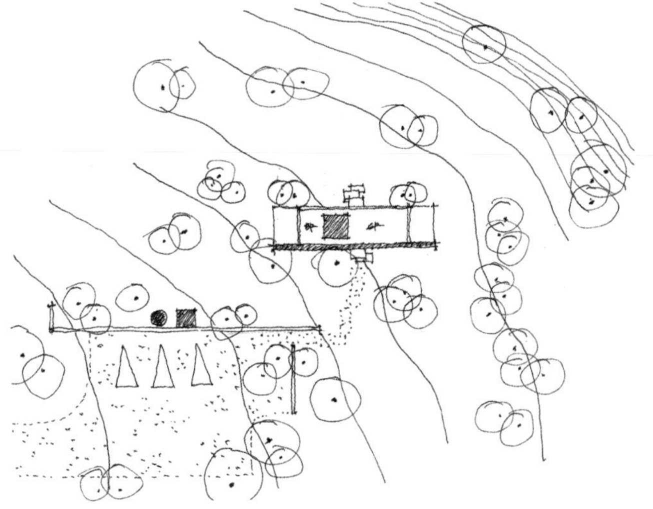

Site plan

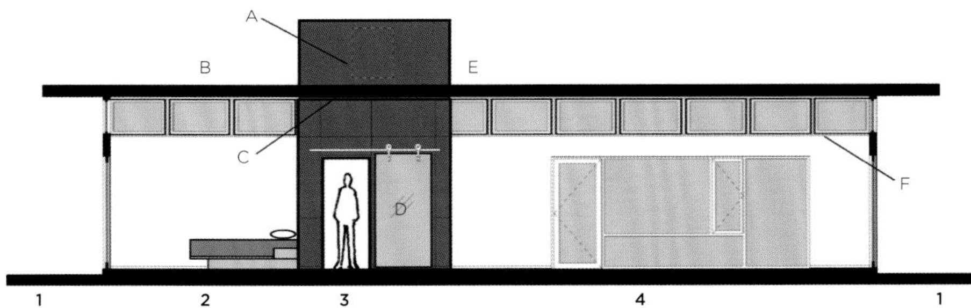


Building secion through hallway

1. Patio
2. Bedroom
3. Bathroom
4. Living area

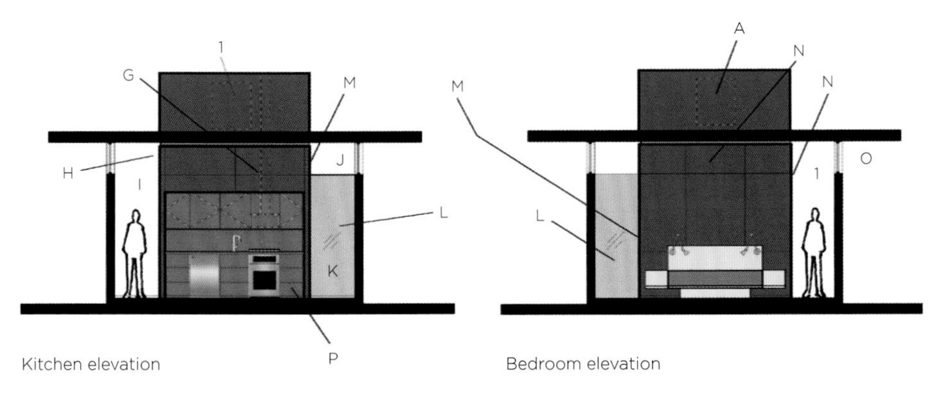


Kitchen elevation

Bedroom elevation

A. A/C compressor inside
B. 6"-thick insulation roof
C. 1/2"x1/2" recess along perimeter of wood core at ceiling
D. Frosted glass rolling door
E. Roof mechanical screen to hide A/C compressor, flues for range, hood, dryer, and plumbing vent
F. 1"x2" wood trim or 1"x8" shelf to run around interior perimeter of the house
G. Range hood and flue hidden inside cabinets
H. Walnut wood panels matching cabinets to wrap around corner and continue down hall to bedroom wall, creating a wood "core" unit
I. Hall open to living area
J. Open to bedroom
K. 42"-deep recess
L. Sandblasted glass panel instead of sheetrock wall
M. Walnut panels to matching cabinets to wrap around corner to 12" recessed wall
N. Walnut panels to wrap around corner from hallway
O. Clerestory window
P. Bold color kitchen recessed into walnut wood core

## THE OUTPOST

Fredericksburg, Texas, United States // Lot area: 44 acres; building area: 2,400-sq ft living space; 700-sq ft garage.

The Outpost is a weekend house on forty-four acres in rural Gillespie County in Texas. The house is geared for outdoor living and embracing the landscape. It is composed of three separate units connected by a cloister and organized around a central courtyard that opens onto a grove of oak trees. Each unit houses different functions: living and eating, sleeping and bathing, working and exercising. The living/eating unit opens onto a covered porch to the south and the courtyard to the north. With twenty-four-foot-wide sliding glass panels, it can become an open pavilion. The garage has twenty-foot overhead doors on both ends, so it can be used as a spacious covered entertainment area that opens onto the central courtyard. Nestled into a hill at the edge of the tree line, The Outpost affords views of the meadows, oak groves, wild turkeys, deer, and other wild inhabitants.

L'Outpost est une maison de week-end située sur un terrain de quarante-quatre acres dans le comté rural de Gillespie au Texas. La maison est conçue pour vivre en plein air et embrasser le paysage. Elle est composée de trois unités distinctes reliées par un cloître et organisées autour d'une cour centrale qui s'ouvre sur un bosquet de chênes. Chaque unité abrite différentes fonctions : vivre et manger, dormir et se laver, travailler et s'exercer. L'unité de vie/mangeoire s'ouvre sur un porche couvert au sud et sur la cour au nord. Avec des panneaux de verre coulissants de vingt-quatre pieds de large, elle peut se transformer en pavillon ouvert. Le garage est équipé de portes basculantes de vingt pieds de large aux deux extrémités, ce qui permet de l'utiliser comme un vaste espace de divertissement couvert qui s'ouvre sur la cour centrale. Nichée dans une colline à la limite de la ligne d'arbres, The Outpost offre des vues sur les prairies, les bosquets de chênes, les dindons sauvages, les cerfs et autres habitants sauvages.

The Outpost ist ein Wochenendhaus auf einem achtundswanzig Hektar großen Grundstück im ländlichen Gillespie County in Texas. Das Haus ist auf das Leben im Freien und die Einbeziehung der Landschaft ausgerichtet. Es besteht aus drei separaten Einheiten, die durch einen Kreuzgang verbunden und um einen zentralen Innenhof angeordnet sind, der sich zu einem Eichenhain hin öffnet. Jede Einheit beherbergt verschiedene Funktionen: Wohnen und Essen, Schlafen und Baden, Arbeiten und Trainieren. Die Wohn-/Esseinheit öffnet sich zu einer überdachten Veranda im Süden und zum Innenhof im Norden. Mit vierundzwanzig Fuß breiten Glasschiebeelementen kann sie zu einem offenen Pavillon werden. Die Garage verfügt an beiden Enden über zwanzig Fuß lange Sektionaltore, so dass sie als geräumiger überdachter Unterhaltungsbereich genutzt werden kann, der sich zum zentralen Innenhof hin öffnet. Eingebettet in einen Hügel am Rande der Baumgrenze bietet The Outpost einen Blick auf die Wiesen, Eichenhaine, wilde Truthähne, Hirsche und andere wilde Bewohner.

The Outpost es una casa de fin de semana en dieciocho hectareas en el condado rural de Gillespie, Texas. Pensada para vivir al aire libre y abrazar el paisaje, se compone de tres unidades separadas conectadas por un claustro y organizadas en torno a un patio central que se abre a un bosque de robles. Cada unidad alberga diferentes funciones: vivir y comer, dormir y bañarse, trabajar y hacer ejercicio. Con paneles de vidrio deslizantes de veinticuatro pies de ancho, el salón-comedor puede convertirse en un pabellón abierto, orientado a un porche cubierto al sur y al patio al norte. El garaje tiene puertas basculantes de veinte pies de ancho en ambos extremos, por lo que puede utilizarse como una amplia zona de ocio cubierta abierta al patio central. Enclavada en una colina al borde de la arboleda, The Outpost ofrece vistas de los prados, los robledales, los pavos salvajes, los ciervos y demás habitantes silvestres.

Floor plan

1. Flagstone patio
2. Pavilion
3. Powder room
4. Storage and pantry
5. Porch
6. Master bedroom
7. Master bathroom
8. Bathroom
9. Bedroom
10. Courtyard
11. Garage
12. Laundry room
13. Exercise room

A. 24" roof overhang
B. 2 x 2 steel tube post-and-beam patio structure and corrugated steel roof
C. Tankless gas water heater
D. Water softener and RO filter
E. Electronics panel
F. Corrugated metal doors
G. Perforated Corten gates
H. No corner post at sliding glass doors
I. Corrugated metal siding
J. Frameless glass and door
K. Covered walkway
L. Hidden door in paneling

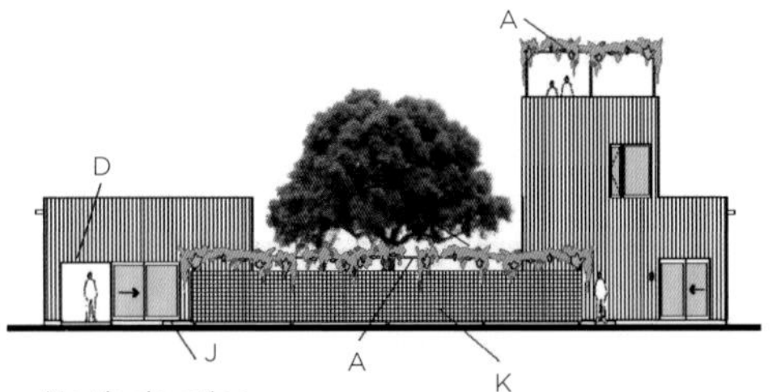

North elevation

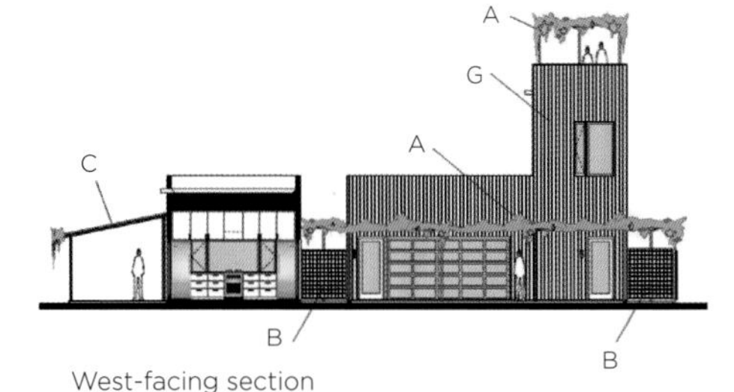

West-facing section

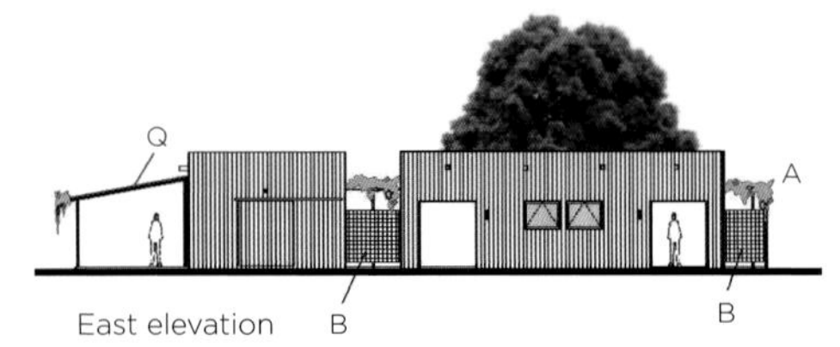

East elevation

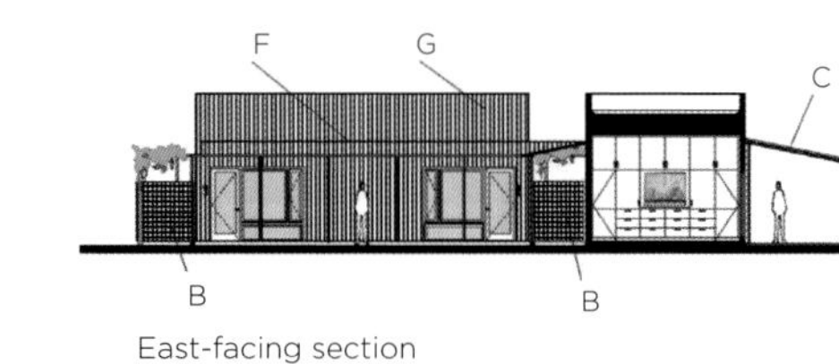

East-facing section

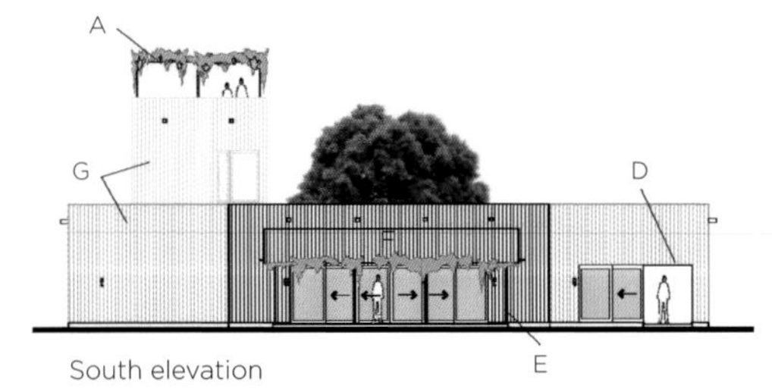

South elevation

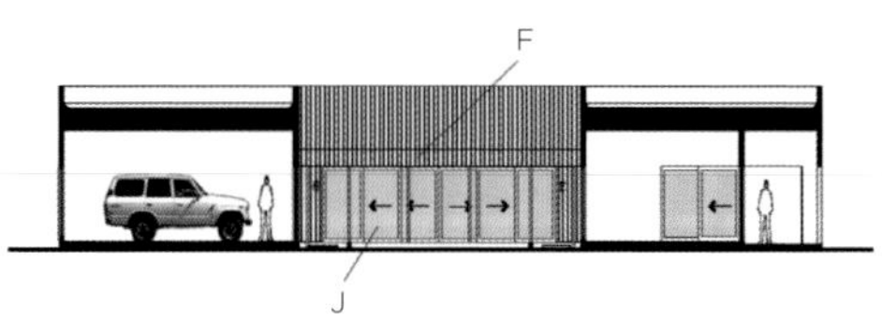

North-facing section

Section through tower

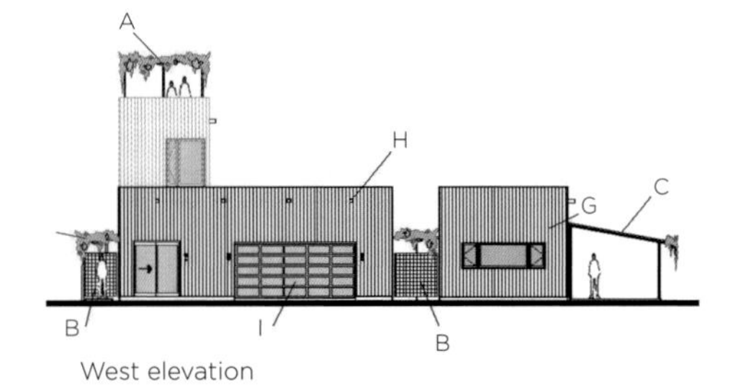

West elevation

A. Steel tube trellis with galvanized hog panels on top
B. Perforated Corten steel pivot gate over 2" x 2" steel tube frame
C. Corrugated Galvalume steel roof
D. Furred down top of porch openings to match top of sliding door openings
E. Square steel tube posts and beam
F. Sloped corrugated metal roof
G. Corrugated Galvalume steel siding
H. 6"x 6"x12" Galvalume metal scuppers
I. Aluminum and glass overhead door
J. Stock size sliding glass doors
K. Perforated Corten metal fence
L. 1"x6" wood decking
M. 30"x60" roof hatch
N. Ship's ladder
O. 1/4" steel plate shade box around windows
P. Mini-split A/C condenser unit

# JAY CORDER ARCHITECT

266
v

**CRESTWAY**

Architect:
Jay Corder Architect
Interior Designer:
Rachel Mast Design
Structural Engineer:
Brad Farris/ARCH Consulting Engineers
Photographer:
© Dror Baldinger

270
v

**KENNELWOOD**

Architect:
Jay Corder Architect
Structural Engineer:
Greenearth Engineering
Photographer:
© Chase Daniel

274
v

**LAMPASAS RANCH**

Architect:
Jay Corder Architect
Landscape Architect:
Alisa West/Westshop
Interior Designer:
Kasey McCarty Interior Design
Structural Engineer:
Brad Farris/ARCH Consulting Engineers
Photographer:
© Chase Daniel

www.jaycorder.com @jaycorderarchitect

Jay Corder

I didn't stumble into architecture. In fact, I don't think there was a time when I didn't know this was what I wanted to do. I started down the path to becoming an architect early when my only-child life spurred me to be creative and imaginative. My mother had a designer's eye and fostered that creativity. That formative experience helped me develop a lens on the world that allows me to dream big, see solutions first, and find joy in the creative process. Today, being an architect is an innate part of my personality entwined with my personal life. It's sort of a selfish passion for helping people bring their dreams to life. But the privilege of doing that comes with responsibility, and it's on me to develop a trustworthy partnership with each of my clients by making sure I understand their desires, dreams, and goals. To get there, I developed a design process that sets clear expectations, establishes optimal momentum, prioritizes value, and generates predictable outcomes while providing beauty, joy, confidence, and peace.

Ich bin nicht in die Architektur gestolpert. Ich glaube nicht, dass es eine Zeit gab, in der ich nicht wusste, dass ich das machen wollte. Der Weg zum Architekten begann schon früh, als ich als Einzelkind kreativ und phantasievoll war. Meine Mutter hatte das Auge einer Designerin und förderte diese Kreativität. Diese prägende Erfahrung hat mir geholfen, eine Sichtweise auf die Welt zu entwickeln, die es mir erlaubt, große Träume zu haben, Lösungen zuerst zu sehen und Freude am kreativen Prozess zu finden. Heute ist der Beruf des Architekten ein fester Bestandteil meiner Persönlichkeit, der mit meinem Privatleben verwoben ist. Es ist eine Art egoistische Leidenschaft, Menschen zu helfen, ihre Träume zu verwirklichen. Aber das Privileg, dies zu tun, bringt auch Verantwortung mit sich, und es liegt an mir, eine vertrauensvolle Partnerschaft mit jedem meiner Kunden aufzubauen, indem ich sicherstelle, dass ich ihre Wünsche, Träume und Ziele verstehe. Um dies zu erreichen, habe ich einen Gestaltungsprozess entwickelt, der klare Erwartungen setzt, eine optimale Dynamik erzeugt, den Wert in den Vordergrund stellt und vorhersehbare Ergebnisse schafft, während er gleichzeitig Schönheit, Freude, Vertrauen und Frieden vermittelt.

Je ne suis pas tombé dans l'architecture par hasard. En fait, je ne pense pas qu'il y ait eu un moment où je n'ai pas su que c'était ce que je voulais faire. J'ai commencé à m'engager sur la voie de l'architecture très tôt, lorsque ma vie d'enfant unique m'a incité à être créatif et imaginatif. Ma mère avait l'œil d'un designer et a encouragé cette créativité. Cette expérience formatrice m'a aidé à développer une vision du monde qui me permet de rêver grand, de voir les solutions en premier et de trouver de la joie dans le processus créatif. Aujourd'hui, le métier d'architecte est une partie innée de ma personnalité qui se mêle à ma vie personnelle. C'est une sorte de passion égoïste pour aider les gens à donner vie à leurs rêves. Mais le privilège de faire cela s'accompagne de responsabilités, et il m'incombe de développer un partenariat fiable avec chacun de mes clients en m'assurant que je comprends leurs désirs, leurs rêves et leurs objectifs. Pour y parvenir, j'ai développé un processus de conception qui fixe des attentes claires, établit une dynamique optimale, donne la priorité à la valeur et génère des résultats prévisibles tout en apportant beauté, joie, confiance et paix.

No me tropecé con la arquitectura. De hecho, creo que no hubo ningún momento en el que no supiera que esto era lo que quería hacer. Empecé a recorrer el camino para convertirme en arquitecto muy pronto, cuando mi vida de hijo único me impulsó a ser creativo e imaginativo. Mi madre tenía ojo de diseñadora y fomentaba esa creatividad. Esa experiencia formativa me ayudó a desarrollar una visión del mundo que me permite soñar a lo grande, ver primero las soluciones y encontrar la alegría en el proceso creativo. Hoy en día, ser arquitecto es una parte innata de mi personalidad entrelazada con mi vida personal. Es una especie de pasión egoísta por ayudar a la gente a hacer realidad sus sueños. Pero el privilegio de hacerlo conlleva una responsabilidad, y de mí depende desarrollar una asociación de confianza con cada uno de mis clientes asegurándome de que entiendo sus deseos, sueños y objetivos. Para conseguirlo, he desarrollado un proceso de diseño que establece expectativas claras, establece un impulso óptimo, prioriza el valor y genera resultados predecibles mientras proporciona belleza, alegría, confianza y paz.

## CRESTWAY

Austin, Texas, United States // Lot area: 19,927 sq ft; building area: 4,226 sq ft

The remodel of an existing modernist house took inspiration from the neighborhood houses and, per the client's request, much of the existing structure was reused. The design came together with a palette of forms and textures that gave the house a contemporary look while maintaining its original modernist aesthetic. The project posed two challenges: One, the main floor of the house is below street level, and the site has a significant slope; two, the existing house had a walk-out basement with low ceilings that opened to a pool. By raising the main floor of the house about two-and-a-half feet, the ceiling height of the walk-out could be increased and the slope to the street from the main floor reduced. This increased the sense of space and let in generous daylight. Overall, Corder changed the scale of the house, improving its views without overpowering the neighboring homes.

Le remodelage d'une maison moderniste existante s'est inspiré des maisons du quartier et, à la demande du client, une grande partie de la structure existante a été réutilisée. Le projet s'est concrétisé par une palette de formes et de textures qui a donné à la maison un aspect contemporain tout en conservant son esthétique moderniste d'origine. Le projet a posé deux défis : D'une part, le rez-de-chaussée de la maison se trouve en dessous du niveau de la rue et le site présente une pente importante ; d'autre part, la maison existante avait un sous-sol avec des plafonds bas qui donnait sur une piscine. En surélevant le rez-de-chaussée de la maison d'environ deux pieds et demi, la hauteur du plafond du sous-sol put être augmentée et la pente du rez-de-chaussée vers la rue réduite. Cela a permis d'accroître la sensation d'espace et de laisser entrer une lumière naturelle généreuse. Dans l'ensemble, Corder a changé l'échelle de la maison, améliorant ses vues sans dominer les maisons voisines.

Der Umbau eines bestehenden modernistischen Hauses wurde von den Nachbarhäusern inspiriert und auf Wunsch des Kunden wurde ein Großteil der bestehenden Struktur wiederverwendet. Das Design kam mit einer Palette von Formen und Texturen zusammen, die dem Haus ein zeitgemäßes Aussehen verliehen und gleichzeitig seine ursprüngliche modernistische Ästhetik beibehielten. Das Projekt brachte zwei Herausforderungen mit sich: Erstens liegt das Erdgeschoss des Hauses unter dem Straßenniveau, und das Gelände weist eine erhebliche Neigung auf; Zweitens hatte das bestehende Haus einen begehbaren Keller mit niedrigen Decken, der sich zu einem Pool hin öffnete. Durch Anheben des Hauptgeschosses des Hauses um etwa zweieinhalb Fuß konnte die Deckenhöhe des Ausstiegs erhöht und die Neigung vom Hauptgeschoss zur Straße verringert werden. Dadurch wurde das Raumgefühl erhöht und großzügiges Tageslicht hereingelassen. Insgesamt änderte Corder den Maßstab des Hauses und verbesserte seine Aussicht, ohne die Nachbarhäuser zu überwältigen.

La remodelación de una casa modernista existente se inspiró en las casas de barrio y, por pedido del cliente, se reutilizó gran parte de la estructura existente. El diseño se completó con una paleta de formas y texturas que dio a la casa un aspecto contemporáneo manteniendo su estética modernista original. El proyecto planteaba dos retos: por un lado, la planta principal de la casa está por debajo del nivel de la calle, y el terreno tiene una importante pendiente; por otro, la casa existente tenía un sótano con techos bajos que se abría a una piscina. Al elevar el piso principal de la casa unos dos pies y medio, se podría aumentar la altura del techo de la salida y reducir la pendiente hacia la calle desde el piso principal. Esto aumentó la sensación de espacio y permitió la entrada de abundante luz natural. En general, Corder cambió la escala de la casa, mejorando sus vistas sin dominar las casas vecinas.

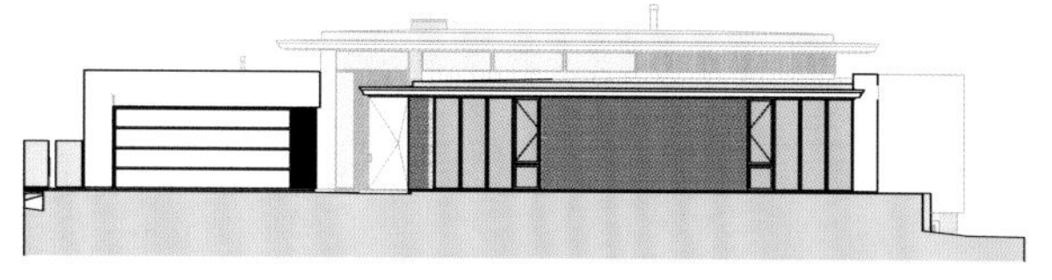

Front elevation

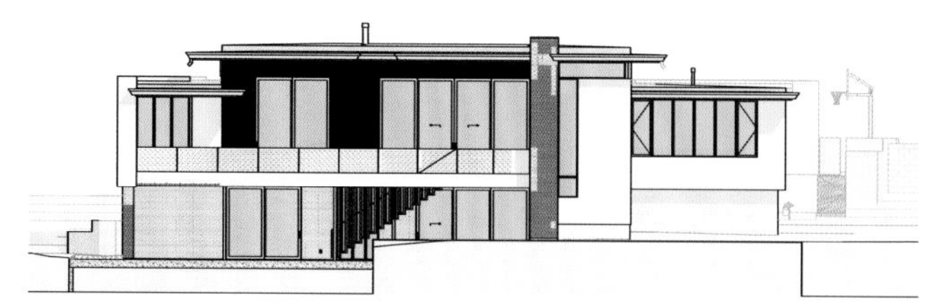

Rear elevation

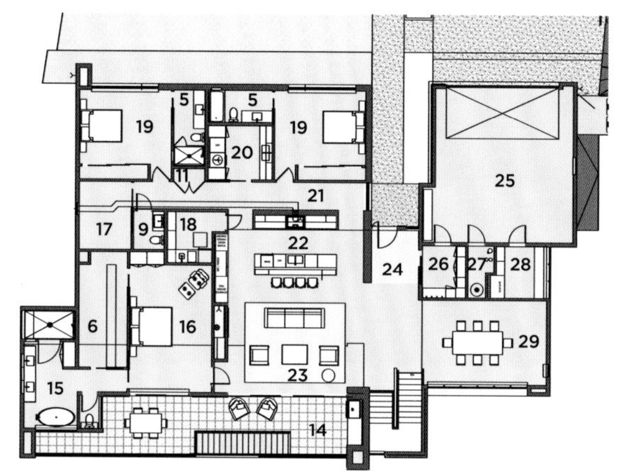


Upper floor plan

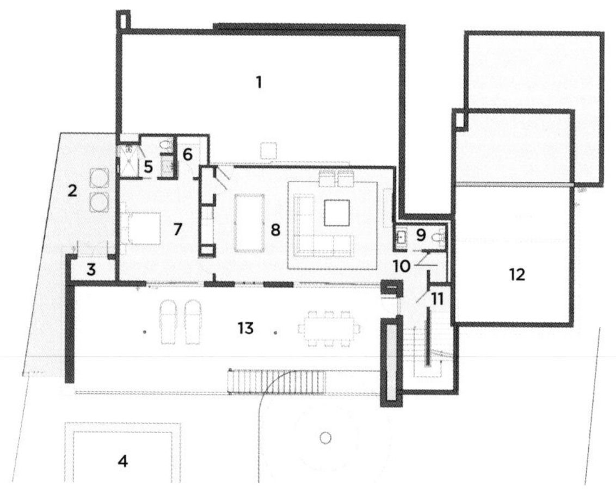


Lower floor plan

1. Crawl space
2. Utility area
3. Pool storage
4. Pool
5. Bathroom
6. Walk-in closet
7. Guest room
8. Family room
9. Powder room
10. AV closet
11. Storage
12. Slab foundation/ crawl space
13. Covered patio
14. Covered porch
15. Master bathroom
16. Master bedroom
17. Office
18. Pantry
19. Bedroom
20. Laundry room
21. Hallway
22. Kitchen
23. Living area
24. Entry
25. Garage
26. Mud room
27. Mechanical room
28. Fly room
29. Dining area

## KENNELWOOD

Austin, Texas, United States // Lot area: 11,137 sq ft; building area: 6,730 sq ft

Gossett and Company, LLC—a home builder and development firm for some of Austin's top residential properties—approached Jay Corder Architects to design a speculative home that felt like a forest hideaway. The property is on steep terrain with ancient trees that needed to be preserved per code. Corder and his team designed the home in the modern transitional style, embracing open-concept living, capitalizing on the views, and connecting the interior to the outdoors. To that end, floor-to-ceiling windows at the front and back of the house allow generous daylighting and highlight the open feel of the home while framing the views of the majestic old trees and beyond. Neutral finishes for the exterior complement the property's natural surroundings and provide a blank slate for the interior, allowing the homeowner to personalize their hideaway.

Gossett and Company, LLC - un constructeur de maisons et une société de développement pour certaines des meilleures propriétés résidentielles d'Austin - a fait appel à Jay Corder Architects pour concevoir une maison spéculative qui ressemble à un refuge dans la forêt. La propriété se trouve sur un terrain escarpé avec des arbres anciens qui devaient être préservés conformément au code. Corder et son équipe ont conçu la maison dans un style transitionnel moderne, en privilégiant les espaces ouverts, en tirant parti des vues et en reliant l'intérieur à l'extérieur. À cette fin, des fenêtres allant du sol au plafond permettent un éclairage naturel généreux et soulignent l'aspect ouvert de la maison tout en encadrant les vues sur les vieux arbres majestueux et au-delà. Les finitions neutres de l'extérieur complètent l'environnement naturel de la propriété et offrent un espace vierge pour l'intérieur, permettant au propriétaire de personnaliser son refuge.

Gossett and Company, LLC - ein Hausbauer und Erschließungsunternehmen für einige der besten Wohnimmobilien in Austin - wandte sich an Jay Corder Architects, um ein spekulatives Haus zu entwerfen, das wie ein Versteck im Wald wirkt. Das Anwesen befindet sich auf einem steilen Gelände mit uralten Bäumen, die gemäß den Vorschriften erhalten werden mussten. Corder und sein Team entwarfen das Haus im modernen Übergangsstil, der ein offenes Wohnkonzept vorsieht, die Aussicht nutzt und das Innere mit der Außenwelt verbindet. Zu diesem Zweck ermöglichen raumhohe Fenster eine großzügige natürliche Belichtung und betonen den offenen Aspekt des Hauses, während sie den Blick auf die majestätischen alten Bäume und darüber hinaus einrahmen. Neutrale Oberflächen für das Äußere ergänzen die natürliche Umgebung des Grundstücks und bieten eine leere Tafel für das Innere, die es dem Hausbesitzer ermöglicht, seinen Rückzugsort individuell zu gestalten.

Gossett and Company, LLC -una empresa constructora y promotora de algunas de las mejores propiedades residenciales de Austin- se puso en contacto con Jay Corder Architects para diseñar una casa que se sintiera como un refugio en el bosque. La propiedad se encuentra en un terreno escarpado con árboles centenarios que debían preservarse de acuerdo con la normativa. Corder y su equipo diseñaron la casa en un estilo moderno, con un concepto diáfano, aprovechando las vistas y conectando el interior con el exterior. Para ello, ventanales del suelo al techo permiten una generosa iluminación natural y resaltan la sensación de amplitud de la casa, a la vez que enmarcan las vistas de los majestuosos árboles viejos. Los acabados neutros del exterior complementan el entorno natural de la propiedad y proporcionan una pizarra en blanco para el interior, lo que permite al propietario personalizar su refugio.

South elevation

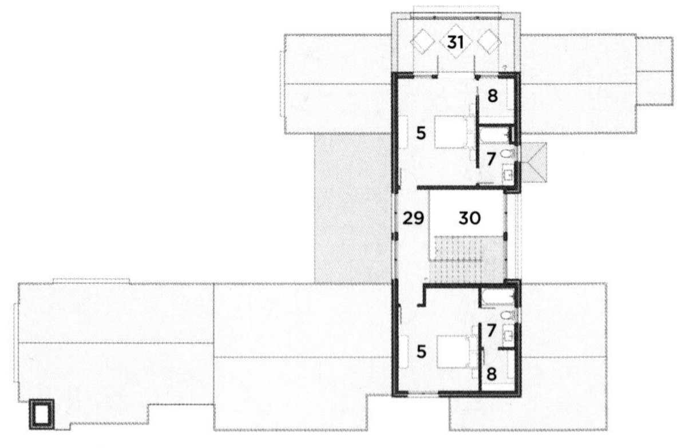


Second floor plan

North elevation

First floor plan

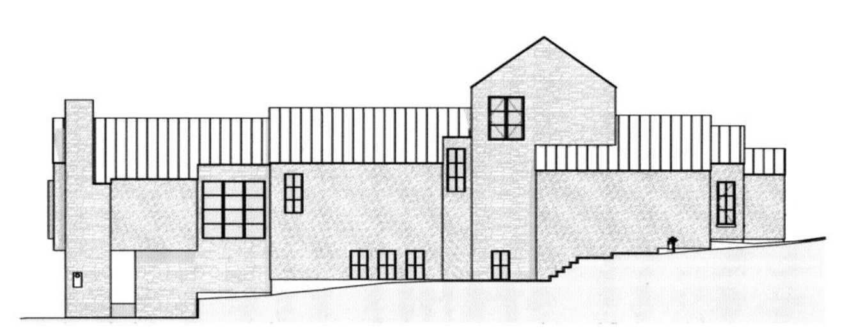

East elevation

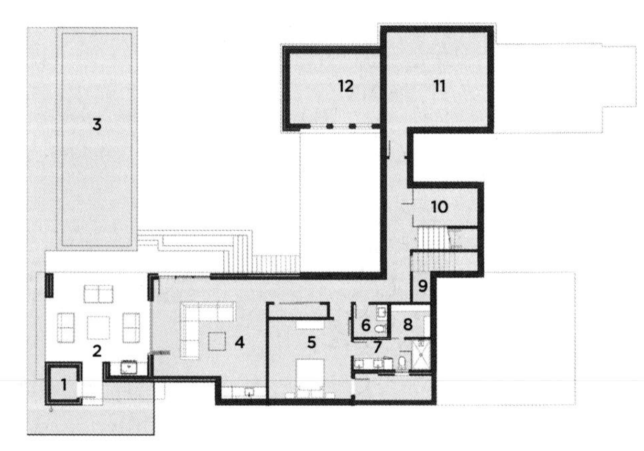


Basement/pool level floor plan

1. Pool storage
2. Terrace
3. Pool
4. Family room
5. Bedroom
6. Powder room
7. Bathroom
8. Walk-in closet
9. Mechanical room
10. Wine cellar
11. Exercise room
12. Crawl space
13. Living area
14. Dining area
15. Kitchen
16. Pantry
17. Utility room
18. Storage
19. Mud room
20. Garage
21. Entry
22. Porch
23. Hall
24. Master bedroom
25. Master bathroom
26. Master walk-in closet
27. Guest bedroom
28. Guest bathroom
29. Catwalk
30. Open to below
31. Balcony

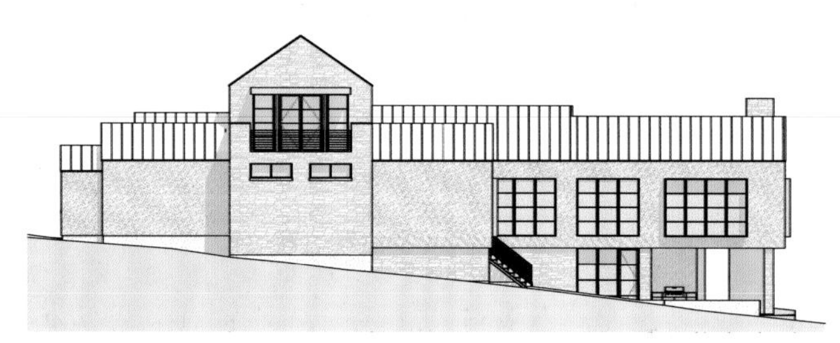

West elevation

## LAMPASAS RANCH

Lampasas, Texas, United States

Confronted with the renovation of a house designed by architect Frank Welch—the father of Texas regional modernism—Jay Corder and his team approached the project with great reverence, creating a sleek but comfortable home with a focus on regionality and durability and improving the views. Interior designer Kasey McCarty took a similar approach, using modern materials that brightened the interiors and lifted some of the original heaviness from the space. The house's signature Frank Welch gestures—concrete columns, a distinctly simple roof atop an orthogonal box-like volume, and clear hierarchy of tight detailing and receding covered porches—were all retained and refined. The kitchen was moved to the heart of the house in response to the family's love of cooking and entertaining, while its open plan allowed the structure of the house to come to the fore.

Confrontés à la rénovation d'une maison conçue par l'architecte Frank Welch - le père du modernisme régional texan - Jay Corder et son équipe ont abordé le projet avec beaucoup de respect, créant une maison élégante mais confortable, axée sur la régionalité et durabilité et en améliorant les vues. L'architecte d'intérieur Kasey McCarty a adopté une approche similaire, en utilisant des matériaux modernes qui ont égayé les intérieurs et supprimé une partie de la lourdeur originale de l'espace. Les gestes caractéristiques de la maison de Frank Welch - colonnes en béton, un simple toit sur un volume orthogonal, hiérarchie claire de détails serrés et porches couverts en retrait - ont tous été conservés et affinés. La cuisine a été déplacée au cœur de la maison en réponse à l'amour de la famille pour la cuisine et les réceptions, tandis que son plan ouvert a permis à la structure de la maison de venir au premier plan.

Bei der Renovierung eines Hauses, das vom Architekten Frank Welch - dem Vater der regionalen Moderne in Texas - entworfen wurde, gingen Jay Corder und sein Team mit großer Ehrfurcht an das Projekt heran und schufen ein elegantes, aber komfortables Zuhause mit Schwerpunkt auf Regionalität und Langlebigkeit und verbesserten die Aussicht. Die Innenarchitektin Kasey McCarty verfolgte einen ähnlichen Ansatz, indem sie moderne Materialien verwendete, die die Innenräume aufhellten und dem Raum etwas von seiner ursprünglichen Schwere nahmen. Die charakteristischen Gesten von Frank Welchs Haus - Betonsäulen, ein einfaches Dach über einem orthogonalen Volumen, eine klare Hierarchie strenger Details und zurückgesetzte überdachte Veranden - wurden alle beibehalten und verfeinert. Die Küche wurde als Reaktion auf die Liebe der Familie zum Kochen und zur Unterhaltung in das Herz des Hauses verlegt, während ihr offener Grundriss es der Struktur des Hauses ermöglichte, in den Vordergrund zu treten.

Al enfrentarse a la renovación de una casa diseñada por el arquitecto Frank Welch -el padre del modernismo regional de Texas- Jay Corder y su equipo abordaron el proyecto con gran reverencia, creando una casa elegante pero confortable, centrada en la regionalidad y la durabilidada y mejorando las vistas. La diseñadora de interiores Kasey McCarty adoptó un enfoque similar, utilizando materiales modernos que iluminaron los interiores y eliminaron parte de la pesadez original del espacio. Los gestos característicos de Frank Welch -columnas de hormigón, un tejado claramente sencillo sobre un volumen ortogonal en forma de caja, y una clara jerarquía de detalles ajustados y porches cubiertos en retroceso- se mantuvieron y refinaron. La cocina se trasladó al corazón de la casa en respuesta al amor de la familia por la cocina y el entretenimiento, mientras que su planta abierta permitió que la estructura de la casa pasara a primer plano.

# megamorphosis

280
v

**DUSK RESIDENCE**

Architect:
John Pearcy, AIA/megamorphosis
Structural Engineer:
Mendoza Engineering
Photographer:
© Documentación Arquitectónica

284
v

**ARROYO COLORADO RESIDENCE**

Architect:
Chris Sias, RA/megamorphosis
Structural Engineer:
Casa Engineering
Photographer:
© Onnis Luque

288
v

**POOL HOUSE**

Architect:
John Pearcy, AIA/megamorphosis
Photographer:
© Documentación Arquitectónica

www.megamorphosisdesign.net megamorphosis.inc

John Pearcy, AIA

Jesse Miller, AIA

Chris Sias, RA

Established in January 1995, Meg Foster Jorn began providing residential architecture and interior design services as a sole proprietorship under the name of **megamorphosis Design**. In 2006 John Pearcy joined the firm. John contributes to the diversity and quality of projects **megamorphosis** delivers. In 2008 John became a partner, and the firm incorporated, which led to the firm's name changing to **megamorphosis**, Inc. Following the tragic loss of Meg Foster Jorn in 2017, we continue her legacy of dedication to the betterment of the community through considered design. Chris Sias became a partner in 2018, adding depth and capacity to the firm through his talent for communication and thoughtful design. Jesse Miller became a partner in December 2019, increasing our firm's ability to engage communities and serve our clients. Our steady growth in workload has brought us to our current staff of eight talented professionals. **megamorphosis** remains committed to environmentally conscious projects with unique solutions and regional sensitivity.

Meg Foster Jorn wurde im Januar 1995 als Einzelunternehmen unter dem Namen **megamorphosis Design** gegründet und bot zunächst Dienstleistungen in den Bereichen Wohnarchitektur und Innenarchitektur an. Im Jahr 2006 trat John Pearcy in das Unternehmen ein. John trägt wesentlich zur Vielfalt und Qualität der Projekte von **megamorphosis** bei. Im Jahr 2008 wurde John Pearcy Partner und die Firma wurde in eine Aktiengesellschaft umgewandelt, was zu einer Namensänderung in **megamorphosis**, Inc. führte. Nach dem tragischen Verlust von Meg Foster Jorn im Jahr 2017 setzen wir ihr Vermächtnis fort, sich durch durchdachtes Design für die Verbesserung der Gemeinschaft einzusetzen. Chris Sias wurde 2018 zum Partner ernannt und bereichert das Unternehmen durch sein Kommunikationstalent und sein durchdachtes Design. Jesse Miller wurde im Dezember 2019 zum Partner ernannt und verstärkt damit die Fähigkeit unseres Unternehmens, sich in den Gemeinden zu engagieren und unseren Kunden zu dienen. Unser stetig wachsendes Arbeitspensum hat uns zu einer Belegschaft von derzeit acht talentierten Fachleuten geführt. **megamorphosis** bleibt umweltbewussten Projekten mit einzigartigen Lösungen und regionaler Sensibilität verpflichtet.

Établie en janvier 1995, Meg Foster Jorn a commencé à fournir des services d'architecture résidentielle et d'aménagement d'intérieur en tant qu'entreprise individuelle sous le nom de **megamorphosis Design**. En 2006, John Pearcy a rejoint l'entreprise. John contribue à la diversité et à la qualité des projets que **megamorphosis** réalise. En 2008, John est devenu associé et l'entreprise s'est constituée en société, entraînant le changement de nom de l'entreprise en **megamorphosis**, Inc. Après la perte tragique de Meg Foster Jorn en 2017, nous poursuivons son héritage de dévouement à l'amélioration de la communauté à travers un design réfléchi. Chris Sias est devenu associé en 2018, ajoutant de la profondeur au cabinet grâce à son talent pour la communication et le design mesuré. Jesse Miller est devenu associé en décembre 2019, augmentant la capacité de notre cabinet à engager les communautés et à servir nos clients. Notre croissance régulière nous a amenés à notre personnel actuel de huit professionnels talentueux. **megamorphosis** reste engagé dans des projets respectueux de l'environnement, des solutions uniques et une sensibilité régionale.

Establecida en enero de 1995, Meg Foster Jorn comenzó a brindar servicios de arquitectura residencial y diseño de interiores como empresa unipersonal bajo el nombre de **megamorphosis Design**. En 2006, John Pearcy se unió al estudio contribuyendo a la diversidad y calidad de los proyectos que ofrece **megamorphosis** . En 2008, John se convirtió en socio y la empresa se incorporó, lo que llevó a que el nombre de la empresa cambiara a **megamorphosis**, Inc. Tras la trágica pérdida de Meg Foster Jorn en 2017, continuamos con su legado de dedicación a la mejora de la comunidad a través de un diseño inteligente. Chris Sias se convirtió en socio en 2018, agregando profundidad al estudio a través de su talento para la comunicación y el diseño reflexivo. Jesse Miller se convirtió en socio en diciembre de 2019, aumentando así la capacidad de nuestro estudio para involucrar a las comunidades y servir a nuestros clientes. Nuestro crecimiento constante nos ha llevado a nuestro personal actual de ocho profesionales dedicados y talentosos. **megamorphosis** sigue comprometida con proyectos ambientalmente conscientes con soluciones únicas y sensibilidad regional.

## DUSK RESIDENCE

Brownsville, Texas, United States // Lot area: 18,860 sq ft; building area: 2,623 sq ft

The residence on Dusk Drive is tucked into a corner of an ordinary subdivision and responds to the site and the owner's desire for a mid-century modern-inspired refuge. Oriented to true north instead of the subdivision street grid, the massing and deep roof overhangs mitigate the harsh south Texas sun, while providing expanses of glazing that connect the interior and exterior. The post and beam typology embraces modern building envelope standards and warm regional materials. The low-fired Mexican brick—which is a hallmark of the region—, the stained pine ceilings, and engineered lumber beams provide continuity from inside to out. Straightforward architectural strategies provide layers of prospect and refuge that allow an unremarkable suburban tract to become a home beloved by the owner and her three canine companions.

La résidence sur Dusk Drive est nichée dans un coin d'un lotissement ordinaire et répond au site et au désir du propriétaire d'un refuge d'inspiration moderne du milieu du siècle. Orientée vers le nord véritable plutôt que vers la grille des rues du lotissement, la masse et les profonds débords de toit atténuent le dur soleil du sud du Texas, tout en offrant des étendues de vitrage qui relient l'intérieur et l'extérieur. La typologie poteau-poutre adopte les normes modernes d'enveloppe de bâtiment et les matériaux régionaux chaleureux. La brique mexicaine à basse température - qui est une caractéristique de la région -, les plafonds en pin teinté et les poutres en bois d'ingénierie assurent la continuité entre l'intérieur et l'extérieur. Des stratégies architecturales simples offrent des couches de perspective et de refuge qui permettent à une parcelle de banlieue ordinaire de devenir une maison apprécié de la propriétaire et de ses trois compagnons canins.

Das Wohnhaus am Dusk Drive liegt versteckt in einer Ecke eines gewöhnlichen Wohngebiets und reagiert auf den Standort und den Wunsch des Eigentümers nach einem modern inspirierten Zufluchtsort aus der Mitte des Jahrhunderts. Das Haus ist nach Norden ausgerichtet und nicht nach dem Straßenraster der Subdivision. Die Masse und die tiefen Dachüberstände mildern die grelle Südtexas-Sonne und bieten gleichzeitig Glasflächen, die das Innere und Äußere verbinden. Die Pfosten-Riegel-Typologie berücksichtigt moderne Standards für die Gebäudehülle und warme regionale Materialien. Der niedrig gebrannte mexikanische Backstein - ein Markenzeichen der Region -, die gebeizten Kieferndecken und die Holzbalken sorgen für Kontinuität von innen nach außen. Geradlinige architektonische Strategien bieten Perspektiven und Zufluchtsschichten, die es einem unauffälligen Vorstadttrakt ermöglichen, ein Zuhause zu werden, das von der Besitzerin und ihren drei Hundegefährten geliebt wird.

La residencia en Dusk Drive está ubicada en una esquina de una subdivisión ordinaria y responde al terreno y al deseo del propietario de un refugio de inspiración moderna de mediados de siglo. Orientado hacia el norte en lugar de la cuadrícula de la subdivisión, la masa y los profundos voladizos del tejado mitigan el duro sol del sur de Texas, a la vez que proporcionan extensiones de acristalamiento que conectan el interior y el exterior. La tipología de postes y vigas adopta las normas de construcción modernas y los materiales cálidos de la región. El ladrillo mexicano de baja cocción, que es un sello distintivo de la región, los techos de pino teñido y las vigas de madera de ingeniería proporcionan continuidad desde el interior hasta el exterior. Las sencillas estrategias arquitectónicas proporcionan capas de perspectiva y refugio que permiten que un terreno suburbano se convierta en un hogar amado por la propietaria y sus tres compañeros caninos.

Site plan

Floor plan

1. Entry
2. Living/ dining area
3. Deck
4. Pool
5. Kitchen
6. Powder room
7. Pantry
8. Laundry room
9. Garage
10. Bedroom
11. Bathroom
12. Master suite
13. Office
14. Dog porch

## ARROYO COLORADO RESIDENCE

Rio Hondo, Texas, United States // Lot area: 94,545 sq ft; building area: 3,970 sq ft

After a devastating fire destroyed their house and extensive art collection, the owners of this residence decided to build their own work of art in the exact same location. Situated on the bank of Arroyo Colorado, the house is arranged with private spaces on the ground level and public spaces above, offering elevated views of the arroyo. The exterior elevations and fenestrations respond to the building's site and orientation, with windows minimized on the west, deep roof overhangs on the south, and large expanses of glass along the water. Casement windows are strategically located to allow the southeastern prevailing breeze to cross-ventilate the home. This residence on the Arroyo Colorado is more than just a home. It stands where, not long ago, laid ashes and rubble and is a testament to the owner's spirit and the importance of place.

Après qu'un incendie dévastateur ait détruit leur maison et leur vaste collection d'art, les propriétaires de cette résidence ont décidé de construire leur propre œuvre d'art au même endroit. Située sur la rive de l'Arroyo Colorado, la maison est aménagée avec des espaces privés au niveau du sol et des espaces publics au-dessus, offrant des vues surélevées de l'arroyo. Les élévations extérieures et les fenestrations répondent au site et à l'orientation du bâtiment, avec un minimum de fenêtres à l'ouest, de profonds débords de toit au sud et de grandes étendues de verre le long de l'eau. Les fenêtres à battant sont placées à des endroits stratégiques pour permettre à la brise dominante du sud-est de ventiler la maison. Cette résidence sur l'Arroyo Colorado est plus qu'une simple maison. Elle se dresse là où, il n'y a pas si longtemps, se trouvaient les cendres et les décombres, et témoigne de l'esprit du propriétaire et de l'importance du lieu.

Nachdem ein verheerendes Feuer ihr Haus und ihre umfangreiche Kunstsammlung zerstört hatte, beschlossen die Besitzer dieses Wohnhauses, ihr eigenes Kunstwerk an genau demselben Ort zu errichten. Das am Ufer des Arroyo Colorado gelegene Haus verfügt über private Räume im Erdgeschoss und öffentliche Räume im Obergeschoss, die einen erhöhten Blick auf den Arroyo bieten. Die Außenfassaden und Fenster entsprechen dem Standort und der Ausrichtung des Gebäudes, mit minimalen Fenstern im Westen, tiefen Dachüberhängen im Süden und großen Glasflächen entlang des Wassers. Die Flügelfenster sind strategisch so angeordnet, dass die vorherrschende Brise aus Südosten das Haus querlüften kann. Dieses Haus am Arroyo Colorado ist mehr als nur ein Haus. Es steht dort, wo vor nicht allzu langer Zeit noch Asche und Schutt lagen, und ist ein Zeugnis für den Geist des Besitzers und die Bedeutung des Ortes.

Después de que un devastador incendio destruyera su casa y su extensa colección de arte, los propietarios de esta residencia decidieron construir su propia obra de arte en el mismo lugar. Situada en la orilla del Arroyo Colorado, la casa está dispuesta con espacios privados en la planta baja y espacios públicos en la parte superior, ofreciendo vistas elevadas del arroyo. Las elevaciones exteriores y las aberturas responden al emplazamiento y la orientación del edificio, con ventanas minimizadas en el oeste, profundos voladizos en el tejado sur y grandes extensiones de vidrio a lo largo del agua. Las ventanas abatibles están estratégicamente situadas para permitir que la brisa predominante del sureste ventile la casa. Esta residencia en el Arroyo Colorado es más que una casa. Se levanta donde, no hace mucho, había cenizas y escombros y es un testimonio del espíritu del propietario y de la importancia del lugar.

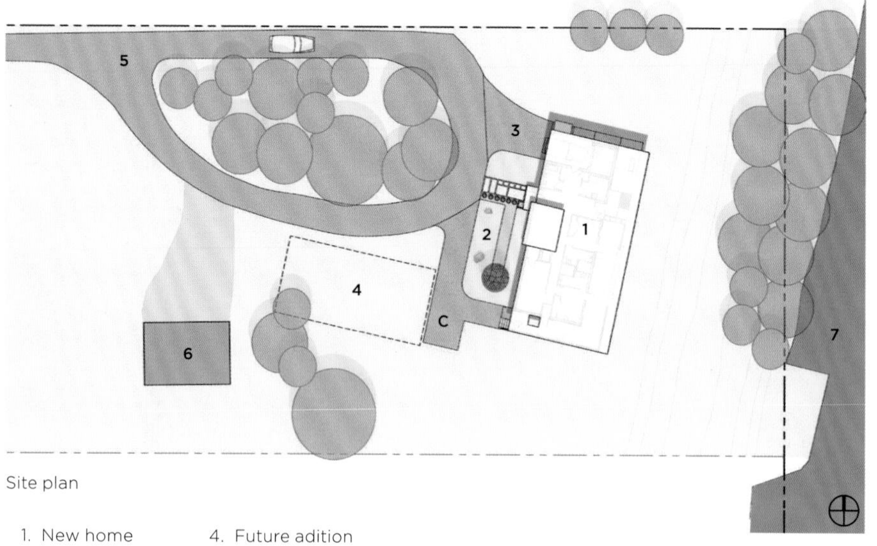


Site plan

1. New home
2. Japanese rock garden
3. New drive
4. Future adition
5. Existing drive
6. Existing garage
7. Arroyo Colorado

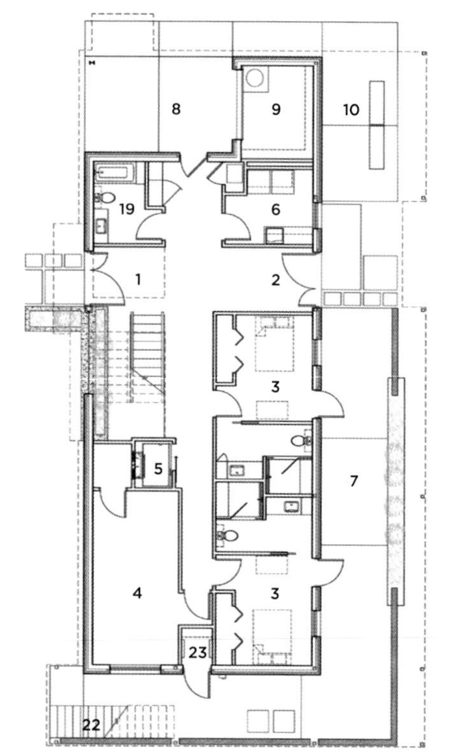


Ground floor plan

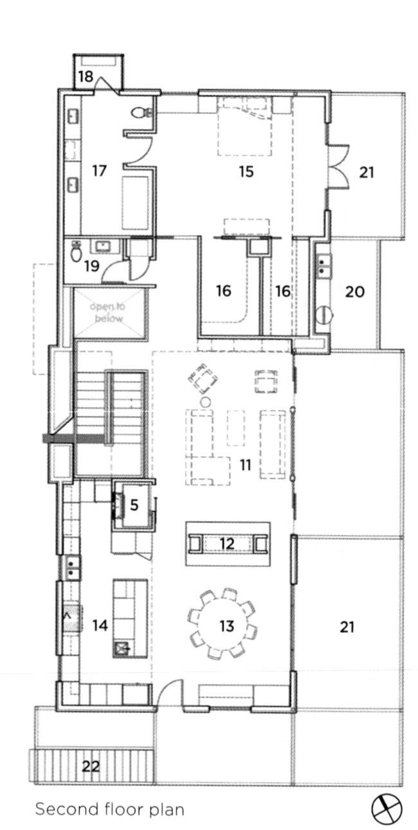


Second floor plan

1. In from the hustle
2. Out to the calm
3. En suite
4. Media room
5. Elevator
6. Laundry room
7. Private patio
8. Carport
9. Solar equipment room
10. Sitting area
11. Living area
12. See through fireplace
13. Dining area
14. Kitchen
15. Master suite
16. Walk-in closet
17. Master bathroom
18. Shower with a view
19. Guest bathroom
20. Outdoor kitchen
21. Arroyo deck
22. Stairs
23. Electrical room

## POOL HOUSE

Harlingen, Texas, United States // Lot area: 75,110 sq ft; building area: 1,087 sq ft

Set in a residential compound with a native brush frontage along the Arroyo Colorado, this project stitches together an outdoor activity zone consisting of a pool, tennis court, garage, and trailhead. This discrete zone provides a transition from the main residence to the arroyo through variations in paving, landscape, and architecture. Programmatically, this secondary structure serves as a guest house, game room, party hub, and place to nap among the existing live oak trees. Exterior covered spaces provide crucial shade while allowing seasonal sea breezes from the nearby Gulf of Mexico. Spatial efficiency drove the architectural response to maximize views and create a pavilion-like atmosphere through large expanses of operable glazing. Massing and location were carefully articulated to maintain the health of the decades-old existing trees.

Situé dans un complexe résidentiel avec une façade de broussailles indigènes le long de l'Arroyo Colorado, ce projet réunit une zone d'activités extérieures comprenant une piscine, un court de tennis, un garage et un départ de sentier. Cette zone discrète offre une transition entre la résidence principale et l'arroyo grâce à des variations dans le pavage, le paysage et l'architecture. Cette structure secondaire sert de maison d'hôtes, de salle de jeux, de centre de fêtes et de lieu de sieste parmi les chênes verts existants. Les espaces extérieurs couverts fournissent une ombre cruciale tout en laissant passer les brises marines saisonnières provenant du Golfe du Mexique tout proche. L'efficacité spatiale a guidé la réponse architecturale pour maximiser les vues et créer une atmosphère de pavillon grâce à de grandes étendues de vitrages ouvrants. La masse et l'emplacement ont été soigneusement articulés pour préserver la santé des arbres existants, vieux de plusieurs décennies.

Dieses Projekt befindet sich in einer Wohnsiedlung mit einheimischem Buschwerk entlang des Arroyo Colorado und umfasst einen Außenbereich, der aus einem Pool, einem Tennisplatz, einer Garage und einem Wanderweg besteht. Dieser diskrete Bereich bildet durch Variationen in der Pflasterung, der Landschaft und der Architektur einen Übergang vom Hauptwohnsitz zum Arroyo. Diese sekundäre Struktur dient als Gästehaus, Spielzimmer, Partyzentrum und Ort, um zwischen den bestehenden lebenden Eichen ein Nickerchen zu machen. Die überdachten Außenbereiche spenden den entscheidenden Schatten und lassen gleichzeitig die saisonale Meeresbrise des nahe gelegenen Golfs von Mexiko herein. Die architektonische Antwort auf die räumliche Effizienz war die Maximierung der Aussicht auf das Grundstück und die Schaffung einer pavillonartigen Atmosphäre durch großflächige Verglasungen. Masse und Lage des Gebäudes wurden so gewählt, dass der jahrzehntealte Baumbestand erhalten bleibt.

Situado en un complejo residencial con una fachada de matorral autóctono a lo largo del Arroyo Colorado, este proyecto une una zona de actividades al aire libre que consiste de una piscina, una pista de tenis, un garaje y un sendero. Es una zona discreta que sirve como transición entre la residencia principal y el arroyo mediante variaciones en la pavimentación, el paisaje y la arquitectura. Esta estructura secundaria sirve de casa de invitados, sala de juegos, centro de fiestas y lugar de descanso entre los robles existentes. Los espacios exteriores cubiertos proporcionan sombra a la vez que dejan pasar las brisas marinas del cercano Golfo de México. La eficiencia espacial impulsó la respuesta arquitectónica para maximizar las vistas y crear una atmósfera de pabellón a través de grandes extensiones de acristalamiento operable. La masa y la ubicación se articularon cuidadosamente para mantener la salud de los árboles existentes, de varias décadas de antigüedad.

Location map

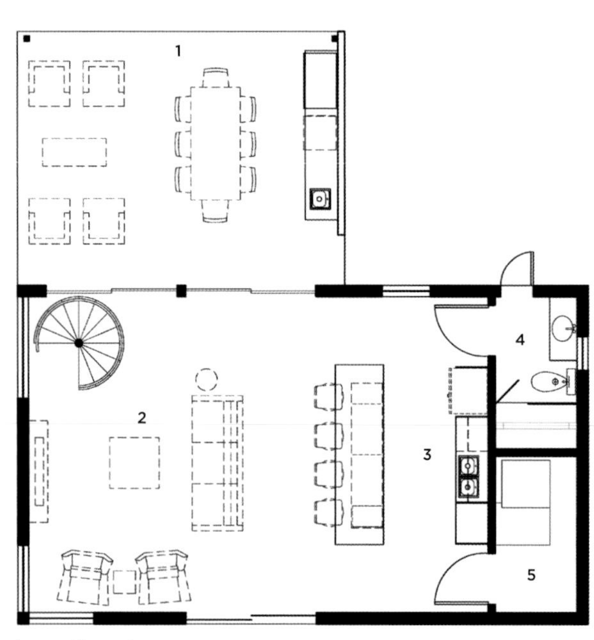


Lower floor plan

1. Deck
2. Living area
3. Kitchen
4. Restroom
5. Mechanical room
6. Upper deck
7. Game/ nap room
8. Balcony
9. Roof below

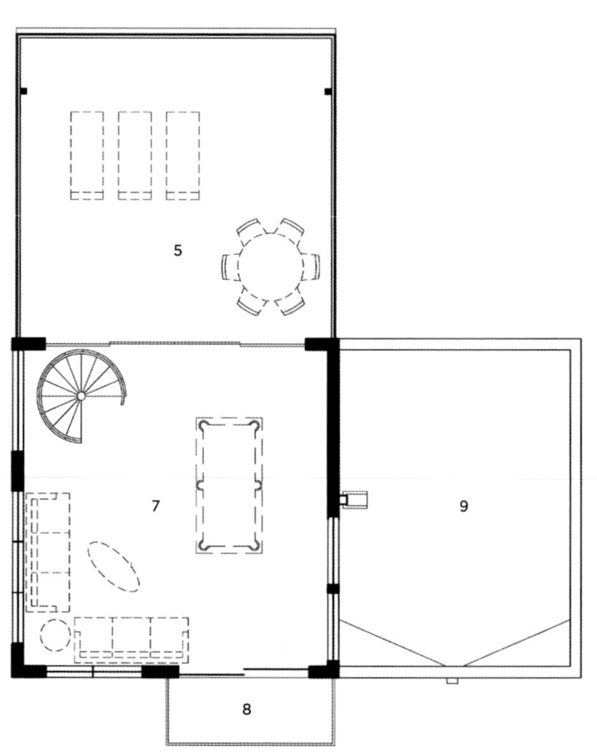


Upper floor plan

# smitharc

## ARCHITECTURE + INTERIORS

294
v

**SOUTHWESTERN RESIDENCE**

Architect:
Smitharc Architecture + Interiors
Lansdscape Architect:
David Rolston
Builder:
Kienast Homes
Photographer:
© Stephen Karlisch

298
v

**SHORECREST RESIDENCE**

Architect:
Smitharc Architecture + Interiors
Fenestration:
Anderson Windows
Photographer:
© Stephen Karlisch

302
v

**SAINT ANDREWS RESIDENCE**

Architect:
Smitharc Architecture + Interiors
Lansdscape Architect:
Hocker
Lighting Designer:
byrdwaters DESIGN
Structural Engineer:
Architectural Engineers Collaborative
Builder:
Coats Homes
Fenestration:
Orama Minimal Frames
Kitchen Design:
Bulthaup
Photographer:
© Nathan Schroder

www.smitharc.com @smitharcarchitects

Walking through a home designed by **smitharc** is not about moving between rooms. It's about experiencing spaces. Architecture has a responsibility to do more than function. It invites and rewards exploration, provoking emotions. Our process starts by listening to our clients describe how they aspire to live. They trust us to translate their thoughts into elevated, artful designs tailored to their unique and layered lives. Collaboration and communication with our clients and with our design and construction partners are essential to execute bold ideas with creativity, vigor, and consistency. While every **smitharc** home is a bespoke design, some common themes arise. A **smitharc** structure leverages nature to harmonize indoor and outdoor spaces. It exhibits the refined skills of talented craftspeople. It sets the stage with lasting detailing and cinematic places.

Bei einem Spaziergang durch ein von **smitharc** gestaltetes Haus geht es nicht darum, sich zwischen Räumen zu bewegen. Es geht um das Erleben von Räumen. Architektur hat die Aufgabe, mehr zu leisten als nur zu funktionieren. Sie lädt zur Erkundung ein, belohnt sie und weckt Emotionen. Unser Prozess beginnt damit, dass wir unseren Kunden zuhören, wenn sie beschreiben, wie sie leben wollen. Sie vertrauen uns, dass wir ihre Gedanken in anspruchsvolle, kunstvolle Entwürfe umsetzen, die auf ihr einzigartiges und vielschichtiges Leben zugeschnitten sind. Die Zusammenarbeit und Kommunikation mit unseren Kunden sowie mit unseren Design- und Baupartnern ist unerlässlich, um kühne Ideen mit Kreativität, Elan und Konsequenz umzusetzen. Obwohl jedes **smitharc**-Haus ein maßgeschneidertes Design ist, gibt es einige gemeinsame Themen. Eine **smitharc**-Struktur nutzt die Natur, um Innen- und Außenräume zu harmonisieren. Es zeigt die raffinierten Fähigkeiten von talentierten Handwerkern. Es setzt die Bühne mit dauerhaften Details und filmischen Orten.

Se promener dans une maison conçue par **smitharc** ne consiste pas à se déplacer entre les pièces. Il s'agit de vivre des espaces. L'architecture a la responsabilité de faire plus que fonctionner. Elle invite et récompense l'exploration, en provoquant des émotions. Notre processus commence par l'écoute de nos clients qui nous décrivent comment ils aspirent à vivre. Ils nous font confiance pour traduire leurs pensées en conceptions élevées et astucieuses adaptées à leur vie unique et multicouche. La collaboration et la communication avec nos clients et avec nos partenaires de conception et de construction sont essentielles pour exécuter des idées audacieuses avec créativité, vigueur et cohérence. Bien que chaque maison **smitharc** soit une conception sur mesure, certains thèmes communs se posent. Une structure en **smitharc** tire parti de la nature pour harmoniser les espaces intérieurs et extérieurs. Il expose le savoir-faire raffiné d'artisans talentueux. Il prépare le terrain avec des détails durables et des lieux cinématographiques.

Caminar por una casa diseñada por **smitharc** no se trata de moverse entre las habitaciones. Se trata de experimentar espacios. La arquitectura tiene la responsabilidad de hacer más que funcionar, invita y premia la exploración, provocando emociones. Nuestro proceso comienza escuchando a nuestros clientes describir cómo aspiran a vivir. Confían en nosotros para traducir sus pensamientos en diseños ingeniosos adaptados a sus vidas únicas y en capas. La colaboración y comunicación con nuestros clientes y con nuestros colaboradores de diseño y construcción son esenciales para ejecutar ideas audaces con creatividad, vigor y consistencia. Si bien cada hogar **smitharc** es un diseño personalizado, surgen algunos temas comunes. Una estructura de **smitharc** aprovecha la naturaleza para armonizar los espacios interiores y exteriores. Exhibe las habilidades refinadas de los artesanos talentosos. Prepara el escenario con detalles duraderos y lugares cinematográficos.

## SOUTHWESTERN RESIDENCE

Dallas, Texas, United States // Lot area: 9,000 sq ft; building area: 3,900 sq ft

This modestly scaled courtyard design is located on a quiet corner in an established bungalow community. It is tailored to its empty-nester owner's craving for an airy, open-plan design that afforded privacy from the street and indoor-outdoor connections complementing their casual lifestyle. In keeping with the low-slung scale of the neighboring cottages, the standing seam metal-roofed volumes step up in a pinwheel arrangement from the front to the back of the property while creating a naturally ventilated porch. Interior efficiency is maximized via built-in furnishings such as the kitchen island-cum-banquette seating. Warm, natural materials imbue a calming atmosphere that serves as a canvas for dancing dappled shadows. Cozy spaces like the primary bathroom and atrium are located in the quieter, rear portion of the lot to create an even more serene sanctuary.

Cette conception de cour de taille modeste est située dans un coin tranquille d'une communauté de bungalows établie. Elle a été conçue sur mesure pour répondre au besoin de son propriétaire, un homme au foyer vide, qui souhaitait une conception aérée et à aire ouverte offrant une certaine intimité par rapport à la rue et des connexions intérieures-extérieures correspondant à son style de vie décontracté. En accord avec l'échelle basse des cottages voisins, les volumes de la toiture en métal à joints debout s'élèvent en forme de roue d'épingle de l'avant à l'arrière de la propriété, créant ainsi un porche ventilé naturellement. L'efficacité de l'intérieur est maximisée grâce à des meubles intégrés tels que l'îlot de cuisine avec banquette.. Les matériaux naturels et chaleureux créent une atmosphère apaisante qui sert de toile de fond à la danse des ombres portées. Des espaces confortables comme la salle de bains principale et l'atrium sont situés dans la partie arrière du terrain, plus calme, pour créer un sanctuaire encore plus serein.

Dieser bescheidene Innenhof liegt an einer ruhigen Ecke in einer etablierten Bungalowsiedlung. Das Haus ist auf die Wünsche seiner Besitzer zugeschnitten, die sich nach einem luftigen, offenen Design sehnen, das Privatsphäre von der Straße bietet und eine Verbindung zwischen Innen- und Außenbereich schafft, die ihren lockeren Lebensstil ergänzt. In Anlehnung an die niedrigen Häuser in der Nachbarschaft sind die mit Stehfalz-Metalldächern bedeckten Volumen von der Vorderseite bis zur Rückseite des Grundstücks in einer Pinwheel-Anordnung aufgestockt, wodurch eine natürlich belüftete Veranda entsteht. Die Effizienz des Innenraums wird durch Einbaumöbel wie die Kücheninsel mit Sitzgelegenheit maximiert. Warme, natürliche Materialien sorgen für eine beruhigende Atmosphäre, die als Leinwand für tanzende Schatten dient. Gemütliche Räume wie das Hauptbadezimmer und das Atrium befinden sich im ruhigeren, hinteren Teil des Grundstücks, um einen noch ruhigeren Zufluchtsort zu schaffen.

Este diseño de patio de escala modesta está ubicado en un rincón tranquilo en una comunidad de bungalows. Está diseñado para culminar el anhelo de su propietario por un diseño espacioso y de planta abierta que brinde privacidad desde la calle y conexiones entre el interior y el exterior que complementen su estilo de vida informal. De acuerdo con la escala baja de las cabañas vecinas, los volúmenes con techos de metal de costura vertical se elevan en un arreglo de molinete desde el frente hasta la parte trasera de la propiedad creando un porche con ventilación natural. La eficiencia interior se maximiza con muebles integrados, como la isla de la cocina con banquetas. Los materiales cálidos y naturales imbuyen una atmósfera relajante que sirve como lienzo para las sombras moteadas danzantes. Los espacios acogedores, como el baño principal y el atrio, están situados en la parte trasera, más tranquila, para crear un santuario aún más sereno.

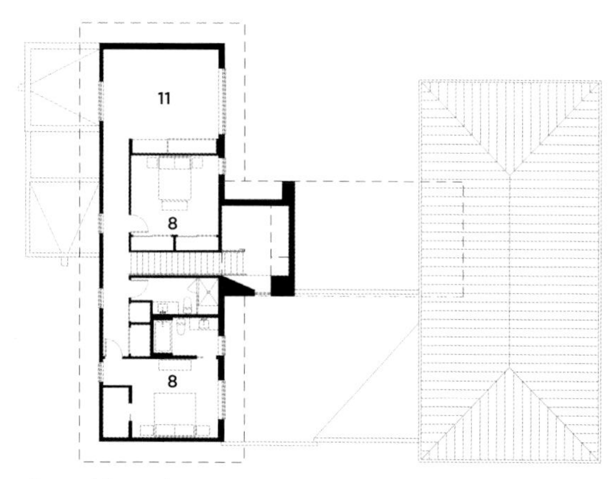


Second floor plan

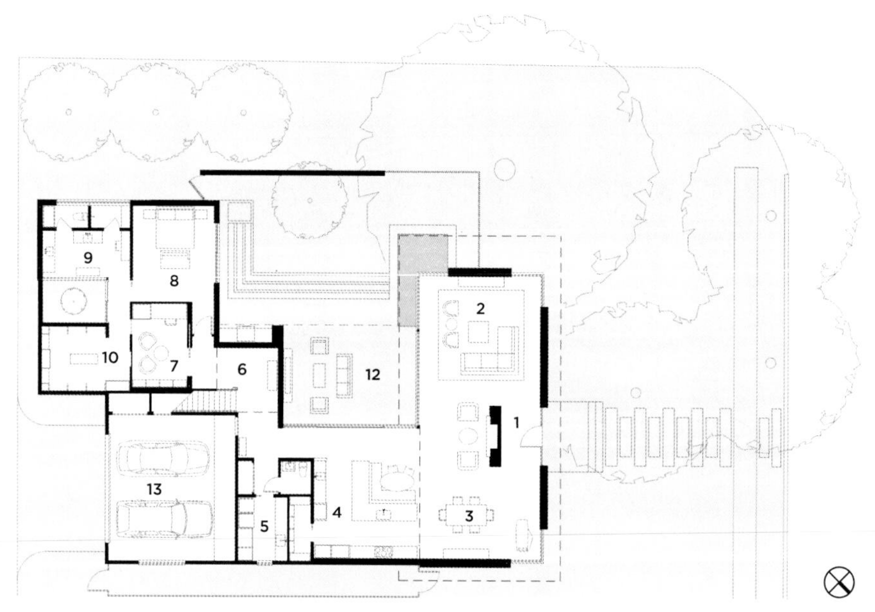


Ground floor plan

1. Entry
2. Family room
3. Dining area
4. Kitchen
5. Laundry room
6. Gallery
7. Study
8. Bedroom
9. Bathroom
10. Closet
11. Den
12. Outdoor living
13. Garage

## SHORECREST RESIDENCE

Dallas, Texas, United States // Lot area: 27,700 sq ft; building area: 4,100 sq ft

This home choreographs a sequence of indoor and outdoor spaces providing privacy from the street and transparency to the north-facing garden and creek. Environmentally sensitive design features include geothermal HVAC, 100% recyclable zinc metal shingles, and locally sourced limestone. Expanses of high-performance glass provide ample natural daylighting throughout the interiors. Sited in a recently redrawn flood plain, the structure had to be elevated five feet above the existing grade. This maximized views but proved to complicate the integration of the new two-story home into the neighborhood's relatively low-slung ranch house vernacular. The architecture reinforces long horizontal lines, planes, and volumes. The scale of the forms is further delineated by the precisely crafted graphite-green zinc shingles juxtaposed against the weighty and tactile buff limestone.

Cette maison chorégraphie une séquence d'espaces intérieurs et extérieurs offrant une certaine intimité par rapport à la rue et une transparence vers le jardin et le ruisseau orientés au nord. Les caractéristiques de conception respectueuses de l'environnement comprennent un système de chauffage, de ventilation et de climatisation géothermique, des bardeaux métalliques en zinc 100 % recyclables et de la pierre calcaire d'origine locale. Des étendues de verre à haute performance fournissent une lumière naturelle abondante à l'intérieur. Située dans une plaine inondable récemment redessinée, la structure a dû être surélevée de cinq pieds au-dessus du niveau existant. Cela a permis d'optimiser les vues, mais a compliqué l'intégration de la nouvelle maison à deux étages dans le style relativement bas des ranchs du quartier. L'architecture renforce les longues lignes horizontales, les plans et les volumes. L'échelle des formes est encore délimitée par les bardeaux de zinc vert graphite précisément travaillés, juxtaposés à la pierre calcaire buffle lourde et tactile.

Dieses Haus bildet eine Abfolge von Innen- und Außenräumen, die Privatsphäre von der Straße und Transparenz zum nach Norden ausgerichteten Garten und zum Bach bieten. Zu den umweltfreundlichen Konstruktionsmerkmalen gehören eine geothermische HLK-Anlage, 100 % recycelbare Zinkblechschindeln und Kalkstein aus der Region. Flächen aus Hochleistungsglas sorgen für reichlich natürliches Tageslicht. Da das Gebäude in einem kürzlich neu ausgewiesenen Überschwemmungsgebiet liegt, musste es fünf Fuß über das bestehende Niveau angehoben werden. Dies ermöglichte eine optimale Aussicht, erschwerte jedoch die Integration des neuen zweistöckigen Hauses in die relativ niedrige Ranchhaus-Architektur des Viertels. Die Architektur betont die langen horizontalen Linien, Flächen und Volumen. Der Maßstab der Formen wird durch die präzise gefertigten graphitgrünen Zinkschindeln, die dem schweren und fühlbaren Kalkstein gegenübergestellt werden, noch deutlicher hervorgehoben.

Este hogar coreografía una secuencia de espacios interiores y exteriores que proporcionan privacidad desde la calle y transparencia hacia el jardín y el arroyo al norte. Entre las características de diseño respetuosas con el medio ambiente se encuentran la climatización geotérmica, las tejas metálicas de zinc 100% reciclables y la piedra caliza de origen local. Las extensiones de vidrio de alto rendimiento ofrecen una amplia iluminación natural. Situado en una llanura recientemente rediseñada, la estructura tuvo que elevarse cinco pies por encima del nivel existente. Esto permitió maximizar las vistas, pero complicó la integración de la nueva casa de dos plantas en la arquitectura de rancho relativamente baja del barrio. La arquitectura refuerza las largas líneas horizontales, los planos y los volúmenes. La escala de las formas queda aún más delineada por las tejas de zinc verde grafito, elaboradas con precisión, que se yuxtaponen a la pesada y táctil piedra caliza.

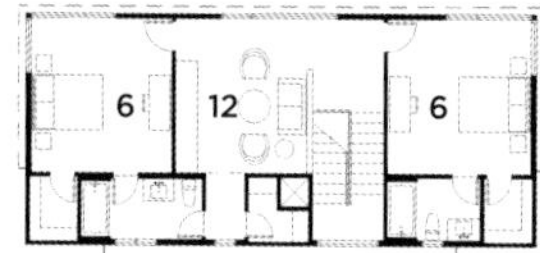


Second floor plan

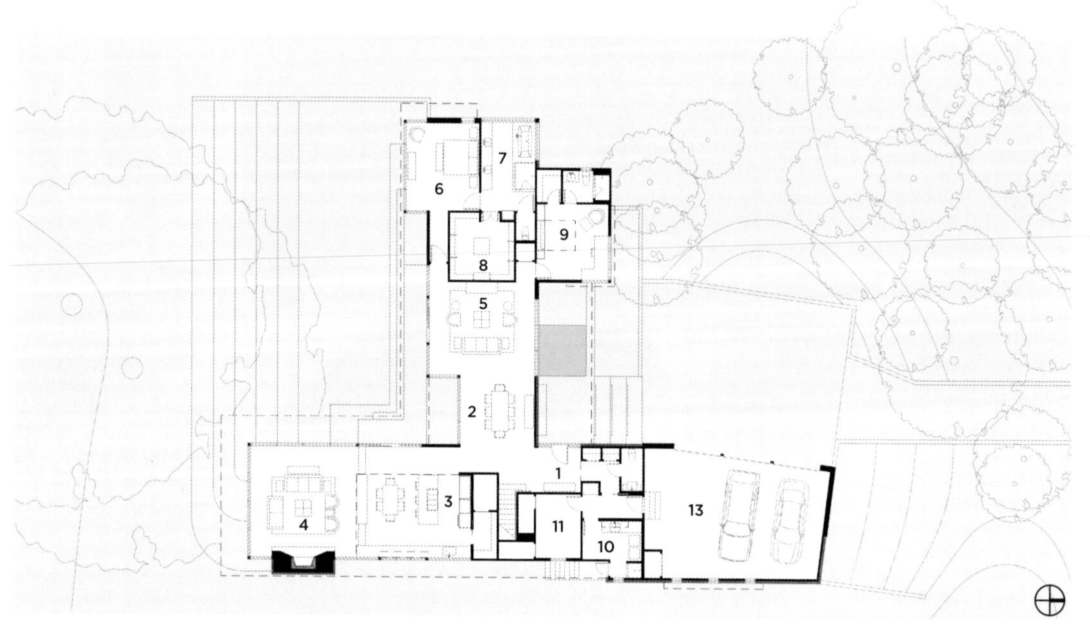


1. Entry
2. Dining area
3. Kitchen
4. Family room
5. Salon
6. Bedroom
7. Bathroom
8. Closet
9. Study
10. Laundry room
11. Exercise room
12. Den
13. Garage

Ground floor plan

## SAINT ANDREWS RESIDENCE

University Park, Texas, United States // Lot area: 17,800 sq ft; building area: 9,000 sq ft

This home for a young family of five is sited to take full advantage of the pie-shaped lot opening up along its street edge to sweeping views of a neighboring golf course. The boundaries of the front and back yards are blurred by the glazed pavilion situated between the two. When the sliding glass walls are opened, the home interior merges with the landscape. The owners wanted a place where they could experience their property's full breadth and width. A space where the tranquil mirror fountain and terraced turf outdoor living room situated on the golf course side of the home are within conversation distance of the interior TV den. An environment that leverages the seasons and can be as inviting as a 4th of July party and still transform into an elegant event space for a daughter's engagement *fête*.

Cette maison pour une jeune famille de cinq personnes est située de manière à tirer pleinement parti du terrain en forme de tarte qui s'ouvre, le long de la rue, sur des vues panoramiques du terrain de golf voisin. Les limites des cours avant et arrière sont brouillées par le pavillon vitré situé entre les deux. Lorsque les parois vitrées coulissantes sont ouvertes, l'intérieur de la maison se fond dans le paysage. Les propriétaires souhaitaient un endroit où ils pourraient profiter de toute la largeur de leur propriété. Un espace où la fontaine miroir tranquille et le salon extérieur en gazon en terrasse, situés du côté du terrain de golf de la maison, sont à portée de conversation de la salle de télévision intérieure. Un environnement qui tire parti des saisons et qui peut être aussi accueillant qu'une fête du 4 juillet et se transformer en un espace événementiel élégant pour les fiançailles d'une fille fête.

Dieses Haus für eine junge fünfköpfige Familie ist so platziert, dass es die Vorteile des tortenförmigen Grundstücks voll ausnutzt, das sich entlang der Straßenkante zu einem weiten Blick auf den benachbarten Golfplatz öffnet. Die Grenzen zwischen Vorder- und Hinterhof werden durch den verglasten Pavillon verwischt, der sich zwischen den beiden befindet. Wenn die Glasschiebewände geöffnet werden, verschmilzt das Innere des Hauses mit der Landschaft. Die Eigentümer wünschten sich einen Ort, an dem sie die ganze Weite ihres Grundstücks erleben können. Ein Raum, in dem der ruhige Spiegelbrunnen und das terrassierte Wohnzimmer im Freien auf der Golfplatzseite des Hauses in unmittelbarer Nähe zum inneren Fernsehzimmer liegen. Eine Umgebung, die die Jahreszeiten nutzt und so einladend sein kann wie eine Party zum 4. Juli und sich dennoch in einen eleganten Veranstaltungsraum für die Verlobungsfeier der Tochter verwandeln lässt.

Esta casa para una joven familia de cinco miembros está situada para aprovechar al máximo la parcela en forma de tarta que se abre a lo largo del borde de la calle con amplias vistas a un campo de golf vecino. Los límites de los patios delantero y trasero quedan difuminados por el pabellón acristalado situado entre ambos. Cuando se abren las paredes correderas de cristal, el interior de la casa se funde con el paisaje. Los propietarios querían un lugar en el que pudieran experimentar toda la amplitud de su propiedad. Un espacio en el que la tranquila fuente de espejos y la sala de estar exterior con césped situada en el lado del campo de golf de la casa estuvieran a poca distancia de la sala de televisión interior. Un entorno que aprovecha las estaciones y que puede ser tan acogedor como una fiesta del 4 de julio y transformarse en un elegante espacio para eventos, como la fiesta de petición de mano de su hija.

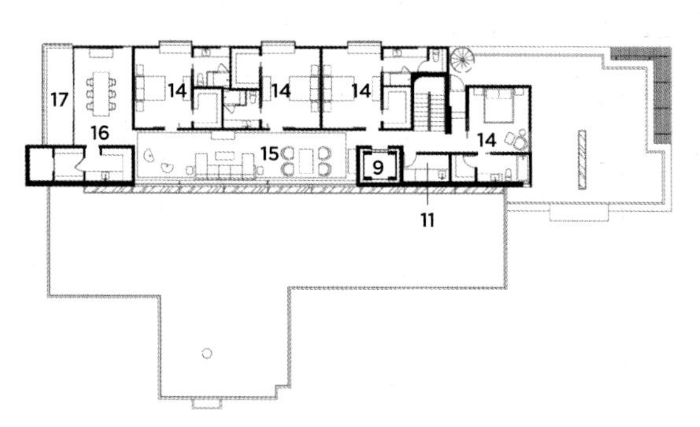

Upper floor plan

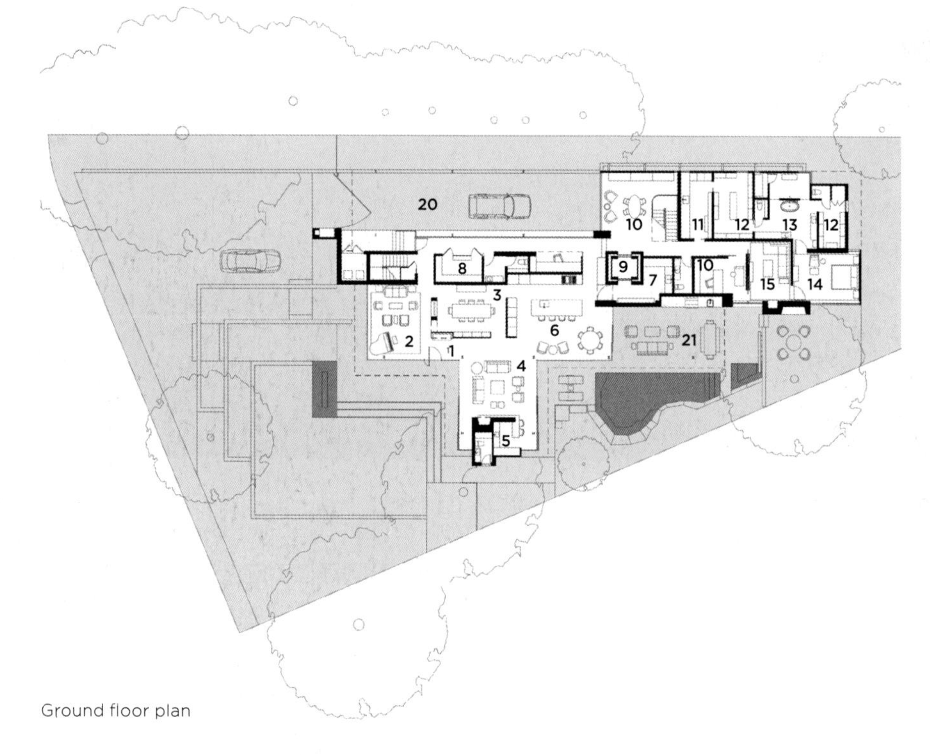

Ground floor plan

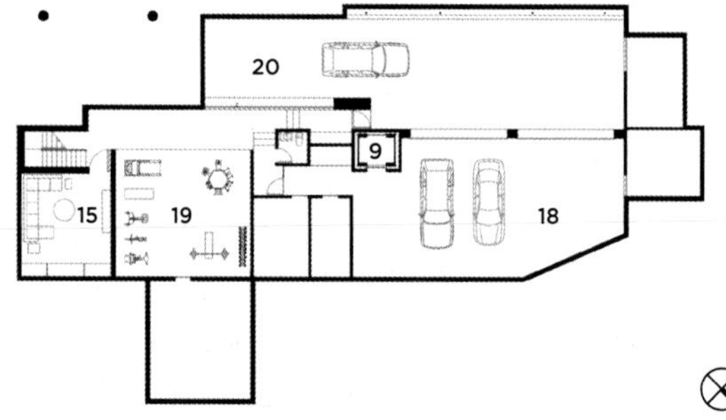

Lower floor plan

1. Entry
2. Salon
3. Dining area
4. Family room
5. Bar
6. Kitchen
7. Scullery
8. Mud room
9. Elevator
10. Study
11. Laundry room
12. Closet
13. Bathroom
14. Bedroom
15. Den
16. Art studio
17. Balcony
18. Garage
19. Athletics
20. Driveway ramp
21. Outdoor living and kitchen

# M-GRAY
# ARCHITECTURE

308
v

**LENNOX**

Architect:
M-Gray Architecture
Landscape Architect:
Archverdi
Interior Designer:
Moore Design Group
Builder:
Tatum Brown Custom Homes
Structural Engineer:
Jensen Engineers
Photographers:
© Costa Christ, Dan Piassick

314
v

**SUNNYLAND**

Architect:
M-Gray Architecture
Landscape Architect:
Agave Landscape Environments,
Waterscapes
Interior Designer:
Yours by Design
Builder:
The Newport Group, inc.
Photographer:
© Costa Christ

318
v

**WOODFIN**

Architect:
M-Gray Architecture
Landscape Architect:
Robert Bellamy Design,
AquaTerra Outdoors
Interior Designer:
Client
Builder:
M-Gray Architecture
Structural Engineer:
Bury Partners
Photographers:
© Costa Christ, Wade Griffin

www.m-gray.com @mgrayarchitecture

Like our business, our story is close to our hearts.
In the summer of 2001, both Mark and Maurie moved to Texas. Maurie, a Texas native, received her Bachelor of Environmental Design from Texas A&M University and her Master of Architecture from Clemson University; Mark graduated from Southern Illinois University with a Bachelor of Architecture. They met in a human resource meeting at an architecture firm, having both started that very same day. They worked together, fell in love, and eventually were married. Later Mark branched off to start his own architectural design firm. A couple of years and a couple of kids later, Maurie decided to team up with Mark's firm full-time. The Gray partnership was formed, and M-Gray Architecture was born. M-Gray Architecture works on a wide range of projects of varying scope and style throughout Dallas and Fort Worth in Texas and beyond.

Wie unser Unternehmen, so liegt auch unsere Geschichte uns am Herzen.
Im Sommer 2001 zogen sowohl Mark als auch Maurie nach Texas. Maurie, ein gebürtiger Texaner, erhielt einen B.S. in Umweltdesign von der Texas A&M University und einen M.S. in Architektur von der Clemson University; Mark erhielt einen B.S. in Architektur von der Southern Illinois University. Sie lernten sich bei einer Personalbesprechung in einem Architekturbüro kennen, da sie beide am selben Tag anfingen. Sie arbeiteten zusammen, verliebten sich ineinander und heirateten schließlich. Später machte sich Mark selbstständig und gründete sein eigenes Architekturbüro. Ein paar Jahre und ein paar Kinder später beschloss Maurie, Vollzeit in Marks Firma einzusteigen. Die Gray-Partnerschaft wurde gegründet und M-Gray Architecture war geboren. M-Gray Architecture arbeitet an einer breiten Palette von Projekten unterschiedlichen Umfangs und Stils in Dallas und Fort Worth in Texas und darüber hinaus.

Comme notre entreprise, notre histoire nous tient à cœur.
Au cours de l'été 2001, Mark et Maurie ont déménagé au Texas. Maurie, originaire du Texas, est titulaire d'un B.S. en conception environnementale de l'université A&M du Texas et d'un M.S. en architecture de l'université de Clemson ; Mark est titulaire d'un B.S. en architecture de la Southern Illinois University. Ils se sont rencontrés lors d'une réunion des ressources humaines dans un cabinet d'architecture, car ils ont tous deux commencé le même jour. Ils ont travaillé ensemble, sont tombés amoureux et se sont finalement mariés. Mark s'est ensuite lancé dans la création de son propre cabinet de conception architecturale. Quelques années et deux enfants plus tard, Maurie a décidé de rejoindre le cabinet de Mark à plein temps. Le partenariat Gray a été formé et M-Gray Architecture est né. M-Gray Architecture travaille sur un large éventail de projets d'envergure et de style différents dans tout Dallas et Fort Worth au Texas et au-delà.

Al igual que nuestro negocio, nuestra historia está cerca de nuestros corazones.
En el verano de 2001, tanto Mark como Maurie se mudaron a Texas. Maurie, nativa de Texas, se licenció en Diseño Medioambiental en la Universidad A&M de Texas y obtuvo un máster en Arquitectura en la Universidad de Clemson; Mark se licenció en Arquitectura en la Universidad del Sur de Illinois. Se conocieron en una reunión de recursos humanos en una empresa de arquitectura, ya que ambos empezaron ese mismo día. Trabajaron juntos, se enamoraron y acabaron casándose. Más tarde, Mark se independizó para crear su propia empresa de diseño arquitectónico. Un par de años y un par de hijos más tarde, Maurie decidió unirse a la empresa de Mark a tiempo completo. Se formó la sociedad Gray y nació M-Gray Architecture. M-Gray Architecture trabaja en una amplia gama de proyectos de diverso alcance y estilo en todo Dallas y Fort Worth en Texas y más allá.

## LENNOX

Dallas, Texas, United States // Lot area: 99,564 sq ft; building area: 26,984 sq ft

Lennox is a stunning compound on a large property highlighting self-sufficient living and a strong connection to its context through a palette of locally sourced materials. The U-shaped house surrounds a courtyard with a pool at its center. A seamless connection between the interior and the exterior through large sliding glass panels is the organizing motif of the house design, promoting outdoor living and entertainment. To this end, the property includes a clay tennis court with an adjacent pro shop, a covered basketball court, a full-scale spa and exercise room, a large theatre room, and a complete guest house. Yet perhaps the most impressive aspect of the design is the use of sustainable features, including an expansive solar panel roof, an underground rainwater harvesting system, and geothermal heating and cooling.

Lennox est un superbe complexe situé sur une grande propriété qui met en avant un mode de vie autosuffisant et un lien fort avec son contexte grâce à une palette de matériaux d'origine locale. La maison en forme de U entoure une cour avec une piscine en son centre. Une connexion transparente entre l'intérieur et l'extérieur grâce à de grands panneaux de verre coulissants est le motif d'organisation de la conception de la maison, favorisant la vie en plein air et les divertissements. À cette fin, la propriété comprend un court de tennis en terre battue avec un pro-shop adjacent, un terrain de basket intérieur, un spa et une salle d'exercice grandeur nature, une grande salle de théâtre et une maison d'hôtes complète. Mais l'aspect le plus impressionnant de la conception est sans doute l'utilisation d'éléments durables, comme un grand toit équipé de panneaux solaires, un système souterrain de collecte des eaux de pluie et un système de chauffage et de refroidissement géothermique.

Lennox ist ein atemberaubender Komplex auf einem großen Grundstück, bei dem autarkes Wohnen und eine starke Bindung an den Kontext durch eine Palette von lokal beschafften Materialien im Vordergrund stehen. Das U-förmige Haus umgibt einen Innenhof, in dessen Mitte sich ein Schwimmbad befindet. Eine nahtlose Verbindung zwischen Innen- und Außenbereich durch große Glasschiebetüren ist das Gestaltungsmotiv des Hauses und fördert das Leben im Freien und die Unterhaltung. Zu diesem Zweck verfügt das Anwesen über einen Sand-Tennisplatz mit angrenzendem Pro-Shop, einen Indoor-Basketballplatz, ein komplettes Spa und einen Fitnessraum, einen großen Theatersaal und ein komplettes Gästehaus. Der vielleicht beeindruckendste Aspekt des Entwurfs ist jedoch die Verwendung nachhaltiger Elemente, wie z. B. ein großes Dach mit Sonnenkollektoren, ein unterirdisches Regenwassersammelsystem und geothermische Heizung und Kühlung.

Lennox es un impresionante complejo en una gran propiedad que destaca la vida autosuficiente y una fuerte conexión con su contexto a través de una paleta de materiales de origen local. La casa en forma de U rodea un patio con una piscina en su centro. Una conexión perfecta entre el interior y el exterior a través de grandes paneles deslizantes de cristal es el motivo organizador del diseño de la casa, promoviendo la vida y el entretenimiento al aire libre. Para ello, la propiedad incluye una pista de tenis de tierra batida con una tienda profesional adyacente, una cancha de baloncesto cubierta, un spa y una sala de ejercicios a gran escala, una gran sala de teatro y una casa de invitados completa. Pero quizá el aspecto más impresionante del diseño sea el uso de elementos sostenibles, como un amplio tejado con paneles solares, un sistema subterráneo de recogida de agua de lluvia y calefacción y refrigeración geotérmicas.

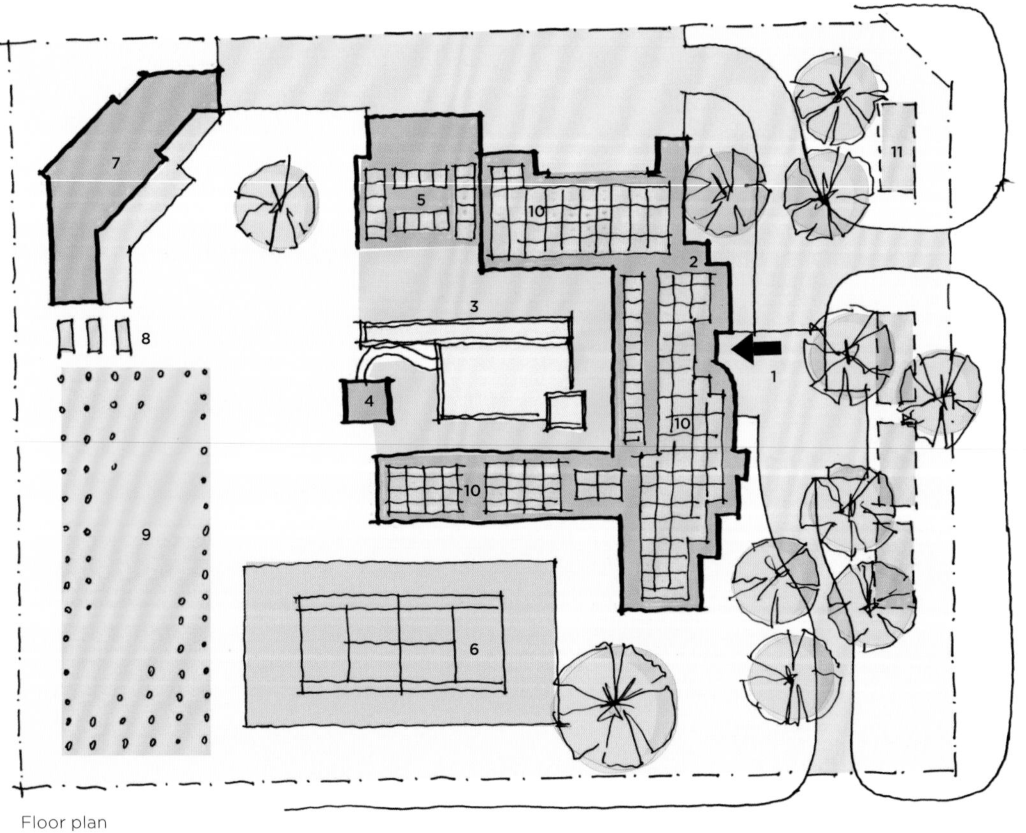


Floor plan

1. Front Entry
2. Primary residence
3. Lap pool
4. Fort
5. Basketball court
6. Clay tennis court
7. Guest house
8. Garden
9. Geothermal field
10. Solar panels
11. Rainwater harvesting tanks

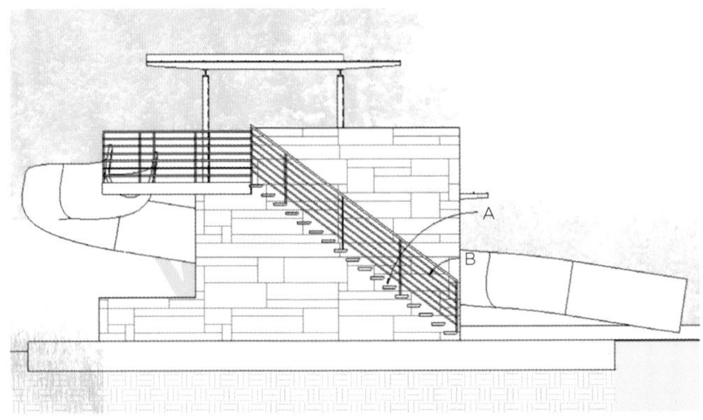

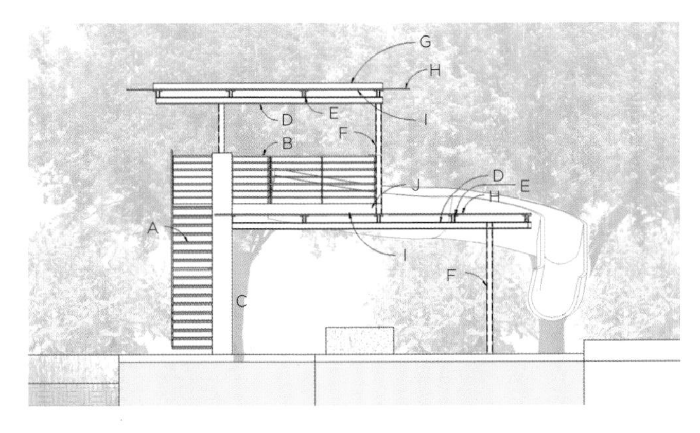


Fort elevations

A. Floating 1-1/2"-thick ipe stair treads supported by steel embedded into wall
B. 42" stair rail
C. 4" stone both sides on 8" CMU
D. I beam
E. L bracket
F. Column
G. TPO roof/ballast and flashing to match existing house
H. 1" round rod
I. Ipe ceiling
J. Ipe deck on 2 x 8 framing

A MAN & HIS WATCH
Love, Cecil
ENTRYWAYS OF MILAN
INGRESSI DI MILANO

## SUNNYLAND

Dallas, Texas, United States // Lot area: 11,043 sq ft; building area: 5,345 sq ft

Sunnyland presented a challenging lot shape and configuration at the end of a street, which resulted in a unique design, treating the front yard as the primary outdoor entertainment space, with a swimming pool as its centerpiece. The home captures views of an adjacent creek and grove of trees that offers some privacy from the street. The "industrial chic" aesthetic featuring red slurried brick, cast stone pillars, parapet walls, and large dark windows—a nod to warehouse windows—was inspired by the homeowners' midwestern roots. The two-story house is connected to a separate single-story multi-purpose room via a covered loggia with a fireplace. This outdoor connector offered the possibility of creating a private trellis-covered terrace—also with a fireplace—off of the primary suite at the second floor.

La forme et la configuration de la parcelle de Sunnyland, située au bout d'une rue, constituaient un défi, ce qui a donné lieu à une conception unique, faisant de la cour avant le principal espace de divertissement extérieur, avec une piscine comme pièce maîtresse. La maison surplombe un ruisseau adjacent et un bosquet d'arbres qui offre une certaine intimité par rapport à la rue. L'esthétique "industrielle chic", avec des briques rouges, des piliers en pierre moulée, des parapets et de grandes fenêtres sombres - un clin d'œil aux fenêtres des entrepôts - a été inspirée par les racines des propriétaires dans le Midwest. La maison à deux étages est reliée à une salle polyvalente de plain-pied par une loggia couverte avec une cheminée. Ce connecteur extérieur offrait la possibilité de créer une terrasse privée couverte par un treillis - également avec une cheminée - à côté de la suite parentale au premier étage.

Sunnyland zeichnete sich durch eine schwierige Grundstücksform und -konfiguration am Ende einer Straße aus, was zu einem einzigartigen Entwurf führte, bei dem der vordere Innenhof als Hauptbereich für die Außenbewirtung diente, mit einem Swimmingpool als Herzstück. Das Haus blickt auf einen angrenzenden Bach und eine Baumgruppe, die etwas Privatsphäre von der Straße bietet. Die Ästhetik des "Industrial Chic" mit rotem Backstein, Kunststeinsäulen, Brüstungen und großen dunklen Fenstern - eine Anspielung auf Lagerhausfenster - wurde von den Wurzeln der Eigentümer im Mittleren Westen inspiriert. Das zweistöckige Haus ist mit einem einstöckigen Mehrzweckraum durch eine überdachte Loggia mit Kamin verbunden. Dieser Außenanschluss bot die Möglichkeit, eine private, von einem Spalier überdachte Terrasse - ebenfalls mit einem Kamin - vor dem Hauptschlafzimmer im ersten Stock zu schaffen.

Sunnyland presentaba una forma de parcela y una configuración difíciles al final de una calle, lo que dio lugar a un diseño único, tratando el patio delantero como el principal espacio de entretenimiento al aire libre, con una piscina como pieza central. La casa tiene vistas a un arroyo adyacente y a una arboleda que ofrece cierta privacidad desde la calle. La estética "industrial chic", con ladrillos rojos, pilares de piedra fundida, parapetos y grandes ventanas oscuras -un guiño a las ventanas de los almacenes- se inspiró en las raíces del medio oeste de los propietarios. La casa de dos plantas está conectada a una sala polivalente de una sola planta a través de una logia cubierta con chimenea. Este conector exterior ofrecía la posibilidad de crear una terraza privada cubierta por un enrejado -también con una chimenea- de la suite principal en la segunda planta.

6730

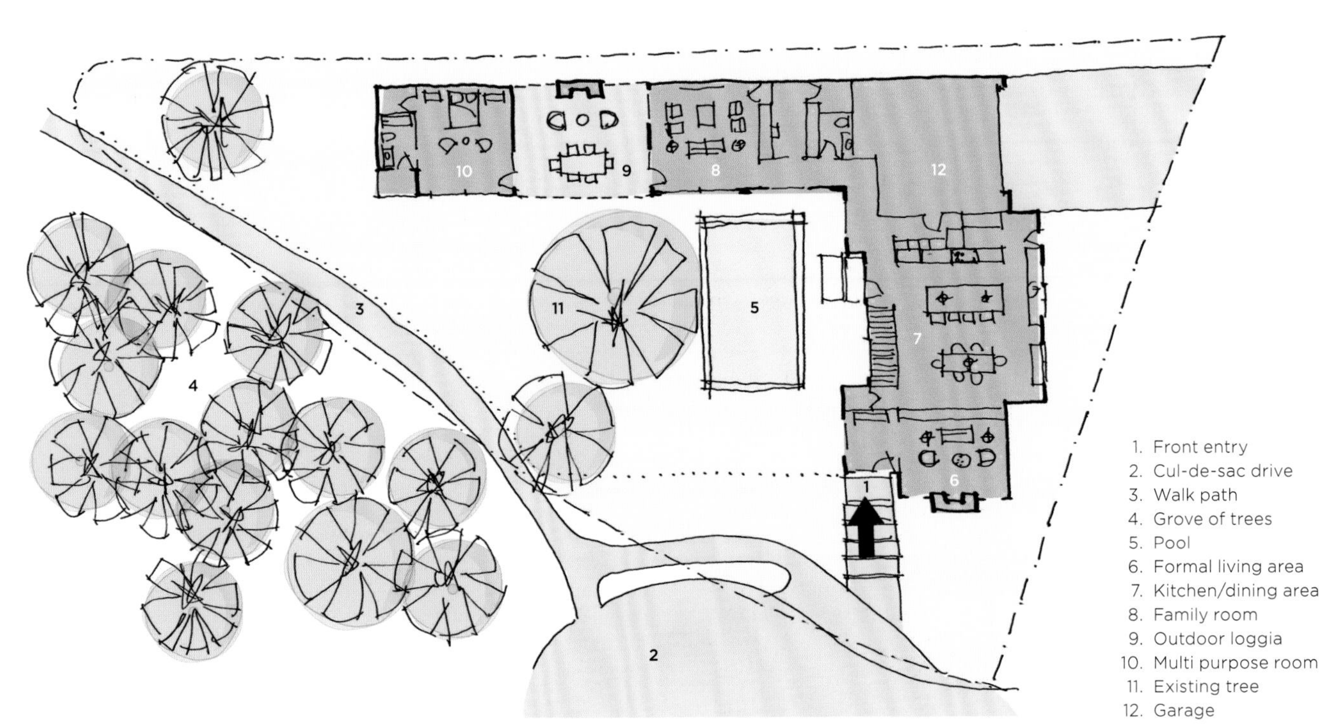


1. Front entry
2. Cul-de-sac drive
3. Walk path
4. Grove of trees
5. Pool
6. Formal living area
7. Kitchen/dining area
8. Family room
9. Outdoor loggia
10. Multi purpose room
11. Existing tree
12. Garage

Ground floor plan

## WOODFIN

Dallas, Texas, United States // Lot area: 34,201 sq ft; building area: 9,998 sq ft

The natural topography was the *raison d'être* of the design of this home, which showcases an effortless integration of the built work into the landscape utilizing large expanses of glass. The program also required a substantial amount of wall surface for the display of an art collection. One of the design highlights is the use of a bridge as a design solution to tie together the private and public areas. This feature also addresses the need for natural drainage and the preservation of a 100-year-old oak tree around which the house is arranged. A separate orchid sanctuary and greenhouse structure serves as a prominent backdrop to a loggia, perfect for outdoor dining. Its clear multi-wall polycarbonate panels not only promote optimal growing conditions but also offer a great degree of transparency, reflecting the aesthetics of the main dwelling.

La topographie naturelle a été la raison d'être de la conception de cette maison, qui s'intègre sans effort dans le paysage grâce à de grandes surfaces vitrées. Le programme nécessitait également une grande surface murale pour l'exposition d'une collection d'art. L'un des points forts de la conception est l'utilisation d'un pont comme solution de conception pour relier les zones privées et publiques. Cet élément répond également au besoin de drainage naturel et à la préservation d'un chêne centenaire autour duquel la maison est organisée. Un sanctuaire d'orchidées indépendant et une structure de serre forment la toile de fond d'une loggia, parfaite pour les repas en plein air. Ses panneaux en polycarbonate transparent favorisent non seulement des conditions de culture optimales, mais offrent également un haut degré de transparence, reflétant l'esthétique de la maison principale.

Die natürliche Topografie war der Grund für den Entwurf dieses Hauses, das sich durch große Glasflächen mühelos in die Landschaft einfügt. Für das Programm wurde auch eine große Wandfläche für die Ausstellung einer Kunstsammlung benötigt. Einer der Höhepunkte des Entwurfs ist die Verwendung einer Brücke als gestalterische Lösung zur Verbindung der privaten und öffentlichen Bereiche. Dieses Element trägt auch der Notwendigkeit einer natürlichen Entwässerung und der Erhaltung einer jahrhundertealten Eiche Rechnung, um die das Haus angeordnet ist. Ein freistehendes Orchideenhaus und ein Gewächshaus bilden die Kulisse für eine Loggia, die sich perfekt für Mahlzeiten im Freien eignet. Die transparenten Polycarbonatplatten sorgen nicht nur für optimale Wachstumsbedingungen, sondern bieten auch ein hohes Maß an Transparenz und spiegeln die Ästhetik des Haupthauses wider.

La topografía natural fue la razón de ser del diseño de esta casa, que muestra una integración sin esfuerzo en el paisaje utilizando grandes extensiones de vidrio. El programa también requería una gran superficie de pared para la exposición de una colección de arte. Uno de los aspectos más destacados del diseño es el uso de un puente como solución de diseño para unir las zonas privadas y las públicas. Este elemento también responde a la necesidad de un drenaje natural y a la preservación de un roble centenario en torno al cual se organiza la casa. Un santuario de orquídeas y una estructura de invernadero independientes sirven de telón de fondo a una logia, perfecta para comer al aire libre. Sus paneles transparentes de policarbonato no sólo favorecen unas condiciones de cultivo óptimas, sino que también ofrecen un gran grado de transparencia, reflejando la estética de la vivienda principal.

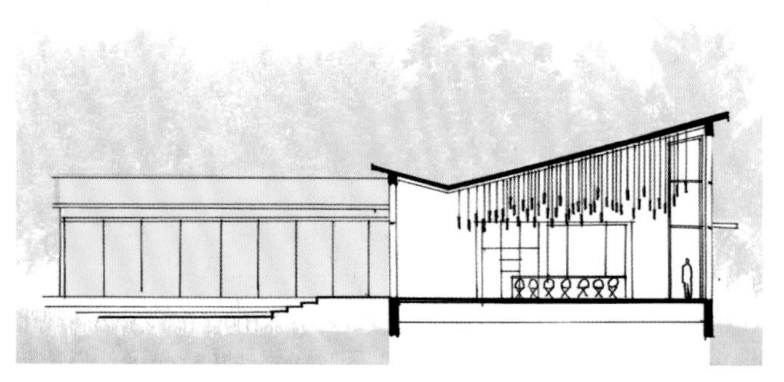

Section through dining room

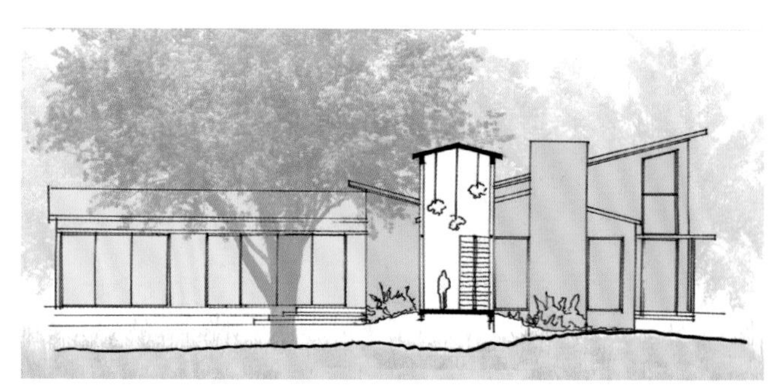

Section through stairs hall

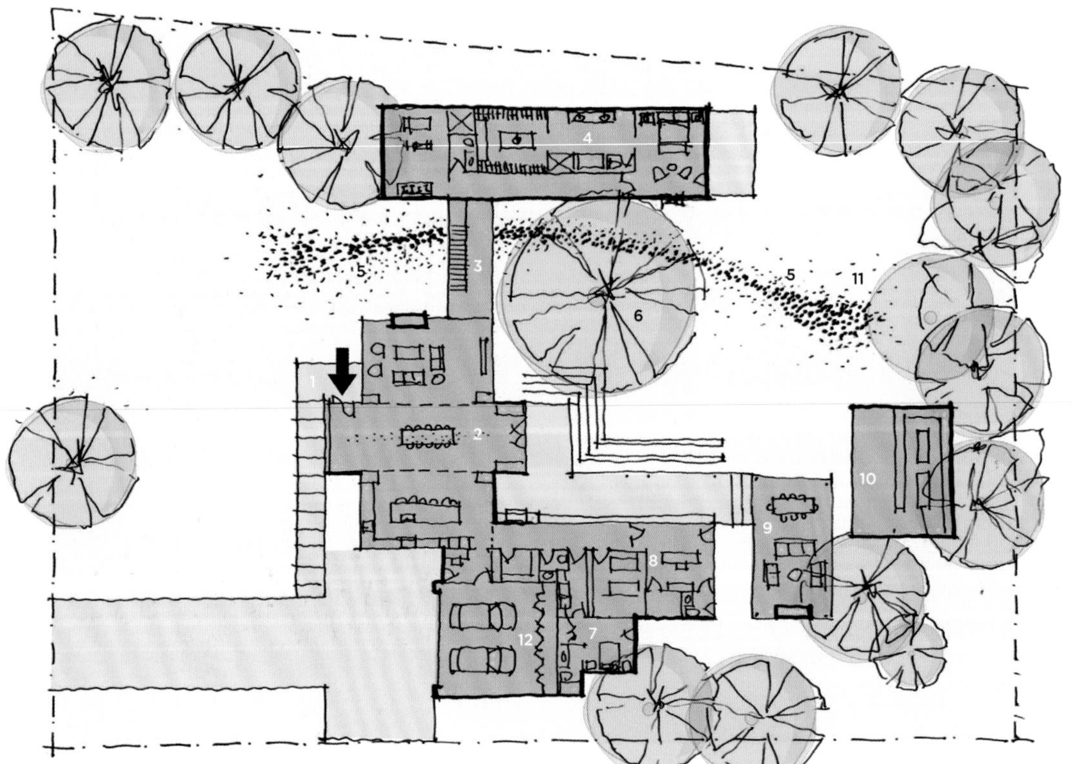

1. Front entry
2. Kitchen/dining area
3. Bridge
4. Primary suite
5. Natural drainage
6. Existing oak tree
7. Support zone
8. Family room
9. Loggia
10. Greenhouse
11. Pond
12. Garage

Floor plan

# LEVY DYKEMA

324
v

**FRIO RANCH**

Architecture Design Team:
LEVY DYKEMA
Builder:
Huband-Mantor Custom Homes
Photographers:
© Rob Gómez, Rachel Ramey

328
v

**SOUTH TEXAS RANCH**

Architecture Design Team:
LEVY DYKEMA
Builder:
DLR Builders
Photographer:
© LEVY DYKEMA

332
v

**SUNSET RANCH**

Architecture Design Team:
LEVY DYKEMA
Builder:
Showcase Builders
Photographer:
© LEVY DYKEMA

www.levydykema.com @levydykema

Stephen V. Levy

Bibiana B. Dykema

John R. Dykema, Jr.

LEVY DYKEMA designs are defined by its signature **Texas Contemporary™** brand, a balance of innovative, simple elegance of present-day architecture with unique elements of Spanish and Mexican agrarian forms. The spirit of **Texas Contemporary™** fuels the culture and productivity of the firm's creative and sustainable designs that extend beyond Texas. The award-winning firm, founded by Architects Stephen V. Levy, Bibiana B. Dykema, and John R. Dykema, Jr., boasts a fifty-year portfolio that has enhanced the lives of those who have experienced the artful spaces designed by the firm. LEVY DYKEMA has helped catapult Texas and the Southwest into a new era of architecture and design leadership through its residential, ranches, multi-family, hospitality, retail, and more. The team's collaborative process with clients stimulates a shared vision of creativity and discipline, producing exceptional results.

LEVY DYKEMA-Designs werden durch die charakteristische Marke **Texas Contemporary™** definiert, eine Balance aus innovativer, schlichter Eleganz der heutigen Architektur mit einzigartigen Elementen spanischer und mexikanischer Agrarformen. Der Geist von **Texas Contemporary™** treibt die Kultur und Produktivität der kreativen und nachhaltigen Designs des Unternehmens an, die sich über Texas hinaus erstrecken. Das preisgekrönte Büro, das von den Architekten Stephen V. Levy, Bibiana B. Dykema und John R. Dykema, Jr. gegründet wurde, verfügt über ein fünfzigjähriges Portfolio, das das Leben derjenigen verbessert hat, die die kunstvollen Räume erlebt haben, die von entworfen wurden Feste. LEVY DYKEMA hat dazu beigetragen, Texas und den Südwesten in eine neue Ära der Architektur- und Designführerschaft durch seine Wohnhäuser, Ranches, Mehrfamilienhäuser, Gastgewerbe, Einzelhandel und mehr zu katapultieren. Der kooperative Prozess des Teams mit Kunden stimuliert eine gemeinsame Vision von Kreativität und Disziplin und führt zu außergewöhnlichen Ergebnissen.

Les conceptions de LEVY DYKEMA sont définies par sa marque **Texas Contemporary™**, un équilibre entre l'élégance innovante et simple de l'architecture actuelle avec des éléments uniques de formes agraires espagnoles et mexicaines. L'esprit de **Texas Contemporary ™** alimente la culture et la productivité des conceptions créatives et durables du cabinet qui s'étendent au-delà du Texas. Le bureau primée, fondée par les architectes Stephen V. Levy, Bibiana B. Dykema et John R. Dykema, Jr., possède un portefeuille de cinquante ans qui a amélioré la vie de ceux qui ont fait l'expérience des espaces astucieux conçus par le cabinet. LEVY DYKEMA a contribué à propulser le Texas et le sud-ouest dans une nouvelle ère de leadership en architecture et en design grâce à ses résidences, ranchs, logements multifamiliaux, établissements hôteliers, commerces de vente au détail, et autres. Le processus de collaboration de l'équipe avec les clients stimule une vision partagée de la créativité et de la discipline, produisant des résultats exceptionnels.

Los diseños de LEVY DYKEMA se definen por su marca distintiva **Texas Contemporary™**, un equilibrio entre la elegancia simple e innovadora de la arquitectura actual y elementos únicos de las formas agrarias españolas y mexicanas. El espíritu de **Texas Contemporary™** alimenta la cultura y la productividad de los diseños creativos y sostenibles del despacho que se extienden más allá de Texas. El estudio galardonado, fundado por los arquitectos Stephen V. Levy, Bibiana B. Dykema y John R. Dykema, Jr., cuenta con una cartera de cincuenta años que ha mejorado la vida de quienes han experimentado los espacios artísticos diseñados por el estudio. LEVY DYKEMA ha ayudado a catapultar a Texas y el suroeste a una nueva era de liderazgo en arquitectura y diseño a través de sus residencias, ranchos, viviendas multifamiliares, establecimientos hoteleros, comercios de venta y demás. El proceso colaborativo del equipo con los clientes estimula una visión compartida de creatividad y disciplina, produciendo resultados excepcionales.

## FRIO RANCH

Real County, Texas, United States // Building area: 3,827 sq ft

The Frio Residence fits the lifestyle of its owners, who desired a Texas Hill Country home in a unique setting, where they could entertain friends and family while enjoying the sweeping views from the hilltop location. They envisioned a spacious contemporary structure that would provide space and inspiration for their artistic endeavors and work. The material palette includes standing seam metal roofing above wood and metal-clad walls. Spatially, the open plan living spaces display the simple yet elegant exposed structure and generous glazing. The master suite includes a large bedroom with panoramic views of the valley below, a master bath, walk-in closets, and a library/office area. Overall, the design captures the essence of what the owner sought to achieve, including comfort, dramatic spaces, a contemporary look, and all with energy efficiency.

Le Ranch Frio correspond au style de vie de ses propriétaires, qui souhaitaient une maison dans la région des collines du Texas, dans un cadre unique où ils pourraient recevoir leurs amis et leur famille tout en profitant de la vue imprenable sur les collines. Ils ont imaginé une structure contemporaine et spacieuse qui leur fournirait l'espace et l'inspiration nécessaires à leurs activités et travaux artistiques. La palette de matériaux comprend un toit en métal à joint debout sur des murs en bois et en métal. En termes d'espace, les salles de séjour ouvertes mettent en valeur la structure apparente simple mais élégante et le vitrage généreux. La suite principale comprend une grande chambre avec vue panoramique sur la vallée, une salle de bains principale, des vestiaires et une bibliothèque/bureau. Dans l'ensemble, la conception capture l'essence de ce que le propriétaire voulait obtenir, notamment le confort, des espaces spectaculaires, un look contemporain, le tout avec une efficacité énergétique.

Die Ranch Frio entspricht dem Lebensstil ihrer Besitzer, die sich ein Haus im texanischen Hill Country in einer einzigartigen Umgebung wünschten, in der sie Freunde und Familie bewirten und gleichzeitig die weitläufige Aussicht auf die Hügel genießen konnten. Sie wünschten sich ein modernes, geräumiges Gebäude, das Raum und Inspiration für ihre künstlerischen Bemühungen und ihre Arbeit bieten sollte. Die Materialpalette umfasst ein Stehfalzdach aus Metall über holz- und metallverkleideten Wänden. Die offenen Wohnräume zeichnen sich durch eine schlichte, aber elegante Sichtbetonstruktur und großzügige Verglasungen aus. Die Master-Suite umfasst ein großes Schlafzimmer mit Panoramablick auf das Tal, ein Master-Bad, Ankleideräume und eine Bibliothek/Büro. Insgesamt entspricht das Design dem, was der Eigentümer erreichen wollte: Komfort, dramatische Räume, ein modernes Aussehen und Energieeffizienz.

Ranch Frio se ajusta al estilo de vida de sus propietarios, que deseaban una casa en la región de las colinas de Texas en un entorno único, donde pudieran recibir a amigos y familiares mientras disfrutaban de las amplias vistas de la colina. Imaginaron una estructura contemporánea y espaciosa que les proporcionara espacio e inspiración para sus esfuerzos artísticos y su trabajo. La paleta de materiales incluye un tejado de metal con juntas alzadas sobre paredes revestidas de madera y metal. En cuanto al espacio, las salas de estar de planta abierta muestran la sencilla pero elegante estructura expuesta y un generoso acristalamiento. La suite principal incluye un gran dormitorio con vistas panorámicas del valle, un baño principal, vestidores y una biblioteca/oficina. En general, el diseño capta la esencia de lo que el propietario quería conseguir, incluyendo comodidad, espacios espectaculares, un aspecto contemporáneo, y todo ello con eficiencia energética.

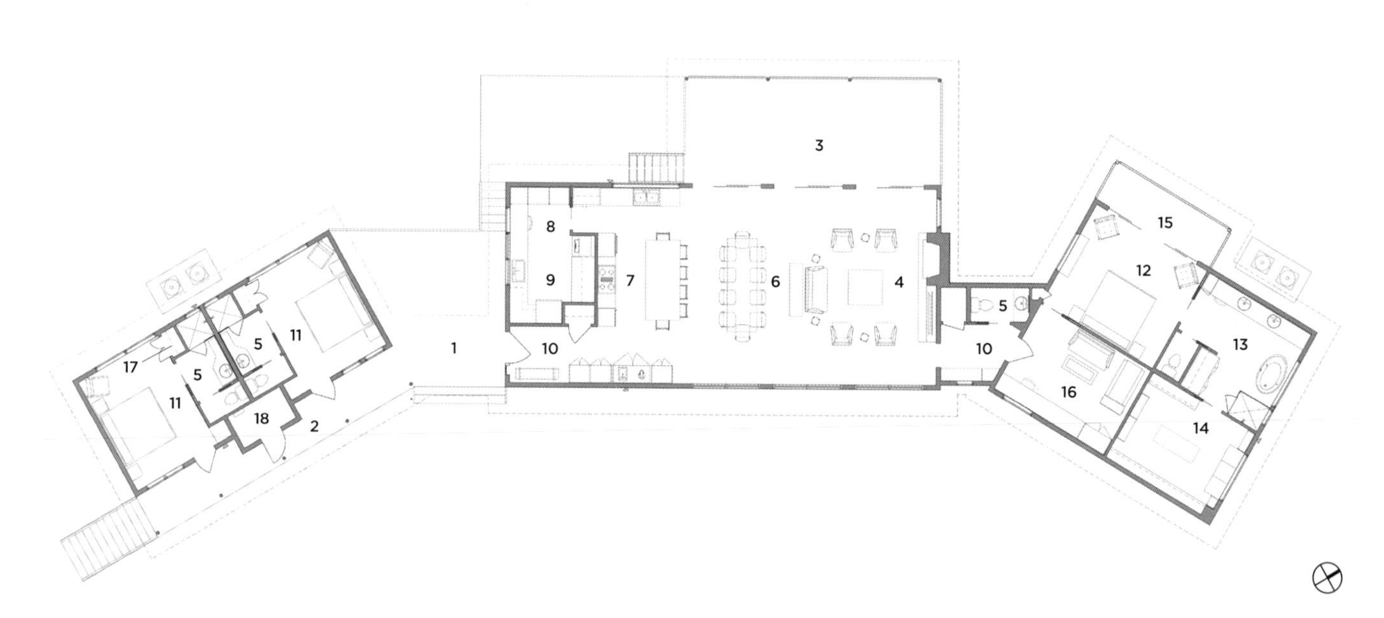

Floor plan

1. Entry porch
2. Porch
3. Main deck
4. Living area
5. Bathroom
6. Dining area
7. Kitchen
8. Pantry
9. Laundry room
10. Hall
11. Bedroom
12. Master bedroom
13. Master bathroom
14. Master closet
15. Master deck
16. Study
17. Closet
18. Storage

## SOUTH TEXAS RANCH

Jim Hogg County, Texas, United States // Building area: 13,146 sq ft

The South Texas Ranch was designed to serve as a family and guest retreat and hunting lodge in the beautiful countryside of southern Texas. It takes advantage of an attractive central courtyard with its existing mature oaks that provide an intimate environment. On one side of the courtyard overlooking a large pond, the main house stands with generous living spaces and porches suited for entertaining. Two guest houses along two other sides of the courtyard accommodate the owner's children, grandchildren, and occasional guests. A dramatic gun room and lounge for hosting hunting activities sits along the fourth side. The intimate central courtyard combines with the expansive landscape providing the building compound with a wonderful sense of place. Limestone walls, metal roofs, concrete floors, vaulted ceilings, and generous glazing embody the Texas country style.

Le South Texas Ranch a été conçu pour servir de lieu de retraite aux familles et aux invités, ainsi que de pavillon de chasse, dans la magnifique campagne du sud du Texas. Il tire parti d'une cour centrale attrayante avec ses chênes matures existants, offrant un cadre intime. D'un côté de la cour, donnant sur un grand étang, se trouve la maison principale, avec des espaces de vie généreux et des porches adaptés aux réceptions. Deux maisons d'hôtes situées de part et d'autre de la cour accueillent les enfants, les petits-enfants et les invités occasionnels. Le long du quatrième côté se trouve une salle d'armes spectaculaire et un hall pour accueillir les activités de chasse. La cour centrale intime se fond dans le vaste paysage, donnant au complexe immobilier un merveilleux sentiment d'appartenance. Les murs en pierre calcaire, les toits métalliques, les sols en béton, les plafonds voûtés et les vitrages généreux incarnent le style rural texan.

Die South Texas Ranch wurde als Rückzugsort für Familien und Gäste sowie als Jagdhaus in der wunderschönen Landschaft von Südtexas konzipiert. Es profitiert von einem attraktiven zentralen Innenhof mit seinen alten Eichen, die für eine intime Atmosphäre sorgen. Auf der einen Seite des Hofes, mit Blick auf einen großen Teich, befindet sich das Haupthaus mit großzügigen Wohnräumen und Veranden, die sich für Gäste eignen. Zwei Gästehäuser an den beiden anderen Seiten des Hofes beherbergen Kinder, Enkelkinder und gelegentliche Gäste. An der vierten Seite befinden sich eine spektakuläre Waffenkammer und ein Saal für die Durchführung von Jagdaktivitäten. Der intime zentrale Innenhof fügt sich in die weitläufige Landschaft ein und verleiht dem Gebäudekomplex einen wunderbaren Sinn für den Ort. Kalksteinwände, Metalldächer, Betonböden, Gewölbedecken und großzügige Verglasungen verkörpern den ländlichen texanischen Stil.

El Rancho del Sur de Texas se diseñó para servir de refugio familiar y de invitados, así como de pabellón de caza, en la hermosa campiña del sur de Texas. Aprovecha un atractivo patio central con sus robles maduros existentes que proporcionan un ambiente íntimo. En uno de los lados del patio, con vistas a un gran estanque, se encuentra la casa principal, con generosos espacios habitables y porches adecuados para el entretenimiento. Dos casas de invitados a lo largo de otros dos lados del patio alojan a los hijos, nietos e invitados ocasionales. A lo largo del cuarto lado se encuentra una espectacular sala de armas y un salón para albergar actividades de caza. El íntimo patio central se combina con el extenso paisaje, dotando al complejo de edificios de un maravilloso sentido del lugar. Las paredes de piedra caliza, los tejados metálicos, los suelos de hormigón, los techos abovedados y los generosos acristalamientos encarnan el estilo rural de Texas.

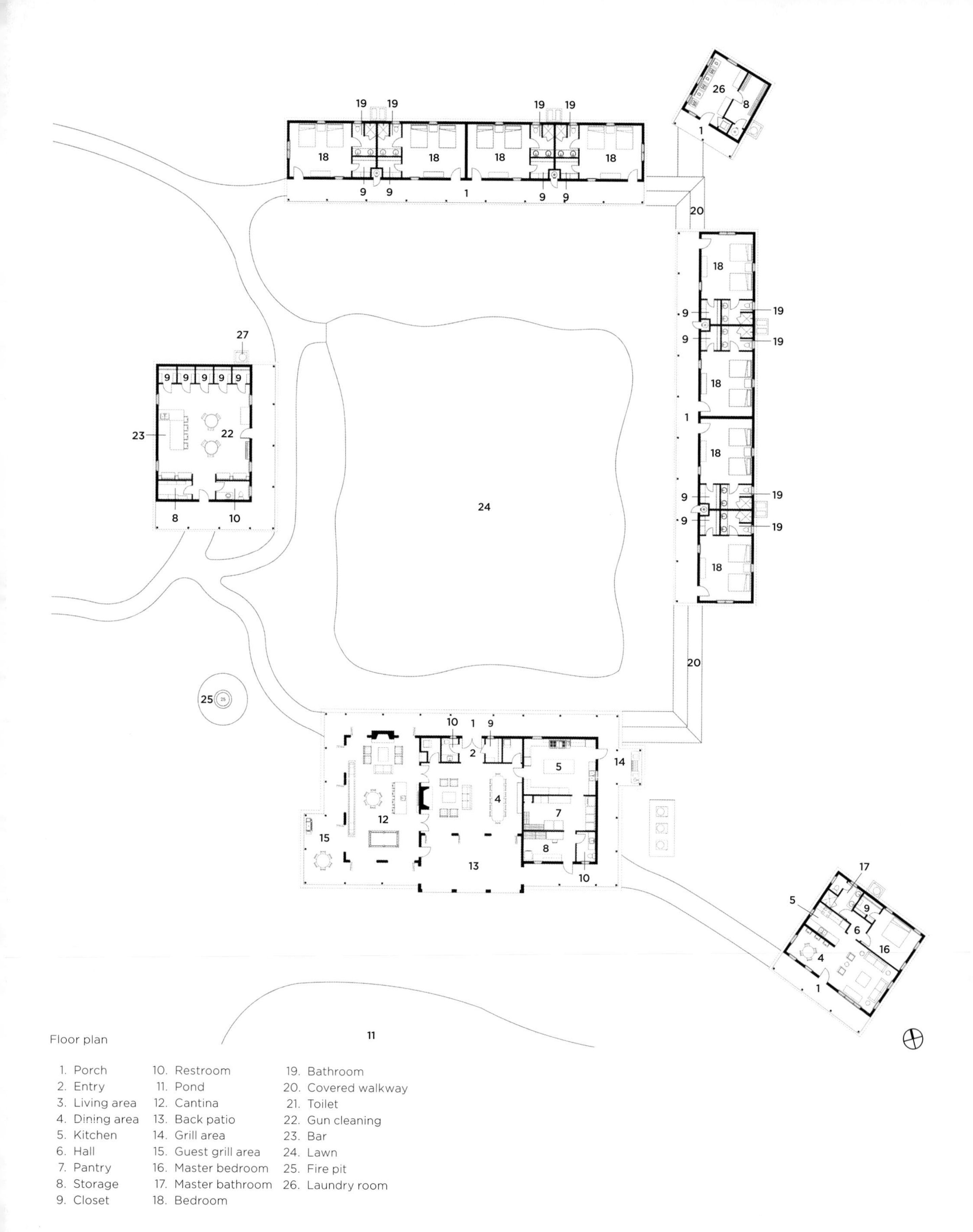

Floor plan

1. Porch
2. Entry
3. Living area
4. Dining area
5. Kitchen
6. Hall
7. Pantry
8. Storage
9. Closet
10. Restroom
11. Pond
12. Cantina
13. Back patio
14. Grill area
15. Guest grill area
16. Master bedroom
17. Master bathroom
18. Bedroom
19. Bathroom
20. Covered walkway
21. Toilet
22. Gun cleaning
23. Bar
24. Lawn
25. Fire pit
26. Laundry room

## SUNSET RANCH

Burnet County, Texas, United States // Building area: 6,660 sq ft

The site is adjacent to a former ranch home on the tip of a peninsula, forming a private compound on Lake Lyndon B. Johnson. The home had complex design criteria for a family of four with two dogs. It needed to serve as both a lake house and a ranch house while embodying **Texas Contemporary™** at its best. A modern-day dogtrot visually connects the ranch and the lake while providing a sheltered outdoor living room under a rainwater-collecting gable roof. The front of the house facing the ranch is clad with locally sourced large limestone slabs and metal panels in contrast with the rear, which takes in the views of the lake through large expanses of glass. The home served the family well during the peak of the COVID-19 pandemic while they enjoyed being off the modern-day grid.

Le site est adjacent à une ancienne maison de ranch à l'extrémité d'une péninsule, formant ainsi une enceinte privée sur le lac Lyndon B. Johnson. La maison avait des critères de conception complexes pour une famille de quatre personnes avec deux chiens. Elle devait servir à la fois de maison de lac et de ranch et incarner le **Texas Contemporary™** à son meilleur. Une passerelle couverte moderne relie visuellement le ranch et le lac, tout en offrant un espace de vie extérieur abrité sous un toit à pignon qui récupère l'eau de pluie. La façade de la maison, qui fait face au ranch, est revêtue de grandes dalles de pierre calcaire d'origine locale et de panneaux métalliques, contrairement à l'arrière, qui jouit d'une vue sur le lac à travers de grandes surfaces vitrées. La maison a servi d'abri à la famille au plus fort de la pandémie de COVID-19.

Das Gelände grenzt an ein altes Ranchhaus an der Spitze einer Halbinsel und bildet ein privates Gelände am Lake Lyndon B. Johnson. Das Haus hatte komplexe Planungskriterien für eine vierköpfige Familie mit zwei Hunden. Es sollte sowohl als Seehaus als auch als Ranch dienen und den **Texas Contemporary™** in seiner schönsten Form verkörpern. Ein moderner überdachter Steg verbindet die Ranch optisch mit dem See und bietet gleichzeitig einen geschützten Außenwohnbereich unter einem Giebeldach, das Regenwasser auffängt. Die der Ranch zugewandte Vorderseite des Hauses ist mit großen Platten aus lokalem Kalkstein und Metallpaneelen verkleidet, während die Rückseite des Hauses durch große Glasflächen den Blick auf den See freigibt. Das Haus diente der Familie während des Höhepunkts der COVID-19-Pandemie als Unterkunft.

El emplazamiento es adyacente a una antigua casa rancho en la punta de una península, formando un recinto privado en el lago Lyndon B. Johnson. La casa tenía criterios de diseño complejos para una familia de cuatro personas con dos perros. Tenía que servir tanto de casa en el lago como de rancho y encarnar el **Texas Contemporary™** en su máxima expresión. Un moderno pasadizo cubierto conecta visualmente el rancho y el lago, a la vez que proporciona una sala de estar exterior protegida bajo un tejado a dos aguas que recoge el agua de lluvia. La parte delantera de la casa que da al rancho está revestida con grandes losas de piedra caliza de origen local y paneles metálicos en contraste con la parte trasera, que disfruta de las vistas del lago a través de grandes extensiones de vidrio. La casa sirvió a la familia de refugio durante el apogeo de la pandemia de COVID-19.

LOVE
YOU
MORE

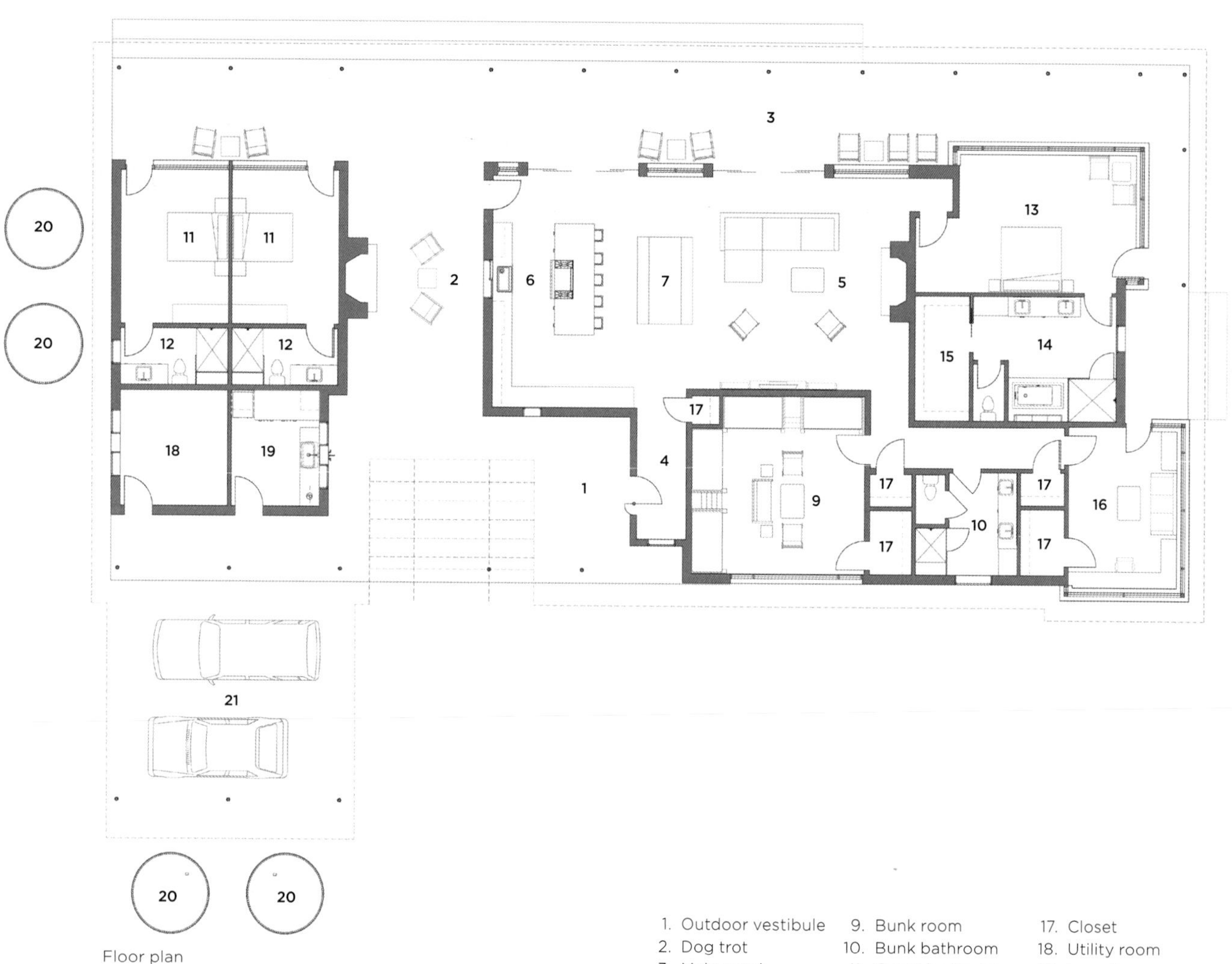


Floor plan

1. Outdoor vestibule
2. Dog trot
3. Main porch
4. Gallery
5. Living area
6. Kitchen
7. Dining area
8. Hall
9. Bunk room
10. Bunk bathroom
11. Guest bedroom
12. Guest bathroom
13. Master bedroom
14. Master bathroom
15. Master closet
16. Study
17. Closet
18. Utility room
19. Laundry room
20. Rainwater collection tank
21. Carport